PEROT
AND HIS
PEOPLE

★ ★ ★ ★ ★ ★

Disrupting the
Balance of
Political Power

PEROT
AND HIS
PEOPLE

★ ★ ★ ★ ★ ★ ★

Disrupting the Balance of Political Power

Carolyn Barta

THE SUMMIT GROUP
FORT WORTH, TEXAS

THE SUMMIT GROUP

1227 West Magnolia, Suite 500, Fort Worth, Texas, 76104

97   96   95   94   93   5   4   3   2   1

Printed in the United States of America.

Publisher's Cataloging in Publication
(Prepared by Quality Books Inc.)

Barta, Carolyn.
        Perot & his people / Carolyn Barta.
        p. cm.
        ISBN 1-56530-065-3

        1. Perot, H. Ross, 1930- 2. Presidential candidates—United States—Biography. 3. United We Stand (Political organization) 4. Political parties—United States.   I. Title.   II. Title: Perot and his people.

        E840.8.P427B37 1993   973.928'092
                                                                    QBI93-1052

★ ★ ★ ★ ★ ★ ★ ★ ★ ★

CONTENTS

Preface   ix

Introduction   xv

PART I: THE PEOPLE'S REBELLION

1   In the Ring: Larry King Live   3

2   Will Somebody Please Answer the Phone?   25

3   Texas Petition Drive
    ("Dad, They're Here, They're Everywhere") 45

4   Voter Alienation:
    A Western Union Frame of Mind   63

5   Deep Pockets and High Technology   81

6   On the Air and on the Ballot   99

7   Who Are these People?   119

8   California High   145

9 The Pros, the Press, the Problems   171

10 Beginning of the End   201

11 Getting Out   229

PART II: UNCONVENTIONAL CAMPAIGN

12 Heartbreak: The People React   257

13 The Second Wave—
Issues Book and Fifty State Ballots   285

14 Mountain to Mohammed—
Back in the Race   311

15 Five Weeks to Finish—
Infomercials and Debates   329

16 Crazy—Perot and People Power   363

PART III: THE NEW AMERICAN POLITICS

17 Communications Revolution:
New Media vs. Old Media   385

18 Lessons for the Future
and Third-Party Politics   407

19 United We Stand America   425

20 The Shadow Presidency   455

Appendix   477

CONTENTS

Bibliography   481

Index   485

★ ★ ★ ★ ★ ★ ★ ★ ★ ★

PREFACE

In April of 1992, when the Perot Phenomenon began rolling though Texas, I was astonished by the citizen reaction to a few televised speeches by Dallas billionaire Ross Perot. In twenty-five years of following politics, as a writer and editor, I had never seen anything like it. And from casual observation of Ross Perot, as a journalist in his backyard, I knew he had been cut from a different cloth than other "politicians." In Texas vernacular, they threw away the mold when they made him. I was intrigued. After interviewing some of the local volunteers and assessing the mood of the country along with the potential impact of a Perot candidacy—including how he might run a presidential race—I was convinced there was a book in it.

I took my ideas to Sharon Holman of Perot's staff, who was handling media inquiries, and asked for assistance in setting up interviews on various aspects of the operation—from high technology to ballot access to the potential candidate himself. "Fax it to me," she said. (Little did I know that everything would be faxed in Perotland.) I faxed her a list of requested interviews and subject matter. She informed Perot, and the word came back from him, "Tell her to talk to the volunteers. That's the story."

Perot did me a big favor. None of the interviews I requested in that initial overture were granted. But I began talking to volunteers, and more volunteers, and the more I talked to, the more I was persuaded that a political movement unparalleled in recent history was sweeping the nation. Perot was not as incidental to it as he would have people believe. Without his money and the force of his personality, the movement likely would have sputtered and died. But it was the people who were building the pyramid, one stone at a time.

It turned out to be a fascinating journey, albeit one with interruptions and numerous bends in the road. For all of the people who helped me get around another corner, I am grateful. I am particularly grateful to my publisher, The Summit Group of Fort Worth, which was willing to take a flyer on a book New York didn't want. New York publishers wanted investigative or "sassy." I wanted to chronicle, as fairly and non-prejudicially as possible, the most extraordinary political phenomenon I had ever witnessed.

Without the gracious help of Sharon Holman, this project would never have been launched. I eventually was able to interview most of the major players and many who were a rung or two down the ladder whose roles were no less important. To all of those who gave so freely of their time, I am grateful. To all of those I never connected with, I apologize for those gaps in my knowledge. The scores of volunteers who were willing to share their experiences, their hopes and their concerns, enriched both my work and my life.

Among those to whom I am indebted for sharing their observations in interviews—some briefly on the campaign trail, but many more lengthy interviews, both during the campaign and after—include: Charles

Donnelly, Anthony Shea, Ruthie Garrett, Jim Ash, Lewis Manson, Alida Anton, Ophelia Mounce, Jay Franklin, Bob Eisele, Bubba Eppes, Michelle Kaihani, Sharon Holman, Jim Serur, Karoline Wilson, Rose Roberts-Cannaday, Ed Campbell, Roy Vokey, Judy Follett, Eric Skidmore, Norma Crabb, Libby Craft, Margaret E. Wright, Paul Howell, John Thompson, Willie Nelson, John Arens, Mike Foudy, David Rhodes, Lynda Riley, Jack Gargan, Nina Vetter, Mark Green, Tom Luce, Bruce Dobie, Patrick Hennessy, Nancy Peterson, Steve Fridrich, Adam Tanner, John Seigenthaler, Marcy Ferren, Ray Davis, Joanne Laufer, Toni Skilman, Roni Bates, Merrick Okamoto, John Baker, Gene Waldman, Monique Mainferme, Mary Oakes, Rae Zeldin, Timothy and Joy Foraker, Linda Aust, Len and Janet Wayne, Joe Balli, Fran Masterson, Dorothy Butler, Stephen Osterman, Bobbie Snavely, Jack Brodbeck, John Jay Hooker, Miller Hicks, Pam Shannon, Yolanda Odom, Michael Kerr, Connie Smith, Gordon Black, Lionel Kunst, John Anderson, Cecil Heftel, Lucy de Barbin, Susan Esser, George Christian, Peggy Douglass, Gaynor Miller, Rosemarie Sax, Noell Custer, Kristen Silverberg, Clay Mulford, Joan Vinson, Richard Winger, Bill Anderson, Hope Walters, John P. White, Dick Norman, Darcy Anderson, Frank Luntz, Eleanor Clift, Kurt Koenig, Bill Frost, Howard and Barbara Mann, Pat Muth, David Meyerson, Russ Monroe, Wick Allison, Gloria de la Cruz, Jim Squires, Joe Canzeri, Yvonne Conway, Orson Swindle, Jeff Zucker, Dennis McClain, Ed Rollins, Charlie Leonard, Kevin Phillips, Stuart Rothenberg, Richard Fisher, William Schneider, Tommy Attaway, John Mashek, Clay Mulford, Doug Bailey, Robert Novak, Mick Ulakovic, Ross Perot, Steve Bost, Debbie Howlett, Murphy Martin, Carolyn (C.J.) Barthelenghi, Hamilton Jordan, Karen

Frost, Joyce Shepard, Alex Rodriguez, Cindy Schultz, Miriam Grayboff, Dee Zuber, Ken Kendricks and Walt Peters.

On one Perot trip, I by chance met Jo Streit, a Dallas video producer who was free-lancing a documentary— trying to capture the same thing on film I was with words. I am indebted to Jo for sharing hours of her unedited tapes, and to Howard Mann, the Dallas phone bank volunteer who was rarely without his video camera. Both provided important pieces to the puzzle and interviews I would not otherwise have had.

While I personally conducted dozens of interviews, much of the research was secondary, from the print and broadcast media. I therefore must thank the first recorders of history, all of the journalists and publications and television news shows that are liberally quoted in this book. *The Dallas Morning News* and *The New York Times* were foremost sources. My job was made easier by the *Political Hotline*, the daily briefing on American politics published by the American Political Network, Incorporated in Falls Church, Virginia. News organizations and political analysts across the country subscribe to the *Hotline*, which excerpts television news shows and the mass of political stories in the nation's major newspapers on a daily basis. Much of the valuable material which enabled me to give a national flavor to the people's movement was obtained from excerpts and quotes in the *Hotline*.

I also owe a special thank-you to Dallas phone bank volunteer Karoline Wilson, who checked names and facts, and who provided special anecdotes and much-needed friendship and support in the final weeks of writing. Other valuable support was provided by *Dallas*

Morning News columnist Jim Wright, who offered his keen editor's eye for the book's first read. Taking this project to conclusion would not have been possible without the generous support of my bosses at *The Dallas Morning News*, vice president and editorial page editor Rena Pederson, and editor and publisher Burl Osborne, who allowed me to take the time necessary to complete the work. Nor would it have been possible without the daily support of my husband, Joe Barta, who lovingly ignored me for hours, days—no, for weeks, as I sat immobilized in front of the computer.

And finally, I must thank Ross Perot, who has opened new doors in American politics and given us something to write and talk about.

June 29, 1993

INTRODUCTION

Jim Serur, Texas campaign chairman, stood at the podium at Ross Perot's Election Eve rally at Reunion Arena in Dallas—the climax of his own eight-month odyssey into Ross Perot's exercise in democracy. "What started out as a normal interview on 'Larry King Live' launched the most massive grass-roots crusade in this nation's history," he said. "People from all walks of life joined together in a crusade to address several issues facing this nation and to give it back to the people. What the framers intended was government of, by, and for the people—not by the special-interest groups and people in high places and for those same people. We want to restore this country to what the framers intended. You decide who runs this country and how they run it. Ross Perot planted the idea in our minds that united we can make a difference."

The Ross Perot presidential candidacy was the defining time in the lives of tens of thousands of people. As Serur went on to say: "This experience has changed my life dramatically. It won't be business as usual for me when this campaign is over, because we will have just begun."

Perot's campaign proved to be erratic; his mercurial personality both attracted and repelled. When he blew up his own foxhole, he took a lot of the newly converted with him. But even after he took himself out of the race on July 16, 1992, it was not without leaving his imprint—arguably handing the reins of power from the Republican incumbent, George Bush, to the Democratic challenger, Bill Clinton.

Clinton, the Arkansas governor who started his road to the White House as a weak Democratic candidate, ended up winning the presidency over the incumbent who was never able to offer a coherent message to justify his reelection. Clinton's message was simple: the need for change. But it was not Bill Clinton who threatened the American political system with real and lasting change. Nor will 1992 be remembered most for the failed campaign of a once-popular incumbent, George Bush. It will be remembered as the year of Ross Perot, the independent candidate whose unconventional campaign often overshadowed those of the major party candidates.

Indeed, the political story of 1992 was Ross Perot, the maverick billionaire accused of having an ego to match his bank account, but who had a common man's appeal that spurred a citizens' renewal in the political process. His call to arms, followed by his withdrawal, reentry, and final five-week campaign resulted in 19.7 million votes, or almost one-fifth of the 104 million voters. It was his presence that gave energy and excitement to the race. In raw numbers, he drew more votes than any previous third party or independent candidate for president. And he proved that, without the need for continual fundraising, a shorter, more innovative campaign can be conducted. This is the story of the citizens' rebellion, the communications revolution, the changes in presidential campaigns, and the potential changes in the American political system wrought by the candidacy of Ross Perot and the people who answered his call.

Perot carried no state, but emerged from the election with an enormous power base resulting from the grass-roots efforts which placed him on the ballot in fifty states. It was a grass-roots effort he fertilized with his own funds. He hired hundreds of workers, in some instances recast the volunteer organization with leaders more to his liking, and provided a sophisticated communications system for networking. Yet, Perot's strength and the charm of his campaign were provided by hundreds of thousands of ordinary and unpaid people, many of whom combined a naiveté with absolute commitment. "He inspired us to do more than we ever dreamed we could do," said Susan Esser, Michigan Perot chairman.

Perot spent $69 million between February and December, 1992, leading some to argue the need for a twenty-seventh amendment to the Constitution—a "Perot Amendment"—that would preclude a rich, self-invented savior from bankrolling his own campaign. While some of his money oiled the volunteer movement, most of it went for thirty-minute doses of television time in the last days of the campaign.

The straight-talking but canny outsider might have gone all the way to the White House had he not voluntarily removed himself from the race in July, quashing at midcourse the Perot-mania he had unleashed.

"Looking back on it," wrote John Sears, former campaign manager for Ronald Reagan, "Perot could have captured the presidency this year had he stayed in the race and picked a proper running mate. And who can doubt that his vote totals might have been substantially higher had he not digressed into the political morass of alleging a conspiracy to disrupt his daughter's wedding during the last ten days of the campaign."

But what are the implications for the future? Some, such as former Perot communications director Jim Squires, argue that Ross Perot didn't really want to be president in 1992, and will never want the full burden of the job. Psychologists can find ample evidence of self-sabotage in his campaign. That notwithstanding, this outspoken Texan has given every indication he intends to continue to be a burr under the nation's political saddle for as long as he can get away with it. As Sears said, "While Clinton and Bush were busy trying to get elected, Perot ran off with the power."

Who can guess where the Perot movement might yet go? On election night 1992, Perot was jubilant. In a North Dallas hotel ballroom, he implored his cheering supporters to stay involved. "Let's forget this election; it's behind us. The hard work is in front of us," Perot said. He charged them not to lose their enthusiasm or their idealism. "Don't feel, 'Gee, I'm powerless again.' We will stay together, and we will be a force for good for our country."

By early 1993, the organization United We Stand America—formed in midsummer to keep the Perot movement alive when he retreated as a candidate—had launched a membership drive to broaden its efforts as a "citizens' lobby" and to try to become financially independent as a permanent political force. Whether funded by Perot or its citizen-members, the organization carried the threat of being the vehicle for another presidential try by Perot, developing into a third party, or at the least being a force for reform to be absorbed by one of the major parties.

Democrats such as New York Governor Mario Cuomo suggested that Perot would be a player in 1996 only if President Bill Clinton and the Democrats fail. But Clinton went to the White House with only 43-percent support from the American people—leaving 57 percent to turn him out of office if he does not perform to expectations. He garnered only 23.3 percent of eligible voters, the smallest mandate of any president since John Quincy Adams in 1824. Perot is well positioned to call attention to a Clinton administration that failed to make its highest priority getting the deficit under control and putting the cuffs on the arrogance of power in Washington. Certainly, Clinton's attraction to governmental programs and public investment provided ample fodder in the spring of 1993 for Perot to continue talking about his own vision of a smaller, leaner government of the people, one that is a better steward of the public purse.

The Republican party, meanwhile, is in a vulnerable condition and could be reduced to third-party status unless it is revitalized. Missing the glue of the Cold War and the threat of communism that has held it together since World War II, the GOP is a party in search of a new core of defining principles—even as it faces an internal struggle over the soul of the party and the threat of dominance by its right wing. By capturing only 38 percent of voter support for its presidential candidate, Republicans fell to a level not experienced since Bull Moose Theodore Roosevelt bolted the party in 1912.

One journalist asked about Perot: Why was his the kiss that awoke the middle class from its slumber? The answer was simple: Because he talked the language of the average American. If Bill Clinton's youthful dynamism reminded some people of John F. Kennedy, Perot's plain-spoken manner invoked the memory of a former president who typified the average man: Harry Truman. He was neither a career politician, like Clinton, nor to the manor born, like Bush. Son of a cotton broker, he grew up in a family of average means in Texarkana, Texas, breaking horses and delivering newspapers, steeped in traditions of God, family and country. After graduating from the U.S. Naval Academy and a stint in the Navy, he combined a strong work ethic with sales ability and technological savvy to form the computer company that would make him a multi-millionaire by the age of thirty-eight. To his adoring volunteers, he offered a rare combination of common sense, discipline and patriotism. And he talked about what people cared about—how they could regain control of a government usurped by the politicians and special interests who had borrowed the country to the brink of oblivion.

The revolt of 1992 was also an uprising against the business of politics. "The crisis in politics is a crisis of disconnection," said Don Eberly, a former congressional and White House aide now serving as president of a think tank in Pennsylvania. "The reason people find politics so remote is because it has evolved into a highly calibrated business; one in which a fairly permanent governing class is both the producer and consumer of what takes place. The public increasingly sees everyone in politics, including activists, as exploiting issues for their own, not society's good...It is a system whose occupants all appear to have collaborated in closing everyone else out."

That disconnection and sense of powerlessness was felt even more keenly because it came at a time when Americans could see democratic traditions sweeping the world. E.J. Dionne, Jr., wrote in *Why Americans Hate Politics*, "At a time when the people of Poland, Hungary and Czecho-

slovakia are experiencing the excitement of self-govern-
ment, Americans view politics with boredom and de-
tachment." And, as political consultants Peter D. Hart
and Doug Bailey wrote for the Centel Public Accountability Project, "At the very moment when communism
has fallen to democratic aspirations in the Soviet Union,
American democracy faces a crisis of confidence among
American citizens. People across the United States increasingly have come to doubt whether our political
system works, either as a vehicle for expressing their
will or as an effective mechanism for confronting the
nation's problems. Many citizens, even those who still
vote, have concluded that they do not exercise real authority over the political system. Americans desperately
want to believe that theirs is a government of, by, and
for the people; deep down, however, very few think we
have that today."

From the beginning, Perot turned conventional wisdom on its head. He showed that a candidate doesn't
have to milk cows and chase pigs in Iowa or slosh
through the snows of New Hampshire, followed by
minicam mobs. He became a master manipulator of the
media he detested, for the most part cutting through
the filter of journalists to talk directly to the people. He
accomplished one reform lawmakers have talked about
for years—free TV—by opening up access to the TV
talk shows and morning shows. With the use of both
free and paid TV, his public campaigning was minimal.
During his periods of active candidacy in the fall, Perot
attended only eight crowd events. He refused to daily
stroke the pack journalists, having only a handful of
press conferences. He produced what voters said they
wanted, a shorter campaign. And he increased interest
in the process. A thirty-minute "infomercial," in which

he used simple cardboard graphs, outdrew a Major League Baseball playoff game.

Perot changed the dynamics of the race, getting out on the eve of Bill Clinton's acceptance address, getting back in just before the debates. He set the tone for political rhetoric. As a businessman, he was able to make the economy a more credible issue against George Bush than Bill Clinton could have done alone, as a politician. He awoke the American populace to Washington's over-whelming absorption with power, perks and influence-peddlers. He pushed some voters away from their traditional Republican allegiance, thus denying George Bush his expected second term. Despite all the furor over conspiracies, dirty tricks and political intrigue, he served to focus the race of 1992 and perhaps American politics for years to come.

The political year of 1992 was a year marked by the weakening of the parties—caused by the growing separation between campaigning and governing and the dominance of the media. Perot, however, would change the concept of the media, introducing the new media of talk shows and infotainment to the political domain. The old media, by contrast, were characterized by the national political correspondents, validated by Timothy Crouse in his 1972 campaign journal, *Boys On The Bus*, and the inside-the-Beltway media elite whose power and influence (and arrogance) had grown over the last two decades. Perot popularized other new ideas of communicating—the electronic town hall meeting, 1-800 telephone numbers, facsimiles and computer bulletin boards that would usher in the kind of "direct communication" that was the hallmark of the New World Order.

Alan Brinkley, who teaches American history at Columbia University, predicted in mid-1992 that the Perot movement would facilitate the passage to a new political order—one controlled by the people instead of the special interests, and one in which the parties and institutions of government would be forced to confront their growing irrelevance to many American voters.

Some Americans remain convinced that Perot is a dangerous demagogue, motivated by nothing more than a giant ego—that he's little more than a charismatic speaker who has captivated a huge but weird collection of groupies. It was, after all, by his own hand that the Perot Phenomenon unraveled in the summer of 1992. By stimulating people to get involved in the political process and then stepping back when he didn't fancy it going all his way, he became the super flake, feeding the very cynicism he said he was trying to allay.

Perot is demonstrably unpredictable, and prides himself on being so. That quality makes it even more difficult to predict his impact on the future of politics. Yet, who can deny that Ross Perot demanded, and got, political change: call it Politics as Unusual. As stated by Orson Swindle, the first executive director of United We Stand America: "Whether you're pro-Perot or anti-Perot, if you're really thinking, you've got to give him credit for heightening the awareness of people in the elections process and heightening their awareness of what's going on in government. It's gotten people involved, and they're going to be involved whether the two parties like it or not. It's a changing point in American politics."

Perot, at the very least, has marked the path to a new American politics that is grounded in the empowerment of people and the communications revolution. He may now embrace his role as political gadfly, serving as a watchdog over those in power, but not without leaving his mark on the process. Or he may do more.

The real impact of the Perot candidacy in 1992—on the parties, the issues, and the American political process—may not be clear until 1996. If the '92 election was the result of lessons learned in 1988, then 1996 will be the result of lessons learned in 1992. Tom Luce, Perot's longtime attorney and chairman of his spring petition campaign, predicts Ross Perot is not going away. "He may not be president, but he will be a major player." And it is entirely conceivable that, come 1996, Perot will be back in the arena asking American voters the question: "Okay, are you ready to get serious now?"

PART I
THE PEOPLE'S
REBELLION

1

★ ★ ★ ★ ★ ★ ★ ★ ★ ★

IN THE RING:
LARRY KING LIVE

THE DATE WAS FEBRUARY 20, 1992, two days after the New Hampshire primary officially opened the quadrennial race for the Democratic and Republican presidential nominations. Television viewers were idly watching the "Larry King Live Show" on Cable News Network (CNN), unaware that political lightning was about to strike. If, as the great Victorian poet Matthew Arnold wrote in 1864, the creation of a masterwork of literature requires "the power of the man and the power of the moment, and the man is not enough without the moment," surely the same could be said about politics. Those tuned into the nation's most popular television talk show were about to witness the meeting of the man and the moment. The man was Ross Perot, and the moment was the 1992 presidential election.

Unsuspecting viewers had no idea at the beginning of the program that a new political movement was about to be launched. But as the interview unfolded, they began to feel a sense of tension, a sense of expectation that something profound could be happening. As the rhythmic intensity between interviewer and guest grew, Larry King appeared to inch forward in his seat with each half-question, each staccato interruption of Perot's soliloquy. Viewers, detecting the chance, however slight, to affect the course of the presidential campaign, were glued to their sets. As one journalist would later write, in the crowded theater of American politics, H. Ross Perot was about to stand up and shout, "Fire!" Usually apathetic Americans no doubt bolted upright in their La-Z-Boys, as Ross Perot conditionally made himself available as a presidential candidate.

It began with an announcer's introduction: "Tonight: He's rich; he talks straight; he doesn't care who gets mad; and he says he knows how to fix America. Millionaire, corporate critic, and folk hero—H. Ross Perot. Now, here's Larry King."

Larry King, shirt sleeves rolled up and suspenders showing, leaned into the camera, welcomed viewers to his nightly interview and call-in show, and began:

"About a third of the voters in New Hampshire's primary said that they wished somebody else were running, and some undoubtedly have this guy in mind. The idea of pulling the lever for H. Ross Perot seems to get people's juices flowing. A Tennessee businessman is trying to talk him into it—even sent Perot rules for getting on the ballot in all fifty states. A retired PR man in Florida wants to draft him because, in his words, Perot's the only guy in the country who owes no favors to anybody."

Turning to Perot, he fired the first shot. "Are you going to run?"

"No," said Perot. "Flat no?" asked King. Perot never answered the "flat-no" question, embarking instead on a Perot-arama of the nation's ills, from the political system to fundamental economic problems such as the deficit and the tax system, to the need for a strong family unit in every home and a law prohibiting

4

ex-government officials from becoming lobbyists. He and King parried on government, Desert Storm and President Bush.

"I'd say let's cut out the adversarial relationship between government and business, and have an intelligent supportive relationship. I don't mean subsidize business. I don't mean burp them and diaper them. But I mean let's stop breaking their legs first thing every morning," Perot said.

King: Do you think President Bush sees this problem?

Perot: In all candor, I don't think he understands it. He's interested in international affairs—doesn't understand business; doesn't like to work on domestic issues. I think he realizes now he's got to get into it."

Perot and King fielded a half dozen call-ins, and the populist billionaire who frequently railed against politics of the sound bite, got off a good one himself, on tax law. "My advice—very simple—to Congress: Throw your old tax law out. It's like an old inner tube—full of patches. Let's replace it with a complete new set of tax laws."

Looking back at that program, one sees the thread of themes that would be hallmarks of the Perot campaign: his infatuation with electronic town hall meetings, his belief that the people are the "owners" of the country and that the people must "stay in the ring" after the election to keep from having a government taken over by the special interests and political action committees.

"We can have a revolution in this country," he said. "I urge you to pick a leader that you're willing to climb in the ring with, stay with, stay the course. Then that leader, with your support, will have the kind of effectiveness with the Congress that allows us to work together as a team, as a nation, and go from where we are to where we want to be. But you're going to have to be very, very active at grass roots level, and not just some sort of puppet that dances to Washington's string."

Toward the end of the hour-long program, King returned to the candidacy question for a third time, as he and Perot engaged in an "I won't dance, don't ask me" sort of duet, leading to Perot's final bow to the people. Here's the script:

King: By the way, is there any scenario in which you would run for President? Can you give me a scenario in which you'd say, "OK, I'm in"?

Perot: Number one, I don't want to.

King: I know, but is there a scenario...

Perot: Number two, you know, nobody's been luckier than I have. And number three, I've got all these everyday folks that make the world go 'round writing me in longhand...

King: Is there a scenario?

Perot: Now that touches me. But I don't want to fail them. That would be the only thing that would interest me. And so I would simply say to them and to all these folks who are constantly calling and writing, if you feel so strongly about this, number one, I will not run as either a Democrat or a Republican, because I will not sell out to anybody but to the American people—and I will sell out to them.

King: So you'd run as an independent?

Perot: Number two, if you're that serious—you, the people, are that serious—you register me in fifty states, and if you're not willing to organize and do th —

King: Wait a minute. Are you saying—? Wait a minute.

Perot: —then this is all just talk.

King: Hold it, hold it, hold it, hold it, hold it...

Perot: Now stay with me, Larry...

King: Wait, wait, wait. Are you saying...

Perot: I'm saying to the ordinary folks—Now I don't want any machine...

King: This is a "Draft Ross Perot on an independent..."

Perot: No, no, no, no. I'm not asking to be drafted.

King: Okay.

Perot: I'm saying to all these nice people that have written me—and the letters, you know, fill cases—if you're dead-serious...

King: Start committees...

Perot: —then I want to see some sweat...

King: —in Florida, Georgia...

Perot: —I want to see some sweat. Why do I want to see some sweat? I said it earlier. I want you in the ring. Why do I want you in the ring? Because I can't do the job, and nobody can do the job, unless you will go in the ring...

King: Well, wait a minute. Are you saying groups all across America—all across America—can now, in New York, Illinois, California, start forming independent groups to get you on the ballot as an independent, and you would then—If this occurred in fifty states with enough people, you'd throw the hat?

Perot: I'm not encouraging people to do this—

King: If they did...

Perot: —but the push has to come from them. So, as Lech Walesa said, "Words are plentiful, but deeds are precious." And this is my way of saying, "Will you get in the ring? Will you put the gloves on? And do you care enough about this country to stay the course?" Now

I want your promise, also that, if we, you know, got lucky and climbed the cliff, you wouldn't climb out of the ring the day after election. You're going to have to stay there for the fight. Then all of these changes could be made. Now recognize, you're listening to a guy that doesn't want to do this, but if you, the people, will on your own—Now I don't want some apparatus built. I don't want two or three guys with big money around trying to do it. If you want to register me in fifty states, number one, I'll promise you this: Between now and the convention we'll get both parties' heads straight. Number two, I think I can promise you're going to see a world-class candidate on each side. And number three, by the convention you might say, "Cripes, you know, it's all taken care of." But on the other hand, we're set, and if you're not happy with what you see and you want me to do it, then I don't want any money from anybody but you, and I don't want anything but five bucks from you because I can certainly pay for my own campaign—no ifs, ands, and buts—but I want you to have skin in the game. I want you to be in the ring. Now then, God bless you all who have written me and called me. The shoe is on the other foot.

Ross Perot would later say that he gave an "impulsive answer" to King. But two weeks before, Perot had made almost the identical statement about people getting him on the ballot in fifty states on a visit to Nashville, Tennessee.

Perot had been invited to appear on a talk show on WLAC radio in Nashville on February 6 to discuss "what's wrong with America." He had been interviewed by the station more than a year before on the Gulf War. Station manager Patrick Hennessy said, "We just invited him up. He loves talk radio." A coffee-and-croissants reception was planned at the station after the show, and fifty or so business and community leaders were invited. Perot mingled awhile and then climbed some stairs so he could see out over the group as he made a few remarks and answered questions.

He told the business leaders that the only way to fix a system currently run by the special interests was "to get the American people squarely behind you...get them into the ring and get them to stay in the ring until the job is finished."

Nancy Peterson, chairman of Peterson Tool Company, was in the audience. Ms. Peterson, who had been named U.S. Businesswoman of the Year in 1990 by Veuve Clicquot, voted for George Bush in 1988, but thought Perot had some interesting ideas. She said to him that it was very easy to Monday morning quarterback; most of his suggestions came "after the game." Her question was: "One, are you going to run for head coach? Two, if that answer is no, why not? Three, if the answer is no, who do you recommend we get to coach, because unless we get a good leader, we can't win the game."

Perot's initial response was that he would be a "square peg in a round hole." Several persons attending remember Perot saying something to the effect that he might respond to a draft, if the people took it upon themselves to put him on the ballot. During the Q&A session, chairman emeritus of *The Tennessean*, John Seigenthaler, leaned over to Adam Tanner, a business writer from *The Tennessean*, and suggested he ask the presidential question in an interview.

Perot then stepped into a tiny room off the lobby for the pre-arranged interview with *The Tennessean*. "I really am not interested in being in public life," Perot said at first, noting that there was no public "groundswell" for him to seek the presidency. Under repeated questioning, however, he began to waver. "If there were a groundswell...I'd say fine. If you feel so strongly about this, register me in fifty states. If it's forty-nine, forget it," he said. "If you want to do fifty states, you care that much, fine, then I don't belong to anybody but you. I would not want to run in any of the existing parties because you would have to sell out."

The draft method would "have others sweat" on his behalf to get on the ballot, he explained. "I learned a long time ago if you offer advice, nobody's interested; if you're asked for advice, everybody listens," he said. Perot understood that people would feel a stake in the outcome if they worked to get him on the ballot—if they had some sweat equity in it. Perot also talked about one of his favorite ideas: interactive television used to promote democracy. "It's the town hall in its purest form," he said.

The next day, *The Tennessean* had a business story based on the interview which focused on General Motors (the company which paid $750 million to rid their board of Perot) and the nearby Saturn car plant. In a sidebar story, *The Tennessean* reported Perot's willingness to run for president if citizens put him on the ballot in fifty states. It was the first published account that Perot was ripe for public picking. Reporter Tanner later would say, "Clearly the mythical account of him spontaneously saying it on 'Larry King Live' is not true."

Another person at the WLAC breakfast was Bruce Dobie, editor of the *Nashville Scene*, an alternative news weekly. Dobie knew that John Jay Hooker of Nashville had been talking to Perot since November, pleading with him to run. Perot had, in fact, been talking rather seriously for several months with a man from Florida and with Hooker, a colorful, sixty-one-year-old millionaire aristocrat with a taste for Panama hats, gold pocket watches, three-piece suits and politics. Hooker had told Dobie he thought he was persuading Perot. "Bruce," he said, "it's like dating a woman. She's lifting her skirt a little more every day." Dobie wrote a story, which appeared February 13, 1992, in the *Nashville Scene*. He also phoned Dallas friend Peter Elkind, editor of another alternative weekly, telling him something was going on with Hooker and Perot.

The Dallas Observer, the alternate newspaper ridiculed by Perot as "something they give out in restaurants" reported six weeks later that the Larry King appearance followed dozens of phone conversations Perot had with Hooker, a flamboyant businessman. Hooker had served as chairman of STP Oil and publisher of the *Nashville Banner*, before embarking on an unsuccessful business venture, Minnie Pearl's Fried Chicken. He was an also-ran in races for governor, legislature and the U.S. Senate in Tennessee.

Hooker and Perot had become acquainted via telephone. Hooker frequently called Perot to discuss the nation's problems. "The whole thing of calling him and continuing to talk to him was born of my own defeats in politics," Hooker said. Hooker was convinced the time was right for an independent challenge. "To begin with, I called him because I was convinced the country had reached a deadlock; the Democrats and Republicans were not going to be able to work it out. The situation was such in America that one political party could only win by blaming the other one. The success of one was based on the failure of the other; therefore, you had all this name calling, bashing and trashing. You needed to get through that problem, and the way to get through that was to have a third person, an independent candidate."

Hooker was talking to other people around the country, including some who thought Perot should run as a Democrat. Pat Caddell, Jimmy Carter's pollster when he ran for president and Hooker's pollster when he ran for governor, kept saying that what America was looking for was an independent.

The first time Hooker asked Perot if he would run, Perot said, "No, period." Then Hooker asked him if he believed the country is governable. Perot responded, "Oh, yeah, I think it is." He said it all begins with jobs, with growing the markets, getting back into manufacturing and realizing the country's potential. "He seemed so confident that the American people had the resources, the intellect and the energy, that we could do what we needed to do," Hooker said. "As he talked through that, getting America back to work, I began to feel this fellow really ought to be president of the United States."

"We communicated, and I became more and more interested in him. He handled himself in such a gracious manner. He never told me once a self-aggrandizing story," Hooker said. "It was very clear he had no ambition to do it. He told me categorically, "No." If he told me once, he told me twenty times."

Hooker kept telling Perot that what Eisenhower was to the post-World War II era, Perot was to the 1990s. "I told him if he would let the American people know, they would draft him just as they drafted Eisenhower. He said, 'But I'm no Eisenhower.' I kept telling him Eisenhower had expertise about the military, you have the expertise about the economy, and the economy is now the subject." During the Nashville visit, they talked again about Ike, and when Hooker drove Perot to the airport, he began to believe that Perot might make himself available. But the question remained as to how to get the word out.

Back on the phone again, they discussed various avenues, including the *New York Times*, *Los Angeles Times* and *Wall Street Journal*. Both preferred Larry King. Hooker says the actual call to "Larry King Live" was made by John Seigenthaler. CNN says the King show initiated the appearance.

Perot gets huffy at any implication that the "Larry King Live" appearance was a setup to launch his candidacy. "He (King) invited me to talk about the economy. I've been on the show three times before. I gave an impulsive answer. Have you got the transcript? Among other things I said was that this won't happen."

When did he begin to realize that it might, in fact, happen? "My first clue was when CNN's switchboard gridlocked that night. Mine gridlocked the next day. I said it would go away by Monday. It gridlocked on Monday."

Certainly, the themes Perot espoused on the King show were not new themes for him. In speech after speech for several years, in some cases dating back twenty years, Perot had been singing verses of the same song. Encouraging the people to take back their government was a familiar refrain for him. Indeed, for several years, people had suggested to him in offhand conversations and in letters that he seek the presidency. He was such a hit when he addressed the National Governors Association in 1987 that the chairman told him he ought to run for president. The chairman that year was a young governor from Arkansas named Bill Clinton.

Perot was frequently asked by the press if he would ever consider running. The feisty billionaire industrialist with the blunt speech patterns had stoked the fires of such speculation by his harsh criticism of the political process, the administration and Congress; he repeatedly had tried to shake up the American people.

Perot made a major speech in Tampa, Florida, on November 2, 1991, before the Coalition for Better Government and T.H.R.O. (for Throw the Hypocritical Rascals Out) in which it appeared obvious that he had thought about the presidency and was fanning the flames of discontent.

To a receptive audience of two to three thousand, he said: "This is a country that stands squarely on the broad shoulders of ordinary people. You are the steel and concrete that holds our country together. Never forget it. You are givers in a greedy world filled with takers. You are very special people—the people who do the honest work in our country. de Tocqueville was talking about you when he concluded that America is great because her people are good.

"You say, 'Well, I'm just an ordinary person.' We don't have a prayer without you, and I'll explain why in a minute. You're paying the bills for everything we do. You're paying the bills for our mistakes. You're the majority of the electorate.

"Let's look at where our great nation is. First off, let me just say this: It's a situation where nobody's taken out the trash here at home for a long time, and nobody's cleaned out the barn...

"We're the largest debtor nation. We have a debt of $3.5 trillion we admit to and another $6 trillion that's kind of like a crazy aunt we keep in the basement. All the neighbors know she's there, but nobody talks much about it. If we're not financially strong, we cannot solve our problems at home. We cannot defend ourselves and others throughout the world. If we want to help other people in other nations in need, we must have money. That means we've got to get our country back on a sound financial footing."

Perot went on to say, "If you want to know why I'm here, I'm really concerned about the world my children and grandchildren will live in. I feel rotten that I am spending their money. I feel I have a tremendous obligation as a private citizen while I'm here to try to pay that debt off and give them the opportunities that all of us had throughout our lives.

"Okay, it's going to take action and not talk. In all fairness to our elected officials—they are generally good people—they are not the problem. Our system of government is the problem. If we threw them all out, put a new crop in, if we went up there within twelve months, having these guys running around tickling you behind the ear telling you how great you are and handing you money, we'd be just like they are. You've got to change the system!"

In the Tampa speech, which was broadcast on C-Span, Perot talked about some of the ideas that would become part of his standard boilerplate: cutting the deficit, getting rid of political action committees (PACs), cutting the election campaign down to five months, free television time for candidates, a line-item veto for the president, holding elections on Saturday and Sunday instead of Tuesday, putting congressional raises on the ballot, and prohibiting former federal officials from serving as lobbyists for foreign countries.

At the end of the speech, Jack Gargan said: "Let me ask you, do you feel the same way I do? This is the guy that ought to be the next president of the United States!" Gargan had extended the invitation to Perot to speak and had provided placards that said, "Perot for Prez." The audience chanted, "Run, Ross, Run."

Gargan, a sixty-one-year-old former Tampa financial planner, had—like John Jay Hooker—been urging Perot to run for president. While Hooker began his conversations with Perot in November, though, Gargan had been talking to the Dallas industrialist since May 1991.

Gargan was the founder of T.H.R.O. and was active in the Coalition to End the Permanent Congress. In 1990, Gargan had taken $45,000 from his savings to buy a half-dozen full-page newspaper advertisements calling for the ouster of all incumbent members of Congress. The headline on the ad was: "I'm Mad as Hell and I'm Not Going to Take It." The ads—which deplored the federal deficit, the savings and loan ripoff and the "shady dealings" of Congress—resulted in a phone call from Perot, who offered to lend his support. That call led to a meeting in Dallas in May 1991, when Gargan told Perot he intended to launch a Draft Perot movement at a six-state meeting of the Coalition to End the Permanent Congress in Kansas City. On Saturday after the May 29, 1991, meeting, the *Kansas City Star* carried a story on Gargan's speech, which began: "You heard it here first: A campaign to draft H. Ross Perot for president of the United States was launched at 4:16 p.m. Saturday in Kansas City." This was eight months before the "Larry King Live" appearance.

Two weeks after Perot's rousing speech in Tampa, on November 16, 1991, *The Dallas Morning News* carried a front-page story headlined: "Perot for president? Billionaire says 'no chance,' but talk persists." The story, by Dan R. Barber, noted a brief mention in *Newsweek*, quoted Gargan and quoted Bob Balkin, editor for *The Hotline*, a daily political journal published in Washington, D.C. Balkin said, "Something's brewing. The word on the guy is keep an eye open for a possible independent candidacy."

Perot told *The Dallas Morning News*, "The answer is no. We can cover that in one word. There's no chance." He said he didn't like politics; it involved too much talk, too many ceremonies and not enough action. "I don't want to be driven around in a motorcade, and I don't want to be led around by the Secret Service. I don't need the ego stroke of a title. I don't want people playing 'Hail to the Chief' every time I go somewhere." Perot also said he didn't think being president played to his strengths, and that he couldn't run and belong to "anybody but the people. You can't get there unless you sell out, and I'm not going to sell out."

Gargan insisted, however, that Perot might run under the right circumstances—which would be a draft by the American people. "I think that's the only way he'll run. It'll take a flood of letters and phone calls from all over the nation, telling him that his country needs him."

Gargan told Perot's hometown newspaper that he and Perot discussed the idea for ninety minutes in May 1991 in Dallas. They even debated the merits of three or four possible running mates, he said, even though Perot insisted, all the while, that he wouldn't be a candidate.

According to Bob Balkin of *The Hotline*, Perot's name had surfaced on two polls in the spring of 1991. In April 1991, Maguire Associates in Boston included Mr. Perot's name on a survey of New Hampshire voters. And in May 1991, Political Media Research in Columbia, Maryland, added Perot's name to polls in California and Florida. Although support for Perot registered in the "bottom tier," he nonetheless did better than Arkansas Governor Bill Clinton and Virginia Governor Doug

Wilder, both of whom later announced for president.

Tom Luce, Perot's longtime Dallas lawyer and friend, said, during a June 1992 interview, that he couldn't remember the first conversation that he and Perot had about a presidential candidacy. "Ross and I'd had several conversations over the last three or four years about the fact that people were urging him to run for president," he said, "both as a Democrat and as a Republican." Luce said Perot was approached before the Iowa caucuses in 1988 to run. During that time period, he and Perot talked almost every day. "I would know that this was going on and we would talk about it. On every occasion that we would bring it to conclusion, Ross would say he isn't going to do it."

Luce recalled, however, that Perot did talk to him about running as an independent after the speech in Tampa. He was curious as to what would be involved. Luce said he had no idea, other than he knew that the rules were different in every state for getting on the ballot. Hooker eventually contacted Richard Winger, a former Libertarian Party candidate in California and a ballot access expert, asking for information on how to get on the ballot in fifty states. He forwarded the information to Perot and Luce.

Perot had long lived the life of the mythical, larger-than-life Texan. A graduate of the Naval Academy, he went to work for IBM on his discharge from the Navy. But after failing to convince IBM that there was a huge market not just in selling computers but in helping people figure out how best to use them, he struck out on his own. With $1,000 of his wife Margot's savings from teaching, he founded Electronic Data Systems in 1962. Six years later, shortly after he took EDS public, it was valued at $375 million. Perot developed a reputation for doing things his way, which caught up with him in 1984 when he sold EDS to General Motors for $2.5 billion and a place on the GM board of directors. Perot so badgered GM management to remake the company according to his image that by 1986, GM was willing to pay him royally (more than $700 million) just to get him out.

In 1988, he started another computer company, Perot Systems. While Perot Systems was relatively small in comparison to EDS—it had 1991 revenues of $200 million compared to EDS' $7.1 billion—it was growing quickly. The company employs about five hundred people in Dallas, four hundred in Herndon, Virginia, and three hundred in the Detroit area. But Perot's business interests went well beyond computers. The Perot Group handles real estate operations, investments and other businesses. One of those businesses is the $50 million Alliance Airport northwest of Dallas, a project headed by his son, Ross Perot, Jr. Alliance is the world's first industrial airport; it handles no passenger traffic. In the Perot tradition, it's original, huge and designed to make millions. Surrounded by seventeen thousand acres of Perot land, the airport is being marketed to manufacturers who will locate plants near the runways so they can receive parts and ship finished goods by air.

But it was his penchant for the dramatic, the patriotic and the heroic that drew him the most acclaim. His adventure stories have been widely told. In 1969, when he thought the U.S. government was not making enough of an effort on behalf of prisoners of war, he flew a planeload of food, medical supplies and Christmas gifts to Vietnam for distribution to POWs in Hanoi. He told a reporter at the time that he did it because "The United States belongs to its people, and each person in the

United States has an obligation to do whatever he can within his limits to make it a better country." That was the introduction of Ross Perot to the American people. At the time, ABC-TV's Barbara Walters regarded him as "some eccentric whack," she recalled on an April 1986, edition of "20/20." While he was denied access on that mission, his efforts on behalf of the POWs and MIAs would continue for several years. He hired and paid the salary for a former network TV newsman, Murphy Martin, to work full time seeking the release of the POWs and accounting of the MIAs. He was credited with getting letters and communications into POWs, with improving conditions for them and with gaining the release of some.

Ten years later, Perot was involved in another adventure during the height of the Iranian revolution. In the midst of the anti-Americanism that raged in the streets of Teheran, two of Perot's employees, Paul Chiapparone and Bill Gaylord, were taken prisoner. Once again, Perot found U.S. efforts insufficient. He called in Colonel Bull Simon, a retired Army rescue specialist, and assembled a team from his company to rescue the men. Their raid, which resulted in the dramatic rescue of the two EDS employees, became the basis for Ken Follett's book, *On Wings of Eagles*, which was made into a TV miniseries starring Richard Crenna as Perot.

In the days to follow, Crenna's portrayal of Perot would be the one most familiar to many Americans. For some, when talk began of a possible independent presidential candidacy, it was all they needed to know about the man. Barbara Walters told these two adventure stories and about Perot's success in building a worldwide computer communications system empire at EDS in her April 1986, interview, during which she asked him his thoughts on Vietnam and military intervention.

"I'll tell you one thing. If we ever start into that again, you'll see a lot of me, because I am absolutely determined that we will never send our men out to die unless our nation is committed. And my motto will be, 'first commit the nation; then commit the troops.' And if you and I don't care enough about it, we can't send our sons out to fight and die."

True to his word, when President George Bush dispatched troops to the Persian Gulf in August of 1990, Perot hit the speaking circuit. In three months, he spoke to more than eight thousand people. His most famous speech of the period was to the National Press Club on December 6, 1990. He urged Congress to undertake a full debate on a declaration of war and, once again, said: "The lesson of Vietnam is, first commit the nation, and then commit the troops." He reminded the national press and the American public, tuned in via C-Span, that "only Congress can declare war and commit troops to death on the battlefield. Read the Constitution. Congress declares war, the president carries it out."

But he said a whole lot more, planting seeds in the minds of the American people, and raising questions about the efficacy of the George Bush administration. Perot talked about the administration's pattern of covering up past mistakes by going to war—such as with Panama over Noriega, and then with Saddam Hussein in the Middle East—and about the growing debt.

"Everybody's running all over the world, trying to get votes for this and that, and nobody is home taking care of the store. So, our biggest single problem is, folks, we're going broke. The ordinary fellow is about to figure that out. I figure it costs $500 million a day to keep 450,000 troops in the Middle East...We just have been so rich for so long, we think we can do anything we want to, and we'll have the money to come up with it. But we had a great economic engine. We let it slip away. We've got to be careful."

Perot said the people were disillusioned that the White House and Congress had covered up the savings and loan crisis until after the 1988 election, when it was obvious in 1986. "The delay, driven by personal political ambitions, increased the size of this problem from $50 billion to $500 billion, and the burden for paying for this mess rests squarely on the shoulders of the ordinary citizen. Who was in charge of deregulation at this time? Vice President George Bush."

Perot went on to say that the ordinary citizen's frustration reached a new high during the 1990 budget and tax negotiations. Whatever happened to "Watch my lips—no new taxes"? he asked. "Our president blames the recession on the war in the Middle East. Don't be fooled. The recession is the result of ten years of gross excess spending and mismanagement in our country."

This speech, followed by an appearance on "The McNeil/Lehrer Report" and a January 8, 1991, appearance on "Phil Donahue," showed that Perot had his ear to the ground and could hear the stampeding hooves of an angry public, even when there was hardly a rustle in the air. He was doing his part to stir the herd.

He told Donahue, in another slap at George Bush, that "there are many ways to deal with these problems, and getting your ego involved and immediately rushing in to prove your manhood across the desert is certainly not the best approach in this particular case." The American people, he warned, needed to go beyond their "Super Bowl mentality" to understand that Americans would be blown apart in combat.

Perot presaged another couple of points that would become important tenets to his presidential campaign: his appreciation of mass media outlets that attracted real people and his belief that Congress worked for those very people. "You've got ten million people watching this program," he told Donahue. "They can determine how Congress votes. Congress is going to be responsive to the people. The elected officials in this country are our servants. We own this country. They work for us."

It's clear that there was some public consciousness of Perot as a potential candidate at the time of his opposition to the War in the Gulf and the "first Commit the Nation" speech to the National Press Club in December, 1990. The first question posed to him in the question-and-answer session following that speech was, "Mr. Perot, isn't it time you run for president of the United States?" Even while he was saying he didn't have the temperament, he was urging people to stay in touch by calling him in Dallas "or you can write me at P.O. Box D—that's 'D' like in Dallas—Dallas, Texas."

In hindsight, there's little question that Ross Perot had long entertained thoughts of getting in the ring. The only question was how to get the people in there with him. "Larry King Live" on February 20, 1992, would open the floodgates.

$\star$ $\star$ $\star$ $\star$ $\star$ **2** $\star$ $\star$ $\star$ $\star$ $\star$

WILL SOMEBODY PLEASE ANSWER THE PHONE?

EARLY FRIDAY MORNING AFTER THURSDAY NIGHT'S "Larry King Live" show, Perot pulled his 1984 red Oldsmobile into the parking garage at the Merit Drive building in North Dallas where his offices are housed. About the same time, employee Sharon Holman pulled in and parked. Ms. Holman had worked for Perot off and on since 1969, and was once his personal secretary. She was employed in the real estate division of the Perot Group, working with Ross Perot, Jr., on Alliance Airport and other special projects, doing marketing, video materials and community relations. Walking from the garage into the office with her boss of many years, she remarked: "Well, you took us by surprise last night."

Still the reluctant candidate and, in truth, not knowing whether the people would pick up the gauntlet he had thrown down the night before, he responded: "It will all have blown over by Monday."

He had told his wife Margot the same thing the night before in the Washington hotel where they stayed after the King show. But, she was not so sure. She later told Barbara Walters on ABC's "20/20" that she was "stunned" when Perot said he would run. Perot also told Clay Mulford, his son-in-law in Dallas, by phone from Washington after the King show that "Nothing will come of it."

But Perot's office was flooded with phone calls the day after the King show, and again on Monday, and for days on end. "His secretaries couldn't do anything but answer the calls. Everybody was at their wit's end," Holman said. "People were being incredibly ingenious about finding the number. There was no 800 number, and Mr. Perot isn't listed in the telephone book as Ross Perot. People were calling the Dallas Public Library, the *Dallas Morning News*, Texas Instruments, anyone they knew in Dallas to get the number."

Within a week of the Larry King appearance, Perot's secretaries had logged calls from people in forty-six states volunteering their assistance.

A Dallas woman and her husband, Judy and Russ Follett, were among the viewers watching "Larry King Live" on February 20, 1992. Transplanted Texans from Indiana, they had long been admirers of Mr. Perot and became excited when Perot offered himself to the people. On Friday morning, Judy Follett called Dallas information for any listing with the name Perot in it. She was given the number for the Perot Group, and her call was one of the first fielded by secretaries who became known to her only as Marilyn and Virginia.

"I left my name and number," Judy Follett said, "and I didn't hear anything for days, so I called back. I was told the calls are pouring in, and they didn't know what to do. I told them to give the people my number."

For the next couple of days, Marilyn and Virginia gave out the number for Judy Follett, who managed an apartment complex in far North Dallas, where she and her husband lived. The calls started coming in as fast as they could pick up the phone. After a day or so, Judy

Follett put a message on her answering machine: "If you would like to put Ross Perot on the ballot in November, send me a stamped, self-addressed envelope."

She was astonished by the volume of the mail. "My mailman could not believe it. It was just phenomenal, just phenomenal. We got hundreds of letters, but we didn't have a petition."

A few miles away in Dallas, Roy Vokey, a semi-retired bookkeeper, and his wife, Virginia, also watched the "Larry King Live" show and were impressed. When Perot said he would run if the people would get him on the ballot in fifty states, Virginia Vokey pointed her finger at the television set and said: "You're on, Ross." At 8:30 a.m. the next day, she called the Texas secretary of state's office to get a petition. She was sent incorrect forms, and it took almost a week to get the right forms. Virginia Vokey, who is disabled and in a wheelchair, was calling friends, trying to establish a pyramid system to get the petitions out in the community. She also established contact with Perot's personal secretary, Sally Bell. The Vokeys began getting calls at home, from in and out of state, and were contemplating having an organizational meeting of their own, when Perot's office took action.

Like most of the early Perot enthusiasts, Roy Vokey didn't know Ross Perot. He ran into him once in a Dallas drugstore, just before the Gulf War began. "I introduced myself to him, and told him I wanted him to be president. He said, 'No, no, I'm a businessman, I'm not suited for it.'" At the time, however, Perot was speaking out against the Gulf War, calling for Congress to have formal debate on a declaration of war if the United States was going to move militarily into the Persian Gulf. Mr. Vokey had heard Perot interviewed on television and knew he was being asked about a presidential candidacy. "There was a strong pulse beating out there, even then," he said.

Meanwhile, Judy Follett was also calling the Texas secretary of state's office, without much success. It took her several days to obtain valid petitions. Then she wrote out instructions and started mailing the petitions. She and her husband worked day and night, she said, "from a quarter to seven in the morning until 2:00 a.m., and we both had jobs. I made 2:30 a.m. my deadline. We would go to the post office with a garbage bag full of mail." The Perot secretaries stopped giving out her name after the first few days, when they heard about the response she was getting. They were still being flooded with calls. By this time, Judy Follett had been listed as a Perot "contact" in an area newspaper and on a popular Dallas radio station. Her phone number was getting out all over the state. There was no turning back.

"Other cities were calling me," she said. "Houston wanted to know what to do. I said you've got to get a petition. A guy from Austin called me; he put a billboard up. He said, 'What do we need to do? Do we have a meeting?' And I said, 'We just need to pass petitions.' We were really floundering there. People were calling and saying, 'I will do anything'—that's what we were hearing. I had a doctor's wife call me from Houston who had been in a Republican women's club for twenty years. She was fed up and said, 'I'll do anything I can in Houston.' Then the next phone call would be a truck driver. There was a truck driver who said he traveled in seven states and wanted to carry petitions into all seven states. I explained to him that we couldn't do it that way—every state was different. What really impressed me was that we were crossing all lines. It was rewarding; it was phenomenal."

Judy Follett called Marilyn and Virginia every day to tell them what was happening. "I was so excited, I had to touch base with someone. I was on such a high." When she told them of the inquiries she was getting from out of state, they faxed her a list of all the secretaries of state in the country.

On March 10, which was Super Tuesday and Texas primary day, Judy Follett called the Dallas radio stations and asked them to broadcast the message that there was a third choice, and that Texans who voted in the primary could not sign a petition for Ross Perot. "People told me they were on their way to vote," she said, "when they heard it on the radio and decided not to vote. One lady said she was parking her car at the polls, and turned around and went home."

Meanwhile, in Austin, David Garrett Rhodes and his friend, Tom Thoman, had decided to rent the billboard they had been eyeing on the upper deck of Interstate 35, which carries north-south traffic through the capital city. On March 9, the day before Super Tuesday and the Texas primary, their billboard went up: "Let's Draft Ross Perot for President in '92. Make a Real Change." A local phone number was listed, and the two men paid for an answering service for a month. An estimated 125,000 cars a day were expected to pass the billboard at its prime location, and Rhodes figured to get 150-200 callers— some of whom might be willing to circulate petitions. For two days and two nights, the phones rang nonstop. An estimated two thousand calls came in. News stories ran in several Texas newspapers about the billboard. The story went out on the *Associated Press* wire, prompting a call from as far away as Anchorage, Alaska. Rhodes was getting worried. Rhodes was thirty-one, married, had a two-year-old son and a demanding job with a real estate and property management firm. Thoman was a roofing contractor. They were wondering how they would answer all the calls. "I thought, Shoot! What have I done?" Rhodes said. He called Perot's office and got Sally Bell.

In Fort Worth, thirty miles from Dallas, thirty-four-year-old Mark Green was "transitioning" out of his job as director of marketing for a start-up company. He didn't see "Larry King Live," but heard about the possible Perot petition effort in Texas. He was curious. On the day before Super Tuesday, he called the Perot Group office in Fort Worth and was directed to call Judy Follett. He got her answering machine. So he called the secretary of state's office, and was told he couldn't sign a petition if he voted in the Texas primary. Trained as a journalist, he thought that might be newsworthy, so he sent a fax to the *Fort Worth Star-Telegram*. His name appeared in the next morning's edition, and by the time he got home from taking his four-year-old son to school, his answering machine had filled up with calls. Green took some one hundred calls that day; all he had time to do was take down the name and phone number of people who said they were interested. One of the calls was from WBAP radio, wanting to interview him for the noon news. WBAP broadcast that day that Green was heading up the Texas effort. "I wasn't diddly," he said, but he was suddenly thrown headfirst into the movement.

The Texas primary, highly touted as a major event in the 1984 and 1988 Super Tuesday collection of southern primaries, drew an abnormally low turnout. The contest for the presidential nomination in the two major parties drew fewer Texans in 1992 than the hotly contested gubernatorial primary two years prior.

Sharon Holman went to the polls on primary day and later cited that as one illustration that the draft effort was not planned. She did, however, cast a write-in vote for Ross Perot. But the woman who would become an important cog in the campaign machine couldn't sign a petition when the petition-signing began in earnest—which was almost immediately.

Judy Follett finally called the Perot secretaries and told them that hundreds of calls and people were being lost, and that she needed help. She had done a little Republican volunteer work back home in Terre Haute, Indiana, but "nothing like this," she said. "It was bigger than I ever dreamed. One woman said she had her phone on redial for three hours to get through. A lot of people think, 'Well, he started this, he was behind it.' He wasn't at all. It truly was grass roots all the way. Finally, I called and said, 'I can't do this anymore. It's more than I can handle, and we're letting people down.'"

Other volunteers, later on, would venture that Perot was intuitive enough to know that the time was right for him to make his move. It was a movement from the people, all right, but he planted the seed and fertilized it well.

On March 10, the day of the Texas primary, Ross Perot called Sharon Holman and a handful of other associates. He said his office switchboard in Dallas was totally gridlocked and the phones needed to be moved out of the office. Said Holman, "He just said we've got to do something to answer people's questions. We've got to get back to these people."

The next morning at 7:30, Sharon Holman and a team of five other Perot employees met to set up a phone system. The six were Mark Blahnik, Darcy Anderson, Russ Monroe, Mike Poss, Darrell Lake and Holman.

31

They were young, bright and energetic. They all worked for the Perot Group—in real estate, marketing, financing, accounting. Mark Blahnik was Perot's personal right-hand man; he handled special projects and Perot's security. Darcy Anderson, formerly a recruiter with EDS, had worked in real estate development for the Perot Group for five years. Russ Monroe, a CPA, prepared the Perot tax returns and handled the real estate taxes. Mike Poss was also an accountant, a financial man. Darrell Lake had just relocated to Dallas from Atlanta to work in Perot real estate operations. Ms. Holman was a long-time employee. None had any significant experience in politics. They took space on the eleventh floor of the building on Merit Drive where Perot oversees his $2.2 billion empire from the seventeenth floor. They arranged for thirty phone lines, called some volunteers and hired some temporaries to answer phones.

Around this time, Tom Luce, Perot's longtime attorney and friend, got a call in a New York hotel from Perot, asking him to check out the requirements for getting on the ballot in fifty states. "This thing is really building up momentum," Perot told Luce. "I don't want people out there trying to perform an impossible mission." Luce called in some lawyers from the Hughes and Luce law firm in Dallas and attorney Tom Barr in New York (who did legal work for Perot during Perot's nasty divorce from General Motors). They were all asked to do ballot access research. Clay Mulford, Perot's son-in-law and a lawyer with Hughes and Luce, would coordinate the ballot access questions.

Darrell Lake and Darcy Anderson took the information from the lawyers about the different state requirements and saw that the information was passed on to volunteers in those states. Mike Poss became the financial officer. Monroe was in charge of the early phone arrangements and setting up the original data base. And Blahnik eventually would take over the field operations.

One of the first decisions that had to be made was how to answer the phones—"What do we call ourselves?" as Sharon Holman put it. They decided against Draft Perot and selected Perot Petition Committee. Sharon Holman, who later would become a principal media spokesperson for the committee, set about trying to understand the Texas petition system, so that the Dallas office could function as a clearinghouse of information for the rest of Texas.

On the morning of March 13, the toll-free number— 1-800-685-7777—was operational. Calls were flipped from the Perot switchboard. During the first day of operation, MCI estimated that more than six thousand calls to his office were attempted. By then, some fifty Dallas-area residents had asked the secretary of state's office in Austin for packets containing information on getting Perot on the Texas ballot. It was three weeks after "Larry King Live." Perot denied he was setting up a presidential headquarters; he was just responding to calls, he said.

But there were, almost immediately, outgoing calls, also. Temporary workers were hired. Volunteers were sought to man the phones and work on the Texas petition effort. One of the outgoing calls was to Mark Green in Fort Worth. The Dallas team had heard he was "heading up" the Tarrant County effort. Green was invited to come over to Dallas to get petitions and to attend an instructional meeting. David Rhodes got a call in Austin from Darcy Anderson. "Can you come up to Dallas tonight for a meeting?" he asked. The mechanics of circulating petitions would be discussed.

Perot appeared at that first organizational meeting of volunteers and asked them to help handle the incoming calls and just see if the rush died out. It didn't. And the volunteers were ready to move on a petition-signing campaign.

Calls were coming in from New Mexico (an offer of three buildings in Albuquerque and Las Cruces), from Atlanta (a veteran who offered a building), from Florida to Alaska, with people saying, "Tell me what to do. I'll do anything." The first day was so exciting, Follett said, "I didn't want to go home that night."

On the morning of March 13, David Rhodes went to breakfast with Darcy Anderson and Darrell Lake and was asked to organize Austin and the Central Texas area. Returning to Austin he asked his employer for a leave of absence until May 1 so he could concentrate on the petition campaign. Beginning March 13, the third day after the initial 7:30 a.m. meeting of the Team of Six, volunteers were being trained around the clock in how to circulate petitions.

Muffie McCoole had been with an executive search firm and was working as a consultant when the Perot effort began. She signed on early, was soon put on staff, and eventually became the phone bank administrator. She called Ed Campbell, a Dallas friend whose company had recently been sold. He was looking for ways to fill his time. Campbell had worked with volunteers in various civic endeavors; he offered to organize the volunteers. He was soon invited to join the paid staff, as the first head of the volunteer center. When Campbell started, there was a nucleus of about a dozen volunteers. "People began coming in from all over and we had to decide how to use them," Campbell said. "It was totally confusing, but it worked. What I first noticed was the team aspect of the thing." The phones were soon transferred to a larger space on the second floor of the building on Merit Drive, and the system was up-graded.

Training times for volunteers were set up in the office at 10:00 a.m., 12:00 m., 2:00 p.m. and 4:00 p.m." People were demanding to be told what to do," Sharon Holman said. "We had a full room every time we did the training. They would come for training and then stay for the afternoon and volunteer. People would just wander in the door and say, 'What can I do?' It was an incredible time. It was wonderful chaos."

The trainers were temporary workers who were hired. Some didn't last long, but a few stayed for the duration of "Perot I," the spring campaign, under the guise of volunteers—an unnecessary subterfuge, according to one volunteer. The depressed Dallas economy provided Perot with plenty of talent. Joe Barton, Henry Hicks and Gary Ross were all out of work, making their living as temps, when they were hired by Perot. They pretended to be volunteers until July.

Names initially were taken on phone slips, put on a list and then entered into a computer. Lucretia Holmes, a computer specialist, was brought over from Perot Systems to set up the original data base. She wouldn't return to Perot Systems until December, 1992.

The number of phone lines continued to grow, from thirty to fifty to seventy. By March 16, a hundred phone lines had been installed, with a voice-mail system to handle the overflow. Some callers still couldn't get through. The Home Shopping Network in Florida was engaged to handle out-of-state calls. Callers could leave their name, phone number and state. The voice mail was transcribed, then sent back to Dallas to be merged with the out-of-state data bank. By March 20, as many as two thousand calls per hour were being taken on the one hundred phone lines.

When people volunteered to coordinate efforts in their states, they were sent names of other callers from that state from the data bank. "The people from out of state were like we were," Sharon Holman said. "They didn't anticipate all these calls. I got a lady transferred from Mr. Perot's switchboard, a lady in Bethlehem, Pennsylvania, who used to live in Texas. She was quoted in the paper up there, and she started getting calls. She was getting five hundred calls a day."

TENNESSEE QUALIFIES PEROT

Even before the Dallas 800 number had been established, petitions were filed making Tennessee the first state to put Perot's name on the ballot. Only 275 signatures were required—twenty-five names for each of the required eleven electors—and Steve Fridrich, a thirty-five-year-old college chum of Ross Perot, Jr., had volunteered for the job of collecting the signatures. The day after the "Larry King Show," Fridrich was sitting in his office at Fridrich and Clark Realty in Nashville chatting with Bruce Dobie, who worked for Nashville's alternative newspaper. Dobie suggested things were probably crazy in Dallas. Fridrich picked up the phone and called Perot's office, talking with Sally Bell. After a brief conversation, he said he intended to put Perot's name on the ballot in Tennessee. Then he hung up the phone and asked, "What have I done?" He didn't know where to start. With Dobie's guidance, he went to the Election Commission and asked, "What do I do?" A clerk copied five pages from the Tennessee Constitution for him to read.

Fridrich had become acquainted with the Perot family during college days at Vanderbilt. He had followed Ross, Sr., enough "to know what I liked about him, his leadership abilities. Where he stood on stuff wasn't my big concern, it was watching him lead people. When he's around, things seem to get done." Fridrich had isolated the keys to Perot's genius: He's action-oriented and motivates people to extraordinary accomplishments.

By March 5, Fridrich had the necessary number of signatures. He sent out three hundred press releases and received a call from NBC's "Today" show asking for an interview. He immediately called Perot. "I said, 'What's our plan?'" Fridrich related. "His comment was something to the effect, 'It's in y'all's camp—do whatever you think needs to be done.'"

Perot was pleased by the Tennessee effort but nonetheless maintained, "It's a long way from one state to fifty." Texas, for example, required signatures of fifty-four thousand registered voters by early May to put Perot's name on the ballot—a far cry from the 275 names taken in Tennessee. "If Texas doesn't do it, then basically it's over. I would just send the word out," Perot said, "that we didn't make it."

The Tennessee petition effort got front-page coverage and top billing on the evening news in Nashville, and was reported on CNN by Bernard Shaw, in addition to the "Today" show. But the second key media event that turned people on after "Larry King Live," was Perot's speech to the National Press Club on March 18. The phones in Dallas went wild, and a whole new wave of volunteers and potential supporters emerged. The "We Own This Country" speech to the National Press Corps in Washington, telecast on C-Span, laid out the principles and the themes upon which Perot would hammer away during the upcoming days in more on-air appearances: what's wrong with Washington, how Americans could regain control of their government, the danger of the mounting federal debt and growing annual deficit. Quotes that struck a chord with the people included:

- "Unfortunately, this city has become a town filled with sound bites, shell games, handlers, media stuntmen who posture, create images, talk, shoot off Roman candles, but don't ever accomplish anything. We need deeds, not words, in this city."

- "Let's look at where we are. The debts piled up in 1992, just this one year, will exceed the total expenditure of the federal government for the first 155 years of our country's existence. The interest on the national debt just this year exceeds the cost of fighting and winning World War II."

- "The total national debt was only $1 trillion in 1980, when President Reagan took office. It is now $4 trillion. Maybe it was voodoo economics. Whatever it was, we are now in deep voodoo."

Perot went on to say, "I feel as owners of this country, if we're going anywhere, you've got to send them a message: You work for us, we don't work for you. Under the Constitution, you are our servants. Grow up! Work as a team! Serve the people, solve the problem, and move on to the next one. Build a better country and stop throwing away money we don't have.

"All members of Congress and the president ought to have to turn in excess funds from each campaign.

And if Congress wants a raise, it ought to go on the ballot. Get rid of the freebies, the airplanes, the excessive staffs. And stop the hop from federal official to foreign lobbyist. And provide adequate television time for all candidates."

"This is kind of basic simple stuff," Perot said. But it was the kind of stuff none of the other politicians were talking about. The talking heads on national TV started addressing the idea of an actual Perot candidacy. On March 20, Charles Gibson of ABC's "Good Morning America" talked about it with Ginny Caroll, Houston bureau chief for News*week*, and Doug Bailey, publisher of *The Hotline*, a daily political news summary. Ms. Caroll described Perot as "sort of an accomplishments junkie, an action junkie" who wanted the people to come to him. "This is what I call a...grass roots effort that's being very well fertilized," she said, with Perot funds. "This isn't just a unilateral, everybody's-got-to-get-up-and-do-it-on-their-own thing," she said. Ms. Caroll recognized the challenge for Perot. "He loves long shots, and the best way to get his attention is to say, 'You can't do that, Ross Perot.'"

"But does Perot's character fit with what it takes to be a president?" asked Gibson. "Well, if you're looking for a teddy bear, it probably doesn't, and someone who is pleasing to everyone," responded Ms. Caroll. "But this is a man who has considerable accomplishments in his life and who has a history of getting things done. He's an engineer. He sees an objective down the road, and he sees the obstacles in the way."

The National Press Club speech prompted the first round of media appearances by Perot: "This Week with David Brinkley" on Sunday, March 22, when George Will and Sam Donaldson showed obvious disdain for their guest and his political future; Phil Donahue on March 25, which motivated the most people to date to call the Dallas phone number; and "60 Minutes" on March 29. Perot also hit "Larry King Live" again on March 29.

It was the "Donahue Show" on March 25 that created bedlam, largely because Perot's 800 number was flashed on the screen during the show. The Donahue appearance produced 257,280 calls to the Perot phone banks; MCI said 18,000 calls hit at the same instant, when the phone number was shown. The phone bank learned to staff up whenever there was a national TV appearance by Perot.

And there was a plethora of such appearances throughout the next month. As volunteers answered the phones, Perot answered requests from the national TV shows that would offer the widest exposure for his message. It proved to be a winning equation: Whenever Perot appeared on national TV, the phone lines lit up and more names were plugged into the computer for the petition drive.

By the time the Texas petition campaign got into full swing, the phone bank had become a highly efficient operation. On April 27, it was moved overnight—along with other staff offices—to a vast, glassed-in second floor office space in a building on LBJ Freeway, not far from Perot's offices. Not only did the new space provide for better security for a very security-conscious person, it also was large enough to become a permanent campaign headquarters, should the movement continue.

The phone bank was open from 9:00 a.m. to 7:00 p.m. weekdays, 9:00 a.m. to 5:00 p.m. on Saturdays, and 1:00 p.m. to 5:00 p.m. on Sundays, and late shifts on nights of TV appearances. Long tables of phones filled the large room. Volunteers were given permanent badges to clear them with the first-floor security. When they arrived at the phone bank, they checked in at the reception table for volunteers with Karoline Wilson, who provided them their Blue Book of instructions. At the front of the room was a big board which listed upcoming Perot media appearances to pass along to callers; many callers wanted to know when Perot would be on TV again. Supervisors were provided if callers ran into a question the volunteers couldn't answer; and trainers were there for any newcomers. "Most of us who were there all the time had no other life," one volunteer said. But no one was complaining. The camaraderie alone was worth it. And the response provided constant gratification. Karoline Wilson, for example, had a master's degree in counseling and could have used a job because of a recent divorce. But a month after she had wandered in to the Merit Drive office, she said, "I couldn't have left. I was hooked. I just made up my mind I was going to last it out."

Next to the phone bank was a huge "break room," where the volunteers took their coffee and coke breaks. It was filled with vending machines, tables and chairs and had a large-screen TV where Perot appearances could be watched. As the campaign progressed, most of the media interviews were conducted in the "break room."

Volunteers manning the phones took notes on interesting calls, which were filed in a folder on a front table and then stored. One such call was from Jerry Plocek of Berwyn, Illinois, who complained that he had given his address three times for an information packet, but still had not received anything. "I understand that you all are volunteers working hard and I wish you strength," he said. "Whenever my wife and I get to be taken out, we speak up for Mr. Perot. We follow every bit of news from or about him. Since Teddy Roosevelt, Perot is the only candidate I believe in and want to support." The volunteer taking the call, Shin Yeung, had written at the bottom of the sheet, "Mr. Plocek is ninety-six years old."

A banner was strung across the wall at the front of the phone room over a table which held copies of news stories, a brief bio of Perot, and information on vendors selling campaign paraphernalia. The banner said: "Democrats and Republicans, Is that all you know? None of the Above, There's Always Perot."

On a large cardboard poster board was one of Perot's favorite quotations, from David Friend's *The Meaning of Life*:

"The real question to ask is: Why am I here?

"Each of us was placed here for a special purpose. I believe that it is each person's responsibility to determine what he or she can do to make the world a better place—and then go out and do it.

"We are here to:

"Live together peacefully.

"Be honest with ourselves and others.

"Stand on principle, never yield to expediency.

"Take full responsibility for our actions.

"Control our selfish and acquisitive instincts.

"Protect and preserve our home—the planet we live on.

"Maintain and improve the most efficient unit of government the world has ever known—the strong family unit.

"Manage a world driven by rapid change for the benefit of future generations even though an inherent trait of human nature is to resist change.

"Be resolute and unflinching in accomplishing the toughest tasks, where the odds of achieving success are against us.

"Risk failure."

—Ross Perot

It was a weird but compatible cast of characters in Dallas who believed in that motto and put their lives on hold for Ross Perot.

One desk was positioned at the front of the room for the phone bank manager, Rose Roberts-Cannaday. Cannaday, the wife of an assistant police chief in Dallas, had worked as a sportscaster and a talk show host. She had also made commercials. She hired on as a temp shortly after "Larry King Live," and then was put on the paid staff. Over the next few weeks, she said, the callers spanned the spectrum of age, economic condition and geography. "We've heard from Americans living abroad, in England, Australia and Canada, wanting to know what they can do," she said. Cannaday said she had never been involved in anything that was such an adrenalin pump. "I go home and it's hard to come down, it's so interesting," she said, as the spring phone bank boomlet took off. "In the beginning, I didn't know how far he would go. Now I believe he's going to be president."

3

TEXAS PETITION DRIVE ("DAD, THEY'RE HERE, THEY'RE EVERYWHERE")

NINA VETTER AND DOROTHY (DOT) DICKEY, two retired sisters from Oceanside, California, were traveling cross country for an extended vacation in late March. They were planning to enjoy three spring months in Florida when they pulled their RV into the piney woods of East Texas to spend the night. The sisters camped at Tyler State Park, and on the night of March 30, 1992, were watching a tiny portable television when Ross Perot was interviewed on "60 Minutes."

The next morning, Nina and Dot motored away from the Tyler area as scheduled. But they had become so excited by the possibility that Perot might actually consider a presidential candidacy, they could talk of nothing else all the way to the Louisiana border. Once in Louisiana, they stopped to call home to see if they should cancel their vacation plans and return to California to get involved in whatever Perot movement was underway there. The California petition deadline, they discovered, was much later in the summer (August 7). They had decided to move on when they tuned into a Tyler radio station and heard a Tyler volunteer talking about the urgency of the Texas situation. Of all the states, Texas had the earliest deadline for petitions to get on the ballot May 11 and required a huge number of signatures. Fifty-four thousand signatures were needed from registered voters who didn't vote in either party primary to qualify Ross Perot to be on the ballot in November. It was a massive job, and there was less than six weeks until the deadline.

Nina and Dorothy pulled off Interstate 20, turned around and headed back to Tyler, where they called James Hutchinson, the local volunteer they had heard on the radio. They offered their services. The Tyler volunteers had just been offered headquarters space in a shopping center, a vacant hamburger joint, according to local chairman Lynda Riley. The "California Dolls," as they came to be known, signed on the first day and opened up the headquarters for several days thereafter. "You wouldn't believe the people who came in at Tyler. They were enthused. They were excited. You haven't heard that word used regarding an election in a long, long time," Nina Vetter said. The sisters remained in Tyler for three weeks, staying in their RV at the state park and working in the petition headquarters until their mother's illness forced them to return to California.

"It's probably his integrity and the fact that he will really make a difference; he will call it like it is," Nina said in explaining why the sisters gave up their travel plans to work in Texas for Perot. "We'd heard about him when he got his men out of Iran. Our husbands were both in the military—they're deceased now—so we'd heard about what he did for the POWs. We just thought that it was that important for our country. We think something needs to be done about the debt, and none of the other politicians will even admit there is a problem."

Nina and Dot describe themselves as basically Republicans, but they had never done that kind of campaigning before—not for any candidate. "They were like manna from heaven—these two little five-feet tall, grayhaired women, wearing SAS shoes, in their seventies, I'm sure," Lynda Riley said. The Tyler headquarters was able to stay open from 8:00 a.m. to 9:00 p.m. and collected five thousand signatures. The "California Dolls" said they had never felt compelled to do such a thing before.

Nor, in fact, had Lynda Riley been compelled to get into politics for a very, very long time. The last time she had been excited about a candidate was in 1968, when she was a Young Republican for Richard Nixon. "I admire Mr. Bush greatly, and I love Barbara Bush. I think he's a good family man," she said, "However, I think he is in quicksand up to his neck, and the harder he struggles the faster he sinks. And it's not all of his making; he just can't move up there. I feel sorry for him. I still like him. I just feel like he can't do the job right now," she said, during the Texas petition drive.

Riley, a thirty-eight-year-old mother of two, happened to hear Perot on ABC-TV's "Good Morning America" in March. A nurse practitioner, she was dressing for work when she heard the voice of a man who was "saying things that made sense, things I had been saying, that my friends had been saying." Riley called out to her husband, "Wayne, who is that?" It was Ross Perot.

An 800 number flashed on the television while Lynda Riley was watching Perot. When she got to work, Riley dialed the number, but got a continuous busy signal. She began "rotarying down" on the last number. Finally, a man picked up the phone and identified himself as Darcy Anderson. "I asked him if he worked for Ross Perot. He said he did, and I asked for some petitions. I couldn't sign because I had voted in the primary. The petitions had only eight spaces, so I asked him to send me a hundred." Riley put the petitions in the doctor's office where she worked, and word soon spread.

The Tyler volunteer operation, which included an organizational structure, demographic and precinct-level work, went on to become a prototype for other county operations in the state and the hub of the East Texas Perot network. Lynda Riley was contacted by Jim Serur, the Texas state coordinator, and eventually placed in touch with Libby Craft, a Dallas woman and former EDS employee who volunteered to be East Texas coordinator.

Jim Serur had shown up in Dallas on March 13, offering to help, and was put to work with Darcy Anderson sending out petitions to Texans requesting them. Within a few days, the Texas petition effort was turned over to him. A financial advisor, Serur was soon working fulltime on the effort. He spent his time talking on the phone to people all over the state, taking their phone numbers and addresses and providing them with petitions and instructions. People were calling and offering to let their business locations be used for petition signing. One day he received two faxes from Patty Sohocki, who runs P.J.'s Crystal Bowl, a bowling alley and restaurant in Corpus Christi. The first said, "Help! I'm drowning." The second said, "Send more petitions." Serur called her and asked, "How many do you need—fifty?" "No, five hundred," she said.

"None of these people came into this except they wanted Ross Perot on the ballot," Serur said. Looking down his list of people across the state who were circulating petitions, Serur said he had met very few of them, yet they were like "good friends" to him. "The spirit has been contagious," he said. "It's been one of the most exciting experiences of my life."

The names of people circulating petitions across Texas were listed in a loose-leaf blue binder that was given to phone bank volunteers as they checked in with Karoline Wilson at the volunteer reception table. Wilson had become acquainted with Perot when her ex-husband worked at IBM in the late 1950s and early 1960s, at the same time Perot worked for IBM. She explained his appeal for her. "He always marched to a different drummer; he says what he thinks. He is the same guy now he was in 1957, except that he is richer. He goes to church every Sunday he's in town. He loves his family. He brags on his kids. You'll see some people with money change; he hasn't."

Flipping through the Blue Book, which contained instructions to the phone bank volunteers, she said, "Even if I didn't like the guy I'd find it unbelievable, all these Texas people working on the petition drive." Names from people in more than one hundred and fifty Texas towns were listed in the Blue Book. Some towns had several names. Petitions were located at places where ordinary people work: in Beaumont, a siding and remodeling company; in Bastrop, Moore Motor Sales; in Boerne, a mini storage; in Brownsville, a crane and equipment company. There were real estate offices, insurance agencies, a tax service office, motel, country store, tool company, roofing and sheet metal company, bar and grill, restaurants, ranches and grocery stores. Also in the Blue Book were names of contacts in other states.

Coordinators of the Texas petition drive bristled at the idea that the campaign was being orchestrated from Dallas. "The implication that Dallas was running things or that people were taking directions from Dallas is not correct at all," Libby Craft said. "These were all people who had been inspired by some of the things Mr. Perot had said, and they did whatever seemed to make sense to them." Unlike the traditional presidential campaign apparatus where directions are handed down from the top, this campaign bubbled up from the grass roots. Certainly, the Dallas headquarters was devoted to facilitating that grass roots development in any way it could, and Perot personally kicked in $1 million in expense money to finance the telephone and computer systems and the Dallas operations for the first couple of months. But out in the field, no one was funding it; no one was directing it; it was whatever the volunteers wanted it to be.

Texans were circulating petitions by staging "rallies"—which could be anything from a card table set up in a park or shopping center to vans and carloads of volunteers going to such events as ten-kilometer runs and Farm Aid. In Dallas, signs made out of poster board with fluorescent markers appeared at intersections directing motorists to "Perot Petitions."

On April 11, volunteers were circulating petitions in shopping centers in Perot's North Dallas neighborhood. Anthony Shea, twenty-five, was hawking signatures in front of the Tom Thumb Supermarket in the Preston Royal shopping center. Shea saw the National Press Club speech, and said he quit his job the next day and went to Perot headquarters to ask what he could do. Ruthie Garrett marveled at the outpouring of support for Perot: "People are going to be shocked in November."

One mile north at Preston Forest shopping center, Jim Ash manned a sidewalk table in front of the Container Store, just down the street from where Perot goes to the barber shop. Ash, chairman of the board of Wright

Asphalt Products, a company where he had worked for thirty-eight years, was spending forty to fifty hours a week on the phone bank. "It's no Madison Avenue campaign," he said. "I've talked to people from Hawaii, Alaska, from the West Coast to the East Coast, all walks of life, from retired people to college students and professors. If you would spend one hour on that phone bank, you would understand. It's been the inspiration of my life."

"I'm fed up with what's going on in Washington. My grandchildren are going to have serious problems unless something is done with the deficit. If we can get him in Washington, he won't be in anybody's hip pocket," Ash said. "We just want to get somebody in Washington who would address the issues rather than trying to get elected again."

Halfway into Ash's explanation of his anger toward Washington, who walks up but Ross Perot. The fourteenth richest man in the United States and, by now, a media celebrity, Perot appeared without press entourage, bodyguards or campaign aides. He was by himself, driving his own car, out surveying the petition activities. Moments later, people lined up on the sidewalk to shake his hand. "I'm proud to see someone like you running," said a young man holding a baby. Others pledged their support.

Volunteers were working twenty to thirty petition-signing locations in the Dallas area that weekend. And, on April 13, Dallas-Fort Worth area volunteers took a bus to Arlington Stadium for opening night of the Texas Rangers to gather signatures on the parking lot. George W. Bush, President Bush's son, is managing partner of the ball club, so the Perot volunteers, working the parking lot in teams of two, didn't know how welcome they would be. Eric Skidmore, who was manning command central at the bus for volunteers, was terrified they were about to be evicted when fifty uniformed police officers started walking toward the bus. It was a false alarm. The fifty officers had been part of the opening ceremonies and were just filing out. Later on, however, policemen providing security on the stadium parking lot did ask the volunteers to leave, but not until after they had been mobbed by fans who wanted to sign the petitions. In a little over an hour, thirty people took eleven hundred signatures, including some from the policemen who asked them to leave the premises.

Nobody ever saw George W. Bush. "We didn't even know if he was at the game or not," Skidmore said. But back on the bus, volunteer Patty Stark of Fort Worth only half-joked, "If my dad was running for president, I'd have been on the phone saying, "Dad! Dad! They're here! They're everywhere!'"

Within days, according to published reports, George W. Bush was in Washington telling his dad he'd better take the Perot movement seriously.

By this time, the Dallas headquarters had more than two thousand volunteers working on the phone bank and petition effort. There were eighty or ninety signing locations in the Dallas metropolitan area, ranging from David Jay's Ice Cream shop to the drive-in window at a vacant suburban bank building. Charlie Richardson, who lived in a suburban county adjacent to Dallas, drove to different locations with signs on his pickup truck and six clipboards hanging from the truck. He brought in more than two thousand names. "It amazes me, and it thrills me," Ed Campbell said of the grass roots effort. "It's the most incredible thing I've ever done. The enthusiasm of the people is a real shot in the arm."

At a petition-signing site in suburban Plano, a woman walked up and said, "Where do I sign? I wish I could sign a hundred times. My husband was a POW," she explained, "and when he came home from Vietnam after seven years, no one would hire him. Someone told him to call Ross Perot. Mr. Perot helped him find a job."

In College Station, Texas, Jim Raatz manned the Perot petition drive desk near the main entrance to Texas A&M University. He likes to tell of the diversity he found in the people attracted to Perot. Late one April evening, a black pickup truck roared into the parking lot. The truck had big mudgrip tires, hunting lights on the roll bar over the cab, a gun rack with a rifle and a cattle prod, and a Confederate flag license plate. Raatz said the two men who jumped out of the truck looked like they had come from the backwoods of Alabama—dressed in jeans, dingo boots, black T-shirts and gimme caps. They whipped out brand new voter registration cards and signed the petition. As they started to leave, the passenger leaned out of his window and hollered, "Ross Perot is the greatest American to run for president since George Wallace!" Then they roared out of the parking lot in a cloud of gravel and dust. A few minutes later another man approached the petition table. He was in his mid-fifties, with almost shoulder-length graying hair, in jeans, sandals and wearing a "Save the Whales" T-shirt. "This fellow could have just stepped out of an anti-war protest march," Raatz said. "He also produced a brand new voter registration card. When he turned to leave after discussing the issues for a few minutes, he said, 'This is the first time I have felt there was anyone deserving of my vote since Eugene McCarthy ran for president. This will be the first presidential election I have voted in since then.'

"In less than five minutes," Raatz said, "I had seen impassioned enthusiasm for Ross Perot from what I thought were the opposite ends of the political spectrum—a spectrum so wide that I don't believe you could ever combine such diversity into a traditional political party structure. Ross Perot's ability to unite such contrasts is truly one of the most remarkable political stories of this century."

On April 26, a Sunday afternoon five weeks after the beginning of the Texas petition effort, Perot made his first real "people appearance" at a picnic for Dallas area volunteers. It was staged at a Dallas park called (appropriately for super-patriot Perot) Flagpole Hill. The volunteers were buying and selling T-shirts, buttons and other Perot paraphernalia when their hero appeared. Once again, Perot arrived in his red Olds; car parkers didn't recognize the car and directed him to park quite a way off. He said nothing, parked as directed, and walked to the top of the hill. As he made his way to a temporary stage, he was mobbed by supporters who, one after another, thanked him profusely for being a candidate. "Thank you, Ross, thank you...Thank you for running," they said. One commented "When's the last time you heard anybody thanking a politician for running?" One Republican activist in the crowd insisted she was still a Republican—just not for George Bush. "I've got a new grandbaby coming up," she said. "I don't think we ought to dump all this crap on her."

Perot was already moving up in public opinion polls. The week before that Dallas appearance, April 20-23, a CBS News/*New York Times* poll was taken which showed President Bush at 38 percent, trailed by Clinton at 28 percent and Perot at 23 percent. The following week, between April 30 and May 3, a *Times Mirror* survey was conducted showing President Bush ahead with 33 percent in a three-way matchup and Clinton and Perot tied at 30 percent.

Perot considered Texas a key indicator as to whether his campaign had real legs. To gather the requisite signatures in such a short time in the home state of the incumbent president would send a message to the rest of the country that he was viable and that his supporters were dead serious.

Indeed, his fellow Texans proved just how serious they were when they got together for the first time at the rally staged on the Capitol grounds in Austin on May 11, when not 54,000, but 200,000 signatures were turned in. Ed Reynolds, a volunteer who single-handedly collected over 2,300 petition signatures, officially presented the petitions to Texas Secretary of State John Hannah. It had taken seventy people working every day for three weeks to verify the signatures on the Texas petition. And the day before the petitions were taken to Austin, volunteers worked all Sunday boxing the petitions and labelling the ninety cartons.

The Texas rally would prove to be a model for similar rallies in other states, when supporters submitted their petitions. It was the first of only a dozen or so such conventional campaign appearances made by Perot over the next two months. He preferred to do his talking to voters via high-visibility TV talk shows, long interviews on network news shows and TV magazine shows, or on cable and satellite TV.

But the rally in Texas and others that would follow in Kentucky, Florida, Arkansas and Nevada, were important for him to keep up the volunteer momentum. "Let me get it squarely on the record. You are not ordinary people; you are special people," he said, in his best Texas twang, to the crowd of three thousand Texans massed in front of the hundred-year-old pink granite Texas Capitol. "You are part owners of this great country. We all own an equal part. We haven't been very good stewards, but you are setting an example to rebuild this country. Everybody in politics who didn't have a political job called me after 'Larry King Live' and said ordinary people can't organize themselves and get it done, that you have to be told what to do. I've had enough of this and you have, too." Of the two hundred thousand signatures delivered in boxes pasted with Perot stickers, he said: "This is the most precious part. This is your project, and it came from you. You've set the standard for all the big states to come." Praising the organizational efforts that had grown up across the nation in only five weeks, Perot delivered a line he would use again and again: "My role is insignificant; your role is paramount."

As Nina Vetter had said, the Texans were enthused. They were excited. They began assembling at 9:00 a.m. in a downtown park for the 1:00 p.m. march down Congress Avenue to the Capitol, explaining to anyone who asked why they supported Perot. Lewis Manson, a seventy-three-year-old independent oilman from Houston who called himself a Perot Patriot had seen the oil business "go to hell," he said. "There used to be forty-eight hundred oil rigs drilling in the United States, in 1981 or 82. Today, there are three hundred." Manson was talking up the need for a third party, called the Patriot Party, because "the other two parties have had it." Alida Anton of Austin, the mother of two high schoolers, had never voted. She was marching for Perot because "he's not a politician, he's a leader and a delegator." Ophelia Mounce of Fort Worth worked for George Bush's election "and he let me down," she said. "Mr. Perot recruited my son out of college; he went to Iran and worked for EDS and is still with EDS in Europe. I like everything Mr. Perot stands for. We don't need all that platform and stuff; we need someone who's a voice for the people." Jay Franklin, a marketing consultant for one of the big six accounting firms in Houston, talked about the "pervasive dissatisfaction and discontent in this country with politics as usual, corruption as usual, special interests as usual. I think people feel like there is a possibility of a real change this year."

Bob Eisele, a real estate investor and Houston coordinator for the Perot Petition Committee, talked about the effort in Houston—four major signing offices, seventy satellite offices, over three thousand volunteers working in a six-week period. He marveled at the people who just "came in off the streets." Eisele had never met Perot, but was absolutely convinced Perot would win the election because people were "fed up, and ready for a change. He has an entirely different approach to government. Government has always worked from the top down, what he's talking about is from the bottom up. People are convinced he's a leader; they feel he will develop an answer if he doesn't have one. We've seen what the others can do; we can't possibly do any worse." Walking down Congress Avenue behind a banner that said,"We the People Choose Perot," they chanted "Hey, hey, ho, ho, we're gonna vote for Ross Perot." And they rode in the parade on a flatbed truck astride hay bales, carrying the boxes of petitions that were labelled with stickers reading: "Perot in 92, Now there is a choice." Randy Harrill, who produced and donated the stickers, is a special events producer in Dallas who has worked over the years on various special events for Perot. Some

Republicans may describe Perot as ruthless, but to Harrill, he's a thoughtful man of compassion. Harrill was working on an event for Perot twenty years ago and was up on a scaffold when he got word his father had died. Perot sent flowers to his mother. Harrill was convinced: "We have a very good chance of seeing political history being made this year."

They came from all over the state—from Amarillo, Boerne, Bastrop, Midland, New Braunfels, San Angelo, Wichita Falls, Laredo, Fort Worth, Fredericksburg, Kerrville, Henderson, Lubbock, Seguin, Waco, Corpus Christi, Poteet, Emory, Livingston, Llano. When the names were called out of the towns where the petitions had come from, it sounded like an almanac of Texas towns and cities. They came from as far away as El Paso, over six hundred miles to march in the parade and attend the rally.

Bubba Eppes of Arlington, which is near Dallas and some two hundred miles away from Austin, heard about the rally on the radio that morning and said he just turned his car south and "came on down." He explained why. "I'm a real estate broker. Don't tell me about tightening my belt. You can't tell it by looking, but my belt is tightened. I just feel like there is so much change that needs to be made that we need someone who's not a politician to straighten it out." The almost entirely white, middle-class and older crowd, looked like a "Bubba" crowd—in Texas a name that is synonymous with redneck. Perot's appeal was reminiscent of the appeal of the Republican Party's 1990 gubernatorial candidate, Clayton Williams, a West Texas good ol' boy, who had made millions in oil, cattle, real estate and high technology. Williams (whose CB handle was "Lonesome Guv") was asked during the course of his campaign against

Democrat Ann Richards if he was trying to appeal to the "Bubba" vote. "I am Bubba," cracked Williams. Sure enough, he was, but he proved to be a dumb Bubba; shooting from the lip cost him the election. Perot, by contrast, talks the Bubba talk, but he's smart and he's shrewd. And Eppes was right when he called the Perot appeal "much broader than just a Bubba campaign. People are ready for a definite change in our political system. Give it back to the people. Let us have a say in what we need to do."

Lynda Riley, the Tyler chairperson, preceded Perot on the platform in Austin thanking the volunteers for meeting the first state petition deadline. "Ordinary people have listened as he has given voice to our concerns. What we've heard is a voice of hope, that it's not too late to restore purpose and integrity to our government—a government for the people and by the people."

David Rhodes, the Austin man who had put up the billboard, said the culmination of the Texas petition drive was the greatest day of his life—better than running for a touchdown in high school in Round Rock, Texas, or at Western New Mexico University. "Today is the proudest day of my life. I've always been proud to be a Texan. Today I'm proud to be an American," he said, telling the crowd, "To change a system that is well dug in, this is our greatest purpose."

Rhodes had worked on the Austin parade and rally with a committee of about thirty volunteers. "Houston sent twenty-three buses. Imagine that! The logistics were incredible. Dallas called everybody to let them know where and when it would be. We called and faxed out information. But again, it was the volunteers who did it—people coming in and getting on the phone." By the day of the Austin rally, Rhodes had taken indefinite leave from his job and gone on staff, to help coordinate petition drives in nearby states of New Mexico and Colorado.

The Austin rally was planned and executed by the volunteers—amateurs—not professional events planners. It was coordinated by three men from the Dallas headquarters—Ed Campbell, Eric Skidmore and Chris Culver. Skidmore, the thirty-three-year-old crew-cut, mustachioed employee of EDS, took his vacation to work on the event. A data communications engineer, Skidmore had been working his full-time job at EDS and volunteering nights and weekends for the Perot petition committee. Chris Culver was a post office employee who volunteered part-time. And Ed Campbell was being moved from volunteer center coordinator to a field staff position, as three housewives—all volunteers—took charge of the volunteer center: Charlene McClary, Jean Ann Reed, and Kay Bickham.

"No man should be put on a pedestal," Skidmore said, "but he does deserve credit for making people believe they can do more than they think they can." Perot, he said, motivated people to do not just an adequate job but a "standard-setting job." He did that by "so focusing on what needed to be done that he was able to marshal all the resources necessary—but not more resources than he needs."

One person who didn't get to go to the Austin rally, however, was Jim Serur, the Texas petition chairman. He was denied the opportunity to meet his "friends by phone" from all over the state because of a late discovery that names of thirty-two electors had to be submitted at the same time as the petitions. Serur was locating electors as the Texans for Perot were massing to march with their petitions to the Capitol.

Less than two weeks later, a similar petition rally was held at the Kentucky State Capitol. As in Texas, the rally had the ambience of an old-fashioned political rally, complete with ragtime band and staged in front of the granite and limestone courthouse in Frankfort. It drew people from adjoining states; some said they had driven eight hours to see and hear Perot. Supporters delivered to the secretary of state forty thousand signatures, eight times the number needed to put Perot on the ballot in the Bluegrass State. Secretary of State Bob Babbage, a Democrat backing Bill Clinton, said Perot would surely be qualified for the fall ballot. "This is not a joke, this is not a game," he said. "This is a very serious discussion about America, and it's a three-way discussion, and it's going to stay that way." The event preceded the Kentucky primary by three days. Since write-in votes were not allowed, Perot organizers were urging voters to cast ballots for uncommitted delegates. And, in fact, Perot flexed his muscle on primary day, as uncommitted finished second to Clinton, getting 28 percent of the vote in Kentucky. Uncommitted also finished second to President Bush in the Republican primary.

Through the end of April, Perot was consistently vague in response to questions about his views on issues and the ways in which he would go about solving the country's problems. Criticized for offering few specifics on issues, Perot said: "Out in grass-roots America, they're not interested in issues. They're interested in principles. I'll have the positions nailed down by the time the two parties do."

One impact of the Perot candidacy was that millions of people who had not been registered to vote were registered. Once they finished getting petitions signed, Perot volunteers began work on voter registration and were surprised to find that half the population was not registered to vote. Most were not registered for two reasons: either they were disgusted with the choices or they felt their vote made no difference. As Libby Craft put it, "In many cases, they voted faithfully and then the choices diminished, so they began to vote against somebody. Then they felt like there were no viable choices so it wasn't worth the time or effort." Or they felt the choice between either of the traditional parties would not make any difference, so their vote didn't matter.

When the Texas petitions were rendered valid by Secretary of State John Hannah, guaranteeing Perot access to the Texas ballot in November, Libby Craft said: "We have proven through this petition drive how one person can and does make a difference. With the energy and momentum of all these people working toward a common goal, there's not anything they can't accomplish. Texas has proven that."

★ ★ ★ ★ ★ 4 ★ ★ ★ ★ ★

VOTER ALIENATION: A WESTERN UNION FRAME OF MIND

As the 1992 PRESIDENTIAL ELECTION APPROACHED, Americans were in a sour mood. Not in recent history had the American public felt so alienated from its elected leaders, so angry and frustrated with politics as usual in Washington. An economy in recession, growing joblessness, plant closings, a mountain of public debt, legislative gridlock, the arrogance of Congress members and presidential aides, waste and corruption in government, national drift, failing systems of education, spiraling health costs, an epidemic of crime and drugs—all of this unfinished business, all of these unmet needs were the signs of a nation spinning out of control. A president who only one year before was at the height of his popularity following the collapse of communism and America's show of military might in the Desert Storm war was viewed as visionless on the domestic front. And Congress was hopelessly mired in political posturing and games playing. The public doubted that members, absorbed in their own perquisites and reelection campaigns, had any appetite for problem solving, policy making or otherwise focusing on the public good.

As early as the summer of 1991, even as Americans were still cheering the return home of soldiers from the war in the Persian Gulf, a public issues research firm was warning of the disconnect that people felt with the political process. The Harwood Group had conducted a series of focus group discussions in ten U.S. cities for the Kettering Foundation, a nonprofit Ohio research institute that works on problems of government, education and science. The group's research indicated that Americans were not apathetic, but they did feel politically impotent. While Americans still cared about their country, they felt pushed out of the political process; they felt they no longer had a role to play. They saw their elected officials' public meetings, letters and surveys as window dressings, rather than serious attempts to hear the public. According to the study's report, *Citizens and Politics: A View from Main Street America*, citizens felt politics had evolved into a system made up of powerful special interests, lobbyists and political action committees that acted as the real power brokers in politics. Expensive and negative campaigns were increasingly turning people away from the political process. And the media seemed to concentrate on controversy rather than substance.

It wasn't that the people had no sense of civic responsibility. In fact, many were working at the local level, to improve their schools, communities and their environment. But they distinguished this problem-solving activity from "politics." David Mathews, president of the Kettering Foundation, and Richard C. Harwood, principal of the Harwood Group, described politics as "like leprosy—people don't want to be around it."

In *Citizens and Politics*, it was argued that reforms such as term limits, new campaign finance laws and ethics standards—while they would create positive change—would not address the underlying breakdown in the relationship between citizens and the policy process. "American politics will not be healthy again until most Americans feel they have a genuine voice in determining our nation's directions and policies," Mathews and Harwood wrote.

In another study, Centel Corporation, with support from The Joyce Foundation, conducted focus group interviews in Chicago, Tampa and Boston and issued a report in October 1991, titled *People Vs. Politics: Citizens Discuss Politicians, Campaigns and Political Reform*. Democratic pollster Peter D. Hart, and Doug Bailey, president of a Republican political consulting firm, explored the feelings voters and nonvoters had about political issues and reform proposals. Based on their findings, Hart and Bailey ominously warned that "People's frustration with politics is real, and their mistrust of the political process runs very deep. This condition goes beyond the healthy skepticism that has been the hallmark of American politics; it is a corrosive cynicism that threatens to undermine American politics." One of their findings was that people are frustrated by their inability to get either straight talk or reliable, relevant information from elected officials, candidates or the media. Washington and the people back home find themselves on different wavelengths.

At the same time, the term-limitation movement was beginning to gain momentum, spurred by reports of bounced checks, fixed parking tickets and unpaid meal tabs by members of Congress. The Senate Judiciary Committee's handling of the sexual harassment allegations by Anita Hill against Supreme Court nominee Clarence Thomas in October of 1991 only heightened the impression the public had of the arrogance of their elected officials. But the roots of the term-limitation movement went far deeper than the congressional she-nanigans of the fall of 1991. They reached down to the ethics scandals of the Keating Five of savings and loan fame, to U.S. senators giving themselves a pay raise with a middle-of-the-night vote, to the televised disclosures of luxurious trips taken by members of Congress with lobbyists. In 1990, term limits were approved by the first three states—Colorado, California and Oklahoma—and the attraction of the term-limitation idea was grow-ing. As Susan Manes, a vice-president of the citizens' lobby Common Cause said, "It's simple. It's quick. It's the guillotine." People were ready for the axe to drop.

That was the atmosphere, the mood of the nation, as the 1992 primaries approached. With the climactic year in the quadrennial election cycle looming, voters were in a Western Union frame of mind. They wanted to send a message. And they did, beginning with the nation's first primary in New Hampshire on February 18, 1992, when President Bush was jolted by the performance of political commentator-on-leave Patrick Buchanan. The showing of Buchanan, who had never before sought public office, rivaled the 42 percent that Minnesota Sena-tor Eugene McCarthy received in 1968 against former President Lyndon Johnson, an embarrassment that pushed Mr. Johnson to retire from public life. For the next month, Buchanan would continue to draw more than 30 percent against the incumbent president, even in states in which he did not campaign. Although there was never really any doubt that President Bush would be renominated, even in Bush strongholds like Texas and Florida, a sizable minority of Republican primary voters continued to rebuff him. In Texas, about one-third of GOP primary voters told exit pollsters that they disapproved of the way Bush was handling his job. In

Florida, almost one-fifth of Republican primary voters said they would vote for an unnamed Democrat in the fall. Most of the voters' anger was directed at Bush breaking his "Read my lips—no new taxes" pledge and at his handling of the listless economy.

Democrats, meanwhile, were no more enthusiastic about their candidates. Former U.S. Senator Paul Tsongas of Massachusetts barely won New Hampshire over Arkansas Governor Bill Clinton, who was hobbled by the question of whether he evaded the draft and allegations of marital infidelity. Tsongas, however, faltered in the South and would bow out after poor showings in the Midwestern industrial states of Michigan and Illinois.

Washington Post political writer David Broder reported in late March from Illinois that "George Bush and Bill Clinton may have cinched their parties' nominations for president, but they are a long way from convincing voters here—and across the country—that they have what it takes to lead the nation in the next four years." The story in the newspaper's *National Weekly* edition was headlined "A race distinguished by a lack of voter enthusiasm. Clinton vs. Bush: Is it possible to just vote no?" Broder noted that President Bush rated high on honesty and integrity but flunked the test of understanding the problems of average Americans. Conversely, Clinton was seen as more in touch, but his honesty and integrity were in question.

Among Democrats, former California Governor Jerry Brown's bashing of the political establishment and flat tax proposal made him the party's protest darling. On March 24, Connecticut served notice that they were underwhelmed by the potentiality of Bill Clinton, who had become known as "Slick Willie," heading the Democratic ticket; Connecticut favored the maverick Brown.

Clinton continued to be dogged by voter doubt. While he won the New York primary on April 7, close to 60 percent of the voters favored either Jerry Brown or Paul Tsongas, even though Tsongas had suspended his candidacy and did not campaign in the state. Almost two-thirds of those who cast Democratic votes in New York said they wished there were other candidates running. A national poll published in *The New York Times* in early April suggested that the electorate remained uneasy with all the candidates and were hungry for more options. Sixty-seven percent of Democrats said they would like to see someone else enter the race.

Some voted with their feet, walking away from the primary polls in record numbers. In the media-intensive New York primary, voting was down 36 percent from the 1988 primary, and at its lowest rate since 1980. It was bad enough to cause ABC political analyst Jeff Greenfield to ask: "What if they gave an election—and nobody came?" Curtis Gans of the Committee to Study the American Electorate, who has charted declining primary turnout since 1972, blamed the low turnout on the absence of cutting issues which distinguished the candidates in the primaries from one another. Presidential candidates had begun to resemble Tweedle Dee and Tweedle Dum. Texas turned out more primary voters in 1990 to choose gubernatorial candidates—Democrat Ann Richards and Republican Clayton Williams—than in the 1992 Super Tuesday presidential primaries.

This was the mood of the nation as Ross Perot began to penetrate public awareness as a potential presidential candidate via the airwaves and to gain spotty coverage in the mainstream media. A national survey was published April 1, 1992, in *The New York Times* featuring a trial heat between Bush, Clinton and Perot, who was listed as a businessman considering entering the race. Perot got 16 percent against Bush's 44 percent and Clinton's 31 percent. As John J. Hooker of Nashville said, if Perot had any doubts about becoming a full-fledged candidate, the people were making up his mind for him by their reaction to the traditional party candidates in the primaries. "The primaries started, and Buchanan started to do well, Tsongas started to do well, and it became apparent this anti-vote was out there," Hooker said.

Meanwhile, members of Congress were talking of bailing out of Washington in record numbers in the face of voter unrest and distrust. Some were merely getting out while the getting was good, before the voters threw them out. For others, the decision to abandon public service was a painful reflection of their own frustration with a government that had ceased to function in the public interest. In March, U.S. Senator Warren Rudman, New Hampshire Republican and one of the authors of the Gramm-Rudman-Hollings deficit reduction bill, decided to call it quits after two terms because he saw little will in Congress to put partisan politics aside and rein in the huge U.S. budget. Senator Rudman talked of the coming era of $400 billion to $500 billion deficits, which would wreck the country. "We will have foreign governments in a position to dictate terms and conditions of money they will loan us. Interest rates will go higher. The economy will be seriously impaired. The standard of living will decline, and this Congress just seems unable to deal with it. And quite frankly, the last several administrations haven't either," he said. Yet the deficit was not being discussed as a major campaign issue by the leading candidates. Only the unannounced

Perot placed it at the top of his agenda, linking the deficit to continuing national decline–much as David P. Calleo of Johns Hopkins University was doing in his book, *The Bankrupting of America.*

On the other side of the aisle, Senator Kent Conrad, (Democrat of North Dakota), announced from the Senate floor on April 2 he would not be running for reelection. The young first-termer said, "I just didn't like to go to work in the morning. It is so frustrating. The budget is out of control, and I think I'm wasting my time and my life." Within days, on April 8, a former congressman and respected senator, Democrat Tim Wirth of Colorado, who was in the process of planning his reelection campaign, abruptly changed his mind and announced he was bowing out after serving one term in the seat formerly held by Gary Hart. Wirth lamented that he had become frustrated with the posturing and paralysis of Congress. In the Senate, issues had become divided along strict ideological lines. Bipartisanship had been replaced by endless bickering and an increasing number of meaningless votes, usually on symbolic amendments offered to "embarrass the opposition." He dreaded the upcoming expensive, negative campaign. "I even fear that the political process has made me a person I don't like," he said. Wirth's surprise decision followed a week spent largely on fundraising for his anticipated campaign and meeting with fellow senators about what he termed trivial matters concerning perks and reelection tactics. "How could we be wasting our time like this when there was so much to do, in the old Kennedy phrase, to get our country moving again?" he asked. Wirth finally faced reality. "I saw myself about to go through seven months of horror—a negative campaign that would be hurtful to all concerned. And for what? To spend another six years in an institution that didn't work. To continue an insane life that required me to spend the vast percentage of my time doing things I did not want to do."

Wirth went to the Senate in 1987 after twelve years in the House of Representatives hoping to find it a more effective forum for inquiry, reflection and consensus building. What he found was an "unsteadying diet of petty partisan maneuvering, ego clashes and legislative ambushes mounted by single-issue zealots." But the upcoming election year held some promise for change, because of the mounting number of retirements.

While some, such as Wirth, were retiring out of frustration, there were other reasons for the expected exodus from Capital Hill: the fear by check kiters that they would be removed by voters, the unappealing threat of a more Spartan, less privileged existence, and the last opportunity for members to quit and take with them leftover campaign funds before such pocket stuffing was prohibited. Constituents back home were demanding that members give up some of their perks. Some members apparently would just as soon give up their job. By April, the predictions were that due to the number of members who would not seek reelection, the way would be paved for an unprecedented turnover in Congress.

There was a growing awareness that the problems in Washington were pervasive—not just in Congress, but also in the executive branch. *The New York Times* printed a devastating op-ed piece on March 30, 1992, by a Republican who had served in the Bush and Reagan administrations. The administration staffer wrote, anonymously: "The unequivocal message throughout the federal bureaucracy is that nothing is to be accomplished by this government except the creation of good feelings and the illusion of action. We've become a government of Amway-type pyramids, a federal Ponzi scheme led by the Recreation President. Either by design or by default, almost every federal agency has been guilty in the past two years of moving only in accordance with a political reaction to an event—not a moment before and not an inch beyond what is needed to quiet things down...In today's Washington matters afflicting the current and future well-being of Americans are seen only as nettlesome disruptions that must be calmed, not problems that must be solved or responsibilities that must be faced."

By April, as the campaign continued to unfold, political analyst and author Kevin Phillips wrote in a *New York Times Magazine* article that "it is increasingly evident that the United States has entered a period of political alienation and turmoil the likes of which we have experienced only a few times in our history." Phillips identified all the ingredients of previous eras of alienation: economic anguish and populist resentment; mild-to-serious class rhetoric aimed at the rich and fashionable; exaltation of the ordinary American against abusive, affluent and educated elites; contempt for Washington; rising ethnic, racial and religious animosities; fear of immigrants and foreigners, and a desire to turn away from internationalism and concentrate on rebuilding America and American lives. Frustration politics, wrote Phillips, "represents a sort of primal scream by the electorate that major party politics must heed if the center is to hold." Yet, the political leaders of both parties, unable to see the depth of the problems, failed to present a coherent set of policies to alleviate the frustration. Rather, they seemed incapable of grasping the possibility that they, and the system, were failing the people.

While members of Congress worried about the increased cost of their gym and whether they would lose their free prescription drugs, cut-rate hair cuts and free parking at National Airport, the average American had far more serious worries. The politicians were consumed with political perceptions, but average Americans were worried about real life problems—about jobs and making ends meet. One national survey of some twenty-five hundred Americans between the ages of eighteen and sixty-five (who were representative of the country by sex, age and income) indicated the following:

- One person in ten had been laid off in the previous year.
- One person in five had a member of his or her family laid off.
- Among those employed, more than two out of five worked in a company that had laid off someone in the previous year.
- Two out of three were aware of a friend or neigbor who had lost his or her job in the previous year.
- One in three was "very worried" that a major wage earner in the family would lose his/her job.

By May 1992, the alienation, frustration politics, and breakdown of government had been substantiated in books that cracked the public consciousness. They also cracked the national bestseller lists–books such as *Who Will Tell The People* by William Greider, *Reinventing Government* by David Osborne and Ted Gaebler, and *America, What Went Wrong?* by Donald L. Barlett and James B. Steele. *America, What Went Wrong?* was an expanded version of a nine-part newspaper series originally published by the *Philadelphia Inquirer* in October 1991. In the "McNewspaper" age, *Philadelphia*

73

Inquirer readers disputed the cynics who said people wouldn't read such long and detailed stories. The series generated the largest response from readers in the newspaper's history—twenty thousand letters, notes, telephone calls and requests for reprints, proving that Americans craved the beef, and that they cared deeply about what was going wrong in this country. Many of the readers, wrote Barlett and Steele, displayed a clearer grasp of the problems confronting the country than the rule makers in Washington.

Barlett and Steele wrote about the issue that was the pier and beam of Ross Perot's message to the American people—the deficit. "At midnight on Monday, September 30, 1992, the U.S. government will close the books on its twenty-third consecutive year of deficit spending," they wrote. "That is the longest-running streak of red ink in the nation's history. The previous record— sixteen consecutive years—ran from 1931 to 1946, the hard years of the Great Depression and World War II." The $350 billion anticipated deficit in 1992 was expected to exceed the deficits of the 1930s, 1940s, 1950s, 1960s and part of the 1970s—combined.

But it was the Greider book that would presage the Perot phenomenon. Greider's was the manifesto for a new grass-roots political awakening. The blunt message of *Who Will Tell The People* was that American democracy is in much deeper trouble than most people wish to acknowledge. Greider wrote that "What exists behind the formal shell is a systemic breakdown of the shared civic values we call democracy." He laid part of the problem at the feet of the press, and rightly so. Because, he said, political reporters separate "politics" from substantive "issues" as if they were two different subjects. Political reporting had become just another form of sportswriting—who's ahead, who's behind, who's winning, who's losing—rather than providing real understanding of the making of public policy, particularly economic and financial policy. Greider recognized, correctly, that politics ought to be anchored in government, not in campaigns.

Political money and what it buys was another scandalous question dissected by Greider, along with the bankruptcy of the two major political parties. Greider found that a new politics had developed over the last generation that guaranteed the exclusion of most Americans from the debate, with a major industry growing up in Washington around what might be called "democracy for hire." He painted a marvelous word picture when he described Washington as "a grand bazaar—a steamy marketplace of tents, stalls and noisy peddlers. The din of buying and selling drowns out patriotic music. The high art of governing-making laws for the nation and upholding them—has been reduced to a busy commerce in deal making....The rare skills required for politics at the highest level are trivialized as petty haggling, done with the style and swagger of rug merchants." Perot would reduce that thought to the lowest common denominator when he talked about Washington politicians being "for sale."

During this generation, government had become less about representative government and more about raw power. As Greider wrote, "At any neighborhood bar or lunch counter, when citizens talk about politics, they do not talk about the governing process as a rational search for 'responsible' policies. They see it, plain and simple, as a contest ruled by power and they know that they do not have much."

Ross Perot wanted to restore power to the American

people. And he understood the Greider admonition that "Strange as it may seem to an era governed by mass-market politics, democracy begins in human conversation."

In the early days of the campaign, Perot was an enigma, a fresh face, an anti-politician. The more exposure he got, the better people liked him—until that exposure turned tawdry, and his own personal characteristics and eccentricities, past and present, scared people.

John Shelton Reed, a North Carolina writer, would write (in the journal *Chronicles*) later in the campaign, "Some folks I've talked to profess to find Perot a little frightening. But what ought to scare them is the alienation and frustration, the wrecking impulse, that he's tapping. All things considered, it seems to me that voting for Ross Perot is a pretty harmless way for that to surface."

Despite the alienation in the country and the climate that was conducive to a political outsider, Perot would be swimming against strong historical currents if he declared his candidacy and remained in the race through November.

History, in fact, suggests that independents do best in the spring when voters are willing to register a protest. Independent John Anderson was competing with the leading party candidates in the spring of 1980 in public opinion polls. By the time the summer nominating conventions were over, he couldn't beg any media attention. In November, he drew only six percent of the vote, and failed to get a single electoral college vote.

George Wallace in 1968 and Strom Thurmon in 1948, Southern candidates with racial appeals, fared better in electoral college votes but left little more impact than that of protest candidates. Wallace, the former Alabama governor and the American Party nominee, took votes away from Democratic candidate Hubert Humphrey and kept Republican Richard Nixon's popular victory to a plurality. Wallace got 13.5 percent of the popular vote and forty-six electoral votes. Nixon and Humphrey were separated by less than one percentage point in the popular vote, but Nixon walked away with 301 electoral votes to Humphrey's 191.

Likewise in 1948, Democrat Harry Truman easily won the electoral contest with 303 votes, while Thurmon, the States Rights candidate, drew only thirty-nine electoral votes. Thurmon attracted only 2.4 percent of the popular vote, the same as Henry Wallace, the Progressive candidate, running the same year, who gained no electoral votes. However, not since Theodore Roosevelt organized the Bull Moose Party in 1912, after an intraparty dispute with President William Howard Taft, had there been an outside candidate who looked as formidable as H. Ross Perot. There were, in fact, striking similarities between 1912 and 1992, including a dissatisfaction with current political institutions. Like Roosevelt, Perot was a nontraditional party candidate who would enter the race with instant credibility. And, like Roosevelt, he was wealthy, colorful and had a reputation for action. Roosevelt, however, could not be called an anti-politician; he had served as president and as governor of New York. Teddy Roosevelt's 1912 candidacy was the high-water mark for a third-party candidate; he won 27 percent and eighty-eight electoral votes. More importantly, by splitting the Republican Party vote, he kept Taft from gaining a second term, effectively throwing the election to Democrat Woodrow Wilson.

The conventional wisdom is that outside candidates peak when they announce. Indeed, two months after the Ross Perot's grass roots movement began, he was polling in the 30 percent range in nationwide surveys, and was beating the incumbent president George Bush in his home state, according to the Texas Poll released April 21. Poll director James Dyer said that the "conventional wisdom is that this is probably as high as he's going to get. As more specifics are known about him, there will be pressure to return to the traditional candidates."

Yet, within two months of the time Perot appeared on the presidential election scene, the experts were talking about how his candidacy could wreak havoc with the electoral college system. After all, presidents aren't really elected by a nationwide popular vote; they actually are chosen by independent elections in each of the states, according to a complex system designed by the founding fathers.

Each state has electoral votes equal to the combined total of its senators and representatives in Congress. A candidate who gets a plurality wins all of that state's electoral votes. The electors who cast the votes from each state make up what is known as the electoral college. They would meet on December 14 to cast the electoral ballots, with 270 electoral votes needed for election. (The 270 is more than 50 percent of 538 electors, 435 for U.S. representatives, 100 for senators and three electors for the District of Columbia.)

Appearing on "Nightline" on April 23, 1992, Republican pollster Linda DiVall said, "The fact of the matter is that his entry could make it impossible, if he continues at this level he's at right now, for either of the major party candidates to get the 270 electoral votes."

If no candidate garnered 270 electoral votes, the presidency would be decided by a vote of the House, under rules that give Rhode Island as much say as Texas or California. Those rules have been invoked only twice, in 1801 and 1825. But the very idea was enough to send shock waves through the political establishment.

In the four-way race of 1825, Andrew Jackson easily beat John Quincy Adams in the popular vote, 41 percent to 31 percent, but failed to gain an electoral-vote plurality. Jackson, however, won in the House, with pivotal support from another candidate, Henry Clay. Subsequently, Clay was appointed secretary of state, which led Jackson to believe that he fell victim to behind-the-scenes horse trading.

For Perot, however, winning an election thrown into the House would be a little more tricky. The Republican and Democratic candidates would have their partisan support in the House; an independent would have no members of Congress owing him allegiance. The independent therefore might bargain away his electoral votes to the other candidate who pledged to adopt some of his favorite ideas.

If the vote were to go to the House, the outcome conceivably could bear no resemblance to the Election Day outcome, because each state delegation would cast only one vote. One of the questions debated as Perot began to build support among the populace was whether a state would vote according to the party dominating its congressional delegation or according to how the people, the voters, in the state cast their ballots.

All of these questions regarding electoral-college chaos were being raised early in the Perot petition drive—and for good reason. The mood of the country was right; Americans were begging for a change agent, someone unwilling to settle for the status quo. The expected candidates of the major parties—Republican

George Bush and Democrat Bill Clinton—both appeared vulnerable, weakened by the primary process and the perception that the choice was between a president who no longer inspired confidence and a challenger who couldn't be trusted. President Bush was dogged by accusations he had no domestic agenda; Bill Clinton was just dogged by accusations. His ideas for change and for returning the Democratic Party to the mainstream, for rebuilding middle America, were lost in the muddle of charges of womanizing, draft dodging and pot smoking, and his own inept responses to the personal allegations.

Perot had yet to go under the media microscope, to have his business activities and personal characteristics picked apart as chickens were plucked in his boyhood home of Texarkana on the Texas-Arkansas border. He had yet to define many of his own programs or flesh out his positions on a variety of issues that could separate those merely infatuated from the true believers. But he had to know, well before he gained ballot access in his home state of Texas, that his candidacy had the potential for unleashing consequences of great magnitude on the political system.

5

DEEP POCKETS AND
HIGH TECHNOLOGY

IF THERE WAS ONE SINGLE FACTOR THAT SET PEROT'S unconventional candidacy apart from previous independents
and third-party candidates, it was his immense wealth.
Unlike others before him, the self-made billionaire and
fourteenth richest man in the country had the funds to
finance his own campaign and was willing to use them.

Former Tennessee senator and White House chief of
staff Howard H. Baker, Jr., remarked: "We've had all
sorts of third-party and equivalent candidates in the
past. But we've never had one where you combine such
a tide of anti-incumbency and a man who has got two to
three billion dollars. Put those together, and nobody
knows what will happen."

Perot essentially had three things going for him: 1)
there were record numbers of Americans who thought
the country was going in the wrong direction; 2) the
two other candidates were viewed as incredibly weak;
and 3) Perot had almost unlimited funds to spend.

In the course of the petition drive, Perot's net worth
was listed as $3.3 billion. He had built EDS into the
world's biggest and most profitable computer services
Medicaid, before selling it to General Motors for $2.5
billion. FEC reports indicated Perot had enough cash

and convertible assets to spend as much as he wanted on a campaign. Most of his wealth was invested in risk-free securities and Dallas area real estate. Since he would not be accepting federal funds, Perot was unrestricted in the personal grubstake he could provide his campaign. He promised to spend "whatever it takes" to wage a world-class campaign if volunteers got him on the ballot. Some journalists interpreted that to mean $100 million or more.

In 1992, candidates who intended to accept federal funding were allowed to spend $33.1 million in their prenomination campaign. Then came the gravy. The Democrat and Republican candidates would each receive $55 million in federal funds, as soon as they were nominated, and the parties would get $10.3 million more that could be spent in coordination with the nominee's campaign, to make a total of $65.5 million each. But that doesn't count other spending that benefits a candidate, such as party expenditures for voter registration, the so-called "soft money" that is raised and spent by other committees and organizations.

That Perot would bankroll his own election didn't seem to bother Perot supporters. They accepted his contention that it would allow him to be independent, whereas other candidates would have to sell out to special interests in order to raise campaign funds. His pledge was that he was "buying it for the people" because the people couldn't afford it. And, despite his enormous wealth, he received more than seventy-nine hundred contributions of $5 or less before he filed his first campaign finance report in April, from folks who responded to his call to put some "skin in the game."

Former Texas Governor John Connally, a 1980 candidate for the GOP presidential nomination, commented on the "buying the election" question on CNN's "Crossfire" on May 14: "Bush is going to buy it with taxpayer money, Clinton is going to buy it with taxpayer money. I'd just as soon Ross Perot buy it with some of his money...If you all think this is a flash in the pan, you all are misreading the political tea leaves. This is a movement that we haven't seen anything like in this century."

Perot did not become wealthy by being profligate. And he did not spend excessively in the early months of his candidacy. About $2 million was spent during the first three months of the petition drive to comply with state election laws, on the sophisticated telephone system, the leased Dallas office space and some salaries. No money went for advertising. There was no need, with the free television time he was getting. Nor was money being bestowed on huge staffs of advance men to plan events, stir up crowds and get media attention around the country. The team of a half-dozen field people who were flying around the country advising volunteers on state and federal election laws was beefed up to around 25 by mid-to-late April, as the intensity of the petition drive grew. The petition rallies were planned and executed by volunteers in the states.

State organization leaders said money allotted for their use from Dallas was meager. They set up petition offices and headquarters in homes and in donated space. Many sold T-shirts, buttons, yard signs, bumper stickers and other campaign souvenirs to raise money. In conventional campaigns, such paraphernalia is distributed by the campaign organization and the parties; supporters are implored to take and display them. Most Perot supporters were willing to buy their own. Selling Perot paraphernalia became a cottage industry, with souvenir hawkers setting up shop on street corners, at flea markets, at concerts—anywhere a crowd gathered.

It wasn't so much that Perot was being frugal as he wanted a campaign that would build from the bottom up rather than the top down. "That's the beauty of it," volunteers would say, when someone commented on the many different campaign buttons showing up at the phone bank. There was no official campaign slogan or button. Some of the different ones included "It's Time to Clean Out the Barn," "Ross for Boss," "Now We Have a Choice," "We the People Need Perot," "My Declaration of Independence—Perot," "I'm Mad as Hell and I'm Not Going to Take it Anymore! Perot," "Status Quo or Vote Perot." Of course, there were buttons with Perot's picture, with the American flag, and with eagles (Perot's longtime symbol).

One of the first providers of Perot buttons was Norma Crabb of Permanent Promotions in Arlington, Texas— just the kind of small entrepreneur that Perot loved to lionize. Norma Crabb got on the gravy train by sheer luck. Judy Follett, one of the early Dallas petition organizers, found her name in the Yellow Pages. "The Button Lady" (as she came to be known) had an office in her home–two desks and a Macintosh computer—and made buttons in her garage. She had never made political buttons before, but she had to hire extra help when the Perot orders started coming in. She got most of them by referrals. By the last week of May, she had sold forty thousand Perot buttons. On her office wall was a map dotted with red stars on states where she had shipped buttons: Montana, Massachusetts, New Jersey, Connecticut, New York, Pennsylvania, Ohio, Tennessee, Kentucky, Alabama, Virginia, North Carolina, South Carolina, Georgia, Florida, Arkansas, Texas, Oklahoma,

Missouri, Illinois, Michigan, Wisconsin, Iowa, Kansas, Colorado, New Mexico, Arizona, Washington, Ohio and Hawaii.

Unlike conventional candidates, Perot didn't have to squander precious time on fundraising activities. There were no $1,000-a-plate dinners, no flying around the country to attend receptions with the well heeled. Contrarily, fundraising had been a real headache for 1980 independent John Anderson. In just a few weeks time, he had to pay several hundred thousand dollars to a prestigious Washington law firm to handle ballot-access legal activities. Even after he retained a less expensive firm, ballot-access legal work cost his campaign $1.5 million. Despite spending much of the summer of 1980 trying to raise campaign funds, Anderson entered the fall campaign nearly bankrupt, without adequate funds to compete on a level with the major party candidates. That would not happen to Ross Perot.

Perot was the ideal independent candidate. He was almost infinitely wealthy. He had access to such resources as fine lawyers to dissect the legalities of the petition process. He also had loyal employees he could transfer from his personal business to the campaign, and he had plenty of experience in recruiting and motivating personnel. A results-oriented boss, his employees were results oriented, too. His people were known for working around the clock, dreaming up new ways to outfox the competition—whoever that might be. No matter that most of them knew little or nothing about politics.

THE FIRST TEAM
Compared to the conventional campaign staffs, Perot's team was miniscule during the first three months of the

petition drive. It began with the team of six that he transferred over from his business to launch the telephone
bank.

The first one outside of Perot's business—but not
outside of Perot's inner circle—to join the campaign team
was Clay Mulford. A thirty-seven-year-old lawyer married to Perot's eldest daughter, Nancy, Mulford graduated from Amherst and the University of Virginia law
school. He met his future wife in Washington when she
worked in the Reagan White House. At the Hughes and
Luce law firm, he had worked frequently with Tom Luce,
Perot's longtime lawyer and friend, but he had previously stayed away from working on "Perot matters."
Mulford was called in to research petition requirements
in the various states and Federal Election Commission
laws, and became general counsel to the Perot Petition
Drive.

Tom Luce, by contrast, had a career centered in "Perot
matters" for twenty years. In 1974, he had just started a
four-member law firm when Perot summoned him to
New York for an interview which led to Luce's first
attorney-client relationship with Perot—helping to dis-
solve the failing Wall Street brokerage firm Perot had
bought, duPont Glore Forgan. Whether or not to risk
money on airfare was a consideration for Luce in 1974.
Today, he presides over a 150-member firm, Hughes
and Luce, which occupies seven floors in a downtown
Dallas office building. Luce, fifty-one, helped Perot plan
the rescue of two EDS employees imprisoned in Iran,
and later represented Perot in a $16 million breach-of-
contract lawsuit against that country, which he won.
When Perot was tapped by Republican Governor Bill
Clements to head a Texas state task force on drugs, he
called on Tom Luce to serve as chief of staff. Again,

when Democratic Governor Mark White asked Perot to head a task force that would recommend major reforms in the Texas public school system, he called on Tom Luce to be chief of staff of the Select Committee. Luce helped to negotiate the bitter dispute between General Motors and Perot. Whenever Perot had a special project or tough task to negotiate, his standard cry was "Get me Tom Luce." Luce, in fact, would use Perot's summons, "Get me Tom Luce," as one of the slogans of his own unsuccessful campaign for the GOP gubernatorial nomination in Texas in 1990.

Luce was one of only two early campaign staff members—members of the first Team—who had firsthand political experience; he had been a Republican since college days at Southern Methodist University. Earnest almost to a fault, the serious-minded Luce tried to define himself when running for governor by his policy positions, made education a centerpiece of his gubernatorial campaign, and sold himself as the thinking person's candidate—a leader for the "New Texas." He was endorsed by all the major newspapers in the state, but voters in the Republican primary found him colorless. "If the New Texas is that dull, I'll take the old," was a typical Texas GOP opinion. Luce ran third, amassing a $953,000 campaign debt. Perot later paid off the debt of nearly $1 million. Bored with law and needing to recharge his batteries after the gubernatorial race, Luce went to the Kennedy School of Government at Harvard for a brief teaching stint. He was heading up First Southwest Corporation, an investment banking firm, when he got the presidential "Get me Tom Luce" summons from Perot. From Perot's initial outburst on "Larry King Live," he was in daily telephone contact with Luce, seeking his advice and assistance even before it was announced on April 16 that Luce was joining the campaign. He was without title, but functioned as chief of staff.

In Luce's office hung a framed collage of all the newspaper endorsements of his governor's race, and three books in ready range: Greider's *Who Will Tell The People*; Barlett and Steele's *America, What Went Wrong?*; and E.J. Dionne, Jr.'s, *Why Americans Hate Politics*. The latter was Luce's personal manifesto. Dionne had declared that for several years American politics "has been trivial and even stupid," and Luce seemed to agree. Like Dionne, Luce believed that the purpose of democratic politics is to solve problems and resolve disputes. But, as Dionne wrote, "Since the 1960s, the key to winning elections has been to reopen the same divisive issues over and over again. The issues themselves are not reargued. No new light is shed. Rather, old resentments and angers are stirred up in an effort to get voters to cast yet one more ballot of angry protest." Dionne argued that "The abandonment of public life has created a political void that is filled increasingly by the politics of attack and by issues that seem unimportant or contrived." For example, he noted, neither Boston Harbor nor prison furloughs—issues in the 1988 campaign— mattered once President Bush took office. Luce was fond of saying that he slept better at night knowing that Ross Perot would not rise or fall on the basis of thirty-second television commercials about such matters. Perot would talk about problems that needed to be resolved. And, he said, "Either this is a unique time in American history and Ross Perot will be president, or it isn't and he won't be."

By the time Luce signed on full time, Perot's office was inundated with media requests. Luce had met Jim Squires, the former editor of the *Chicago Tribune*, at the

John F. Kennedy School of Government at Harvard University. The first "outsider" to join the campaign, Squires's appointment was announced on April 22. He moved to Dallas in May after completing a teaching assignment at Middle Tennessee State University, near the Kentucky horse farm where he had retired upon leaving the *Chicago Tribune* in 1989. Squires had had a distinguished career in journalism, beginning at the Nashville *Tennessean* and including a stint as a political writer for the *Chicago Tribune,* and editor of the *Orlando* (Florida) *Sentinel,* before being editor of the *Tribune.* But he had become disenchanted with the quality of public discourse, the dialogue of politics. He and Luce had similar complaints about modern politics and the press.

"The survivors of the process are always the people who don't say anything controversial, don't have strong opinions, tailor themselves to what's popular," Squires said. He was intrigued by the idea of a candidate who could be outspoken, and who had the potential to revitalize American politics, partly through unprecedented use of communications technology. With the title of communications director, Squires said from the beginning he had no intention of being a spin doctor or image maker; he would not be a traditional campaign aide. His first job, however, was to deal with a backlog of fifteen hundred media requests.

Squires had been out of the newspaper business long enough to do some writing, teaching and thinking, and his conclusion was that the intersection between the press and the government was one of the worst parts of democracy. He believed the elections process had become a Potemkin Village, where everything the politicians did was designed to manipulate the press, and everything the press did was to respond to that manipulation. He was bothered by the fraudulent nature of campaigning, by the rules that governed the system. The rules had not been planned or thought out, they were just put into play as the game of politics had progressed. Candidates had to have the press conferences, put out the press releases, provide the buses and planes so reporters could follow them around, because the press could only deal with people who run for president in this rigid kind of framework.

How far could Perot go in bucking that system was the subject of early talks between Luce and Squires. They decided to try to go as far as they could go without losing credibility for their candidate—to find the edge, to run an unconventional campaign, to try to make the point that campaigns didn't have to be run the traditional way. After about two weeks in Dallas, Squires discovered that Perot couldn't possibly be a conventional candidate. It just wasn't in him; he felt too strongly about reforming the system.

On Easter Sunday, John P. White, an Eastman Kodak vice-president, got a call at his Rochester, New York, home from Tom Luce. Perot was looking for an issues director and Luce had gotten White's name from colleagues at the Kennedy School of Government. An economist, White had a unique background in business, academia and government. A Democrat, White had worked in the Carter Administration. As assistant secretary of defense, he helped convert the nation's military from a draft to an all-volunteer force. He later transferred to deputy director of the Office of Management and Budget, where he was responsible for budgets at the Pentagon and Departments of State, Treasury and Labor. Before entering government, White had risen from being a research economist to senior vice-president at Rand Corporation in Santa Monica, California. When he left the Carter Administration, he became chairman and chief executive of a software development company, which was acquired by Kodak in 1988.

White was thinking of retiring to do something else when the call came from Luce. After visiting with Perot, he decided to jump in. By early May, White and his wife had packed up and moved to a furnished apartment in Dallas. The *New York Times* reported his hiring on May 7, a couple of days after Perot said he was curtailing public appearances to devote more time to issues. White was charged with forming a team of ten or twelve to flesh out the policy themes on which Perot might base his campaign. When White arrived, he and Squires were the only staff people on board who didn't have a long-term relationship with Perot.

But no one had enjoyed a closer long-term relationship with Perot than Morton H. Meyerson. If Abbott had Costello, if the Lone Ranger had Tonto, Ross Perot had Mort Meyerson. Whenever Perot faced a tough business problem, Meyerson was his point man. The grandson of Russian Jewish immigrants, Meyerson was reared in Fort Worth. He had joined EDS as a low-level computer specialist after graduating from the University of Texas, and worked his way up to president by handling troubled projects. They included being sent by Perot to New York to run the ailing brokerage, duPont Glore Forgan. The loyal Meyerson later was a key player in EDS dealings with General Motors. Meyerson was president of EDS from 1979 to 1986. He left the company a millionaire, but Perot had other rewards in mind for his loyal employee. Perot donated millions to the construction of a new I.M. Pei-designed symphony center in downtown Dallas on the condition that it be named the Morton H. Meyerson Symphony Hall. Meyerson served as chairman of the Dallas Symphony Association building committee, as well as head of the committee which helped to get the Superconducting Super Collider in Texas. He and his wife bought an abandoned power station near Dallas's inner city and turned it into one of the city's most unusual homes, where they enjoyed bringing in musicians and artists when they entertained.

Apolitical by nature, Meyerson was a trusted associate whose judgment Perot valued. He professed to have "no interest" in politics, but "a great deal of interest in America." After being outside of Perot's employ for a few years, he was named chairman of Perot Systems in May 1992, freeing Perot up for the anticipated campaign. He also became an integral part of the campaign's decision-making team.

HIGH TECH

The other early earmark of Perot's unconventional campaign was his fascination with high technology and the use of it in political communications. He had long been enamored with the idea of the electronic town hall, where citizens could view discussion of an issue on TV and react by voice or electronic voting. He called it the modern technology version of Franklin D. Roosevelt's fireside chat. Others called it a kind of "wire-side" chat, which would include television, satellite uplinks, viewer response by touch-tone phone or computer.

Because of his own expertise, his campaign was expected to utilize television, telephones and computers to a greater extent than any candidate ever had. Call it direct-dial democracy or touch-tone rebellion, Perot was convinced that interactive communications had a place in politics and that office holders or, in his case, a candidate, could be linked to the public through TV, telephone and computers. Tom Steinert-Threlkeld wrote in *The Dallas Morning News* in early May that "the experts say Mr. Perot's prospective campaign could profoundly reshape the conduct of U.S. politics, depending on how heavily he draws on his deep expertise in computer and communications technologies. The transformation could be as dramatic as that ushered in by television three decades ago, some experts say."

Perot, of course, didn't invent high-tech politics. Others were playing around with it. Democrat Jerry Brown raised money with his 800 number during the 1992 primaries and communicated with voters through a computer bulletin board. Before Jerry Brown, 800 numbers had been used to market all sorts of products, but no politicians. But whereas callers to Brown's 800 number could pledge a contribution or request information, Perot's telephone system would be far more complex. Democrat Bill Clinton used 800-number hookups to allow journalists to hear major speeches without attending them, and then installed an 800 number so that callers could ask for information, make a suggestion or find out how to attend a rally. He fielded questions from subscribers to electronic bulletin boards. Other candidates also were beginning to use two-way satellite conferences which allowed supporters in several locations to see and hear the candidate on a giant screen. A town hall-style meeting broadcast from the Home Shopping Network headquarters to TV audiences of one hundred to two hundred people per site provided the first two-way video, two-way audio appearance for Clinton in mid-May. The Perot Petition Committee provided state organizations with a program called Campaign Manager II, provided by Aristotle Industries of Washington, to report their financial records to Dallas.

Computer technology was Perot's field, how he made his mark in business—first with EDS, which became a $7 billion General Motors subsidiary, and later with the company he formed to compete with EDS, Perot Systems. He could be the visionary who would take politics off the stump and into the studio. And he had the money to do it; one of the largest obstacles to turning such technology to political uses had been the cost. He was prepared to experiment with satellite technology, with a sophisticated computer-assisted telephone system, with establishing an electronic link with potential supporters instead of the traditional handshake.

The sophisticated phone bank provided the first example of Perot's high-tech politics. Push-button options on the 800-number line allowed callers to find out where to sign a petition, volunteer to help in the petition effort, or find out when his next television appearance would be. Incoming calls were sorted to give priority to those from states with the earliest petition deadlines.

The phone bank also was used to get feedback from the viewing public after Perot made a national TV appearance. Such reaction was unprecedented, and it gave Perot the kind of political structure—direct access to and from his beloved volunteers—that he needed in the absence of a party. It was a way of bonding the candidate with the supporter.

Surely it wasn't a coincidence that offices leased for the phone bank and Dallas headquarters were in a building which formerly housed the Texas operations of Centel Corporation, a telephone company acquired by GTE. The offices were equipped with an advanced electronic switchboard that could capture the number of an incoming call before the call itself arrived. Numbers from incoming calls to the petition committee could be shipped to a database company called Telematch, in Springfield, Virginia, which matched telephone numbers with names and addresses of callers. By early May, the petition committee had names, addresses and phone numbers for seven million Texas voters on compact disks.

MCI Communications helped the petition committee establish its phone bank, which at one point had one thousand lines. The phone bank had handled more than two million calls before the end of April, when it began phasing down as volunteers were getting organized in all the states. By using six MCI routing centers, Perot's 800 number could take incoming calls from anywhere in the country and send them somewhere else, without having them pass through the Dallas phone bank. His 800 number became the highest-volume 800 number in history, with calls from volunteers at one point coming in at a rate of nine hundred an hour.

A government affairs specialist from Austin, visiting the campaign headquarters at 6606 LBJ remarked that "it doesn't look like a campaign office. It looks like someone is preparing for a NASA launch."

The facsimile machine became the standard form of communications by state organizations with satellite petition offices throughout their state and with Dallas. The petition organization could have had another slogan to compete with any of the Elect Perot themes—one which said simply, "Fax to the Max." Information and requests of all kinds kept thousands—maybe hundreds of thousands—of fax machines ignited around the country. All field personnel had cellular phones, so they could be found on a moment's notice by Dallas staff. Electronic databases and bulletin boards were becoming the rage, and that sort of activity was tailormade for Perot supporters, many of whom were called "computer freaks" or "techies." Subscribers to Prodigy could call up information about the campaign, how the petition activities were going. Subscribers to CompuServe could read major speeches on their computers. Prodigy offered an April 9 poll—some thirty thousand subscribers just signed on and voted—which showed Perot leading among the techies, 36 percent to Bush's 28 percent. Brown and Clinton had only 10 percent each. In one week in May (May 16-22), Prodigy's call-in "poll" of customers (one vote per password, with twenty-six thousand voting), had Perot at 63 percent.

Richard Louv, a San Diego writer, discovered a retired Army lieutenant colonel in Colorado who linked together thousands of computer bulletin boards into a huge Perotian network. Louv wrote, "One of the problems with computer-based electronic democracy is that it's too fragmented. Some networks are used primarily by high-end university and business people; then there are the thousands of hobbyist bulletin boards (at least one hundred bulletin boards are dedicated to supporting Perot), and other people log on to expensive commercial systems such as CompuServe."

David Hughes of Colorado Springs linked local and national bulletin boards around the country, using his computers and his own money, so that computer users could dial a local number and join what amounted to a national electronic discussion about Perot. Louv called this branch of electronic democracy "of the modem, by the modem and for the modem."

That Perot was tapping into a new era of communications technology and a motherlode of support along with it was strikingly apparent. Perot had become the first real New Age candidate—a high-tech computer wizard, electronic-media savvy candidate—to run for president. If he didn't lose it on the political end, he could surely win it on the technological end.

The whole approach was unprecedented. "There's never been a candidacy like this in the whole history of the Republic," said Richard Murray, a University of Houston political scientist. "Nobody's ever spent a real fortune to run for the presidency. There never has been communications links like there are now, and there almost never has been political alienation like this. There's a very slight chance he could win—but there's a very good chance he will have an effect on the race."

6

ON THE AIR
AND ON THE BALLOT

FROM THE BEGINNING OF ROSS PEROT'S INCARNATION AS A potential candidate, he promised an unconventional campaign. He did not disappoint.

He never said he was going to "run" for president. "I'm not sure he is ever going to run. I think he's going to stand for the presidency," said Doug Bailey, publisher of *The Political Hotline*. "What he has said is that if people put him on the ballot, he will run, if they build it, he will come...but the moment he changes gear to run for the presidency and seek it eagerly is the moment some people will back off. So I think he's going to make himself available all throughout this but not run the usual campaign," Bailey told "Good Morning America's" Charles Gibson on April 24.

Perot's approach, however, can't be chalked up as mere political strategy. The premise of his campaign was to empower the people, to force them to take back control of their country. A conventional campaign would have run counter to his belief that the whole conduct of presidential campaigns was wrong. As he said on many occasions, "The system has nothing to do with selecting a good president. The system has everything to do with stunts, sound bites, dirty tricks, et cetera, et cetera, et cetera."

His intention was to try to take a message to the people quite separate and apart from the traditional trappings of presidential campaigns. As a self-financed candidate, he would need no fundraisers. As an independent candidate, he would have to gain ballot access by petitioning in every state. If he had a "convention" of his supporters, he promised it would be far different from the national convention extravaganzas designed and constructed by the Democrats and Republicans.

MEDIA CANDIDATE

Perot's aim was to avoid press conferences, press releases, or in any way helping the hordes of press people with an announced schedule or parallel travel arrangements. The press, still caught up in the glamour of the "Boys on the Bus" days of political reporting, liked to travel around the country with presidential candidates, writing about their appearances and inside-campaign strategy talk—although the political story of the 1990s was to be taken from the grass roots and television. Perot believed reporters to be basically lazy, and sucking up to them (as most politicians have learned to do) was beneath him. He particularly saw no reason to court the print media when he believed the wave of communication was in the electronic media, where he could do his own thing without regard for the journalists.

Tom Luce said the rule of thumb in the spring campaign was that "Ross would appear anywhere that would let him talk live and unedited. The more minutes the merrier."

For Perot, there would be no motorcades or other ostentatious shows of importance. If he became president, he promised to dispense with all the regal trappings, including motorcades and renditions of "Hail to the Chief." In his campaign, public appearances would be kept to a minimum. His only appearances outside of Texas, three months into the petition drive, were to a petition rally in Kentucky, at the petition drive headquarters in Washington, D.C., and at a Florida rally which was simulcast to six other states. Ross Perot wasn't going to spend eighteen-hour days jetting from one part of the country to another, cramming in a half dozen appearances per day, designed to get thirty seconds of exposure on the morning or evening news. Nor was he going to devote time and effort doing research to respond to whatever charges might be levelled against him by the press or the opposition.

No, Perot would be the ultimate media, high-tech candidate—going for maximum exposure on leading television programs where he had time to espouse his philosophy and often a chance to interact with the public through call-ins. As they might say in Texarkana, Mama Pee-roh (as they pronounced it back then) didn't raise no fool. Why try to kill two birds with one stone when, using the right weapon, you can kill two hundred thousand? His rationale was simple: more voter bang for the time buck. Perot recognized that the American populace in the 1990s was getting its information not from newspapers, but from television. And he recognized a new phenomenon—the talk show.

No candidate, in fact, had ever received so much free TV time, and in such a short period. The opportunity given Perot, as a potential candidate, to air his views in thirty-minute, one-hour, even two-hour segments was unprecedented. And, when done in talk show format, with the public asking the questions, the journalists could be bypassed. Former Colorado Senator Gary Hart said, in a 1992 interview, that when he was running for the

Democratic nomination for president in 1984, he "would have died" for a two-hour appearance on the "Today" show or "Good Morning America." It just wasn't done, then.

During the months of March, April and May, Ross Perot made at least twenty major television appearances, including the daytime Phil Donahue Show, Sunday evening's "60 Minutes," "20/20" with Barbara Walters and "Both Sides" with Jesse Jackson. He appeared on the three standard network morning news shows and the three network Sunday morning shows. He had appeared three times on "Larry King Live." "He's a television candidate, period," David Brinkley said on his May 24 Sunday morning show. And his major speeches of this period—to the National Press Club, American Society of Newspaper Editors and American Newspaper Publishers Association were broadcast on C-Span.

Besides being all over ABC, CBS, NBC, CNN and C-Span, Perot also was hitting other satellite shows. In one week—the last week of April—he was on National Public Radio's "Diane Rhem Show" and "Talk of the Nation," "Coast to Coast" with Jerry Pippin on Independent Broadcast Network, the "Tom Snyder Show" on National Network, and "Jack Anderson Washington Hotline" on Independent Broadcast Network.

At the same time, Perot was unavailable to most of the "mainstream press," giving a limited number of interviews to the big-name political columnists and to the trendsetting national newspapers and news magazines. Even so, before the first of May, he had been on the cover of Newsweek; in May, he was on the cover of *Time* magazine. His hometown newspaper, *The Dallas Morning News*, was never granted a sit-down interview. He went virtually nowhere except to television studios, as the requests for interviews piled up on his desk. Perot personally determined which shows he would do and which interviews he would grant.

A trademark of his campaign, he said over and over, was that there would be no handlers powdering his nose and creating his image. He wrote his own speeches, and intended to keep doing so. He invariably spoke from notes written on a yellow legal pad, and, if standing at a rally, characteristically had a hand on his hip.

Ironically, while Perot would provide no press plane and no press releases, not even schedule information (he only released the schedule of upcoming TV appearances), he dominated the press anyway. The May 29 edition of the *Washington Post* featured six articles on Perot, only one on Bill Clinton, who was about to lock up the Democratic nomination. In a commentary on CBS Radio, Charles Osgood rhymed, "It will never ever work, all the party pros feel. 'We'll see,' says Perot, 'it will be a different kind of deal.'"

Time magazine's Walter Shapiro, in the May 25 issue cover story on "President Perot?" wrote: "Perot has done the impossible: crafted a credible national campaign out of two dozen TV interviews and half a dozen speeches...Make no mistake: Perot, sixty-one, just might (gulp!) be the next President of the U.S.—a leader unfettered by any party, untested in any office, unclear in his policies and unshakable in his faith that he is right and the entire bipartisan governing arrangement is wrong."

In contrast to Perot's media candidacy, the last independent candidate, John Anderson in 1980, spent the spring and summer of his campaign more conventionally, traveling around the country making speeches and granting interviews to local television and newspaper reporters. Even though Anderson started his independent candidacy (after having run in the Republican primaries) with 25 percent of the vote, his national television exposure was limited, and his national coverage declined along with his ratings in the polls.

Other independent or third-party candidates traditionally receive almost no coverage. In 1980, Barry Commoner was speaking out on issues as a Citizens Party candidate, but was virtually ignored by the press. Uncommon candidates must have an extra "something" to suggest they might indeed be viable to gain the attention of the press. Typically that means zooming up in the polls—an unlikely occurrence because they get no coverage.

While that fact speaks to the power of the press, it also points to the power of the people. The media were paying attention to Perot because their listening audiences were responding to his outspokenness. An April 15 *Wall Street Journal*/NBC poll indicated 28 percent of potential Perot voters cited as the one reason that would most cause them to back him: He is honest and says what he believes. It was the single most prevalent reason. Perot produced good ratings. Because of his TV appearances, people were stirring the political air with their petition-signing activities.

People liked it when he talked back to the talking heads, bluntly telling the TV journalists when he thought they were off base. "Everything you've just said is incorrect," he responded in an interview with David Frost. "If I want one hundred thousand volunteers more, all I need to do is go on some national show with adversarial people...when people are rude or arrogant or condescending, the switchboard just goes nuts for three days," Perot told *Time* magazine.

Media folks joked about the backlash. NBC's Tim Russert had picked apart Perot's deficit-reducing numbers in a Sunday morning encounter. On a subsequent "Today" show, the *Wall Street Journal's* Al Hunt said in a conversation with Russert, "Back in April, he (Perot) was at 22 and 24 percent in the polls. Russert beat up on him and now he's at 34."

Mark Jurkowitz, writing in the *Boston Phoenix*, concluded that circumventing the press might be the cornerstone of Perot's campaign. "When you run against Washington, you also run against the press corps, which is increasingly viewed as the handmaiden to the discredited establishment...Pile that onto the public's already dim view of the press's probing into character issues, and you might have a winning formula in this angry political year."

Larry King expressed this opinion on Perot. "People like him, the camera likes him. He's forceful, dynamic, doesn't shirk and is not afraid to say, 'I don't know.'" King told *Dallas Morning News* TV critic Ed Bark, "See, Perot can get past us. If John Doe in Indiana likes him, it doesn't matter what Larry King thinks, or Sam Donaldson."

Donaldson thought Perot was overrated. "Ross has been having a good time putting reporters down. And if you've got a 250-watt radio station in Des Moines, Ross will get on the telephone and spend an hour with you. These talk show hosts that treat him as though he can walk across Lake Dallas, he thinks they're wonderful people," Donaldson told *The News's* Bark.

While he was being intensely covered, Perot also was taking a beating from the press for not being specific on issues. His response was something to the effect of "Give me a break, fellas, the parties have yet to come out with their platforms."

On "Nightline," Ted Koppel compared him to "Wheel of Fortune" hostess Vanna White. "We probably know less about Vanna—that is, what she thinks and believes—than almost anyone else. So we can project onto her what we would like her to believe. So, too, with Ross Perot. He is enjoying the support of conservatives, liberals and moderates precisely because, like Vanna, Ross doesn't go into much detail."

Perot seemed to enjoy just dismissing certain questions. When asked on one "Larry King Live" appearance whether he thought President Bush should go to the global environmental conference in Rio de Janeiro, he replied, "I don't know a thing about it." When asked on CNN's "Evans and Novak" show whether he favored federal funding for abortion, Perot said he hadn't "spent ten minutes thinking about it." Conventional politicians would have had carefully crafted responses on such issues.

Jim Squires, the former newspaper editor hired by Perot in April to deal with press inquiries, dismissed the criticism by saying the media were not used to dealing with people being themselves. "They're used to dealing with candidates who have been groomed and trained and taught and sent out to do tricks."

Most of the Perot news in the first three months of the Perot petition campaign was generated by the TV shows. His criticism of President Bush during an April 24 public television interview with David Frost drew widespread coverage. Perot accused Bush of ignoring the nation's deepening debt troubles, propping up President Saddam Hussein of Iraq in the years before the Persian Gulf war, and not acting to halt the savings and loan crisis while overseeing deregulation of the industry as vice-president. Perot dynamited "those who are in power, who don't believe anything, who don't stand for anything, who won't admit the problems of the country. Have you ever heard the president talk about the $4 trillion debt? I haven't. Have you ever heard him come up with even a bad plan to work on it? I haven't. All you hear is Lawrence Welk music, 'Wonnerful, wonnerful, wonnerful.'" Perot went on to sarcastically challenge the president to "step forward, surrounded by sixteen handlers and somebody squatted down in front of him, signing and telling him what to say and when to say it. Give him all his aides. Talk about the $4 trillion debt, $3 trillion on his watch—vice-president and president."

With the demand for specifics heating up, in early May, Perot announced during a speech to the American Newspaper Publishers Association that he would curtail his media appearances to spend more time studying the issues. "Night and day, there is saturation bombing, there are Patriot missiles going down airshafts in my office," he said, "all your good reporters wanting to know my positions on everything from mosquitos to ants." His lower profile lasted less than two weeks, however, when he reemerged, feisty as ever, vindicated by his beloved phone bank. "The phone banks are going crazy with working people saying, 'Why are you wasting your time on this? We're not interested in your damn positions, Perot. We're interested in your principles.'"

One staffer speculated that Perot reemerged because, at that point, it was still fun. And he enjoyed nothing better than being unpredictable. Laughing loudly, he told the *Los Angeles Times's* Jack Nelson, "I changed my mind, that's all. This is a beautiful, first-time experience for me."

Upon his "return" to the limelight, he was stung by coverage of a May 29 interview with Barbara Walters on "20/20"—an interview designed to introduce Perot's wife, Margot, to the nation. It wasn't Margot, however, that drew notice from the press. It was Perot's comment that a homosexual should not be appointed to a top Cabinet-level job: "I don't want anybody there that will be a point of controversy with the American people. It will distract from the work to be done." Likewise, it wouldn't be realistic, he said, to allow gays to join the military. Although, he added, "what people do in their private lives is their business."

The *New York Daily News* responded with the headline "No Way on Gays." *USA Today's* header: "Perot: No top jobs for gays, adulterers." (Perot acknowledged that he would not knowingly hire someone who cheated on a spouse. Infidelity, in fact, was grounds for dismissal in the early days of EDS. Perot's long-felt belief was "If your wife can't trust you, how can I?") Published reports based on advance copies of the interview before it was aired caused Barbara Walters and her co-anchor, Huge Downs, to respond on the air. "All day, the press has focused on one facet and that's the hiring of homosexuals and, in headline form, at least, they didn't always get that right," Downs said. Holding up the *Daily News* with the headline on gays, Downs remarked, "That is not really what he said."

While he was being rebuked for lacking "positions on the issues," Perot was continuing to reveal his beliefs through his media candidacy. He told Barbara Walters he believed abortion was the woman's decision, he favored government-funded abortions and parental approval for abortions for fifteen-year-olds. He recommended revising the whole structure of the American embassies, which he called "relics from days of the sailing ships," irrelevant in an era of instantaneous communication around the world. "If some American walks in with a problem, at least in all my experience, you're treated like a nuisance," said Perot, who had fairly intimate knowledge of the State Department. He dealt with it in 1969 and 1970 when he tried to deliver mail, food and medicine to American prisoners in North Vietnam, and when two of his employees were jailed in the Iranian Revolution in 1979. He said it was reprehensible the way senators on the Judiciary Committee treated Anita Hill, and he would have urged Bush to come forward with a more capable person than Clarence Thomas for the Supreme Court.

Barbara Walters cut to the heart of his media candidacy when she asked: "Mr. Perot, you are really using television now to revolutionize the process, aren't you?" His response was: "Well, I don't know a better way. The purpose is to make sure the people really understand what's happening in their country."

Late in April, California Assembly Speaker Willie Brown suggested that the Democratic party might consider turning to Perot if the candidacy of front-runner Bill Clinton faltered. But, said Brown, "I'd keep him off TV." Citing Perot's "short haircut, the ears and the squinty eyes," he told *The Dallas Morning News's* Carl P. Leubsdorf, "He just doesn't fit the profile of a person that inspires love and warmth." Was he ever wrong—at least about Perot's TV appearances and their propensity to generate support for his candidacy.

While the other candidates were still slogging from state to state in search of their daily sound bites, Perot had become the first pure electronic media contender. He had successfully displaced the traditional political mechanisms with television.

George Bush was clearly rattled, his campaign folks flailing about for a strategy to offset Perot's rising strength. Fearing a three-way race with Perot dominating the center, Bush and the Republicans began to shift to the right, anchoring their base to protect at least one-third of the vote. Thus, Dan Quayle's blast of the fictional TV character Murphy Brown for bearing a child out of wedlock, stimulating the "family values" debate. The foundation was being poured for the disastrous Republican National Convention that would be held later in the summer, which pitched the Bush-Quayle campaign farther to the right and away from the mainstream.

While perturbed by the drift of the campaign, Bush still wasn't about to acknowledge that Perot was on to something with his talk-show appearances. "I don't plan to spend a lot of time on 'Phil Donahue' shows...I'm President. I try to conduct myself with a reasonable degree of dignity, seriousness," Bush said in an interview with *The Dallas Morning News's* Kathy Lewis.

Meanwhile, because of the fascination with Perot, Clinton had all but vanished from the media map. ABC political director Hal Bruno summed up the Perot phenomenon on May 22 with this comment: "There has never been anything like the Perot thing before, not in our lifetimes."

BALLOT ACCESS
"On the air and on the ballot" could well have been the motto of the Perot push in the spring of 1992. The condition of his candidacy was that he qualify for ballot position in every state—a formidable undertaking. Each state has its own rules—some of which are bizarre, others just confusing or difficult to comply with. That's because the traditional parties don't want a lot of third party or independent candidates cluttering up the ballot.

In writing about the maze of ballot rules, *The New York Times's* Steven A. Holmes quoted Scripture. "It is easier, the Bible says, for a camel to go through the eye of a needle than for a rich man to go to heaven." Holmes rightly concluded that, rich man notwithstanding, getting on the ballot in fifty states—even for Ross Perot—was only slightly less tricky.

Start with these givens: the number of signatures required for petitions differ in every state; so do the rules regarding who can sign the petitions, who can circulate them and when and where the names can be collected. The deadlines for submitting the petitions vary, ranging from May 11 for the first state—Texas—to September 18 for the last state—Arizona. Nationwide, eight hundred thousand signatures have to be collected. But supporters must over-subscribe their petitions by 1 1/2 or 2-to-1 to guarantee that they have enough "valid" signatures. Most states require that petition signers be registered voters. Some require a person to live in the county in which the petition is signed. A few, such as Texas, disqualify persons who voted in party primaries.

The most difficult states were Texas, North Carolina and New York—Texas because of its early deadline, high number of signatures required, and because primary voters couldn't sign petitions. Also, the Texas primary occurred just at the startup of the petition drive. North Carolina not only requires a high number of petition signatures by an early deadline (two percent of the state's currently registered voters, or 70,543, by June 12), it also requires a filing fee of five cents for each signature. After the petitions are checked by county officials, they must be resubmitted to the state with names in alphabetical order. It's easier to get on the ballot as a third-party candidate, so John Anderson formed the

"Independent Party" to qualify in North Carolina. New York is not only super technical in its petition process, but the window for gathering signatures is compressed into six weeks, beginning July 16 and ending August 27. All sorts of traps are set in New York for independent or third-party aspirants. Candidates have been removed from the ballot for misnumbered petition pages, for signatures from voters who live in a congressional district other than the one listed on the cover sheet, for signatures that look like printed names and for petitions bound by paper clips instead of staples. Thomas D. Barr, a New York lawyer who served as a ballot-access advisor to Perot, told *The New York Times*: "You have to go and look carefully at every damn state."

In Hawaii, signatures must be written in black ink. In Oregon, a candidate can get on the ballot with thirty-six thousand signatures, or with only one thousand if they are obtained at a "single assembly." In West Virginia, if petitions are circulated before party primaries, it's a crime not to tell people they can't vote in the primary if they sign.

"To say it's byzantine is too generous," said Clay Mulford, Perot's attorney son-in-law, another ballot access adviser. "I had no idea how undemocratic it was. It's designed to protect the two-party structure and benefits the people administering the structure," Mulford said.

With the complexities of ballot access, it's almost impossible for new parties to run a full slate of candidates in all fifty states. In Florida, for example, separate petitions signed by 3 percent of registered voters have to be submitted for each office—governor, U.S. senator, U.S. representatives, and state senator and representative.

Richard Winger, who publishes *Ballot Access News* in California, says the complexity of ballot access dates to the insecurity of the depression years of 1930s. People were afraid of the growing Communist party and feared labor unions would start their own party. After Progressive candidate Henry Wallace ran against Truman in 1948, state rules were made even more stringent. In 1968, George Wallace couldn't get on the ballot in Ohio until the Supreme Court ruled that really strict access laws are a violation of the first Amendment's free-speech guarantee. The reasoning was: what good is it to be able to associate with a new political party if you can't support candidates? According to Winger, when it comes to ballot access, the United States is "at the bottom of the heap among countries that call themselves democratic."

George Wallace, Eugene McCarthy in 1976, and John Anderson in 1980 paved the way for Perot's ballot access as an independent. When McCarthy ran, there were a dozen states which had no procedure for an independent candidate to get on the ballot; he had to be nominated by some political party. McCarthy was stubborn and didn't want to create a party, so he sued and won all of his lawsuits.

John Anderson's contribution to ballot access was significant. Anderson didn't decide to be an independent candidate until April 24, 1980, which was too late to turn in petitions in five states. He sued and won in all five states, eventually achieving ballot access in fifty states.

The Perot people knew it could be done because Anderson had done it and, in fact, the little known and sparsely funded Lenora B. Fulani achieved ballot position in fifty states in 1988. But they had to learn the rules.

Jack Gargan, the Throw-the-Hypocritical-Rascals-Out guy from Florida, who had been pushing Perot to run for president, knew Winger was an expert on ballot access and, in early March, paid for Winger to fly to Dallas. In a meeting at a Dallas/Fort Worth Airport hotel, Winger outlined the problems and identified the tough states to seven of Perot's lawyers, as well as Gargan and Lionel Kunst, the chairman of the Coalition to End the Permanent Congress.

Clay Mulford described the situation by saying "Things were beginning to explode around the country," and Perot "didn't want to stand in the way of all the volunteer groups." Even though it was easier to be a third-party candidate, the determination was made that Perot would try to get on the ballot as an independent. "We weren't trying to create a party," said Mulford. "The purpose was, he would be willing to be a candidate if placed on the ballot."

Some states require that the name of a running mate be listed on the petition. To satisfy that requirement, Perot needed a "proxy" vice-presidential candidate, because he didn't want to make his real selection until he nailed down ballot position and became a declared candidate, perhaps even after both parties' national conventions in the summer. So, on March 31, he announced that Admiral James Stockdale would be his "interim" running mate. The sixty-eight-year-old retired admiral, a senior research fellow at the Hoover Institute at Stanford University, was doing his breakfast dishes in his Stanford condo when Perot called to ask his friend of twenty years a favor: "Would you be my stand-in running mate so I can get these petitions filed in the states that require certification of both the presidential and vice-presidential candidate?"

A decorated pilot, Stockdale was shot down in Vietnam in 1965 and spent seven years as a prisoner of war—

the highest-ranking Naval POW of the Vietnam war. Much of that time was in solitary confinement. His leg was twice broken and his ankles kept in leg irons. Perot had worked with Stockdale's wife, Sybil—who helped form the League of Wives of American Vietnam Prisoners of War and moved to Washington to lobby the government—on the effort to free the POWs. Stockdale considered himself a Republican and had supported George Bush in 1988. He and his wife already had volunteered to help in the Perot petition effort, attending one of the first volunteers meetings in California. It took him only a second to answer, "Of course I'd do that, Ross." The only deal they made was that Stockdale would be the stand-in until Perot picked his actual running mate, if he got on the ballot in fifty states.

On several occasions, Perot said that his vice-president would "not be an empty suit that goes to funerals and plays golf" but would be "absolutely qualified to run this country as president."

In mid-to-late March, the theory of Perot's staff was that he shouldn't become too popular until August, because there was so much room for abuse of the petition process by partisan politicians in the various states. However, his popularity worked in the reverse. The enormous response made it easier for him to get on the ballot. State officials were fearful of a public backlash if they denied him ballot position in the face of his mounting support.

The petition task also was easier for Perot than it had been for John Anderson and others because of his enormous wealth and his access to lawyers through his business.

The early focus, of course, was on Texas—for three reasons. Texas had the first deadline. Texas was Perot's home state as well as that of President Bush, and Texas would serve as a pilot for the rest of the country. Once the Perot staff was comfortable that Texas was a "done deal," which was soon after the phone bank began operation, they began working to set up an organizational structure in the other states. Texas had taken off like wildfire, and within a couple of weeks of the start of the petition campaign, Darcy Anderson of the original Team of Six was convinced that "Texas was going to happen." The Perot staffers moved quickly to regionalize the United States. The three young men from the Perot Group divided up three-quarters of the country: Anderson took the West, Darrell Lake the Southeast, and Russ Monroe the Northeast. Ralph Perkins, who had a background in recruiting and human resources and was a friend of Perot's personal aide-de-camp Mark Blahnik, was hired for the Midwest. The team leader was Blahnik.

Very quickly, the regional field leaders saw a need to expand from five to twenty or so field representatives. Many of those hired were former junior-military officers—about half of whom had served in Desert Storm. "We were looking for a profile of a person," said Anderson "who had had good people skills, who had been in a leadership role, and who had the ability to live out of a suitcase and handle the rigors of the campaign." Darcy Anderson, at thirty-six, had served as a U.S. Army officer at Fort Riley, Kansas, before he went to EDS in recruitment management and then to the Perot Group.

Russ Monroe was the first one out in the field. He was twenty-eight, and had joined the Perot Group in 1988 from Arthur Young in Dallas. Monroe had a master's degree in taxation from the University of North Texas and handled the Perots' tax returns. He was the kind of young, hungry and loyal employee Perot liked, although he wasn't a veteran. "We thought we needed to go to the state that had the next deadline, so we headed to Maine, a small state that needed something like five thousand signatures," Monroe said. Two friends who had taken leaves from their jobs to work in the petition drive went with him. "It became laughable later. We thought it important to get out to Maine first. But it was done well in advance of the deadline."

Blahnik, Anderson, Monroe, Lake and Perkins jokingly labelled themselves as the "Young Turks." Over the course of time, that "Turks" label would be one of derision, as volunteers in some of the states objected to any direction from "Dallas." The "Turks" contended that most of the problems were caused by local supporters jockeying for positions of power in the organization—most of whom were bad apples spoiling the barrel for everyone else. Ironically, it was the lack of "people skills" and their youth—two of the requirements for serving as field reps—that were the source of most of the complaints from the volunteers.

Having to qualify for ballot access by petition was a laborious and difficult process in most states, but it had its benefits. It required an intensive grass roots effort that needed enormous volunteer organizations, serving both to reenergize the American public in the political process and to provide Ross Perot with a power structure equal to that of the two traditional parties. One of the unforeseen problems was that the volunteers were so pumped up to perform all the Mission Impossibles to get Ross Perot on the ballot, that once their task was completed, they craved their next assignment. "What do we do now?" they asked. Dallas didn't know.

7

WHO ARE THESE PEOPLE?

FOR THE FIRST THREE MONTHS OF ROSS PEROT'S "maybe-campaign," he had been almost entirely a media candidate. The time had come to get out among the people. It was, after all, the people who would enable him to thumb his nose at the traditional parties, it was the people who would be the backbone for the new American politics. If the people would petition to get him on the ballot, he didn't need a party to nominate him.

As the consummate salesman, Perot knew that the first step in making the sale is to get the customer to take action. By making his candidacy contingent on his name being placed on the ballot in all fifty states, and requiring the people in those states to perform the work, he forced voters to invest in their candidate. Once they signed on, the petitioners became part of a movement. As a movement, it was much more dynamic than present-day political parties.

The fervor of the Perot Phenomenon was evident at Perot's May 29 rally in Orlando, Florida. This was only his third public appearance, following Texas and Kentucky, and he attracted a crowd of twelve thousand people. The event at the Central Florida Fairgrounds marked the achievement of ballot position in eleven states—Florida, Texas, Tennessee, Kentucky, Alaska, Idaho, Utah, Maine, Delaware, New Jersey and Wyoming. Volunteers from each state placed a star on a giant map on stage to signify gaining ballot position for Perot. Supporters also were filing petitions that day in three other states—Alabama, Kansas and Ohio.

"Perot has bypassed all the conventional rules of thumb for how you become president," Merle Black, a political scholar at Emory University in Atlanta told the *Orlando Sentinel.* "Perot is bypassing nomination politics. If he is successful, he could change the structure of American politics."

Perot was also illustrating a new method of campaigning—relying on satellite hookups to avoid travel. Instead of going five different places, Perot beamed the Orlando rally by satellite to petition rallies in five other states—Ohio, Alabama, Kansas, Wyoming and Idaho. While the satellite hookup was to have afforded interactive audio access, it fell short of expectations. Supporters in Orlando could hear crowd noise from other cities, but only one speaker. Perot was the cheerleader: "Let's hear it from Ohio," he said, stimulating a roar. Still, the Orlando event was carried on CNN and C-Span, embodying Perot's strategy of avoiding the filter of reporters and analysts while transmitting his message directly to the people. CNN's Frederick Allen declared on "Inside Politics" that the political loser of the week was the old-fashioned political campaign. "Our winner of the week, the new politics," he said, "Perot campaigns via satellite."

More than three thousand supporters who had helped gather forty-five thousand signatures in Kansas attended the satellite rally in the Performing Arts Center in Topeka. "Who are these people?" Kansas state coordinator Orville Sweet asked from the Orlando podium.

Answering his own question, Sweet described Perot's people as: "A ninety-two-year-old Wichita great-grand-mother who talked her son into taking her for a drive and wound up at a Perot petition party; a retired psy-chologist carrying petitions who said, 'This is for my grandchildren,' and concerned college students writing term papers, holding campus rallies and carrying peti-tions. This is what they said: 'Ross Perot is a man of action—he doesn't mess around.' Another: 'I don't have any trouble hearing and understanding what he says. Mr. Perot gives us hope and will return our country to the people. Also, our country is in moral bankruptcy and is in need of a strong moral leader.'"

"This," said Sweet, "may sound simplistic to the elite media, but it is a dream that is as achievable today as it was two hundred years ago. Our common cause, our mission, our quest is to put someone in the White House with such a strong mandate from the grass roots that Congress won't mess around with him. This may be our last chance to salvage our country and restore it to vigor and health...Let's convince the two-party system and the elite media that Perot is not a phenomenon. He is an idea whose time has come." Indeed, the man and the moment were met.

Business people who said they long ago gave up on the political system got involved in the Perot campaign in Florida. Electrical engineer Don Miller took the day off to direct volunteer parking attendants at the site. Real estate agent Kathleen Dickelman left prospective clients for the day to organize a group of musicians. Ernie Bach, who owns a television production business near Tampa, once worked on Reagan and Bush presi-dential campaigns, but felt disenfranchised by the Bush

Administration. He was heading the petition efforts for Perot in Tampa. After his home and work phone numbers were published as Perot Central, he said he got fifteen thousand calls, burning out two answering machines.

Little evidence of minority support was seen in the first few months of the petition drive. However, Perot's New Jersey state leader, Steven R. Ross, a black owner of a real estate consulting firm, said he signed on with the Perot campaign because he was tired of Bush and felt that Democrats were taking minorities for granted. By the time he appeared at the Florida rally, he was trying to manage twelve thousand New Jersey volunteers. Also at the Florida rally was Ollie Jones, a black woman who had been honored as Teacher of the Year in Alabama.

Persons attending the Florida gathering seemed nonplussed by the fact that Perot had yet to detail his position on specific issues. Over and over, they said it was not Perot's stands on health care or welfare or any other issue that impressed them, but his reputation as a leader.

Pat Muth, a transplant from the Chicago area, had signed on as a regional coordinator in Florida shortly after the "Larry King Show." She would later succeed Ed Hubbard, a former POW and motivational speaker, who was the initial Florida state coordinator. She stood beside Perot on the stage at the Orlando rally and, at one point, he turned to her and said: "There is a lot of work to be done."

"I knew that," she said later. "We were at that first step. There were many steps that had to be accomplished in terms of achieving the goal to change the country."

Pat Muth was attracted to Perot's candidacy because he was the first person to "so succinctly say and pin-

point how things really were in many areas—in education, the economy, government and business." Her background had cut across all those areas. She had seen the
need for education reform as spokesperson for the board
of education in Chicago. She had been a trader at the
Chicago Mercantile Exchange, and knew people in government "didn't have a fix on" what was happening in
the economy. "I sensed we were losing jobs, things were
not as bright and rosy as they would have us believe,
and no one was talking about this." She had tried to
become a small business owner in communications, creating a TV show to aid businessmen working in global
markets, but was unable to obtain financing. A year or
so before, she had moved to Florida. For Pat Muth, there
couldn't have been a better spokesperson for substantial change in the country than Perot. And, she believed
he could win.

After the rally, C-Span featured a call-in show that
indicated not all Americans were so enamored with the
Texas billionaire's brand of politics—including his claim
that he was willing to buy the presidential election for
the people. By not accepting campaign contributions,
Perot was not subject to the $55 million federal spend-
ing limit, so he was free to pour his personal fortune
into the campaign. A Maryland caller to C-Span criticized Perot for being "a lot of talk, little substance," and
added, "it's sort of hard to believe" that he is "buying it
for the people."

A Charlottesville, Virginia, woman told C-Span she
believed Perot was getting too much free media time.
"The major networks and C-Span ought not give him
any more air time until he comes up with positions and
is willing to answer hard questions, like Clinton and
Brown and Tsongas and Bush." She said the American

people are "gullible enough" to go along with Perot because he "vocalizes essentially what they feel. They're mad as hell and they're not going to take it anymore. Unfortunately, they don't know what to do about it."

From Sausalito, California, came this intriguing call to C-Span: "I think this thing about Perot is a personality cult. It's not just his money or they don't like the other candidates; they're mesmerized by his personality. The other personality cults I'm familiar with—Saddam Hussein, Stalin, Hitler—no matter what those persons did, people didn't care. They still liked them. People I see at these rallies are all the same. They're sort of nerdy, sort of dorky, very straight-laced, sort of like people who would show up for the "Gong Show." And I don't know what that means, but that's the way they all are."

Voters caught up in the movement preferred to characterize themselves as ordinary, working, taxpaying, concerned Americans who are dissatisfied with their government and anxious about the country's future. But they also had bought into an enduring American political mythology—perhaps best personified in a couple of old movies—of the self-made hero who is free from the corruption of greedy politicians and who unites the common people.

It was as if Ross Perot saw Gary Cooper in Meet John Doe and Spencer Tracy in *State of the Union* and fashioned his campaign after the movie characters. Gary Cooper in *Meet John Doe* describes the people Perot would captivate. "You'll find us everywhere. We raise the crops, we dig the mines, work the factories, keep the books, fly the planes and drive the buses."

Spencer Tracy describes them in *State of the Union*. "You voters, you farmers, you businessmen, you working men, you ordinary citizens of whatever party, are not the selfish scum that venal politicians make you out to be."

In this Frank Capra classic, Tracy is the business magnate who has no electoral experience, but is rich in patriotic fervor. He decides to bankroll his way into the White House as an alternative to an unpopular president and corrupt, out-of-power politicians. Although he falls briefly under the spell of the back-room bosses, he redeems himself in a dramatic radio address to the people.

Perot was the same kind of folk hero as the fictitious movie characters. His lines could have been out of the same films:

> "I'm just a catalyst that gave these people an outlet for their concern," said Perot. "I'm not surrounded by people writing my scripts, powdering my face, telling me what to say and do."...."We've got all kinds of special interests and people who understand the status quo and don't want it changed, who don't really want the people that involved in the process."

Some of the Perotistas were absolute political neophytes; others had been involved in the political process but had become spent with the two major parties. Some had been Perot-watchers and aficionados for years; others knew next to nothing about him. Many were well educated; others had little formal education.

Colorado lawyer John Schenk, for example, was one of the first callers to Perot's secretary, Sally Bell, after the "Larry King Live" show. Schenk described himself as an independent who had been totally apolitical, except that he voted. He knew very little about Ross Perot, other than he had seen him on C-Span and CNN. "I have two boys, twelve and nine. By the year 2000, one will be twenty, one will be seventeen. I don't know how we make it from here to there. It's totally out of control. We're not going to have the country we had before. Rather than say it's going down the tubes, I'm going to try this, for my boys. I think a lot of people are going to take a flyer on this," he said.

Schenk opened an office on March 23 in Glenwood Springs, Colorado, along with some other Coloradans who were "fed up with the politics of the elite. It isn't an issue of what the government's doing; it's how the government is doing it. It's structural," he said. "It's the system."

Schenk felt that, long term, "Perot is not the answer; the people are the answer." For the moment, Perot was different from the consummate politicians of the day. In previous eras, politicians held views passionately, he said, citing William Jennings Bryan and his Cross of Gold speech. Such politicians "believed in something and fought to convince people to change their minds. Those people were hard set on values. Today we have politicians constantly massaging their message. They don't ask people to change; they constantly change to reflect what the people say."

Hope Marie-Walters, a mother of two who worked in property management, hosted the first meeting in Denver on March 27. She opened the campaign office in Denver, one of three headquarters across the country that never closed throughout the 1992 campaign year and which continued in operation in 1993 with the organization of United We Stand America. She had never been involved in politics before. Among those attending the first meeting in Colorado, however, was a former conservative Republican speaker of the Colorado House, Bev Bledsoe, who worked in the early petition coordination. Diane Rees, who had worked in the 1988 Bush campaign, became media coordinator for Colorado.

Colorado took off like wildfire. A poll published in the *Denver Post* on May 6 showed Perot in the lead. Pollster Paul Talmey said, "Perot isn't just nibbling around the fringes of Mr. Bush and Mr. Clinton's support. He's ravaging both of their core constitutencies, but Mr. Clinton's in particular. The presidential campaign in Colorado appears to be shaping up as a two-man contest—between Mr. Perot and Mr. Bush."

Colorado was one of the most organized states. It has sixty-three counties. By the end of May, the petition drive had steering committees in every county.

In Boulder, a longtime Republican activist who had watched Perot carefully over time, guided Boulder County in accumulating signatures from 18 percent of registered voters—leading the country in county per-capita signatures. Peggy Douglass had spent twenty-four years in the computer business, was with NCR about the time Ross Perot started EDS. Their companies were in competition, and Douglass worked in medical education and government, where Perot made his inroads. "I knew if it took us nine months to get something done, it would take him three," she said.

Now the manager for a nonprofit spiritual foundation, Peggy Douglass was reared in Albuquerque, New Mexico, where her mother was Bernalillo County Democratic chairman. She was brought up in politics. But she cast her lot with the Republican Party, first campaigning for Dwight D. Eisenhower. She also campaigned for Barry Goldwater for president, and for Harrison Schmitt and Pete Dominici from New Mexico for U.S. Senate. Douglass spent ten years in California, working there in 1980 for the independent presidential campaign of John Anderson, the former Republican U.S. senator from Illinois. Peggy Douglass saw a difference in the two independent campaigns: She felt the Anderson campaign was more of a protest movement—it lacked the intensity of the Perot campaign. "And the climate was not as hostile then," she said. "We weren't as far down the drain."

Peggy Douglass was one of the few in her county organization with political experience. "It was totally a grass roots movement. Almost all of our group were (political) virgins." "I've never seen a political movement like this is my lifetime," she said. The youngest Boulder volunteer was a twelve-year-old boy whose parents supported Bill Clinton, and the oldest was eighty-two.

In New Mexico, a longtime political activist was drawn to the Perot campaign from the Democratic side— Ray Hughes, a retired judge living in Deming. At seventy-one, he was occupying his days playing golf and doing a little woodworking. Hughes followed in the footsteps of his father, a county clerk in Luna County who had been active in New Mexico politics. But Hughes had made up his mind he wouldn't vote in 1992 if Bill Clinton was the Democratic nominee and George Bush the Republican nominee. After seeing the "Larry King Live" show, Judge Hughes felt a spark of hope. He went to Las Cruces and put an ad in the paper, asking anyone interested in circulating petitions to call him. The response was so striking that he set up a southern New Mexico headquarters in Las Cruces on March 30, which would cover an eleven-county area. He had no contact with the Perot people in Dallas when he placed the ad, because it had been too hard to get through on the 800 number.

New Mexico got coordinated a little later, with tri-state chairmen. Dr. Steve Vigil, a dentist, became coordinator in Albuquerque and John Bishop in Santa Fe. For John Bishop, involvement in the Perot campaign reconnected him to politics after a long lapse. As a teenager, he served as a page for then-Senator Barry Goldwater, the Arizona Republican. Although his father ran for Congress as a Republican in the 1960s, he drifted out of politics. "I wouldn't say I was a hippie, but I was pretty close to it," says Bishop, who, at forty-five, owned Bandelier Designs. His company manufactures stationery products made from recycled, acid-free paper. In the early 1970s, Bishop was convicted of distributing marijuana, a felony offense. As a result, he couldn't sign the petitions he distributed, nor could he vote for Perot.

Judge Hughes came to the conclusion early in the petition drive that the Perot movement was a no-lose situation. If nothing more, Perot would shake up the two-party system. If Perot didn't win, at least he would have enough influence to change things for the better, Hughes said. But a little more than three months after Perot made himself available, Hughes was firmly convinced that Perot would win—because of the people he had come in contact with. "These people come from everywhere. Right off the bat, we had the vice chairman of the local Republican party of Luna County. Shortly after that, we got the Democratic chairman of Socorro County. He resigned as Democratic county chairman, and three precinct chairmen went with him to work on the Perot campaign, from an entrenched Democratic county. I don't think the political people and the news media understand what is happening here," he said.

In other parts of the country, the movement was also spurred by people who took out newspaper ads. Charles Donnelly, the forty-one-year-old president of a small advertising and public relations firm in Manhattan, spent some $700 to buy a tiny classified ad on the front page of *The New York Times*: "Ross Perot for President. He wants to help Americans and needs your help." A phone number was listed. The ad appeared on March 16, attracting attention and response throughout the country. A week later, when the "Today" show called wanting to shoot the grass roots movement in New York, Donnelly's business partner, Kurt Koenig, called Dallas to get the names of interested people in New Jersey, New York and Connecticut, and tied them together.

Donnelly was concerned about the rolling debt and about the American public being informed. "Both Democratic and Republican parties have nothing to gain by having the American public find out what's going on," he contended. "As institutions, neither will be able to respond and react effectively to domestic and international issues that face the country, and be able to make a difference in how we live the next few years because they're so ingrained in the way they do things."

Within days of Donnelly's ad, Kurt Koenig, a financial planner at Donnelly's agency, sent out a letter on People for Perot letterhead inviting friends to a March 23 meeting—although petitioning for signatures could not begin in New York until July 7. The meeting was designed to build an organization and lay out a battle plan. "Our campaign goal is to restore control of the government to the American people," Koenig wrote. "Politics is a very depressing subject that few people want to discuss anymore. This campaign is something we can all feel good about. We're doing this for ourselves, and we can succeed."

Some seventy-five New Yorkers showed up for the first organizational meeting. They set up shop on the thirty-second floor of the building at 11 West 42nd Street, across the street from the New York Public Library, where Donnelly's ad agency, Castagne Communications, had its office. They began receiving names from Dallas, first by fax, then printouts by overnight mail, and finally by computer modem. Eventually, the New York group had some twenty thousand names on its computer list. They sent out a mailing to raise funds; one contributor was actress Katherine Hepburn.

Cosmopolitan New York was not a place one would expect people to identify with the likes of Ross Perot. But even in Manhattan, there was a growing anti-establishment sentiment. Support was surfacing from the financial district to the penthouses on Park Avenue, along with everyday, ordinary people. "Wall Street flocked here in droves," Koenig said.

One natural area of support for Perot came from veterans and people who had been associated with him through his work on behalf of prisoners of war and missing in action in Vietnam. Joan Vinson of Annapolis, Maryland, was one of those. Her husband, Air Force Colonel Bobby Vinson was shot down in April 1968 and had been listed as MIA. A presumptive finding of death was issued in September of 1977.

Joan Vinson first met Perot in 1969 when he chartered a plane to take POW-MIA family members to Paris on Christmas Eve to meet with the North Vietnamese on Christmas day. The entourage had no luck gaining the meeting with the North Vietnamese, but did see some other people regarding the plight of those missing and imprisoned in Vietnam. From Paris, the group flew back to Newark, New Jersey, where Perot had arranged for hotel rooms and a Christmas celebration for the children. Vinson had taken her four children who, at the time, were five, ten, twelve and fourteen. "I was impressed with his ability to make things happen and do it without a great deal of fanfare." In her role as president of the National League of Families of POWs and MIAs in Southeast Asia, Vinson talked and worked with Perot; she liked the way he tackled problems. She had written him a couple of times suggesting he run for president. When she saw him on "Larry King Live," she immediately called some friends and then Perot Systems in Dallas. She was asked to be Maryland coordinator.

Her name was published in the Annapolis newspaper, and she was overwhelmed with phone calls. She had eight telephones installed in her home and asked people to help answer them for about a month until headquarters space was obtained. "People were just coming to the house; how they found me I don't know— all these strange people walking into the house. One night, at 4:00 a.m., the phone rang and a woman said she wanted to sign the petition. I said, 'Do you have to sign it at four o'clock in the morning?' The woman said she was elderly and had been calling during the day but was unable to get through."

Vinson had pursued a doctorate in political science at George Washington University in Washington, D.C. She had worked in and around Washington, in positions such as director of media relations for the Bicentennial and as a Gerald Ford appointee to the Presidential Clemency Board. She was concerned about the cynicism that prevailed in the capital city.

One book that had inspired her was Walter Lippman's *The Public Philosophy*, published in 1955. Lippman wrote, "The whole vast labor and passion of public life would be nonsense if we did not believe that it makes a difference what is done by parties, newspapers, books, broadcasts, schools and churches." Vinson believed it did make a difference. She also believed Lippman when he wrote, "Faith in an idea can quite literally move a mountain. The idea would have to become, like the idea of winning a war, the object and the focus of the nation's energies. Because ideas have the power to organize human behavior, their efficacy can be radical." Lippman, she believed, did not relinquish the democratic ideal that the people can be rallied in the defense of public interests.

She was therefore excited to see the people rallied—equal numbers of disenchanted Republicans, Democrats and the politically uninvolved who were drawn into the Perot phenomenon. The incredible cross section was inspiring. But she was particularly impressed by the fervor of middle-class, blue-collar workers, whom she described as the backbone of the country, but who are either frequently ridiculed or not taken seriously. "They are not a part of the underclass and they are not a part of the power structure," she said. "They are just out there making a modest salary, raising families, taking responsibility for their homes and neighborhoods and schools and trying to make ends meet. They're out there on the factory floor, driving trucks, working all sorts of jobs from construction to manufacturing, that's what the majority of our citizens are. They're people tired of working hard and having their tax dollars squandered. It's not that they don't want to pay taxes; they don't want their tax money wasted," she said. "People have seen their elected officials—people who have lots of money and power—get by with all kinds of excesses. They think, 'Why should I suffer when those who have it all are not.'"

A frequent spokesman for the national media throughout the campaign, Vinson said, "People are not only angry, they're afraid—afraid for the future. I not only have four children who are adults now, I have six grandchildren. I'm concerned they will not have the same opportunities I and the people of my generation had."

In Annapolis, a community near Washington, D.C., and home of the U.S. Naval Academy, Perot's alma mater, the movement drew heavily from the ranks of retired military. Perot, of course, had long been associated with military causes. Even though he opposed Desert Storm and believed it to be little more than a political war to benefit George Bush (Perot preferred to "take out" Saddam Hussein with a commando force), Perot opened up his checkbook for homecoming parades and events for veterans of the Gulf War. He hired some of them to work in his campaign. His opposition was explained away by veterans who recognized that "though he disagreed with the war, he didn't disagree with the warrior."

Perot also has a military-type, command-and-obey personality. His modus operandi is authoritarian, hierarchal, no-nonsense and mission-oriented. He is decisive, which appeals to military people, and possesses the leadership qualities many military individuals have dealt with much of their lives. He is unwavering in his beliefs, and there's little room for compromise. Military people understood him when he described leaders as being like eagles: "Eagles don't flock, you find them one at a time."

His is also the personality of a pragmatist. Like many Depression-era babies, Perot is interested in what works; action counts.

Some of those imagining what his presidency would be like looked to Harry Truman's expectations of the last non-politician to sit in the White House, General Dwight D. Eisenhower. "He'll sit here and say, 'Do this! Do that!' And nothing will happen. Poor Ike, it won't be a bit like the Army," Truman had predicted. But Truman underestimated both his successor's skills and the efficiency of the Army. And it was Perot's reputation for getting things done that provided part of his attraction to the military minded. Military types also identified with his super patriotism, his straight-arrow idealism, his penchant for commando-style tactics, even his close-cropped hair. Vinson believes military people gravitated to him also because of his message for Americans to work for the common good. "The military has always had to put the nation's welfare above its own," noted Vinson. "I think there is just a common bond there."

The second in command of the U.S. troops in Desert Storm, Army Lieutenant General Calvin A. H. Waller, was a vocal supporter of his Commander in Chief, George Bush, during that war. But after Perot made himself available, General Waller switched allegiances. "I happen to like President Bush," Waller said. "But I happen to think he is out of touch with what is happening in America." Dan Roden, a retired naval aviator working on the petition drive in Colorado Springs said: "He doesn't blink—that's what gives us confidence. My position is to put him on the ballot. After the Democrats and Republicans get through tearing him apart, I'll see what's left." Ron Moretti, an Austin-based disabled vet, noted that Perot had a special appeal to Vietnam veterans. "They feel slighted—that they got no respect when they came home. I think Perot gives these guys respect again."

In the early weeks of the petition drive, a veterans' network was quietly spreading across the country, as calls from veterans streamed in to the phone bank. Roy Vokey, a Korean War veteran who had enlisted in Perot's army on "Day 1," took on the job at the Dallas head-quarters of organizing retired and nonactive military personnel. "We became aware quickly that there is a large block of admirers of Mr. Perot—probably a higher percentage of support than in any other group—in military groups. It's a fertile field," he said, pointing to twenty-seven million veterans and active military personnel.

It didn't take much organization. POW-MIA activists backing Perot were told six times, according to *USA Today*, to take down a Perot banner at the Vietnam Veterans Memorial in Washington D.C. Whenever Perot had a rally or public appearance, vets turned out in full force—particularly those from Vietnam. The black POW-MIA flag became a familiar sign in every crowd.

Paul Howell, president of the Arkansas State Council of Vietnam Veterans of America, said he was supporting Perot "because of his involvement in veterans issues and getting the POWs out of Hanoi. He's stood for veterans all his life." The four thousand-member Vietnam Veterans of America was polled in Arkansas and 92 percent favored Perot in May of 1992. "That's just one organization," said John Thompson of Fayetteville, an Army sergeant and Vietnam vet who has worked with Perot on the POW/MIA issue. While veterans' organizations would not endorse a candidate, members were working one-on-one to build the Perot network. A training coordinator for ABF Freight Systems in Fort Smith, Arkansas, Thompson said: "I've talked to the president of a lot of veterans' organizations, and they all want to see Perot as President."

Perot's appeal for vets and people with military connections no doubt was reinforced by the debate over whether Democrat Bill Clinton had avoided the draft.

Other groups of people who appeared heavily involved in the Perot movement were retirees, entrepreneurs and small business people, baby boomers, the unemployed and people between jobs—many waiting for the economy to pick up.

Mark Green, thirty-four, of Fort Worth, who described himself as a "ticket-splitter," found that most of the people involved in the Perot campaign in the Fort Worth area were not traditional political people. "This is the silent majority coming out in force," Green said. "They feel like they are part of something. They're not sure what—but something." Green predicted that if Perot failed to capitalize on the grass roots organization that had self-started, he would lose the source of his momentum. "We're staging a bloodless coup against the government. It's not the government as it was founded but the government as it has evolved. It's been exciting, but it's depressing, too."

Many of the people Green met in the petition campaign were volunteering because they didn't have anything better to do, i.e., wage-earning jobs. "In a vibrant economy," he said, "many of these people wouldn't have time to do this."

Like the military, the nation's retired population provided natural political bedfellows for Perot. They remembered the country he was trying to recreate. They remembered hometowns not so dissimilar from Ross

Perot's beloved Texarkana, which straddles the Texas-Arkansas border. And they remembered the days before the government reached its present stage of evolution.

Making up another leg of the stool of natural alliance with Perot were the entrepreneurs—obviously because he was an entrepreneur who had made good in a big way. His success in business, establishing EDS with a $1,000 grubstake from his wife's teaching salary, and turning it into a multi-million-dollar business is the dream of everyone who develops a small business. He was a risk taker, as are most entrepreneurs. William Schneider, a political analyst at the American Enterprise Institute in Washington, believes entrepreneurs are more likely to identify with political independents than people in other lines of work. He describes them as "technocratic, sometimes nerdy, believers in technologies, and basically they're problem solvers," he said.

A sampling of Perot activists around the country showed a preponderance of small business people—many of whom had not previously been mixed up in politics. In truth, many of them believed they still were not involved in politics, but rather in a citizens movement to clean up the country.

A *Wall Street Journal*-NBC News poll conducted May 14-19 indicated the billionaire populist was fashioning one of the most unusual political coalitions ever. The survey showed Perot ran best among independents, blue-collar workers, westerners and men. He was so strong in the state of Washington that he captured nearly 20 percent of the primary vote as a write-in candidate. Election officials there said they had never seen so many write-ins in a statewide vote. In Dallas, a demographic study in sixty-four different zip-code areas where petitions were circulated found Perot backers to be solidly middle-class. The median income was $38,240, sixty-five percent were white-collar workers, and the average age was forty-two. A quarter of the Perot Dallas area backers had four or more years college. And ethnically, they mirrored the breakdowns in the area and nation: 76 percent white, 12 percent black and 12 percent Hispanic.

While it was easy to read "common man" and "average American" into almost any group of Perot volunteers, there were those that were uncommon, as well. California's leaders were, by and large, highly educated. The Dallas volunteer force contained F.O.Ps (Friends of the Perots), many of whom, while not quite as wealthy as the Perots, traveled in the same circles and did charity work with Margot Perot. A Dallas-datelined story in *The New York Times* said, "To be sure, there is evidence of the common people on the phone banks and in the blue-gray cubicles here, where retired people, homemakers and sales representatives on vacation are all doing their part. But there are hothouse flowers among the grass roots." *The Times* mentioned several socialites who preside over the charity balls and participate in Dallas's socially correct causes, such as the art museum and Junior League. Some were helping to pay back the Perots for their civic contributions. Ruth Sharp Altshuler, one of the most civic-minded women in Dallas, whose brother was the late Dallas Republican Congressman Jim Collins, said, "They did for me—I want to do for them." Perot is well known for his philanthropy. Mrs. Perot is also known in Dallas for various good works, including her favorite causes, the Salvation Army, United Way and Planned Parenthood. For Anne McKamy, former chairwoman of the Women's Board of the Dallas Opera Guild, working for the Perot campaign had become a full-time job. "I don't have time for anything else now," she told *The Times.*

A surprising show of support developed during the spring that wasn't showing up in the polls, but was apparent to computer junkies across the country ,was college students. Most college campuses are tied in to InterNet, and students were using that computer hookup for much of their communication about Perot. Two students completing graduate school at Harvard were hired at the end of the spring semester and given the assignment of coordinating the youth campaign. "We just tried to catch up with the organizations already sprouting up," said Kristen Silverberg, one of the youth coordinators. "Anybody that tells me young people are apathetic, I would argue with them a long time. We had campaign plans coming in from all over the country. We had organizers in every state." The youth movement was particularly strong in California, a state that, like Texas and Florida, was extremely important to the Perot campaign. "We had a lot of 'techies,'" she said, or "computer nerds," many of whom were graduate students. Many of the students were calling the phone bank and even coming to the Dallas headquarters for instructions.

"The future of America understands what Mr. Perot is saying," said Rose Roberts-Cannaday, the manager of the Dallas phone bank. "They know that when they get out of college, they won't be able to find jobs if things don't change in the country." She also said the college students who call and come to the headquarters "understand the concept of the electronic town hall meeting" as proposed by Perot for gaining the sentiment of citizens. They are much less inclined to be skeptical of electronic innovations and new communications techniques because they've grown up with them. Cannaday found that people were not coming to Perot because of this issue or that issue. In fact, many of the volunteers were on the opposing side of such issues as abortion and gun control. But they were coming together because of the big issue—the search for the American dream.

Who are these people? They're those for whom the American dream seems out of reach. "They're the people who have lost it and the people who haven't had a chance to reach for it who are not sure it's going to be there when they do," she said.

The description of the Perot following by most of the folks involved was a far cry from the way some traditional party people, particularly Republicans, wanted to cast it. U.S. Senator Phil Gramm of Texas, for example, tried in early June to link Perot with the fringe candidates of both parties. "It's clear when you look at who is supporting him (that) it is an unstable coalition of Jerry Brown supporters and Pat Buchanan supporters, and it is a coalition that cannot hold together."

Arkansas provided a good example of the eclectic nature of Perot's appeal. The day after Perot was in Orlando for the rally with satellite hookup, he went to Bill Clinton's backyard in Little Rock for his fourth public event. The state that might have inspired cartoonist Al Capp's Li'l Abner and Daisy Mae, Arkansas had become known for the governor (Orval Faubus) who stood in the schoolhouse door to prevent integration, and in recent years as the headquarters for Wal-Mart stores and the nation's biggest poultry producer, Tyson Foods. By producing a presidential nominee, its twelve-year governor, Bill Clinton, Arkansas would have a new claim to fame. Arkansas had never spawned a presidential nominee, yet that wasn't reason enough for some not to look beyond their home-state candidate to their Texas neighbor. When Perot appeared before supporters in Little Rock, he made only passing reference to Clinton in his speech when he said, "Did you ever think you'd see one boy from Texarkana and another from Hope, Arkansas, in the same campaign?"

But John Thompson of Fayetteville wasn't bashful about giving his support to Perot over Clinton. A member of the Governor's Task Force for POWs/MIAs who had worked with Perot on the POW-MIA issue, Thompson said: "A lot of people in the state of Arkansas think Arkansas is one of the lowest states in poverty, education, and jobs. Clinton's been here long enough to make a change—he hasn't. Bush, the only time he's ever been here during his term was to honor Sam Walton (the founder of Wal-Mart) before he died."

Arkansas had a different process from the rest of the states. It's one of the easiest states in which to qualify for ballot position. There was no need to circulate petitions there. Arkansas law requires only that six delegates—one from each congressional district and two at-large—convene to offer the name of an independent. Perot supporters had been organizing the state by congressional district, holding town hall meetings. The two-day convention was scheduled both to get Perot's name on the Arkansas ballot and to build steam for the campaign. Twenty-five hundred Perot boosters showed up for the meeting that had all the characteristics of a tent revival, with Perot touted as a latter-day Moses.

Only weeks after the Los Angeles riots, Oklahoma City's Larry Jones, president of Feed the Children, stepped to the microphone at the Statehouse Convention Center in Little Rock to deliver this invocation: "The Bible says that a house divided against itself cannot stand. And Lord, we are indeed a house divided. Brother against brother, black against white, rich against poor, party against party. Our land is being torn apart by crime, drugs, violence and scandal. Immorality has become commonplace. Our families are being destroyed. Our children are raised in a world without hope. Our once great nation has been brought to its knees by forces that seem out of control—rampant disease, corruption and greed, strife and discord. We've become a nation adrift without a rudder...Lead us out from this wilderness, this confusion...and to the promised land. The land flowing with milk and honey. Jobs, prosperity, fair prices for our products, hope...and a land where no child goes to bed hungry...Raise up a man to lead this nation out of the wilderness. A man of character. A man of conviction. A man of spiritual principle. You gave the Israelites such a man in Moses. We humbly beseech you today to raise up such a man here in our midst to lead us."

The revival air grew as country singer Willie Nelson sang the old Hank Williams hymn, "I Saw the Light," with his sister, Bobbie, at the piano.

Like the Florida rally, the Arkansas event produced few people of color. Otherwise, however, it yielded a signal example of Perot's ability to cut across the political spectrum, drawing together diverse interests and political alliances.

The state coordinator in Arkansas is a case in point. John Arens is a slight man with graying hair, glasses and a salt-and-pepper beard. But he is youthful, even avant-garde looking, in Levis, boots and a blue blazer. Arens has followed Perot since the Vietnam War, when he served in the First Marines. He has the looks of a liberal Democrat who survived the Vietnam era. Arens is a civil-rights lawyer from Fayetteville. He serves as legal counsel for the American Agriculture Movement, and spends most of his time on lawsuits involving family farmers, grape growers and others who fight the big financial institutions—what he calls the "tall building firms." John Arens was Jesse Jackson's voice in Arkansas in 1980. He doesn't expect it, and knows some Perot supporters wouldn't like it, but he would love to see a Perot-Jackson ticket. "I think we have to be attentive to this serious problem of a large percent of our people feeling left out...the race issue is extremely important to me." Going from Jackson to Perot is not such a leap for him. "Their ideas for me are the same. They're about jobs in America, progressive economic ideas."

Arens had been introduced to Perot-the-politician through the agriculture effort. Some farm leaders had met with Perot's representatives and were convinced that the farm issue would be part of his agenda. Plus, said Arens, "He speaks from the heart. He's the most honest man we've ever had running for president."

Arens and Willie Nelson were old friends; Arens helped Nelson with his tax problems with the Internal Revenue Service. Actually, Arens bought Nelson's Texas farm to try to help him get out of hock with the IRS. So Nelson was more than willing to appear on the platform with his old friend, Arens, and his new friend, Perot. "We have to start from the ground up to rebuild America. We have to help the small farmer and small businessman. Ross Perot is the man to get it started," Nelson said.

After Perot's speech, Arens, the organizer, was elated with the reponse. "This is the closest thing we've ever had to a revolution in this country. You can just feel it."

8

CALIFORNIA HIGH

IF ANY AREA OF THE UNITED STATES WAS SWEPT UP IN Perotmania, it was California. The metaphor used by Tom Luce was that Perot was "riding the wave" of discontent in the country; it was not a wave Perot created. That figure of speech was all the more apropos for the land of surf and sun, because the sun had not been shining on California for a long while. And this fact was particularly important since California accounted for fifty-four electoral votes, or one-fifth of the 270 needed to win the presidency. While California mirrored the problems in other states, things were worse in the Golden State in many cases. While other states were picking up the pace of recovery, California lagged behind. Unemployment was higher there, and the everyday problems people encountered because of the recession were compounded by the high cost of housing in California. The state had lost seven hundred thousand jobs, including two hundred thousand in the aerospace industry. Unemployment in May of 1992 in California was 8.7 percent; it would go up to 9.5 percent in June—the highest of the eleven industrial states. To columnist Kevin Phillips, California was the "post-war mecca for the now-threatened American dream."

But it wasn't just the recession. California was also reeling from riots in Los Angeles after the trial of the L.A. policemen for the video-taped Rodney King beating. The nation's most populous state (one in eight Americans live in California), the Golden State was third in the nation in crime rate. And the political system wasn't working at home any better than it was in Washington; state political leaders were in a budget standoff. The *Washington Post's* David Broder wrote that "with swelling immigration, the state's ratio of dependent children and retirees compared to workers is trending upward. Neglected housing, education and transportation needs are choking the state." Add to those man-made woes the recent natural disasters, two earthquakes and the Oakland Hills fire, and it's easy to see why the California climate was ripe for rebellion.

In a story on the mood of California, the *San Francisco Chronicle's* Jerry Roberts wrote:

"Across the state, blows struck by humans and nature seem to have damaged the native faith in the unlimited potential of the future that has shaped California's psyche since the gold rush.

"The Rodney King riots suddenly but perhaps inevitably exposed a host of long-festering statewide problems—structural declines in a troubled economy and education system, intractable social afflictions ranging from AIDS to welfare, and gaping ethnic and income splits between California's emerging population and those who control its political agenda."

Governor Pete Wilson's communications director, Dan Schnur, agreed. "At this point the only precedents for what we've faced are biblical," he said. "We're running two plagues behind Egypt."

Enter Ross Perot, who promised—more than anything

else—hope for the weary of heart and the restoration of the can-do spirit of California. His maverick candidacy had quick appeal in a state long known for being on the cutting edge of cultural and political change. Californians were big on such populist ideas as initiative and referendum; their initiatives had ranged from Proposition 13 to welfare reform. Petition after petition had been circulated to get various propositions on the ballot, including, just two years before, an initiative limiting the terms of legislators and cutting their staffs. Petitioning for this independent presidential candidate was not that much different. Many Californians had time on their hands, and they were more than willing to get involved in a citizens' revolution. What George Bush seemed never to comprehend was that the Perot petition drive was, for many, the highest and best use of their time; many had nothing better to do, particularly in California.

And Perot was the ideal candidate for California, as described by Los Angeles Democratic consultant Bill Carrick: "vaguely liberal on social issues and vaguely conservative on economic issues." He really defied labels. Like many conservatives, he favored a much smaller federal government and a balanced budget. Like many liberals, he favored gun control and a woman's right to choose an abortion. But specific issue positions mattered little, largely because Californians—like voters throughout the nation—had come to the conclusion that the positions they preached about didn't really matter much to the politicians, either.

Perot was also a disciple of advanced technology in a high-tech milieu. Kevin Phillips wrote: "Perot is speaking to compelling national realities: the high-tech and interacive telecommunications revolution bearing down on us, and the need to transcend a party system linked to corrupt campaign finance and special interests. Here, too, California, with its expertise in populist politics, high technology and new forms of mass communications, must have a role if there is to be a Perot Revolution."

Moreover, Perot's independent candidacy was just the kind to appeal to the state's huge bloc of suburban "swing" voters who were largely white, middle-aged and well educated. At a time when the suburban voter was being looked upon as the most important new voting bloc in American politics, California had 4.6 million of them—more than a third of the state's electorate. Perot was attracting interest from the Democrat-leaning Silicon Valley to Republican Orange County to glitzy Beverly Hills and tinsel-towned Hollywood. Alliance Industries president Betsy Bryant was quoted in *New York Newsday* as saying, "He's the ultimate Silicon Valley fantasy. This is the heart of the entrepreneurial environment in the United States, where Apple took on IBM. This is where change happens." Steven Jobs, who cofounded Apple, had announced that he was backing Perot.

Even before the nation's news media picked up on the grass roots reaction to Perot's availability, the Perot prairie fire was spreading across California. Names were being exchanged by electronic mail, through Prodigy, CompuServe and other on-line services, and people were frantically trying to establish contact with other Perot disciples, both in the state and in Dallas.

On March 8, a dozen or so Californians met in Visalia, coming from areas as distant as San Diego and Sacramento. Phylis Kritchfield, a grandmother from Fairfield, had car trouble on the way, and hired a driver to take her the last few miles. John Gaynor of El Centro drove over four hundred miles to attend the meeting. The group elected Bob Hayden of Ventura chairman and decided to move forward to register Perot on the California ballot, with or without a declared candidate. Their primary goal was to gather two hundred thousand signatures to ensure that 134,781 would be valid. Petitioning efforts could begin on April 24 and had to be completed by August 7. Hayden sent a memo to the Perot Group in Dallas, to inform Perot of the actions under way in California. "Skin is in the game," Hayden wrote, "and we are growing daily in numbers."

By March 31, Jack Brodbeck, a forty-eight-year-old international resort developer from Orange County who had a master's degree in international marketing, received for redistribution around the state the first list of California volunteers who had called the Dallas toll-free number. There were between three thousand and thirty-five hundred names on the list.

On April 4, a headquarters was opened in Orange County. Some eight hundred persons, attracted by newspaper notices, showed up. Other meetings in San Diego and San Francisco each drew more than six hundred volunteers. Handmade signs of neon orange paint pointed the way to the Orange County office, which was squeezed between a delicatessen and a skin-care salon in a small shopping center in Irvine. Outside, a television set stood ready to replay Perot's March 18 rallying cry to the National Press Club in Washington.

One of the people at the Irvine kickoff was Marcy Ferren, forty, who, with her husband, Don, owns a travel agency. College-educated, Ferren had considered herself a staunch Republican until disenchantment had set in over the past three years. She had seen the National Press Club speech, studied the videotape, and was convinced that Perot was "in touch with what's going on" in the country and how the people feel about the economy, health care and the job situation. She became one of three managers for the Irvine office, volunteering more than forty hours a week, leaving her husband to run the travel agency. "The economy has been very stagnant. You notice it in our business," she said. "It's a small, self-sufficient business, and we've been hit very hard."

Toni Skilman was another of the office managers who volunteered the day of the headquarter's opening rally. She was an interior designer, doing well in furniture design when "it just came to a screeching halt two years ago. The design business stopped." She had the free time to devote, along with others who were "in between jobs" or who were job searching. "These people who get into politics have no idea what it's like to live out here in the real world," she said. She was particularly turned off by President Bush's visit to Japan, with automobile company executives making seven-figure salaries in tow. "What are they doing to earn that money? Those companies are going down the tube," she said. "They don't live in the real world either."

Joanne Laufer, who earned an M.B.A. in marketing from the University of Pennsylvania's Wharton Graduate School, scaled back her own consulting business in computer sales and marketing to be manager of the Volunteer Hotline at the Irvine office. She believed the country was in trouble, and that today's politicians don't understand how to manage the problems; they only understand how to get elected. She found what had happened in the 1980s "unconscionable," with the growth of the national debt and the savings and loan crisis. "And we all allowed it to happen," she said.

The Irvine office opening was followed by a meeting on April 8. Darcy Anderson was there from Dallas to give a briefing. The next day, a reporter from the *Orange County Register* tried to reach Sharon Holman, the sole representative authorized to speak for Perot in Dallas; the reporter was told she would be placed on the call-back list—at spot No. 201.

By the third week of April, according to a *Los Angeles Times* poll, Perot was running neck-and-neck with President Bush and slightly ahead of Bill Clinton in California, although he was still little known. The protest movement was well underway.

Volunteers fanned out across California, in shopping centers and flea markets and community events, in front of supermarkets and post offices, getting petitions signed. A sign on the Valley freeway trumpeted "Perot Petition" at the "Next Off Ramp." One of the popular approaches was to use ironing boards, covered with bumper stickers and buttons, as tables. "People don't have card tables anymore," one volunteer explained. "Nobody has time to play bridge." Volunteers carried their paraphernalia in red paint buckets, tied balloons to the paint buckets wherever they set up their ironing boards. They called themselves the "ironing board brigade."

Bobbie Snavely, a seventy-year-old cardiovascular nurse from Foster City, a planned community in the San Francisco Bay area, used her own money to create a weekly statewide newsletter—the *Perot Petition News*— to spread the word of petition signing activities and provide contacts. A May Day rally on the Foster City boardwalk, attended by more than one thousand supporters, provided supporters an opportunity to pen personal notes to the potential candidate on a three hundred-foot letter, which was later strung across a wall in the Dallas phone bank room.

The Perot petitioners were everywhere, with their T-shirts and buttons and rallies and brass bands, signifying an old-fashioned political revival. A signature was a symbol of empowerment for the disgruntled electorate. Some signers said they weren't sure they would vote for Perot, but they wanted him on the ballot.

In San Diego, volunteers gathered on a Saturday morning at the Belmont Park roller coaster, Mission Beach. After a wake-up ride on the historic coaster, they spread out into nearby communities, wearing their Perot Petition Committee T-shirts, to gather signatures.

John Baker, the media relations person for the San Diego area for the petition drive, had no political experience and never expected to have any again. A 1962 graduate of the Naval Academy, he owned a San Diego public relations firm that worked in the high-tech industry. He described San Diego as a "hotbed" of Perotism, fueled by Perot's appearances on TV. "The beauty of the kind of exposure he's getting, like the 'Today' show, is that everybody has a full question and a full answer. That gets people involved rather than just a thin veneer on tonight's news." Baker also said that within the American populace is a "short-temperedness with the press. Part of what's going on that people should be watching is the process. The process is new. Election campaigns will never be the same again. You're seeing a new medium, the talk-show medium. It's different from network news. It comes closer to being real communicating. I don't think you can ever put that genie back in the bottle."

There was talk in California about the eventual formation of a third party. "I'm in it because I want to see this man in the White House," Baker said. "I don't think it's a requirement that there be a third party. If it's going to happen, it should be evolutionary, not something we try and rush into."

Gene Waldman of Los Angeles, who worked for a real estate management company, decided to give up six to seven months of his life to try to change the country by supporting Perot. He figured "We have a small window of opportunity; if we don't change it now, we will lose it." Waldman started working in petition drives when he was nineteen on Proposition 13, and was once an aide to Howard Jarvis. The Perot candidacy would be his fifth petition drive. Waldman thought of trying to reach the disabled community, particularly the blind. He printed Perot biographies and petitions in Braille, and planned to produce audio tapes and big print literature.

By mid-May, the California Poll conducted by the Field Institute showed Perot leading in California with 37 percent, compared to Bush's 31 percent and Clinton's 25 percent. As California approached its June 2 primary, it was clear that even though Perot wasn't on the ballot, he was dominating the California presidential race. R.W. Apple wrote just such a story in *The New York Times*, saying Perot was hogging the spotlight in California, after the primaries in Oregon and Washington where he polled sizable write-in votes. Eric Shockman, a professor of political science at the University of Southern California, told *The Times*, "This guy, this cowboy riding into town on horseback, is absolutely seductive for people in this state. Californians love this junk." Comparing Perot to Ronald Reagan, Shockman said, "This is the mythology of Hollywood come to life, a revisiting of the B-movie actor who gets elected governor and then president."

These were dark days for the Bush and Clinton candidacies. Bush had already locked up enough delegates to be nominated, although he was challenged by Patrick Buchanan in the California primary. Clinton was running against Jerry Brown, and was just short of the magic number of delegates to be nominated. June 2 was the date for the last cluster of primaries in the country, and it was a foregone conclusion that they would put Clinton over the top.

But there was no joy in either of the major party campaigns. Bush was stalked by voter derision over his "grey poupon" approach; he appeared an elitist out of touch with the everyday problems of the people. His response to the Los Angeles riots had been as uncertain and tentative as was his decision-making in dealing with Iraq after Iraq invaded Kuwait, Dan Balz wrote in the *Washington Post*.

"From his body language to the softness of his voice and the hesitancy of his questioning when he talks to inner-city residents, Bush conveys unfamiliarity and a lack of confidence with the issues he faces," Balz wrote.

The strategy of both major party candidates appeared rooted in the hope that Perot would self-destruct. "That's a prayer," said former Democratic National Chairman John C. White. "That's not a strategy."

Clinton, meanwhile, was beginning to show the degree to which he was privately agonizing over how to deal with the Perot phenomenon. Flying to California just before the primary, he was asked by a *Boston Globe* reporter how he would get his message out to voters, given the preoccupation with Perot. His response was: "I don't know. I don't know. I don't know." According to the *St. Louis Post-Dispatch*, he was described by one associate as "upset and self-pitying" because he was not getting the attention or the credit he felt he deserved.

Perot was not on any of the June 2 primary ballots, but as reported in the June 1 *Political Hotline*, surveys showed him leading in four of the six states voting on the last primary day—California, Montana, New Jersey and New Mexico—tied in Ohio, and running behind Bush and Clinton only in Alabama.

Sure enough, on Election Day in California, exit polls demonstrated the voter fixation on Perot. Among California Democrats, 35 percent favored Perot, 34 percent Clinton. Among Republicans, it was Bush 47 percent, Perot 43 percent. The CNN's "Morning News" reported on June 3, the day after the last party primaries, "Ross Perot was not on any of the yesterday's ballots, but if he had been, some exit polls indicate that one in three voters would have supported him. Among California Democrats, 34 percent said they'd vote for Perot, 33 percent for Bill Clinton, 24 percent for Jerry Brown...Among California Republicans, 47 percent said they'd vote for Perot, 39 percent for President Bush and 10 percent for Patrick Buchanan." It was hardly the victory lap Clinton had in mind, as he cinched the Democratic nomination, nor did it provide any solace to the incumbent president.

Perot attributed his backing to four voter concerns: (1) a government that comes "at the people" rather than from them, (2) gridlock on Capitol Hill, (3) the $4 trillion debt, and (4) the disintegration of the American dream. And he promised, in an interview with CNN's Tony Clark, that "with that sort of support from the people, I feel a tremendous obligation to keep my commitment to these petition signers and volunteers to run a world-class campaign."

U.S. News's David Gergen said on "The MacNeil-

Lehrer News Hour" on PBS on June 5 that "If the election were held next Tuesday Ross Perot would be
elected...The only person who can beat Ross Perot is
Ross Perot."

And Gergen wrote shortly thereafter in *U.S. News
and World Report* that "Perot is streaking across the political skies so rapidly now that he is more likely to win
outright—or crash and burn long before November. He's
just too hot to stand still. In less than ten weeks, a man
who has no party and no political experience has made
this a race that's his to lose. Both the other candidates
are now copying him in both style and substance."

Clinton hoped to beat Perot at his own game, appearing on "Arsenio Hall," where he played the saxophone,
appearing on NBC's "Today" on June 9 and appearing
on three call-in programs in seven days. But ironically,
according to syndicated columnists Jack Germond and
Jules Witcover, "Just as Clinton and Bush are catching
on to Perot's crafty use of television entertainment talk
shows to bypass the critical press, he appears to have
the capacity through his money and volunteer man-
power to go beyond television communication and put
politics back on Main Street." Germond and Witcover
wrote that not since the campaign finance reform laws
of 1974 and 1976, which channeled presidential campaign spending into paid television, had there been such
a potential for grass roots politicking.

California voters also expressed their displeasure on
Election Day with the way things were going in their
state. Twenty-seven of thirty-two counties voted in favor of a "secessionist" move, providing more fodder for
an effort to split the state into two or three states.

Leaders of the California petition drive knew that
they were on the verge of gathering far more signatures

than were necessary; there was no need to keep the petition campaign going indefinitely. So Ross Perot agreed to attend rallies in both Northern and Southern California on June 18 to accept the petitions. At the rallies—in front of the state capitol in Sacramento and at Lion Country Center at Frasier Park in Irvine—it was announced that California had collected not just the required number of 134,781 signatures, and not just double that amount for good measure, but 1.4 million signatures—more than 10 percent of the state's registered voters. "I can't over-emphasize what your impact has been on the other states," Perot told the thousands who gathered at the Perot Volunteer Appreciation Rally and Family Day in Irvine.

By this time, according to Orange County coordinator Merrick Okamoto, GOP stronghold Orange County had ten thousand people in its data base and six thousand active volunteers. There were sixty-five thousand people in the Southern California data base, and plans were being made for volunteers to go into the precincts, county by county, distributing literature and video tapes and registering voters.

Perot said in Orange County: "I have been asked so many times, Who are these people? I've been asked so many times I want to respond. Number one, these are people who love their country. These are people who understand and love the principles on which this country was founded. And all across this great country, these are people who don't like to see those principles violated. These are just good people who work hard and play by the rules. They rear good children. They've been in the center of ethical behavior. They're active in their schools and communities, and they serve in the armed forces when they're called on," he said.

"Both parties are watching your lips. They are really watching you with great concern now," Perot said. "Both parties have already conducted town meetings, after condemning them. Both parties are talking about the debt and the deficit. You made that happen. Believe it or not, the members of the House and Senate are now talking about getting the debt and the deficit under control."

Among the first to arrive at the Irvine rally were Monique Mainferme and Linda Aust of Phillips Ranch in Pomona. They arrived before 9:00 a.m. and spread their blanket in the only shaded area in front of the platform. The program was scheduled to begin at 2:30 p.m. Beside them was Mary Oakes, who lived near San Diego. She was wearing five Perot buttons and doing needlepoint-like work on plastic canvas. When finished, it would say, in red, white and blue, "Sunshine Soldier" for Perot. "I don't think they (the other candidates) have the slightest clue that we are as angry as we are," she said.

The red-headed Monique Mainferme, who had recently retired from working as a registered nurse, was definitely angry. She had emigrated to this country from Canada in 1958, but she was especially angry about California being "invaded by immigrants."

"All our systems are depleted. Our hospitals are in disarray, taking care of illegal aliens. They come and have a baby, take over our school system. We have no more money for anything. We should close the border, period, and be serious about it. A lot of the rioters were in that group (immigrants). Our jails are crammed with them. They're coming through Mexico, but they're coming from all over the world—by boat, by plane, by foot, by car," she said. She was concerned, as well, about homelessness, AIDS, and an uneducated populace. "Nobody wants to hear Bush. He's a good man, but he has no idea what the people are going through, what the people are suffering." The mother of three grown children, she had collected signatures every Friday afternoon in front of the market. She called it the "easiest job of our lives. People just came to us; they're eager to sign. They think, finally, somebody's listening to the people. They believe he (Perot) will make things happen."

Linda Aust and her husband, at fifty-five, were living at the margin after enjoying a fairly comfortable life. She had owned a talent agency in Beverly Hills, and her husband worked in the fish industry at management levels. The Japanese bought out his company and brought in their own people. So this couple, at mid-life and looking forward to retirement, became independent contractors for international exchange student groups—teaching the students, taking them to tourist attractions. "People you used to feel sorry for, you think, one more step and that's me. I don't remember in thirty-five years of marriage, since the early married days, having to worry about money like this. Are you going to make the month's mortgage? It's not right, dammit. We're willing to work. George Bush is a good man, but he lives in a bubble, he has all his life. He doesn't know what people are going through."

Rae Zeldin, a native of Texas who moved to California in 1944, was a former school teacher living in a senior community in Huntington Beach, Orange County. The previous year, she participated in a discussion group on "What's wrong with America." She introduced the group to Ross Perot, reading excerpts from his November 1991 speech to the Coalition for a Better Government in Tampa. "I feel a lot of guilt about the sin of inaction and the sin of silence. We knew what our legislature was doing, the broad pattern of bribery and corruption in our legislature and the U.S. Congress. So I have thrown myself into this as a way of saying to my children and grandchildren, I sort of did this to you and this is my way to help." Zeldin was a member of a performing group, too, which went to area hospitals and retirement homes with a song-and-dance act, which included a song that began, "Give my regards to Congress; Republican and Demos, too."

"My family thinks I'm crazy; I'm so passionately, fervently involved in this thing. I may not agree with everything he says, but in general I believe he knows how to mobilize the country and bring us together," she said.

Timothy Foraker, president of Automotive Alliance Incorporated in Santa Ynez, California, made sun shields for cars with "Perot 92" on them. To him, it was a revolution, all right, but "it's a quiet revolution, walking down Main Street, on the telephone, over the fax and in the Rotary clubs."

Foraker's wife Joy noted that "History will teach you that when the crisis is severe, great men will emerge. They're there all the time. People have been very complacent. Their attitude has been, let George do it. Let Carter do it. They're too busy with their lives. Now they realize they're going to have to do it. George and Carter are not doing it. People have been disgusted. I can see resiliency in people's minds and hearts."

Len and Janet Wayne were hawking paraphernalia at a booth at the Lion Country Park in Orange County—bumper stickers, T-shirts, visors, key chains. They were offering yard signs at $2 apiece, and people were buying. Wayne worked in the advertising business as a creative consultant. His wife was a nurse in the Orange County burn unit at the University of California at Irvine Medical Center. She had been a nurse in Vietnam and believed Perot did more for the POWs than the government did. Wayne didn't really expect things to get better in his lifetime. "I'm here for my sons," he said, referring to his sons, ages thirty-one, thirty and twenty-nine. "I don't want my sons paying. I don't believe sons should pay for the sins of the father. What the Democrats and Republicans have done to this country is sinful; it makes you cry. We've never been involved in politics. We vote and let it go at that. But look what they've done to us," he said. "What we've let them do," his wife added. "We've got to stop it, and Perot is a way to do it."

This was the crowd Perot was playing to when he said: "When you watch the Democratic and Republican conventions, I want you to look at that multi-million dollar podium that is erected for the giant media event. And when you look at that podium, I hope you like it because you paid for it with taxpayer money." Indeed, the *Houston Chronicle* had reported in early June that the GOP convention manager and his deputy and another consultant were staying in posh apartments—complete with twice-a-day maid service and health club—at the Four Seasons Hotel where rents ranged from $2,000 to $6,000 a month.

He went on to say: "Now, when you watch their TV ads in the fall, I hope you adore every one of them because they're going to be paid for with taxpayer money. Now I love these boys. They've got hard money, they've got soft money, they've got money coming in from overseas, but they're worried to death we'll outspend them. Well, it breaks my heart to tell 'em; they're already outspent because of your brains, your wit, your creative ability. Now I realize that facts don't matter in an election campaign, but here are some interesting facts. At the end of April they had spent $17 million apiece. We spent $1.4 million and we're ahead of them. So if we bought it, I'll say, we sure bought it wholesale."

"But the facts are that it is your great creative ability and initiative that has done this. That's what made this nation great. That's what created all the great inventions, that's what created all the jobs over the years—the brains, the wit, the creative initiative of the American people. In my business career, again and again, I've been the underdog. And I've turned to my people and said, 'We can't match 'em off money, so let's just out-think 'em. And those boys with money always had a disadvantage, because we were there thinking, scheming, planning, figuring out with brains and wit and the creative ability of our people how to win. This will work for this country. You've proved it already here in California."

In the southern California crowd was the usual Vietnam vet carrying a black POW flag. There were family members of POWs and MIAs who have never been found. Fran Masterson of Upland, California, still wears a bracelet for her husband Michael Bat Masterson, who bailed out over Laos on October 13, 1968. A lieutenant colonel in the Air Force, he's been missing since. She's been involved in the MIA-POW issue all these years. "We want to end this now. If they're listed as KIA, we want their bodies back."

It was an overwhelmingly white crowd that greeted Perot at both public events in California, but Perot had spent the day before in private meetings with black, Asian and Hispanic community leaders in Los Angeles in the wake of the riots there. He reiterated, at the rally in Irvine, the plea he had made for racial harmony at prior rallies. "We're a nation of many races and many creeds. We are a melting pot. That's a strength; our diversity is a strength and not a weakness. Every time we have an election we turn it into a weakness. We split the melting pot into all kinds of little special pieces, pander to everybody's fears and special interests. And then everybody wonders why we can't put everybody back together as a united team after the election."

In California, Perot used one of his favorite sayings to close his speech—the words of Winston Churchill, which he recalled were spoken at a critical time during World War II. "Never give in, never give in, never, never, never."

It was an upbeat day for Perot, despite a local group that showed up in Sacramento and chanted during his speech, "Talk about the issues." His northern California crowd was reported to be six thousand, the biggest since President Reagan spoke on the Capitol grounds in 1984. Republican Governor Wilson's communications director Dan Schnur walked among the press at the events, saying: "I came here out of professional curiosity. I've never seen a snake oil salesman before." The only other sour note of the California trip was the report of a *USA Today*-CNN poll which showed Perot had fallen five points, down to 34 percent. He nonetheless remained ahead of Bush and Clinton, and he continued to ride high in other polls. This one, however, was the first indication that there just might be a crack in his armor. Perot's California appearances were the first of a three-day swing that would take him to rallies in Denver, Colorado, and Boston, Massachusetts, to be followed a few days later by another rally in Annapolis, Maryland.

By this time, the *Political Hotline*, using poll data from all fifty states, estimated that Perot was leading in seventeen states, with a total of 243 electoral votes. He was, indeed, on a California High; and he was riding that crest right across the country—the next day at an equally enthusiastic rally in Denver and on to Boston on June 21.

The contrast between the two cultures—California and New England—is marked. They are on opposite coasts, and seemingly opposite cultural poles. Where California is laid-back "new America," Massachusetts is prim and proper "old America." Both geographically and culturally, the two states represent the two extremes of America—California with its Sister Boom Booms, and Massachusetts with its sons and daughters of the American Revolution. Yet, what was remarkable about the movement was that people from both East and West forged a common bond with Ross Perot—whether they embodied the Western frontier spirit or the Eastern fetish for old world traditions and patriotic symbolism.

In Boston, two successful businessmen got together to launch the Perot organization there. Dick Norman, sixty years old, was a Naval Academy grad who had an M.B.A. from Harvard. He had been a small-businessman for twenty years, working primarily in the energy field, most recently developing small scale hydro-electric projects. He had never really been involved in politics. But when Paul Tsongas dropped out, he took a look at the choices and saw none he liked—except Perot. He called Perot's Dallas office and then the 800 number, until he finally got through and was given the name of someone else in Boston who was interested in Perot. That was Bill Anderson, who ran an international aluminum business, shipping goods in and out of the Middle East.

Anderson also had been interested in Paul Tsongas, had read Tsongas's book, *A Call to Arms*, and had offered to get involved in the Tsongas's campaign. He was asked to raise money, which he didn't want to do, so he asked for another assignment and was told, essentially, that the Democrats are well organized; they don't need you. Perot offered the opportunity for citizen involvement, and Anderson grabbed it. He turned his conference room into a small phone bank and held an organizational meeting. It was late March. "A bunch of people showed up," Anderson said. "I asked, how many are Republicans, and a bunch of people threw up their hands. I said, how many are Democrats, and a bunch of people threw up their hands. The same thing, when I asked how many are conservative and how many are liberal. There was no majority. We had to try to build something out of this group." A state steering committee was elected. Norman was named treasurer.

Anderson, Norman and the other volunteers built an organization in Massachusetts in each of the ten congressional districts until each city and town had a coordinator. According to Norman, almost every one of the 351 towns and cities had a coordinator.

One of the congressional coordinators was Larry Williams, a small-businessman from Chatham in Cape Cod. In an interview with Dallas video producer Jo Streit, Williams talked about the wind beneath the sail. "What it is, really, is a motivation of people with the entrepreneurial spirit, the individuals who have the know-how and the ability, and are willing to put the objective ahead of themselves; willing to put the team effort ahead of themselves and get the job done," Williams said. Williams talked about one town which had two coordinators—one came from the top of the Republican town committee, the other from the top of the Democratic town committee. "What motivated these people is that they had a chance to express themselves. For so many years, they haven't had a chance to express themselves."

The support that grew for Perot in Boston and throughout Massachusetts was no surprise to Anderson. "In 1991, the city of Boston alone had lost one hundred thousand jobs," he said. The Dukakis "Massachusetts Miracle" had turned into a nightmare. High-tech companies like Wang and Digital were laying off big chunks of their work force. Massachusetts had thought in the early 1980s that it was bulletproof, but once the economic downturn hit, it hit hard. People were ready to hear Perot's message.

Massachusetts, indeed New England, turned out to be fertile ground for Perot. There had been a strong base of support in Massachusetts for Tsongas, who had served the state as U.S. senator, before retiring to fight cancer. When Tsongas dropped out of the race for the Democratic nomination, his support was ripe for the taking. And, said Dick Norman, treasurer of the state steering committee, in spite of the liberal reputation of the state, "A lot of people were disenchanted with tax-and-spend; they wanted to see a change in government. A lot of people harbored negative feelings about what (former Governor Michael) Dukakis did with state government. Perot represented someone who had the potential to try and make the changes in the national government that the state in part has made and in part wants to make."

Plus, Perot's independence connected with the independent-minded, proud and patriotic New Englanders. He was respected for being self-made, as someone who was willing to stand up and speak his mind. In Massachusetts, more voters call themselves independent than identify with either of the parties; the ultimate independent had a readymade audience.

The high point of the Perot campaign for the Massachusetts volunteers was the June 21 Boston rally that had five thousand people marching in an eight-block parade through historic Boston, the cradle of democracy. After assembling on the plaza at City Hall, they marched by the Granary Burying Ground, the Park Street Church, and on to the Boston Common area where police estimated ten thousand to fifteen thousand turned out to hear Perot speak.

People showed up from all over the state, as well as from Maine, Connecticut, Rhode Island and New Hampshire. They were decked out in Revolutionary dress and militia costumes, complete with muskets, with their colonial bands. All of the rallies were encouraged to be a grass roots show, to call upon their own colloquial uniqueness, and Boston was one of the most colorful, playing to a Revolution-patriotic theme.

The day of the rally, Perot arrived in time to tour the Vietnam Veterans Shelter, a tough-love kind of rehab center for veterans, located in the heart of the historic district. He watched the parade from a room in the Parker House Hotel with Mayor Raymond Flynn and a few staff people. Anderson was amazed to hear later that when his party left the hotel room, Perot asked that the leftover sandwiches be packed up so he could drop them off at the veterans' shelter.

Appearing on the platform at the rally was another veteran Perot had helped—Tom Reed. Reed, who was stationed at Fort Devens (Massachusetts) had lost part of his leg in a land-mine explosion in Desert Storm. Perot took a personal interest in seeing that Reed got the best doctors and prosthesis available. The prosthesis enabled the athletic young soldier to be able to run and play basketball again. It was Reed's daughter that Perot would hold on his shoulders at the end of the rally.

While it was a large and enthusiastic crowd, Perot had his detractors at this event. He appeared somewhat thrown off stride by protestors from the Queer Nation, who tried repeatedly to interrupt his speech. The volunteers played down the trouble as just typical of Massachusetts politics.

"Remember, you're in Massachusetts, this is a hotbed of this stuff," said Williams, the Cape Cod area leader. "It's just part of the Massachusetts tradition. You would be very surprised if you came to Massachusetts not to see some real serious demonstrations of some kind."

But the real trouble in the Perot campaign was just about to start. Perhaps Williams had a premonition. He talked on Jo Streit's documentary footage about what could derail the campaign.

"We talk about sailing," said the volunteer from the Cape Cod area. "It's like a spinnaker. As long as the spinnaker is catching that wind and pushing it, it goes very well, but if it takes a slight tack in another direction, it loses that wind from the sail. I see this as one of the great challenges. It's very difficult for somebody who's going to run a political campaign to know and keep that wind. It's almost impossible to keep that wind in your sails. It's tricky. As long as they keep the sail catching the wind, it's going to sail right on through to November. But lose that and you lose it all."

The wind in the sail, to Williams, was the grass roots, the spontaneous team effort. If that was replaced by a stiffening, a hierarchical, top-down campaign structure, he predicted trouble. The boat would be on the rocks. "Organizationally, if it's a traditional campaign, it's death, it's over. The wind goes out of the sail, (the boat) drifts into the rocks. Those are the uncharted waters."

The boat was about to hit the rocks. Ross Perot was about to go from a California high to a nationwide low.

9

THE PROS, THE PRESS, THE PROBLEMS

THE DAY AFTER THE CALIFORNIA PRIMARY, Perot sent shockwaves through the political community when he planted a foot firmly in both party camps, hiring veteran Republican strategist Ed Rollins and former Jimmy Carter presidential campaign manager Hamilton Jordan as co-managers of his campaign.

It seemed like a good idea at the time. And, in theory, it was. It gave the campaign a bipartisan bouquet: Jordan would show appeal to Democrats and Rollins to Republicans. Their defection reinforced the message that party loyalty was at an extraordinary low, and the Perot candidacy cut across the spectrum of partisan (and nonpartisan) support. It was the kind of coup—drawing big names from both parties—that might encourage other high profile crossovers. Political watchers had been speculating for weeks about whether a Perot candidacy would hurt the Democratic nominee or the Republican. With Jordan and Rollins, the answer was clear: it would hurt both—and, ultimately, both *parties*, unless they were able to deflect the Perot candidacy and captivate his supporters.

Up to this time, the tiny team managing the petition drive had been working from the crack of dawn until midnight, trying to get the job done, with its army of volunteers. It was a crazy, fun time, and they were seeing their man rise in the polls. But it was still a zoo. They were presiding over chaos, and Mort Meyerson and Tom Luce, who were running the campaign, weren't used to chaos. Meyerson thought the zoo needed to be professionalized. The time had come to fish or cut bait; were they going to have a real campaign or not?

The hirings held the promise of injecting some needed professionalism into the operation. After all, Perot did promise a "world-class campaign." Supporters were beginning to ask, what do we do when we finish the petition drive? And, as talented and creative as members of Perot's First Team were, none of them had ever run a presidential campaign.

Raiding the top party ranks also lent credibility to the grass roots movement, which had been largely ignored or belittled by many in the press, despite the depth and breadth of frustration being registered by the American people. If two men who ran previous winning presidential campaigns said it was real, it had to be real. And these two said it was real. "I doubt there's been a time in the recent history of our country when there's been a greater disparity between what the American people want and expect from government, and what both political parties have provided them," Jordan said. Rollins agreed, saying, "There's an awful lot of Americans who just don't feel that the parties represent them any more."

Jordan offered early support to Perot; he was working for Whittle Communications in Knoxville, Tennessee, but he was volunteering his advice to Luce. During April, he came to Dallas for some of the weekend meetings that the First Team held. He was fascinated by the grass roots uprising, and by what the Perot phenomenon might mean to the American political system. He believed Perot would not just work at the margins of the nation's problems but would go for wholesale change.

Jordan had devised and run the maverick, anti-Washington campaign that put peanut farmer Jimmy Carter, a fellow Georgian, in the White House. And while he served as White House chief of staff, he was never regarded as a Washington "insider." Rather he had been something of a playboy in Washington. After Carter's loss in 1980, Jordan had little to do with the political establishment. He returned to Atlanta and was later diagnosed with lymphatic cancer, which he fought off with experimental chemotherapy. He remarried and ran a losing race for U.S. Senate in 1986 before going to work for Whittle.

As Luce and Meyerson discussed bringing in professional support, they looked for a Republican consultant to try to balance the team. Meyerson, in particular, saw a need to offset the "Carterites"—Jordan and Policy Adviser John White. Rollins would be their man. He had been a White House political director and had run Ronald Reagan's 1984 campaign. Two years later, he headed a presidential exploratory committee formed by Jack Kemp. Rollins had become an irritant to the Bush White House by disagreeing with the selection of Dan Quayle as vice-president in 1988, and urging Republican congressional candidates in 1990 to distance themselves from the budget agreement when Bush broke his no-new-taxes pledge. Some fellow partisans charged that he sold out to the highest bidder, that he went with Perot for an exorbitant salary. Others rationalized his taking the job because he was out of favor with the Bush White House and was blacklisted for the Bush presidential race.

Rollins disputed both charges. What he would make in a month with Perot would amount to about what he was making in a month at the Sawyer-Miller Consulting Group in Washington, where he was earning $800,000 to $900,000 a year. Rollins also said that the week before he joined Perot, he was offered work with the Bush campaign if he wouldn't sign up with Perot.

In companion op-ed pieces in the *Washington Post* June 7, the two men explained their breaks from their respective parties. "I do not believe," wrote Jordan, "that it makes any real difference whether Governor Clinton is elected or President Bush is reelected...The answer to our problems is not likely to come from either major party because the nomination processes of both exaggerate the influence of interest groups, reward extreme positions, produce a public discourse that is irrelevant to the average citizen and create a cynicism about the political process that discourages participation."

Jordan believed the system to be badly flawed and that Bush or Clinton could produce only incremental change at a time when the nation's core problems were growing exponentially worse. "While there are real policy differences between Bush and Clinton, those traditional partisan differences are moot as long as the federal budget deficit persists and grows...Traditional partisan arguments about how to divide the pie are moot when there is no pie left to divide," he said. Jordan believed that a Perot administration would "strive for major reforms instead of incremental change and would be built on the simple premise that our national purpose is to create a bright future for our children instead of short-term pleasures for ourselves."

Rollins had been working to elect Republicans for twenty-five years, after growing up in a blue-collar family in California and starting his adult life as a Demo-crat. His special passion had been wooing working-class Democrats to the Republican cause, but he felt Bush had blunted that effort. While he thought of himself, at least psychologically, as an outsider, he was firmly rooted in the Republican party, both philosophically and financially. Working to elect Republicans had provided a good part of his livelihood. After leaving as co-chair of the Republican Congressional Committee in 1991, Rollins became a managing partner in Sawyer-Miller, a tie he had to sever when he joined Perot.

Jumping ship carried serious consequences for Rollins. His wife, Sherrie, felt she had to quit her own prestigious job in the Bush White House. And Rollins was jeopardizing his long-range prospects of ever rep-resenting Republicans again. Rollins tried to offset fu-ture repercussions by declaring that he was a "Republican for Perot," and that he intended to vote for other Republicans in November.

As for Bush, however, Rollins said: "After long and painful deliberation, I do not believe that George Bush and his advisers—who have been at the reins of power and policy for twelve years—can be effective catalysts for change. Ross Perot can."

On "Nightline" on June 4, the day after being hired, Rollins said he believed Bush had lost touch with the American public, "particularly in the last thirty days, in the post-Los Angeles period, I just saw him doing busi-ness as usual...I guess I felt that Mr. Perot would be the only one who could really change the system."

Jordan justified the campaign's hiring of the "odd couple" on the same "Nightline" show. "What Ed and I have in common," he said, "is a concern about some core issues that face the American people, pessimism that those issues will ever be confronted by either of the two major political parties, and a belief that Mr. Perot has a real-life experience and leadership ability to attack those issues. And I think that's been the basis for this unbelievable grass roots movement that's developed in this country over the past ten or twelve weeks in support of his candidacy."

The week that Rollins and Jordan were hired was the same week that Bill Clinton played his saxophone on the "Arsenio Hall" show, illustrating his own outreach to voters through new and different media channels, and President Bush staged a press conference that was boycotted by three major networks and carried only by CNN. Bush wanted to talk about the need for a balanced budget amendment; the press wanted to talk about Perot, the man who was changing the face of American politics.

Rollins and Jordan became the talk of the political talk shows. But Perot's two-headed cow was not universally heralded. Some said it merely symbolized the fact that Perot was trying to be all things to all people. Others found the hirings hypocritical. Rollins, for example, was the product of and had helped perpetuate the system that he was now trying to dismantle. He boasted of being the "architect of the Reagan coalition." One Democratic congressman even charged Rollins with hiding the "truth" from the American people that the Republican economic policies of the 1980s were destroying the country.

But the harshest reproach was: How could Perot decry professional politicians and their handlers, and then turn around and hire two premier handlers? Perot protested that they weren't handlers, only staff strategists. Then he immediately set out to prove that they would never "handle" him.

Perot also made it clear from the beginning that the hiring of Jordan and Rollins was not his idea but that of Tom Luce and Mort Meyerson. Because of the brief period of time between June and November, Perot told CNN's "Morning News," "Tom and Mort felt it would be wise to get the two best people in the business, if they were interested." In the same interview, he reiterated that "this will not be a conventional campaign."

"What we're trying to do is get the talent in here to make sure we can deliver on my commitment to run a world-class campaign. They will not be my handlers. They will not get me up in the morning, dress me, give me words to say, tell me what to do and where to go. That's not their role. Their role is to bring the experience of what's involved in the massive campaign, in the terms of getting it organized and making it work," Perot said.

The hiring of the pros drew mixed reviews from the volunteers. Many welcomed the addition of the professionals, assuming they would bring order and expertise to the campaign. Some resented the hirings from the beginning, because the whole idea ran counter to the "people's campaign." The problem was not so much the idea of the professionals coming in as the reality of their presence—a presence that rocked the soul of the people's movement. The professionals brought a profound change in the flavor of the campaign. New and serious tensions were created that portended disaster.

Jordan and Rollins were about as different as two guys could be. Where Jordan played his cards close to the vest, Rollins enjoyed appearing on TV talk shows and was compulsively candid with the press. Being loose-lipped with the press, in fact, put him in immediate disfavor with Perot. For all practical purposes, Rollins burned his bridge with Perot before he ever started working in Dallas. The *Wall Street Journal* reported the week before the hiring that the purported "co-managers" had met with top Perot aides over the weekend. Hiring a Democrat "with experience at grass roots organizing" and a Republican "with an iconoclastic streak" would be a "stunning coup for Mr. Perot," the story said. Rollins was identified as the leak, and although Perot hired him, he never trusted him.

Acting as co-managers would be difficult even in the best of circumstances, but impossible given an uncooperative candidate—which is what Rollins and Jordan encountered—and given the differences in their own personalities.

Rollins contended that he and Jordan got along fine. Others in the campaign, however, claimed Rollins wanted to be in control. He wanted to be the manager, not co-manager. He moved quickly to take the reins, bringing in his own team and lining up old friends and associates to be subcontractors. Within days, Rollins's loyalists had invaded the campaign; his net was thrown far and wide.

There was little doubt that Rollins and Squires, the communications director, failed to see eye to eye. After the campaign was over, Squires said he had voted against bringing in Rollins during a three-man meeting with Meyerson and Luce, but Meyerson was insistent. Squires said he knew Rollins, and Meyerson didn't. His concern was that Rollins and Perot would lock horns, because Rollins represented the very aspects of campaigning that Perot was against—the slickness, the press manipulation. Squires believed that Rollins had a compulsion to leak information and he couldn't function without talking to the press. It was, according to Squires, the way Rollins validated his existence.

To Rollins, talking to the press was "just a reality of life. It's my job to try to get the best story forward. It's your job (as a journalist) to tell the story you want to write."

Rollins claimed he told Perot before he was ever hired that he was accustomed to appearing on TV and he would expect to continue doing that. Perot had no problem, he said, until he was on the air.

Friction developed right away with Rollins. In a Perot organization, only one person is going to have total control, and that's Ross Perot. Real influence with Perot is built over time. So it was unlikely from the beginning that he was going to take advice from rank strangers. The advice of Rollins and Jordan, after the first few days, was almost always carried to Perot by Luce and Meyerson.

The weekend before the hirings of the pros were announced, Charlie Leonard arrived to get an early start on the job. Leonard had been campaign director for the House Republicans in 1990 and a regional political director for Bush in 1988. Like Rollins, he also worked for Sawyer-Miller in Washington. Leonard had been hired by Luce to be political director, working with the state organizations in making the transition from the petition drive to the campaign. Leonard set up a meeting with Mark Blahnik, Perot's personal aide-de-camp. Blahnik was over the field operation for the petition drive. Blahnik probably spent more time with Perot than anyone in the petition drive effort. He not only worked for Perot, he was like a second son to Perot.

Blahnik was late to his meeting with Leonard, and the two got off to a rocky start. Leonard set down the rules. There would be the volunteer organization, and there would be the campaign organization, and anybody from the volunteer side who wanted to join the campaign side needed to get in line. He might as well have spit in Margot Perot's eye, Squires said, in detailing this story. Blahnik reported back to Perot, who immediately decided that Charlie Leonard would not be in charge of Mark Blahnik. So within the first forty-eight hours of the new, professionalized campaign, the political director was banned from running the field operations. Perot never relinquished his hold on the volunteer organization, through Blahnik.

According to Leonard, Blahnik felt the field organization was something he had built and he wanted to remain in control of it. "Squires thought we came in to try to change the movement. Nothing could be further from the truth. We clearly saw ourselves as in-house advisers. We thought it would be a mistake to try to change the character of the volunteer movement," Leonard said.

When Perot switched gears, Leonard agreed to be deputy campaign manager.

The professionals came in, had meetings and conceived strategy, wrote budgets, wrote manuals for field operations, and hired more professionals, but the campaign continued to be run by Meyerson and Luce. It became almost a full-time job for Luce and Meyerson to try to convince Perot to let Jordan and Rollins do what they wanted to do, and what they thought they had been hired to do.

Rollins and Jordan had laid out the kind of campaign they wanted to run in a meeting with Perot before they were hired. According to Rollins, Perot agreed to the $150 million conventional campaign they proposed, including TV commercials to begin in July. Yet, once on board, they found it impossible to get a decision out of Perot on virtually anything they proposed.

The pros knew what their challenge was and tried to forge ahead, mostly without Perot. "I had thirty to forty people who were anxious to get on with the task," Rollins said.

By then, Luce had hired a research director, a pollster—Frank Luntz, who had done polling for Republican insurgent Patrick Buchanan. Perot, however, never acknowledged that he had a pollster. According to Rollins, the money to fund the polling operation had to be hidden in the budget, or they would have had no polling data.

The pros also immediately went to work planning how they would spend Perot's money—on advertising, direct mail, field operations, etc. That was their biggest mistake. Perot and his money are not easily parted, except for his family and private acts of charity or patriotism. Wasting his money on unnecessary political expenditures was neither patriotic nor prudent to him.

Leonard wrote the budget he said "sent Ross to the ceiling," and then wrote the budget that "brought him back down." The first budget was based, he said, on instructions from Luce and Meyerson and Perot's top finance men. The original $150 million budget included a $60 million ad campaign, $13 million for direct mail, and other high-powered costs of an orthodox campaign, using traditional techniques. But when it was presented to Perot, he "went nuts," Leonard said. The second budget was for $70 million, but it left out all projects after the first thirty days—such as advertising, direct mail, polling and additional hiring. Leonard said he was advised that they would have to go back to Perot later to get more funding in increments. Tom Walter, chief financial officer of the Perot Group, and Bill Gayden, who had been with Perot at EDS, actually presented the budget to him. "These were his money guys inside the companies; they had the most experience in handling Ross. They understood him—here was a man who ran a $300 million business out of a checkbook," Leonard said.

One of those expenses was to produce TV advertising. *Newsweek* reported, apparently based on information given them by Rollins, that San Francisco adman Hal Riney would create the campaign's TV ads. Riney was the creator of Ronald Reagan's "Morning in America" campaign, as well as the popular, off-beat commercials for Bartles & James wine coolers, and General Motors' new Saturn car. Luce had hired Riney to film rallies; he was on board when Rollins arrived. But it was Rollins who told the press about Riney, and he acknowledged that Riney quickly became "my guy," because he believed Riney to be the best in the business. Perot was obsessed with leaks. If somebody said he was going to do something, that was reason enough not to do it. Beyond that, however, Rollins's allegiance to Riney became the source of serious conflict with Perot.

Other big-league political consultants were brought in, among them Sal Russo, one of the Republican Party's most experienced California campaign pros; he would be a senior advisor to Rollins, his former partner. Russo had helped engineer the election of Governor George Deukmejian in California. Tim Kraft, who had done volunteer coordinating for Jimmy Carter, was brought in to perform a similar function in the Perot campaign. Special events man Joe Canzeri, who had worked for New York Governor Nelson Rockefeller and for Vice President Dan Quayle, was brought in to work on events and scheduling.

Russo, Marsh and Leonard came up with what they thought was a great idea for a $1.5 million mailing, which would be a "thank-you" letter from Ross Perot to the volunteers. Leonard said there were seven hundred thousand to eight hundred thousand people who had called the Dallas headquarters who had never been thanked. The mailing would also provide a return card with demographic information that could be put into the data base. Perot's response was: "Why should I spend $1.5 million to say thank you?" according to Leonard.

By the third week of June, seventy-five people had been hired to work on the staff side of the campaign. Rollins told the *Washington Post's* David Broder he had plans to put a campaign coordinator and a press coordinator into each state and hire "eight or nine big-name consultants from both parties" to give guidance and direction to the volunteer effort. He predicted that within two weeks he would have "a better team than either Bush or Clinton."

The professional staff in Dallas officed in high-security space behind locked doors on the same floor as the phone bank, in the Dallas headquarters. Electronic passkeys were required to get into the staff space. Volunteers were not allowed in unless invited. A "war room" in the center was off limits except for top campaign officials. Even at a strength of seventy-five, the paid staff was well below that of the other candidates. Clinton had about two hundred on his full-time staff, and Bush had more than 250. But the rapid escalation of a paid staff—a sort of piling-on at the top—resulted in all sorts of tensions in a campaign that had built up from the bottom.

One would have expected tensions between the professionals who had worked for Democrats and those who had worked for Republicans. Those, however, were negligible. The real strains that developed were between the professionals and the volunteers, and between the professionals and the Perot associates. The first order of business for Perot's longtime associates was to protect and insulate him. The first order of business for the political pros was to get the campaign machine up and running, full speed ahead, damn the torpedoes and the cost, as well.

Almost from the beginning, the Perot folks sensed that the alliance, particularly with Rollins, wasn't going to work. Perot liked Jordan, but not Rollins. Those close to Perot believed that Jordan had been intrigued by the grass roots phenomenon. But Rollins wanted to run a hierarchical presidential campaign structure. He was trying to impose a structure that Perot didn't want. Charlie Leonard wanted to set up a soft money fundraising organization, according to Clay Mulford. But Perot didn't have to raise soft money to get around the FEC; he wasn't using federal funding. And soft money was against his principles; he had no intention of raising soft money, which is money raised and spent outside federal election rules, ostensibly for "grass roots activity." Perot thought his grass roots were doing fine on their own, thank you. Rollins wanted to do focus groups, according to Mulford, to find out how people felt so Perot could appeal to them. Again, that wasn't Perot. "We knew immediately it was not the right kind of ideological match," Clay Mulford said.

Rollins's personal style didn't fit in, either. While Perot prides himself on driving his own '84 Olds, Rollins had a driver. He also had a team of personal assistants ready on a moment's notice to fetch his dry cleaning or do other personal chores. That may have been de rigeur in Washington, but it wasn't the Dallas way. It certainly wasn't the Perot way.

While there was a common mission, conflicts developed because different people had signed on to the campaign for different reasons. Those brought in to work on issues, for example, had no allegiance to Ross Perot. They were brought in because they were researchers, because they had astute minds or a special area of expertise. John White had gone to universities that had major public policy schools—Wharton, Duke, Harvard, Syracuse, Berkeley, Stanford, Rand—to recruit top graduate students. They had to be bright and they had to come recommended. Otherwise, there were only two requirements: White wanted them to be young, because he knew they wouldn't get much sleep, and he wanted them to have worked, although not necessarily in politics. He just didn't have time to teach them how to work. So he had a dozen or so young scholars who were not there because of any burning passion for Ross Perot.

Then there were the political professionals who were hired guns, political vagabonds who make their living in part by going from campaign to campaign. Most had worked for candidates who were ideologically different from Ross Perot—the kind of professional politicians that Perot abhorred. Many of the pros had allegiance to Rollins, not to Perot.

And there were the Perot loyalists, who were there because of professional or personal ties with Perot. They likewise had brought in people. Kristen Silverberg, for example, had met Tom Luce at the Institute of Politics at Harvard, where she was an undergraduate. She gave up her first year in law school to work in the campaign. She became, with Bob Siegel, co-coordinator of the Youth Campaign.

Meyerson brought in some, such as Virginia (Ginny) Fitzgerald, a special-events coordinator from Greenwich, Connecticut, to help with the rallies in the different states.

On June 20, Meyerson also brought aboard an old high school friend from Fort Worth (they had been National Merit Scholars together) to be head of administration. Bill Frost, who had retired as a sales vice-president with AT&T in Houston, had known Perot when he oversaw people who handled the EDS account. He was working as a telemarketing consultant in Houston when Meyerson called and asked him to come in and establish a budget and a payroll system, to take over security, office planning and personnel, and to oversee administration of the volunteer organization. Bringing in the professionals had apparently only produced greater chaos. One of the first things Frost did was to tighten up what appeared to be an already tight security. All the volunteers had to wear badges. "If you came to the front desk to talk to Tom Luce, somebody from the organization would have to walk you back. It was the only way to have control of the facilities," he said.

The Perot loyalists included the Young Turks, who were working as field coordinators out in the states with the volunteers. The head Turks were Perot loyalists, transferred to the campaign from Perot businesses; the others (twenty-five or so) were recruited because they were young, action-oriented problem solvers who didn't mind living out of a suitcase. None of them had any experience in political campaigns.

Finally, there were the people in the campaign who were the true believers—the volunteers. They were the ones who would have walked on broken glass for Ross Perot, who spent all or much of their free time in the petition drive and manning the phone bank, whose other lives virtually stopped during the petition drive. They felt isolated, unimportant and ignored after the pros came in. Some of the volunteers, in fact, had been hankering for paid positions and felt they had earned the right to go on the payroll. Instead, they saw those jobs being taken by political hired guns who had no real allegiance to "their" movement.

Frost encouraged the campaign chiefs—Luce, Meyerson, Jordan, Rollins and Leonard—to walk through the phone bank, even if for only five minutes a day, to "take notice of the worker bees." The volunteers felt they were being locked out by all of these new people "on the other side of the wall."

Campaigns normally start with the professionals, who recruit volunteers. Perot's campaign developed the opposite way, as campaigns did before the emergence of the cottage industry of campaign professionals. For Perot volunteers, it had been a heady time. "The power of the first three months was indescribable—the connection you could make with other people," Dallas volunteer Barbara Mann said. "It was very addictive, very cult-like." As the pros moved in, many of the volunteers felt they were losing their newfound power.

Complaints also were being heard from the field. Local organizations claimed the field representatives from Dallas were running roughshod over them. Factional disputes were developing in the local petition drive offices. Volunteer leaders were anxious to know what effect the professionals would have on their operation.

In an effort to ease tensions in the field, all of the state coordinators were brought to Dallas for a meeting with the "national staff." Rollins briefed them at a Dallas hotel. Charlie Leonard tried to alleviate their concerns that the pros would be "taking over" the states. Leonard said the volunteers were told about successful approaches in other campaigns. Leonard advised them to write their own individual state plans, adapting the ideas they felt would work in their states and rejecting those that wouldn't. He denied they were telling the states what to do. "I have been a consultant to twenty-five campaigns around the country; I understand the role. I give you my best advice. If you choose to do something else, that's your decision," he said.

Even with the problems of the transition, it was an exhilarating time at Perot headquarters during the first three weeks of June. Perot was riding high in the polls, continuing to get on more state ballots, attracting large and enthusiastic crowds at his petition rallies. The excitement was building. There was a sense that he could really win the election, that he would be the next president. When Perot hit 38 percent in June, Frank Luntz, the pollster, became a believer; even he thought Perot might win. When writer Wick Allison came in from New York the last week of June to write the manuscript for the issues book, he thought he was a part of "a moment of tremendous importance. You could feel it in the headquarters. There was a groundswell around the country."

Yet, even as the pros were setting up shop and multiplying by the day, they were being frozen out by the Boss. He dealt with them through intermediaries, ignored their advice, their memos, their work product. He refused to do things the traditional way.

One of Kristen Silverberg's responsibilities was to develop briefing materials on the states that Perot was scheduled to visit. She would call the state coordinators and ask for background on local issues and other information Perot might use on his visit. The local volunteers would turn handsprings preparing packets to send to Dallas, and she would refine the information into briefing papers for Perot. After doing several, she questioned whether they were being read, whether she was wasting her time on the effort. So she went to Luce, who told her, "I'm not really sure Mr. Perot is ready for that."

Meanwhile, Perot still had to finish getting on the ballot in all of the states—and that appeared to be the only thing he was interested in doing, other than appearing on TV, which by now had become an addiction. He thought the TV folks loved him. Why should he spend money to buy commercial time, when the networks wanted him? He would often disappear for days, calling Meyerson from his plane to announce he was on his way to appear on another TV show. He insisted on being his own scheduler and advance man. Rollins thought Perot was getting "over-exposed" and counseled him to cut out his TV appearances for a while. Perot agreed. Soon thereafter, Rollins was flipping through the channels in his office and saw Perot appearing on PBS's "MacNeil/Lehrer News Hour."

"It's very simple," Perot had said when he hired Rollins and Jordan. "If you want to play football in the NFL, you'd better find a coach or two that's played ball before...People running the campaign will be first-timers, but we need the advice and counsel of people who've been there." As it turned out, he virtually ignored whatever advice and counsel came from his "coaches."

THE PRESS
By late June there were other distractions to consider. By then, Perot was almost totally absorbed by negative press reports. The first wave of coverage had been favorable, reflecting Perot's position in the polls, the volunteer support and the anti-incumbent mood that prevailed around the country. As NBC reporter Lisa Myers said, "There was this initial period of uncritical

press—'Here he is, everyone thinks he's wonderful.' What we've seen in the last few weeks," she told the *Washington Post* the third week of June, "is an effort to fill out the picture."

Eleanor Clift of *Newsweek* felt the press never figured out how to deal with Perot; it went from giving him an early free ride to overscrutiny. As long as he was just a blip on the radar screen, the press, collectively, would let Perot have his fun. But when it became apparent that he was a serious candidate, that he had the potential to scramble not just the presidential race but the whole political system, it was time to take a closer look. Perot had bypassed the primary system, where candidates for the nomination are weeded out by the intense press scrutiny. "There was a collective feeling in the media," Eleanor Clift said, "that you don't let him off scot-free. We've got to put him through a primary."

Rollins felt there were two phases of "Perot I," the initial Perot campaign. The first phase was from Larry King to June, when Perot could appear on any talk show, the people were doing all the work for him, and he was treated by the press as a serious political figure, but not as a serious presidential contender. The second phase began about June 1, when he was leading in the polls, he was the hottest political phenomenon in recent history, and he had hired a couple of professionals who knew how to run campaigns. All of that made him a serious presidential contender, so he was treated differently, Rollins felt.

Tom Luce, who dealt with the press when he ran for governor, was unprepared for the intensity of the coverage, particularly once Perot was regarded as a serious candidate. During the second week of June, twelve reporters from *The New York Times* were working on Perot stories. Ironically, *The Times* didn't run a single story on the potential Perot candidacy until one month after the initial "Larry King Live" pronouncement. "Because it started on Larry King, it was not in *The New York Times's* universe," Luce noted, at least not for a while. The first story written in *The Times* was by a business writer. Once *The Times* realized Perot was a legitimate political story, however, it made up for lost time.

Journalists complained that they were having a hard time covering Perot because they had no access to him. The Perot campaign refused to put out a "message of the day"—which was the way the conventional campaigns did it. There was no "offensive press machine" for Perot. Rather, the campaign responded to specific requests for interviews or information. Reporters found little information forthcoming, however, and few interviews granted. There were no press conferences, no new issue positions to report. Tiring of Perot's stock speech and his television comments, and failing to get much out of the Perot Petition Committee, they began looking elsewhere. Since Perot had no political record to exhume, journalists dug into business dealings, Perot's philanthropy, any relationships he had with government, or any other stories—public or private—that could provide an idea of what kind of president this man would be.

Among the stories that began to surface about his past were conflicting accounts of his military career and stories that questioned the propriety of some of his business dealings and employee policies at EDS. He was called the "welfare billionaire" for having built his fortune at EDS processing Medicare and Medicaid claims. He was said to have hounded a competitor, the Bradford National Corporation, out of a signed contract for Texas Medicaid's computer-data work in 1980.

There were stories that Alliance Airport, a Perot project headed up by Ross Perot, Jr., had sought and received federal funds. There was nothing illegal, mind you, but they were described, for example in *Newsweek*, as "handouts" and "favors." *Fort Worth Star-Telegram* publisher Rich Connor charged that, because of a critical story in his newspaper on the Perots and Alliance Airport, Perot threatened him with a photograph of a newspaper staffer in a compromising situation with a city official.

Other old stories were revived, which said Perot had:

- Suggested the police cordon off a Dallas minority neighborhood and conduct a door-to-door search for drugs and weapons.
- Backed a military-style war on drugs, including bombings and espionage operations in Latin America.
- Dressed down a policeman who had stopped his daughter-in-law for speeding and discovered a concealed weapon in the glove box.
- Withdrawn funding from the Reagan Library after a blowup with the Reagan Administration over the POW/MIA issue.
- Canceled an $8 million pledge to the Dallas Arboretum; even asked that his initial $2 million donation be returned.

The whole General Motors-EDS affair was restudied. Perot's relationship with Oliver North and his role in the Iran-Contra affair were reexamined. His work with the Texas Legislature on public education and his involvement with the state's war on drugs were scrutinized. Going back to the 1960s, he was portrayed as an "insider" who was closely allied with the Nixon White

House. As Perot would say, "et cetera, et cetera, et cetera."

Some of the stories were legitimate because they revealed character traits, beliefs or how he worked in the public arena. Others were marginal, at best. Not all of the media bought into all of the old stuff. Commenting on CNN May 19 on Perot's father trying to reduce his Naval commitment after the Korean War, commentator Mark Shields said: "If that's the most serious charge you got against the guy—it's like double parking outside an orphanage on Christmas Eve." Paul Burka, *Texas Monthly* editor, said on the "Phil Donahue" show May 28, "I'm so tired of trying to elect a president on what they did in 1955 or 1960. When are we going to stop this?"

Two of the harshest critics of Perot were magazine writers Sidney Blumenthal of *The New Republic* and Elizabeth Drew of *The New Yorker*. Elizabeth Drew wrote in the May 18 New Yorker: "One is reluctant to use inflammatory words, but Perot's concept has the aura of quasi-fascism: Peron-style, or Mussolini-style fascism, with the hero-leader, backed by 'the people,' breaking down impediments to having his way—all, of course, in their name." Perot's electronic town hall meeting struck her as a "large step toward plebiscitary government with a whiff of mobocracy. It is a formula ripe for demagoguery, and Perot has already shown some demagogic tendencies," she wrote.

Blumenthal, in his piece on "Perotnoia" in the June 15 *New Republic*, called Perot "a man with no fixed political beliefs and, according to many who have had dealings with him, the temperament of a zealot. Above all, he operates according to the principles of loyalty and betrayal, which he applies mercilessly to everyone but himself. His preferred method is paramilitary...Whether from the far right or the far left, Perot is willing to underwrite crackpot schemes as though they were entrepreneurial bright ideas."

Could the anti-politician really campaign without a real press scrutiny? asked Blumenthal. "In every state where he secured a lucrative government contract, from California to New York, there is an unpretty tale of influence for the local media to unearth if they will...What effect the collision of fact and myth will have on Perot's movement, the largest UFO cult in American history, is the great unknown."

Blumenthal concluded that "It's far too soon to write the epitaph of one who is hailed today as a messiah by a plurality of the voters. But historically this sort of figure has been rejected for the same reasons he is popular. Each strength of Perot's character has its jagged side: the righter of wrongs who carries out vendettas; the successful entrepreneur who can't function in any situation he can't completely control; the man of convictions who's paranoid; the one who believes in merit but wins through intimidation; the fearless one who is on all sides of controversial questions; the one who knows best who's an ignoramus; the worshiper of the Founding Fathers who hires soldiers of fortune; the loyalist who betrays his loyalists; the patriot who wants to scrap the American system of government."

Old hands in the press saw cause for alarm. Bill Kovach, once editor of the *Atlanta Constitution* and curator of Harvard's Neiman Foundation was troubled by a kind of reporting that was rooted in Watergate. In a June 14 *New York Times* story, he said the legacy of the Watergate investigative fervor was "an intense focus on the watchdog role of the press, on the 'journalism of exposure.' The press should be ready, he said, 'to not just expose wrongdoing, but expose the characters and the ideas' of politicians, especially Presidential candidates."

Initially Perot dismissed many of the "investigative" stories as just "silly putty" or "Mickey Mouse tossed salad." He said in the spring, "I can't control what people scribble on pads." Even the columnists, he said, had a right to their opinions.

And polls were showing that people distrusted and disliked the media. A Gordon Black poll published in early June indicated 89 percent of those polled feel the newspapers "prefer shots at candidates" rather than helping voters with the issues. Seventy-three percent said they felt the national networks were "out of touch with what Americans think." And 70 percent said the "so-called TV experts don't understand normal concerns."

The stories kept coming, and they got worse. Perot's initial irritation turned to anger as he was portrayed as someone who employed surveillance tactics at will, was consumed with conspiracy theories, and would get rid of anybody or anything that got in his way. The "Billionaire Boy Scout" had become "Inspector Perot."

There was the "tenant story"—Perot had persuaded a judge to permit warrantless searches of a Perot property occupied by a tenant. There was the "Armitage story"—Perot tried to block the nomination of Richard Armitage (who he believed was thwarting his POW efforts) as secretary of the Army because he suspected Armitage had underworld contacts. There was the "Bermuda story"—he wanted to blow up a coral reef near his house in Bermuda so he could harbor his boat near his house.

The straw that broke the camel's back was a June 21 story by Bob Woodward in the *Washington Post*, based on background information that had been given to him by Perot four years before. Woodward wrote that Perot, realizing Bush was not going to help him find remaining evidence of POWs and MIAs in Southeast Asia, had launched a series of investigations of Bush designed to expose Bush as being weak, indecisive and possibly even corrupt. Perot aides claimed that Woodward, four years before, came to Texas to investigate Bush's financial background, called on Perot, and Perot shared some information with him.

According to Squires, Woodward decided he "needed a piece of the Perot story," and his four-year-old conversation had been on his mind for weeks. His 1988 conversation with Perot had been off-the-record, and he called several times trying to get released from his off-the-record commitment. Finally, Woodward called Squires to inform him that the *Post* was going to go with the story and that Perot could respond if he wanted to. Squires tried to get Woodward to come to Dallas to talk to Perot, but Woodward declined; he was on his way to Italy.

This story had far-reaching ramifications. It was repeated across the country, and President Bush even weighed in with a response. Perot was being redefined in a way not at all to his liking. He blamed many of the stories on Republican "dirty tricks," tips to the media from the Bush campaign's opposition research.

As Perot took the lead in the polls, Republicans began a well-orchestrated campaign to paint him as "scary" and "dangerous." The Republicans had conducted focus groups which told them Perot had just such a vulnerability with voters. They discovered a trait that concerned voters, which they described as an authoritarian streak that threatens people's liberties. And they jumped on it—beginning in late May—portraying him as crazy, kooky, temperamental, intolerant and dangerous.

White House spokesman Marlin Fitzwater described him as "a dangerous and destructive personality." Americans are creating a "monster," Fitzwater said. House Minority Leader Bob Michel called Perot a "frightening...demagogue," and warned of his "authoritarianism." Vice President Dan Quayle labelled Perot a "temperamental tycoon who has contempt for the Constitution." Quayle also said that President Bush even described Perot as "a Martian from off our planet" who defies understanding. Bush said he didn't understand why Perot disliked him so much, but suggested it might be because Bush (when he was vice-president) told Perot on the eve of his trip to Vietnam to search for American MIAs that the Reagan administration "did not want him to go."

The surrogate attacks were stepped up during the height of the Inspector Perot stories. On one occasion, Fitzwater crammed three scare words into one sentence about Perot—"shocking, frightening and bizarre." He accused Perot of "thinking he can investigate, harass and intimidate people." And Vice President Quayle said: "Imagine having the IRS, FBI and CIA under his control. Who would be investigated next?" Bush campaign manager Robert Teeter said Perot lacked the "judgment or temperament or respect for our laws to be president." Another Teeterism: "Perot is a guy who's been noted in his public career for doing a lot of things outside the rules." Drug czar Bob Martinez said Perot "advocates reckless, Wild West, covert operations, and he apparently regards the Bill of Rights as little more than an antique inconvenience."

It was written in the *Political Hotline* that, "after months of reported disarray, Bush-Quayle sends uncharacteristically unified message on Perot and civil liberties. Attack ranges from Bush himself to VP to Drug Czar to House floor to state GOPs."

Texas state chairman Fred Meyer went after Perot at the State Republican Convention. He was quoted in the *Dallas Morning News* on June 19 as saying: "There are other countries around the world, during times of, perhaps, concern, that have made the decision to empower people like that—much to their regret." Asked for an example, Meyer cited Mussolini.

Charles Black, a senior adviser to the Bush campaign, confirmed that the decision had been made to allow surrogates to "dust him up a little bit." Describing the effort, he said simply, "Make him risky." The strategy worked. A *New York Times*/CBS News poll, published on June 23, found that, while Perot remained tied with Bush, the percentage of voters who viewed Perot negatively had doubled in a six-week period.

Perot spokesman Jim Squires complained to the *Washington Times's* Hugh Aynesworth about a "scalp-hunting mentality" that had taken over the press. "Today, instead of proving you're the fairest, the most complete, you have to prove you're the toughest — and so you are the one who will get him if he's gotten." And David Gergen, editor-at-large of *U.S. News and World Report*, said in an interview with the *Washington Post*, "What we're seeing now with Perot is what we saw with Bill Clinton: He's emerging as a caricature. There is an effort to find the dark side...I trust we won't lose sight of the fact that he's had a lifetime of many accomplishments."

Squires was also highly critical of the "increasingly hysterical attacks by the Bush character assassins, which is all that's going on in elections these days. This is a system that destroys good presidential candidates." Little did he know at that time that his own candidate was headed for destruction. As it turned out, the combination of the professionals trying to turn the Perot Phenomenon into a conventional campaign, and the "primary" that the press put him through, proved to be a recipe for disaster for the still unannounced Perot candidacy.

★ ★ ★ ★ ★ 10 ★ ★ ★ ★ ★

BEGINNING OF THE END

PEROT LIKED TO SEE SOME LOCAL COLOR—a taste of Norman Rockwell-style American injected into his petition rallies. His petitioners were eager to oblige. On June 24, a flotilla of twenty-four flag-draped boats sailed and motored into the City Dock in Annapolis, Maryland, with petitions bearing one hundred and fifty thousand signatures. The flotilla sailed down the Severn River that empties into Chesapeake Bay and arrived to the strains of "Anchors Aweigh," only two blocks from where Perot had attended the U.S. Naval Academy. As a student leader (he was president of the class of '53), he had escorted President Dwight D. Eisenhower on a tour of the campus.

In Annapolis, for the first time at a rally, Perot was joined by his wife, Margot. Previously, he had said he feared for her safety and loved her too much to put her in harm's way at any public events. In Maryland, however, she was returning to her old stomping grounds as well; she was a student at Goucher College in Baltimore when she met Perot, the young midshipman, on a blind date. It was in Annapolis that Margot had pinned on Perot's ensign's shoulder boards when he graduated from the Naval Academy. Perot floated up to the pier in a battered crab boat behind the armada. He boarded the excursion boat, Annapolitan, shook hands with volunteers dressed as Uncle Sam and Betsy Ross, and addressed his supporters. Standing under banners that read, "Soar with an Eagle," and "We the People," Perot exclaimed to the crowd of six thousand: "People like you are excited about taking their country back!"

Maryland coordinator Joan Vinson and other volunteer leaders liked to call the Perot campaign the second American revolution. "John Adams said the Revolutionary War did not begin in Concord. It began in the hearts and minds of the people, fifteen years before," she said. "One of the most important things Ross Perot says is that if you're dissatisfied with your government, look in the mirror. As citizens, we have been too lax in our civic duties; we've just been asleep at the wheel. A lot of people felt they didn't have power. The strong word now is empowerment," she said.

It should have been a day for Perot to bask in, a day celebrating his getting on the ballot in a state with sentimental ties. Instead, he spent it denying charges that he had investigated everyone from President Bush, to Bush's children, to his own employees and his own children.

Perot had been on the defensive for days about his reported tendency toward surveillance techniques and use of private investigators, conspiracy theories and strong-arm tactics. The day before, in a *Washington Post* story, Perot strenuously denied a report in the opinion journal *New Republic* that he had investigated his own children, now in their twenties and thirties. He called it a "fairy tale of the highest order." He acknowledged, however, that during his children's college years, he had security experts "take precautions to see that where they lived was safe, where they parked their cars was safe." At the time, he was involved in investigations of drug dealing and feared for his own safety. "In every way, we wanted them to have a normal college life," he said. "That's gotten turned upside down."

In an effort to diffuse the attacks, he held his first news conference in two months following the Annapolis rally. During the hour-long press conference, he denied that he had conducted investigations of Bush, the president's children and his own children. To thwart the story that he had investigated the Bush offspring, Perot produced a handwritten note from then Vice President George Bush thanking Perot for letting him know about rumors concerning Bush's sons. Perot claimed the incident was twisted by the Republican "dirty-tricks" campaign. "There has been a ninety-day effort to redefine my personality by a group called opposition research of the Republican Party. They're generally known as the dirty-tricks crowd."

The press conference was full of reporters who had driven over from Washington for the day, many of whom had not previously covered Perot. Some were impressed. The *Houston Chronicle's* Cragg Hines wrote that "Perot's good-natured, unblinking performance in the hour-long wrangle with journalists probably reinforced his popularity with voters drawn to his take-charge image." David Gergen of *U.S. News* and the *Boston Globe's* John Mashek remarked at what a great job he had done in a room of fairly hostile journalists. Other journalists in the *Washington Post* and *Newsday* depicted him as "at times furious, at times jovial and at times darkly suspicious" or "clearly rattled by the onslaught of criticism from the White House." The overall impact, however, ended up being negative as people saw him on television sparring with the press over these harmful stories.

Perot was in the midst of a media blitz to counteract the offensive against him. He started the day on the "Today" show and ended on "Larry King Live." Republican surrogates were definitely making progress in their efforts to define Perot as a weird and dangerous person, inclined to ride roughshod over people's civil liberties.

It was clearly an orchestrated effort. Republican National Chairman Rich Bond sent a memo to Republican leaders across the country on June 16 outlining some "talking points" to be used by Republican leaders across the country in their speeches and conversations with the press. "Ross Perot's way vs. the American way," the memo said. "But how does Perot get what he wants? Several cases indicate that he resorts to using private detectives, surveillance photos and tough tactics." The *Los Angeles Times* reported that Bond wrote that Perot "is assuming mythical proportions—not unlike the Great Wizard of Oz, who Dorothy discovered was no more than a manipulative man behind a curtain." It was no coincidence that Republicans across the country were using the same words and the same comparisons—Perot to the Wizard of Oz and Mussolini.

Bond, however, denied that there were any "dirty tricks" involved. And, in fact, this was politics as usual for the Republicans. They had been successful in their organized efforts to define Democrat Michael Dukakis four years before. It was a tactic that worked, so why not continue to use it? It was part of their strategy that had been stated in the press: rattle Perot early. Not only did they want to define Perot, they wanted to make him uncomfortable with the whole process. As stated in the

Wall Street Journal: "They (Republicans) calculate that their best tactic is to rattle him early, in part by reminding him of the petty intrusions and indecencies that are part of a political campaign."

Bond even called in on the "Larry King Show" the night of the Annapolis rally to dispute Perot's charge that Republicans were engaged in "dirty tricks." The scrap that took place bears repeating. As excerpted by the *Political Hotline*:

King: Did you expect to happen what has now happened—the back-biting, the stories?

Perot: I said I do not want to engage in personalities. We've got one group whose whole life is in character assassination and personality distortion. There's nothing I can do about that. I just ignored it as long as I could, and finally I felt that I had to answer their specific untrue allegations...

King: The *Washington Post* story Sunday, false? Bob Woodward was wrong? Because that broke in the Post, not in the Republican Party.

Perot: They all break in some newspaper, Larry. You understand how the system works. But the point being, I never investigated the president's children. I have told this story several times today.

(Enter Rich Bond, an unexpected call-in to the show.)

King: Is that you, Rich?

Bond: Hey Larry, how are you? Then to Perot: I feel you have made some very wild and unsubstantiated charges about dirty tricks by the Republican Party over the last couple of months. Now these charges are simply untrue; they are fiction and they are fantasy...Do you have one shred of evidence, do you have any proof right now to back up your allegations of dirty tricks?

Perot: Oh, sure. I've got more than I need. And at the

right point in time, if you guys keep it up, I'll cover it...This is not the place and the time. When I'm ready, I'll do it. I'll pick my time; I'll pick my place. Now are you telling me you don't have a huge number of people in opposition research? You're telling me you don't have a huge number of people going through every shred of evidence they can find about anything relating to me?...

Bond: ... That's not a dirty trick to track your words and evaluate your contradictions out there.

Perot: But is it a dirty trick to distort the truth? Is it a dirty trick to lie?

Bond: Mr. Perot, we have no desire to distort the...

Perot: Well, wait a minute. You called in. If you don't have the—wait a minute, you called in; you called in. You wanted to climb in...

Bond: Larry, he has no substantiation, and he knows it. He has not one shred of proof to offer that the Republican Party has engaged in dirty tricks. Now, Mr. Perot, I respect you, okay? And I liked what you said about your high regard for the constitution. But in my America, Mr. Perot, people are innocent until they are proven guilty. Now I'm just asking you right now—right now—can you offer one shred of proof that the Republican party has engaged in dirty tricks?

Perot: Yeah, I can spend till midnight, but...

Bond: Well, let's go then.

Perot: Well, because I'm not going to do what you want done on your terms. I'll do it on my terms when I think it best serves my purposes. But I'm delighted that you're on the record now, and I'm delighted that we have this transcript...the thing that I think the American people and anybody listening, it's obvious, number one, you won't come up with a single specific. I asked you to; you ducked that. Number two, you ducked all over the place about how big your opposition dirty tricks is and where it's located and who runs it.

King: He said there is none.

Perot: Oh, give me a break—who runs it and who they report directly to, etc. etc....I'm going to give you the benefit of the doubt. Maybe you don't know it's there; you don't know it's there...but, believe me, it's alive and well, and it just comes up with one fairy tale after another, poorly constructed.

Bond: ...this is fantasy.

King: Can we put away one thing, though, tonight? Can we say that Mr. Perot has safely answered the charge about investigating the children?

Bond: Oh, I wasn't even talking about that. ...It's freedom of speech, in case I need to remind you. The Republican Party didn't print that story. The *Washington Post* did. ...We haven't broken one story, Mr. Perot. Name one.

Perot: He's living in an isolation booth...I don't respond to a competitor on his terms. I will wait and wait and wait, and at the right time and the right place I'll do it.

Even as the King show was being aired, Frank Luntz, the pollster hired by Tom Luce, was conducting his nightly tracking poll on Perot. The news was not good. It was the first bad night for Perot since the tracking survey had been started. Luntz believed the sixty-five-minute Annapolis press conference, carried live on CNN, had gone on too long, and Perot had been too testy. His humor had been hard-edged.

The *Baltimore Sun* wrote that while Perot "may have pulled himself out of the fire for the moment, the Sherlock Holmes image may trail him as doggedly as

Mr. Clinton's 'Slick Willie' label." R.W. Apple wrote in *The New York Times* that "much will depend on whether there is more to come." Apple wrote that political reporters were "working on hundreds of leads" on past Perot activities. "If their investigations result in an avalanche of believable articles, it could well bury Mr. Perot's political future."

Most of the volunteers around the country, however, had no notion of the turbulence inside the campaign, and how deadly the blows from the press had become.

The day after Annapolis, Perot continued to do his thing—speaking at yet another petition rally. At the rally in Hartford, Connecticut, Perot noticed a Norman Rockwell poster in the audience. He asked that the poster be sent up to the podium, and that an eight-year-old Boy Scout stand beside him and hold the poster during his address. At the end of the rally, he hoisted the Boy Scout to his shoulder—signifying that the petition effort and his candidacy was "for the children." It had become a familiar picture.

Perot's movement was at its zenith—about to begin its descent. At the time, despite his imbroglio with the press and Republican name-calling barrage, Perot commanded enough electoral votes to win the election outright. The *Political Hotline's* weekly scoreboard said polls in forty-two states gave Perot a majority in the electoral college of 284 electors (with 270 needed to win) in twenty-two states. Bush was given fifteen states with 158 electors and Clinton only two states with sixteen electors. Perot was even leading in Bill Clinton's home state of Arkansas.

Clinton's campaign appeared unworried by the polls. Spokesperson Dee Dee Myers said, "You've got a couple of Texas millionaires out there spitting at each other and we're here talking about the details of our economic plan. I think that's a pretty good position to be in." And so it proved to be. There was a growing contrast between the rosy picture that the volunteers were seeing on the outside and the turmoil on the inside.

On Saturday, June 27, Ross Perot turned sixty-two. He always had a fondness for doing big things on his birthday; many had speculated he would choose that day to declare his candidacy. The day came and went, however, and still there was no official Candidate Perot. The man had an aversion to doing the "expected." He had said in Annapolis: "We still have major states to get the petitions signed in, and so when that gets done we'll announce."

Perot also claimed in Annapolis that the Republicans had been preoccupied with the possibility that he might announce on his birthday—thus the massive assault launched against him the previous week. He told Larry King it was the week that the Republicans "had carefully orchestrated for weeks to take me out."

Washington Post reporter David Von Drehle wrote that "instead of a triumphant fanfare as his sixty-second birthday approached, a grinding of gears was almost audible as Perot's machine, which had zipped along in the fast lane last week from rally to rally, downshifted for a slog through more traditional political mires. He had made so few unstaged appearances in the past month some reporters were calling him the 'stealth candidate,' but suddenly Perot was on every screen, blasting Bush early on NBC's "Today" show, at the midday news conference (in Annapolis), and late on King's phone-in show."

The only bright spot surrounding Perot's birthday was the party thrown by the Dallas volunteers on June

26, the day before Perot turned sixty-two. A huge crowd congregated in the phone bank area at the headquarters to eat birthday cake and see a show put on by the Dallas volunteers. They called it, "The People Want Perot Productions." The cake was a replica of the White House, complete with rose garden made of pieces of strawberries. Bernice Meyerson (Mort Meyerson's mother and a dedicated phone bank volunteer) pointed out the garden of strawberries to Perot, since he had said he would never have a press conference in the Rose Garden. In contrast to the hostile media environment and the chaos "behind the wall" where the professional staff worked, spirits were high among the volunteers. A dozen women—wearing red T-shirts which said "Perot Girls"—had been practicing for days their chorus-line rendition of the old Johnny Mercer tune, "Something's Got to Give." The song was capped with the words, "Something's gotta give—Bush has gotta go—the people want Perot."

The party was planned by Karoline Wilson, who manned the check-in table for volunteers at the phone bank—always. One day she was standing at the front of the phone room talking about needing the help of a musician for the birthday party when another volunteer introduced himself. Brett Basnett worked in marketing for America Video Productions, a local firm which was video-taping the petition rallies. He was also a musician. Basnett became the producer of the show, Karoline Wilson was the director, and Allison Wetsel, a dance major at Southern Methodist University, was the choreographer. Basnett also wrote an original song for Perot's birthday party, "Don't Tread On Me, I'm American." At Perot rallies, there were always original songs, but this one was Perot's favorite. Months later, Perot was still playing a tape of "Don't Tread on Me" at his appearances. Some of the words were:

> In the hearts of many millions
> There are doubts and there are fears
> They've lost their courage to believe
> Their future seems unclear
> Built from all of this uncertainty
> A movement has been stirred
> By volunteers throughout this land
> Who have quickly spread the word.
>
> Don't tread on me,
> I'm American.
> Keeper of this land,
> Protector of my family.
> I offer you my hand,
> And swear as American,
> To leave a better place
> For the children of this world,
> With our Father's Grace
> From on High.

At the end of the program, when Perot talked about the kids being our future, he lifted up Amanda Gossick, the five-year-old daughter of volunteer Pam Gossick, who lived in a Dallas suburb.

The party was fun for the dedicated Dallas volunteers and for Perot, but it was a far cry from what volunteers around the country had hoped for—a huge event at which Perot would officially declare his candidacy. And the fun didn't last long.

"This is the week that was"—the week Perot believed the Republicans were systematically trying to take him out—was followed by more critical media coverage. On Monday night, June 29, Perot agreed to appear on a special late-night town hall meeting on ABC-TV called "Peter Jennings Reporting: Who is Ross Perot?" Members of the campaign's professional staff were dumbfounded when they walked into Perot's office four days before and found him negotiating the appearance.

The town hall originated from New York and was connected by satellite to nine other cities. Before questions were asked by persons in the audience, however, a news report was aired which depicted Perot's efforts on behalf of POWs and MIAs, his involvement in the building of Fort Worth's Alliance Airport, his fight for education reforms in Texas and his relationship with General Motors. *Dallas Morning News* TV critic Ed Bark wrote the day after the Jennings program that Perot's "fight to get Fort Worth's Alliance Airport built was portrayed as borderline ruthless by correspondent John Martin." Martin had reported that Perot had "no hesitation about using power and influence" and pulled strings in Washington to get action back home. In John McWethy's segment on POWS and MIAs, wrote Bark, "Perot was portrayed as an easy mark for unscrupulous soldiers of fortune who wanted him to believe that the government was hiding the truth."

Perot objected to part of the portrayal, claiming "I have never once said there was a conspiracy (regarding the POWs and MIAs). I do claim we left men behind." Perot said that his son, Ross, Jr., played the lead role in developing Alliance Airport, and that the airport had paid more in federal taxes than it had received in federal grants. He also noted that it was helping to reindustrialize America by supplying thousands of jobs in the Dallas-Fort Worth area.

But it was clear from the skeptical questions in the town hall portion of the program that Perot was developing a new image as the Teflon Texan. A Washington minister suggested Perot had "a great history of investigating people" before posing his question: would he "take the cameras to our bedrooms." Perot's reply was: "You're a victim of reading the Washington papers...I've used investigators three or four times...I do not run around with Sherlock Holmes's hat and a magnifying glass." At one point in the show, a heckler in the New York audience shouted, "You're a bigot for what you said so far about gays and lesbians...You're a bully, Mr. Perot, nothing but a pint-sized bully!"

The ratings for the Peter Jennings show were high: 19 percent of the total audience for the first segment; the second segment drew 9.76 percent of total TV homes and 30 percent of the sets in use, double the normal rating for ABC's "Nightline." But Perot was bloodied about the head and shoulders. Rowland Evans and Bob Novak wrote in their syndicated column that the turning point for the campaign may have been the June 29 "town hall" on ABC. "In hindsight, Perot was taken to the cleaners," the columnists said. "The 'Who is Ross Perot' documentary preceding the candidate's appearance, in the opinion of a stunned Luce and Meyerson, was so negatively one-sided that it stacked the decks against him before a huge prime-time television audience."

It was as if Perot had been hit by a scud missile. He had allowed himself to be defined by his opponents, as had Michael Dukakis. Even as he tried to answer all of the charges against him, the accusations were taking on a life of their own. The flak would not let up. Perot was spending more and more of his personal time trying to research each and every one, with only the help of David Bryant, a former Perot Systems employee who had some institutional memory of prior days.

The dust-up between Perot and the Republicans, and Perot's portrayal in the media, served to benefit Bill Clinton. Clinton, left alone after the primaries, retreated to his neutral corner in Little Rock to regroup, iron out his economic positions, select a vice-presidential running mate and get ready for the Democratic National Convention. The result: an ABC News/*Washington Post* poll published at the end of June showed that Clinton, miraculously, had edged ahead in a three-man race. The poll showed Clinton with 33 percent, Perot with 30 percent and Bush with 29 percent support, although when the margin of error was taken into account, the three candidates remained bunched.

Squires agreed that the Republicans were out to eliminate Perot—so they could turn their attack on Clinton—and they were doing it through the press. Part of the strategy was to make Perot look intolerant "by taunting him in front of the TV cameras, with the gays attacking him, and the press getting on his nerves to the point he explodes," Squires said.

Perot's position on gays, as stated to Barbara Walters, was one piece of evidence that could be disseminated to the "media elite" to substantiate the accusation of intolerance. The other story being spread around was the "Jewish professor" story. It had to do with a romantic interest of Perot's daughter, Nancy, when she was a student at Vanderbilt several years before with a professor. (Nancy by this time had been married for several years to Clay Mulford and had her own family.) Squires confirms that Perot didn't like the relationship between Nancy and the professor because she was nineteen and he was thirty-two. But the spin being put on the story fed to the "opinion-makers" was that he didn't like it because the professor was Jewish. There were several different twists to the rumors going around, including one that Perot had employed private detectives to "spy" on the student and her prof. The Dallas press office was receiving hundreds of inquiries about the "Jewish professor" story. Squires tried to dispute the supposition that Perot was anti-semitic by pointing out that two of his closest associates were Jewish—his trusted executive Mort Meyerson and Dallas advertising executive Lanier Timerlin. Meyerson had even sent a letter to the Anti-Defamation League of B'nai B'rith to defend EDS's firing of an employee in 1983 for growing a beard in violation of company policy. The employee, an Orthodox Jew, refused to shave the beard for religious reasons.

Squires believed the Republicans were feeding writers and columnists that would pick up on the intolerance angle—namely, Jewish writers and columnists—with these particular stories.

The strategy to paint Perot as intolerant had consequences inside the campaign as well as in the public eye, because it served as a distraction to the "Pentagon"—as the campaign's upper staff had come to be called—and because it upset Perot.

Rollins recalled one evening having dinner with Tom Luce when Luce was repeatedly called away from the table to take telephone calls from Perot. Perot, he said, was "going crazy" over the threatened airing of the Jewish professor story. Each time Luce returned, he was more ashen-faced. According to Rollins, Perot was disturbed because he did have the professor under surveillance, and for security reasons had used surveillance on his children—which they never knew.

On July 2, Perot was off to Olympia, Washington—a hotbed of support—for another of his petition rallies. This time, fifty-five thousand signatures were turned in. While they needed only two hundred signatures, volunteers in Washington had staged 204 conventions on the same day—in homes, churches, wherever people wanted—to gather a one-day record of fifty-five thousand signatures. A special sign-in station was placed at a rest stop in Chehalis, where hundreds of bikers stopped during a bike-a-thon from Seattle to Oregon. The July 2 rally, along with the petition drive, was designed to unite eastern and western Washington state, across the "Cascade Curtain" of the mountain range which divides the state. People from across the state, and from Oregon, attended the rally—some six thousand people.

The backdrop for the scene on the steps of the Washington Capitol was two hundred American flags held aloft by volunteers. Yvonne Conway, petition delivery event chairman, had borrowed the flags from a cemetery. The spectacle of all those flags against the blue sky, said Conway, "took your breath away." But the perfect setting was marred by a small group of protestors. A handful of members of Act Up, an advocacy group for people with AIDs, briefly took the stage and disrupted the rally. Perot met with several in the group and promised to address gay issues.

Afterward, Conway wrote *The Olympian* newspaper that "July 2 was a historical day in our city, county, state and nation. It was done in good taste with the help of six thousand concerned citizens minus the dozen or so non-supporters the media concentrated on."

As at other rallies, this one showed what volunteers with no budget could do. A seventeen-piece band, platform, sound system, tables and chairs were all donated.

The only expense was $32—for decorated petition boxes.

But all was not well in the volunteer organization everywhere. All sorts of pesky problems were bubbling up out in the states. Conflicts had developed between the Young Turks and the volunteers out in the field. Disputes broke out within state organizations, with people vying for leadership positions. The disputes had to be settled by the field representatives from Dallas, whose job was to facilitate the volunteers in getting Perot on the ballot and to make sure they followed the Federal Election Commission rules and state law. Volunteers in some of the states complained that the Dallas field reps were taking over their campaign. Much of the grumbling came where there had been factional squabbles and leadership strife within local organizations.

In Colorado, longtime volunteers claimed they had been ousted by David Rhodes, the thirty-one-year-old from Austin who had become one of the "Young Turks." The Denver headquarters was reorganized and moved; Rhodes blamed the whole thing on a disgruntled employee. And John Schenk, one of the original Perot organizers in that state, dismissed the volunteers' complaints as the grumbling of ambitious people who didn't get their way, the *Los Angeles Times* reported.

In Arizona, two factions—one based in Tucson, the other in Phoenix—were vying for control of the state organization. That dispute included allegations of vandalism and a lawsuit charging slander.

In Illinois, organizers had thrown out one thousand signatures and had started anew because of questions about the loyalty of four Perot candidates to the electoral college listed on the petitions, according to state coordinator Ted Pincus.

In Missouri, state coordinator Sandy McClure was forced to throw out the first one thousand signatures because petitions failed to fit the form required by state law; volunteers had to return to the streets. The *St. Louis Post-Dispatch* reported that ex-coordinator Kevin Laughlin had been "ousted" by McClure and her backers because he "mishandled the first drive and failed to cooperate with Perot leaders elsewhere."

In Oklahoma, one petition gatherer, who claimed he feared a takeover by emissaries from Dallas, reportedly stashed thirty-five thousand petition signatures in a bank vault.

And, in Virginia, thousands of signatures were thrown out because of technical errors. Election law specialists were dispatched from Dallas to try to iron out the difficulties. Other disputes were reported to have cropped up in the midst of the transition to a campaign run by the paid professionals.

Some state organizations were complaining that their plans were ahead of Dallas. California, for example, had elaborate plans for speakers' bureaus and other volunteer activities. The California organization had sent to Dallas a twenty-six-page manual on volunteer deployment.

Ginny Fitzgerald, who had been brought in by Meyerson to assist the volunteers in planning and staging the petition rallies where Perot spoke, observed the Turks at work. Her job was to "fine tune" the events, to keep the volunteers motivated and happy, and to make sure that the rallies were spontaneous, but didn't turn to chaos—an impossible job had it not been for the volunteers, she said. Volunteer Howard Mann videotaped her saying: "I was pretty unhappy about the way some of these extraordinary people, volunteering their time and energy and money were being treated by some of the Dallas people. Inside they were referred to as the Turks, outside they were called the White Shirts. They were a group of young men who definitely had only one color of shirt in their closet," she said.

Fitzgerald, a fiftyish mother of grown children, described many of the volunteers as being "peers of mine. They took exception to being told what to do by a twenty-four-year-old. These guys didn't see that."

Gloria de la Cruz, a staff member responsible for Hispanic outreach assigned to the volunteer organization, said the phone bank was getting reports that the young Turks were inconsiderate, that they were insulting and offending the "masses of people who were contributing their time." She attributed it to "inexperience or the wrong kind of experience—college or military." "They were all very young," de la Cruz wrote in a memo to Tom Luce telling him of the alienation between the field forces and the masses. "If we don't change this," she said, "we will self-destruct."

Russ Monroe, Perot's twenty-eight-year-old former tax man who was responsible for the field reps in the Northeast region, said: "I don't think anybody ever treated anyone intentionally badly." But if a volunteer became destructive to the organization, he said, the field rep had to be firm. The bad apple had to be separated from the barrel; the problem had to be solved. But Monroe emphasized: "We couldn't fire anyone, we didn't hire anyone. We never empowered anyone, so we couldn't unempower anyone. These people empowered themselves. When people empower themselves, sometime you have more than one group—not just in the same city or county or state, but sometimes in the same city block—who want to be in control." When people feel they're taking back their country, taking control of their destiny, he said, they don't want to relinquish that control. "You're talking about a handful of people, five percent, but sometimes a handful of people can be very damaging...If you have five thousand people spending their nights and weekends getting signatures, going door to door, sitting on street corners, I felt it was my responsibility to see that their efforts weren't wasted by a few self-serving individuals. We weren't going to let them screw it up."

One volunteer said that Meyerson, Luce and Squires were "wrapped up in a bubble" once the professional campaign began to grow, and that the Turks became autonomous, left too much to their own devices. As described by one staffer, "they were very decent people, they just got way too caught up in the allegiance to Caesar; they were very suspicious."

But the professionals were in greater disarray than the troops in the field. They couldn't get any answers from Perot, so they were doing work to no avail. Rollins could frequently be found in his office reading the *Washington Post*. "I couldn't get a decision on anything. We would prepare stuff, get the staff all geared up, and then go in, and we couldn't get a decision," Rollins said.

One ball being bounced back and forth was the question of who would handle the press, and how. When Rollins was brought in, Squires said Rollins ought to handle the press. After all, that's what he did best. He was the ultimate spin doctor. He loved to feed the animals. Squires knew there would be trouble if he was working the front door with the press and Rollins was working the back door. By then, however, Squires had a pretty good relationship with Perot—although not necessarily with the press—and Perot wanted Squires to handle the press. Squires and Luce didn't want to do the traditional press thing—which included regular briefings and press conferences, and providing buses and planes for members of the press to follow the candidate around. Perot didn't like to be followed around. And he didn't like motorcades, which are required if you're being followed around by several press buses. His public appearances were so few that Luce and Squires figured the press could make their own arrangements to get there. According to Squires, Rollins's philosophy was that the press had to be catered to and taken care of, i.e., if you stroke them and feed them stories, they will be nice to you. That whole idea was alien to Ross Perot, whose typical response was, "Why do you want to do that?"

Rollins saw it a little differently. He contended Perot needed a "first-class press operation" and Squires didn't want to do it. He said Squires would only take care of his "old friends" in the press and that he had "absolute disdain" for the "new breed of reporters." According to Rollins, Squires would "crumple up their phone messages and throw them in the trash." Squires, according to Rollins, kept telling Perot, "You don't have to do it that way. Don't give them a plane, screw the bastards, let them get there on their own." Rollins feared the press would "write bad stories if they're irritated." To the charge that he was only interested in the caring and feeding of the press, Rollins responded: "No, I'm interested in the care and feeding of my candidate."

Rollins argued that, if Squires didn't want to do the job—providing a "first-class" press operation—"let me bring someone in, a George Stephanopoulos-type guy." (Stephanopoulos was the boy wonder of the Bill Clinton campaign, who was replaced as White House Communications Director by old-hand David Gergen four months into the new administration.)

Rollins's propensity to be quoted in the media and to appear on TV at first irritated Perot and later infuriated him. According to Rollins, he told Perot at the outset: "One of us has to be on the air on a regular basis—the candidate seldom goes on—talking about the game. It's all a part of the game. I'm on TV a lot, I would expect to do that. He said, 'Fine.' The moment I was on, there was strenuous animosity. Perot said, 'You don't know my positions.' I said, 'I'm talking about the game, and I know more about the game.' I was talking about the (political) environment. He said, 'You gave away our strategy.' I had said we had to win it three ways: we have to win a majority of states, 270 electoral votes, and we have to win congressional district by congressional district." (If the election were to be decided by the House, each member of Congress would vote in their state delegation, and presumably would be influenced by the vote in their home district on Election Day.) Rollins said he told Perot, "'That's saying the obvious, that's not a secret.' I said, 'Ross, I promise you, that's not a strategy. We never had a strategy.'"

Luce and Meyerson eventually bought into Rollins's concept that something had to be done to try to muzzle the negative press. It was less than a week before the opening of the Democratic National Convention. Perot's staff remained in shambles, and his public support was continuing to drop, according to nightly tracking polls. So, on July 7, changes were announced in the press operation, changes which amounted to a 180-degree turn for Perot. Luce announced that there would be a daily press conference. As he explained it, "We realized that we have a huge number of people assigned to cover us on a regular basis, and those people have to have a story every day," he said. "That's just a fact of life. One way or the other, they are going to have a story." Sharon Holman would perform as the press secretary, Luce announced.

The announcement of the new press approach was made the same day Perot and his wife, Margot, lunched at a Dallas hotel with three hundred celebrities and business/professional/community leaders from across the country who were being recruited for Perot's National Advisory Panel. The lunch was planned by a Dallas Perot friend, Ruth Sharp Altshuler, and New York friend Tom Barr. The idea, according to Barr, was to combat the "dirty tricks brigade" from the Bush administration by coming up with substantial people from all parts of the country who were signing on to the Perot campaign. Perot told them he would probably announce his candidacy after the Republican National Convention in mid-August.

Among those attending the platform-power session were Paul Nitze, ex-Reagan arms negotiator; Bernard Marcus, co-founder of Home Depot; Samuel Butler, managing partner of Cravath, Swaine and Moore; country singer Willie Nelson; Hollywood producer Martin Jurow; former football star Paul Warfield; the Reverend Calvin Butts, pastor of the Abyssinian Baptist Church in New York City; Leonard Lauder, president of Estee Lauder Inc.; Andrew Tisch, chairman and chief executive of Lollilard Inc.; Ace Greenberg, chairman of the New York investment banking firm Bear Stearns Incorporated; Arthur Temple, the Texas lumber magnate and former *Time* board member; Martha Stewart, the decorating and entertainment author; and Kathryn Thompson, a leading Republican fundraiser from Orange

County, California. Invited but failing to appear were retired football star O.J. Simpson and actress Katherine Hepburn.

Kathryn Thompson had been a member of Team 100, people who contributed $100,000 to the Republican National Committee for the 1988 campaign. But she had become disenchanted with the administration. She also used the word that was becoming de rigeur with the Perotistas when talking about the grass roots movement; it had "empowered" people who had not been in the political mainstream. Thompson, chief executive of a development corporation in Aliso Viejo, California, said she wasn't worried about losing her Republican ties by lining up with Perot. "I've come to the conclusion that being an American is more important than being a Democrat or a Republican," she said.

After hearing Perot speak at a luncheon, the attendees split into groups to exchange ideas on issues. As Perot called it: "just visiting, brainstorming." The Perot camp was still wrestling with coming up with a platform, or at least position papers on issues. The "advisers" were supposed to help Perot come up with his "platform." The discussion leaders and topics included Tom Barr, crime-abortion-legal issues; John White, economy-budget-health care; Dallas investment banker and ex-Carter adviser Richard Fisher, foreign policy-foreign trade; Ed Rollins, campaign issues; Mort Meyerson, women's issues-gay and lesbian issues; and former journalist Marilyn Berger, Middle East-Israel.

While reporters raced around trying to grab participants in the hall as they moved from lunch to the issue discussions, Hal Riney and his crew of twenty-seven were busy one floor up filming sit-down conversations with the participants for use in campaign commercials.

Members of the professional staff, emerging from the lunch, appeared tight-lipped and tense—and probably for good reason. Perot was not happy about the ad crew. The professionalization of his campaign had not gone to his liking. And the "gay issue" wouldn't go away. Mort Meyerson and his son, David, who was a campaign aide, had been working for weeks to try to mitigate the problems that had begun with Perot's statement to Barbara Walters on May 29. Perot had told Barbara Walters he thought it would be difficult to appoint an openly gay person to a high cabinet position, and that it would not be realistic to have gays in the military. The two Meyersons had met with gay activists and had been working with California civil rights lawyer Gloria Allred to develop a new position. The position they finally came up with sounded very much like the Clinton position in that it called for removing the ban on avowed homosexuals in the military. Squires and Luce didn't like it. That's a "double back," warned Squires. Not only is it recanting a prior position Perot had taken—which you can only do a handful of times without losing total credibility—but the whole idea of meeting with special interest groups and bowing to their demands is not Perot's style. Squires also believed that it was a mistake for Perot to change his position on gays in the military because it would have shaken the trust placed in him by veterans, the military and the military-minded—the very core of his support.

After the lunch, Luce and Squires met in a corner with Meyerson to object to the new statement. Meyerson then went off to negotiate it with Perot. When Perot reviewed the statement, he removed the portion that referred specifically to gays in the military. The statement that was released said Perot would not rule out

naming someone to a cabinet position who was homosexual, and that "any discrimination based on gender,
race, religion or sexual orientation will not be tolerated"
in a Perot administration. "What people do in their private lives is their own business." But it did not speak
directly to the military ban against homosexuals.

The press wouldn't let it alone. Reporters wanted
further clarification.

On July 10, the day after Bill Clinton named Al Gore
as his running mate, Perot went to Lansing, Michigan,
for a rally to celebrate the collection of three hundred
thousand signatures in the state that was once the automotive manufacturing center of the country. "You have
created pure panic in both parties, which is healthy for
this country," Perot said. "All over Washington, the
mood is, the barbarians are at the gate." One person in
the audience shouted back, "And the barbarians are
hungry."

The pros wanted Perot to start rolling out the issues.
Since his bitter battle with General Motors had become
a $700 million legend, it made sense that he talk about
free trade and manufacturing while in Michigan. He
used the occasion to pledge to make America "the car
capital of the world" again. Auto workers from GM's
Willow Run plant, scheduled to be shut down one year
later as part of GM restructuring, joined the rally on the
steps of the Capitol. According to a volunteer, half of
Willow Run's nineteen hundred employees had signed
petitions to get Perot on the ballot. They liked his criticism of free trade talks with Mexico and respected his
efforts to shake up GM. "Our country right now, in plain
Michigan talk, is where General Motors was in the mid-
1980s," Perot told the crowd. "Now, while we're still
relatively strong is the time to fix it." Despite the fact

that Perot companies had never been unionized, the auto workers liked his emphasis on revitalizing manufacturing, "I don't know if he is anti-union or not. All I know is he is for keeping manufacturing jobs in this country, and that's what matters most to us," said a Willow Run worker.

As usual, the press was playing catch-up. Many had to fly into Detroit and drive more than two hours to get to Lansing. However, special events coordinator Joe Canzeri was allowed to schedule a "press availability." At the airport, a spot was marked on the tarmac with an X where Perot was supposed to stand. Perot, of course, disliked sidewalk press conferences; he thought them unruly. And he had scorned the kind of public disruptions created by traditional presidential candidates at airports.

But the pros thought this would be a good time to "roll out an issue" and get the press to pay attention. The issue was free trade, making Detroit the car capital again, and how this country would deal with Japan. Perot was going to call for reciprocal trade with the Japanese—if they wouldn't give America the same deal they were getting, then Japanese cars wouldn't be allowed off the boat. The pros figured that if Perot said that in his speech, the press would want to know how he was going to do it. It didn't quite work out that way.

At the airport, Perot eyeballed the X, then refused to stand on the tape on the tarmac. ABC's Mort Dean asked the first question—requesting a clarification on the previous day's story in *The New York Times* regarding Perot's position on homosexuals serving in the military. Perot responded that the statement would speak for itself and that he had nothing to add to it. He wanted to talk about something else. Next, the *Boston Globe's* John Mashek asked about dissension within his volunteer organization. Volunteers in such states as Michigan, Florida and Colorado were complaining that their role was being eclipsed by paid professionals. Perot blew.

"Only in America, when you look at the miracle that the volunteers have created in the last few months, would you focus on the tiny little problem in these people who self-selected themselves and self-selected their leaders," he said.

"He was mad as hell about the tenor of the questions," Mashek said later. "As he was leaving, somebody shouted another question and that angered him."

Perot finally stalked off to his plane, muttering, "I'll never do *this* again."

The man who people thought would stand up to Congress and the bureaucracy was not keeping his cool. He was not reacting in what might be viewed as a stable, strong way to difficulty. Under pressure, he reacted with hostility. He was defensive, evasive and nasty. One of the top ten rules of politics is: Don't let 'em see you sweat. Perot was starting to sweat—and it showed.

As it happened, Democratic pollster Geoffrey Garin had been quite prescient when he said on ABC's "Nightline" on May 27, "As you watch this campaign unfold, if he's forced to play by the conventional rules in the conventional way, his candidacy is going to be a failure. If he gets to play by his own rules, his candidacy could do quite well."

Perot was no longer writing the rules. The undertow of conventional politics was about to sweep him under.

★ ★ ★ ★ ★ 11 ★ ★ ★ ★ ★

GETTING OUT

THE PROFESSIONALS WERE CONFOUNDED. There was no strategy. Perot refused to finalize announcement plans. There was no permanent vice-presidential candidate to replace Admiral Stockdale. There was no platform; there were no policy papers. They didn't know when or if they were going to hold a convention. They had no control over budget; they could authorize no expenditures. Ed Rollins and Hamilton Jordan were stymied. The highly touted co-managers of the campaign had almost nothing to do.

Rollins figured there were four aspects of a presidential campaign: field operations, press operations, scheduling and advance, and television advertising. He had no control over any of those. On the day of the Lansing rally, Rollins wrote a memo to Perot laying out three options: (1) he could run a "world-class" presidential campaign, as promised; (2) he could continue to run a "non-campaign," in which case he didn't need a professional staff and in which case he would surely lose, or (3) he could quit.

Perot categorized the volunteers on one side and the professionals on the other, Rollins said, "never understanding that we believed in a lot of the same things the

229

volunteers did, but with a more jaundiced eye." Basically, Rollins had insisted from the beginning that Perot needed to avoid being defined by the media, and the way to do that was to start advertising in the summer. Perot simply didn't see it that way.

"After Perot started getting bombarded, his mood and the environment changed dramatically," Rollins said. "To a certain extent he blamed us—he blamed me—for bringing that on him. It would've come no matter who he brought in or if he brought no one in. All of a sudden the spotlight fell on him in a different way."

Perot couldn't stop the negative press, and he was obsessed with the Republican "dirty tricksters." Rollins kept telling him that the problem was not the Republicans. "Your problem," Rollins told Perot, "is *The New York Times*, CBS, ABC—all of the investigative reporters looking into you as a serious presidential candidate."

"Perot never understood that," Rollins said. "Perot just said, 'I never had bad press in my life until I hired you guys.' To him, the campaign was a great campaign until the professionals came on.'"

Rollins was vindicated on the matter of Perot letting others define him. But the role played by the Repubicans was not insignificant. As quoted in the July 6 issue of *Time*, a senior advisor to the Bush campaign said: "It's done. Perot is now defined, and he is more than just quirky and eccentric. What we have to do now is drive a wedge in there and cleave away from Perot's core support those voters who are independents and Republicans."

On the day after the Lansing rally, Perot was in a crabby frame of mind when he flew from Dallas to Nashville to speak to the NAACP. He had agreed to go, although he didn't want to. The top staffers had encouraged him to go. After all, Rollins said, it was one of four groups that presidential candidates always speak to. And he had agreed to let Jim Squires draft a speech for him. Squires spent the July 4 weekend working on a speech called "The Three Deficits." But Squires knew Perot wasn't going to deliver the speech as he wrote it; Perot believed "another man's words can't come from his heart." But he conceded to let Squires give him some ideas, which he would put in his own words.

Jim Squires remembers that day well. Perot, he says, "was tired of listening to Mort (Meyerson), so he threw him off the plane to the NAACP." According to Rollins, he also threw Joe Canzeri off the plane. So he was winging his way to Nashville solo to make his first campaign appearance before a predominantly black group. Squires said: "He always called me from the plane—he'd be writing what he was going to say. On Saturday, I got up early and was in my office by 6:30 a.m. I wanted to tell him not to tell those old stories. But he never called. He didn't call me until after five o'clock, after the total wreck. When he did, he said, 'Well, I guess I just went up there and wasted my whole day.' I said, 'Well, I guess the hell you did!'"

The reaction to the NAACP speech was swift, and it was harsh. Perot had come across as patronizing when he twice used the phrase "your people." Talking about the nation's economic problems, Perot said, "Financially, at least, it's going to be a long, hot summer. I don't have to tell you who gets hurt first when this sort of thing happens, do I? You, your people do. Your people do." He later said it was "your people" who suffer most from rampant crime.

Benjamin Hooks, the group's outgoing executive director, tried to play down the offensive words, saying

"It's something we all have to work on, but I don't think it's a sign of irreparable failure. None of us liked that language, but we don't want to lose the emphasis of the speech over one thing. I hate to see his appearance here marred." Hooks called it "a matter of education. I've educated a lot of white folks."

New York City Mayor David Dinkins, appearing on "Both Sides with Jesse Jackson" the day of Perot's speech, said, "I don't accuse him of racism...But I accuse him of being completely out of touch with the African-American community."

Perot talked on the theme suggested by Squires, economic injustice in America, but used only two lines of his draft. And he did tell "those old stories" about how his father paid poor blacks after they had retired from working for him, his mother's insistence on feeding Depression-era hobos, and how as a child he loved to go to the black church and hear the choir sing. The stories fell flat on an audience that regarded them as condescending. But the "your people" remark is what caused a fire storm. It was played all day on CNN, until finally Perot called in and offered an apology. "I sincerely regret if anyone was offended by my choice of words," he said. "'You'—I was referring to the people in the audience; and 'your people'—I was referring to the people they represent...If I offended anybody in any way, I certainly apologize." Perot appeared badly rattled; it was the first crack many Americans saw in their iron man's veneer.

The press was gathering in New York City for the Democratic National Convention, scheduled to begin on Monday. Many watched the NAACP speech in their work spaces in or near Madison Square Garden, hooting over

Perot's faux pas, anxious to comment in their Sunday editions of July 11, or to scare up reaction from the Democrats in New York on Perot's blunder. Some journalists reported that they had heard Perot say "you people," which sounded even more sinister. Some, recalling the flap over the gay issue, reported that it was the second time in a month that Perot had offended a major voting bloc. Some saw Perot's miscue as coming at the very worst time for him, as Clinton was taking center stage with his new running mate at a well-oiled convention.

The next day on NBC's "Meet the Press," Jesse Jackson (who had been predisposed toward Perot all along) was conciliatory about Perot's remarks. "That gaffe was not intentional or a politically motivated or racially calculated statement," he said. "I think it would not be fair to try to judge someone of his character on that. It was an unfortunate choice of words," he said, adding "to come up with a lot of hot tears over that misstatement would be a terrible diversion."

And the Reverend Calvin Butts, one of New York City's most prominent black pastors who had just been announced as New York Perot co-chair, largely stood by Perot. On the "Today" show on Monday, July 13, he said: "He needs more help in terms of interpreting the sensitivities of people of African descent in America. However, I think when he talked about the economic conditions in this country and who gets hit the hardest by it first, he was right on target."

The minority outreach leaders who were attached to the volunteers in Dallas were not offended by the NAACP speech. Shelton Cotton, an African-American and a Dallas area consultant who was working as a laison to African-American communities, attended the NAACP convention on behalf of the campaign. He believed what

Perot said was blown way out of proportion. He saw it as "an opportunity for the media to try to smear some dirt on the petition drive or his potential presidential bid." Cotton's assignment was to try to build bridges between Perot and African-American communities, and the NAACP speech did not dissuade him from continuing the job; he didn't believe Perot was racist.

Gloria de la Cruz, the campaign staffer who was building bridges to the Hispanic community, was not offended because, she said, "I know Ross Perot and men like him. He did what was natural for a man of his generation. All my life, I have heard men of his generation, if they're talking to the Rotary Club or whatever, say 'you people' or 'you guys' or 'y'all'—it's just an expression they use. I know how he talks and I knew he didn't mean anything by it."

But there was no way to put Liquid Paper on that speech. Perot had offended many blacks. He had embarrassed himself. And he had created a political uproar on the eve of the Democratic convention. He was out of his milieu.

Yet, there was even more trouble in Perotville. Things had come to a head over one of the major internal conflicts of the campaign since the professionals came on board—television advertising.

Perot and Hal Riney never "clicked," partly because Perot thought he was outrageously expensive. He wanted to know from Riney how much a commercial would cost. Riney explained that it depended on the commercial; it wasn't like a creation by cookie cutter. Rollins recalls the conversation going something like this: "You mean you can't tell me what your product costs to make?" Perot demanded. Then he asked the cost of a film crew per day. Riney said some crews cost

$60,000 a day. "Sixty thousand dollars a day, for those high school dropouts with earrings and long hair?" Perot responded. Finally, Riney told him that twelve commercials for Saturn cost $15 million—or an average of $1.25 million. "I don't want to spend one penny more than $5,000. Can you do that?" Perot asked. "Sure," said Riney. "I'll go down and buy a Beta cam and I'll shoot it myself." Perot said: "Hal. We've got a problem. We've made a big mistake here. You want a Rolls Royce and I want a Volkswagon."

Rollins believed Perot just didn't understand advertising. He wouldn't sit still for talks about concepts, script-writing or story boards. He just wanted somebody to go out and "shoot the rallies." Meanwhile, Murphy Martin—the former anchorman who had worked for Perot years before on the POW issue—told his former boss there were a lot of unemployed film guys around and he could get him a two-man crew for $12,000 a day. To Perot, that sounded more like it. To Rollins, it was just not professional.

The week before the Democratic convention, Rollins had enlisted Ross, Jr., to go to his father and make the case for Hal Riney. But Perot hated the turn the campaign had taken. He thought Rollins had brought in a bunch of unnecessary and over-paid people. And now, here was his son, carrying water for the top campaign echelon, the so-called "Pentagon." To say the least, it didn't sit well with Perot, senior. In fact, Perot was so angry, according to Squires, that he banished Ross, Jr. from the campaign. (Ross, Jr., of course, didn't stay banished. He was very much a part of the campaign later on.)

Perot wanted Riney gone, and made that perfectly clear. Rollins was mortified. He had been talking up this big advertising campaign to his contacts in the media, and Riney's exit surely showed a campaign in disarray, he thought. On Monday, July 13, the *Wall Street Journal* reported that Riney had been fired. When Perot had met with Riney the previous Thursday, only three people had been at the meeting—Rollins, Riney and Perot. Perot called Riney and asked if he had talked to the *Wall Street Journal*; Riney said "No." "Well," he said, "I guess we know who did." At that point, the final nail was poised on the top of Rollins's coffin.

The *Wall Street Journal* reported that Perot was outraged at the likely cost of the ad campaign and dissatisfied with the content of one ad. When Perot had viewed the sample ads, Perot reportedly kept saying sarcastically to Meyerson, "Take a guess how much this cost. Guess what that shot cost." He stormed out of the meeting.

Rollins told the *Journal* that the ads were "as good as the ads he did for Ronald Reagan in 1984." The big problem was, Ross Perot was not Ronald Reagan. The ads were too slick for Perot. He had no intention of being packaged and sold as Reagan had been. And his instincts were correct: The staged and showy, Hollywood-style campaign techniques of the Reagan era were out of touch with the public mood in 1992.

Perot wasn't alone in not liking the ads. Hamilton Jordan had called together a group of twenty or so key volunteers at the Dallas phone bank and a few staffers to preview the ads. The screening participants were given evaluation sheets for each ad. After viewing and evaluating three, they could discuss them. One ad featured Mort Meyerson; they found it boring. Another featured Perot's sister, Bette; they found her nasal twang "terrible." The third sample spot featured a POW's wife.

"It was that soft Reagan-Bush thing," complained one volunteer. All of the ads were panned. "We didn't think that was Perot," said one volunteer. We thought they were good for the Reagan years, maybe even for Bush. But they were not dynamic like Ross. He should just get on the tube and talk to the people. That's what the people love—Ross."

Perot had asked a Dallas advertising friend what it would cost to shoot such ads and was told, if you really throw money at it, the figure would be about one-fourth of what Riney wanted to charge. Perot believed he was being ripped off.

Squires said, "Perot has been the object of every slick shark artist in the country. These California ad guys were kindergarten people in comparison. They couldn't slick him. You're not going to slick Ross Perot. He might like you and give you something, but you're not going to get your hand in his pocket. He has a remarkable facility to throw money at something he likes and be very cautious not to let people take advantage of him."

Squires also viewed the political process with some disdain. "The economics of political campaigns is that you go out and raise money from people who want to buy influence, and take taxpayer money, and then you blow it out the ceiling. You spread it around the political image-making community."

Perot wasn't about to spread it around to a bunch of people he figured made money by milking the political system. He thought he was being taken advantage of by the political pros. And the whole operation was abhorrent to him.

Understandably, both Rollins and Jordan were frustrated by Perot's tendency to override their advice. Rollins had said Perot would announce in July, but Luce

and Squires continued to say no date had been set for
an announcement. Rollins had publicly advocated an
earlier timetable for choosing a vice-presidential candidate than Perot wanted. Luce and Meyerson were calling the shots, according to whatever Perot told them.

And Rollins and Squires clearly were at opposite
poles. "Squires kept saying I was trying to run a conventional campaign in an unconventional year. I'd been
in eight presidential campaigns and never run the same
one twice, every one was different. The conflict started
in the whole media area. Perot didn't understand the
difference between the "Today" show, "Good Morning
America," "CBS Morning News" and "Larry King Live."
He thought if he was on the "Today" show everyone
watched the "Today" show. Each had an audience all
its own. He balked at buying TV. He balked at what Hal
Riney cost. It was just a mindset. I kept saying, you only
have a certain amount of time; most presidential campaigns are a full year of running full bore." Rollins kept
telling Perot he needed to buy some time to get his
message out.

The fact was that Perot didn't want to spend his
money in July. He didn't want to spend more than Bush
and Clinton, and if he started spending $30 million a
month in July, he would have spent more. He felt he
didn't need to waste his money when he was getting
free exposure. And besides that, he felt "a full year of
running full bore" as a presidential candidate was ri-
diculous.

When Hal Riney was released, as far as Rollins was
concerned, the campaign was over. Rollins told Riney:
"Tell your kids this is the day the Perot campaign
ended." Luce thought the flap over Riney was over-
blown. He said Riney was brought in to do some film-

ing and that task was finished. Riney had made some sample commercials and the campaign decided not to go forward with the project, he said. In the overall scheme of things, this was just not that important. As Luce said, "To take a matter of whether you go on television this week, or next week and at what hour and with what commercial, I don't think rises to the level of national importance as to what we ought to do about the budget deficit in this country."

The *Wall Street Journal* reported that rumors were circulating that one of the co-managers—either Jordan or Rollins—would leave the campaign, that their roles had been eclipsed by Luce and Meyerson. Some commentators were ready to kiss off Perot. On CBS on July 13 political writer Fred Barnes said, "I think there's a remote possibility that this guy will not announce. You couldn't get a date from Tom Luce, they keep putting it off, he's sinking fast."

On Tuesday of convention week, Meyerson informed Rollins that Perot "is not going to do it your way and he won't quit. He's not going to abandon the volunteers." Rollins's response was that Perot was going to let the competition have a two-to-three-month jump start and he would never recover. At that point, Rollins hadn't talked to Perot since the blowup over Riney, almost a week before.

Rollins was correct about one thing. He had warned Luce that Perot would continue to be in the fishbowl during the week of the Democratic National Convention, even though it was Bill Clinton's convention. "Luce had never been to a convention. I told him, 'Here you have fifteen hundred reporters and ten thousand political junkies, and all they're talking about is politics for one solid week. You know what the politics of 1992 is?

It's not George Bush. It's a little bit of Bill Clinton. The politics of '92 is Ross Perot.'"

Many of the commentators and analysts were starting to write Perot's obituary. They were talking about the NAACP speech, about the Perot campaign being in turmoil, the rumored resignations of the professionals, and about Perot's inability to attract a top-flight running mate.

For six weeks, Jordan and Meyerson had been working on the vice-presidential selection, trying to come up with a short list of potential running mates. Discussions actually had begun in the spring by a committee consisting of Luce, Clay Mulford, Jordan and a couple of other Perot associates, who were looking for a running mate who would serve as a chief of staff to a President Perot.

But there was disagreement, once again, in Perotland. The tussle was over whether to have an established politician to "balance" Perot, or whether to have a woman outsider.

Of the "established politicians," Warren Rudman, who was quitting the Senate in protest over process, and Paul Tsongas, who had run for the Democratic nomination on a tough economic agenda, were the most popular. While Tsongas was never asked, the campaign spent a lot of time courting the former Massachusetts senator who had been the Democratic Don Quixote in the primaries, touting a shared-sacrifice, honesty-first, deficit-reducing economic plan. Rollins was into "bold strokes." He liked Rudman, and thought Tsongas would be a "bold stroke." Rudman, however, was angered by apparent background checks on him and said he had no interest in running with Perot.

Colin Powell, chairman of the Joint Chiefs of Staff, was a favorite of all the top Perot staffers, but there was never any indication that Powell wanted to be the first black candidate on anyone's national ticket. Virginia Governor Doug Wilder, an African-American, did indicate some interest, but there reportedly were no discussions.

There was a great deal of interest in finding a woman running mate. Jeanne Kirkpatrick was the woman most often mentioned in media speculation. According to Rollins, Kirkpatrick was a "closet Perot supporter" and let it be known that if Perot could find no other suitable choice, she might be willing to do it. Kirkpatrick said publicly she would not consider being Clinton's vice-president, but if "Ross Perot were to ask me, that would be very serious." The problem with Kirkpatrick was that as an internationalist and strong supporter of a foreign policy based on a strong defense, she might not provide the appropriate balance for Perot. He was already perceived as pro-military.

Rollins also said Luce met twice with former cabinet member Elizabeth Dole, and "they were ready to ask her" when she let it be known she didn't want to be asked. According to Squires, among the top women on the list were Bernadine Healy, head of the National Institute of Health, a black judge in New York named Amalya Kearse, and Planned Parenthood ex-president Faye Wattleton. (Margot Perot was a dedicated worker in Planned Parenthood.)

The speculation in the media was endless: Former baseball commissioner and Los Angeles cleanup czar Peter Ueberroth, former Democratic presidential candidate Jesse Jackson, independent governor of Connecticut Lowell Weicker, General Norman Schwarzkopf of Desert Storm fame, Chrysler ex-chief executive officer Lee Iacocca, ex-Labor Secretary Ann McLaughlin, former television news anchor Walter Cronkite, former Republican senator and budget watchdog William Proxmire, Boston mayor Ray Flynn, television commentator Bill Moyers, financier Warren Buffet, Housing and Urban Development Secretary Jack Kemp, Democratic presidential also-ran Bob Kerrey, and on and on. There was no indication, however, that the Perot camp talked seriously with any of the above about a potential vice presidency.

The commentators were saying that the Perot camp couldn't find anyone of substance willing to go on the ticket. Democratic strategist Bob Beckel said on CNN's "Crossfire" the Friday before the Democratic convention began, "A Perot person told me their biggest problem is they can't get anybody of substance to get on the ticket with the guy...the farther he goes down in the polls, nobody with any standing is going to jump on a losing ship...they have a credibility problem right now."

But Perot told his staff all along he didn't want to make the choice until after the Republican National Convention in August. Even while Rollins was urging an earlier announcement, Luce said on the July 9 "Today" show that the target date for announcing a vice-presidential selection was mid- to late-August.

Squires is convinced that Perot wanted Stockdale. "Perot was not going to get rid of Stockdale. That would have been a concession. He was a war hero. Nobody was beating up on him because they thought he was a stand-in. And Perot didn't want to change. He liked the idea of having a nonplastic man," he said.

As usual, Rollins had a different interpretation. Rollins felt Perot didn't want to name a running mate because he didn't want to share the limelight. "He didn't want a strong second choice to share the spotlight," said Rollins.

Others said Perot found fault with many of those suggested as potential running mates. Perot wasn't making news with his vice-presidential selection, but Bill Clinton was. The week before the Democratic National Convention, Clinton announced his selection of Tennessee Senator Al Gore as his running mate. Several days of glowing coverage boosted Clinton just as he was going into the convention, which was expected to boost him even more.

The convention was going splendidly for the Democrats, and Perot's support was dwindling. Perot was losing one to two points each night from the time of the Gore announcement, according to tracking polls being taken nightly by research director Frank Luntz. There was a bulletin board in the "war room" at Dallas headquarters, where Perot's support was posted in each state. The numbers had to be changed every day. But even though his popular support was collapsing, Perot was still winning in the electoral vote. The experts thought he needed to get on the air or he would be down to 25-28 percent by the end of the Democratic convention on the night of July 16. While Rollins felt he would never recover if he continued going down, Frank Luntz believed that even if Perot was down to the mid-twenties in percentage of support in September, he could still blast the other two candidates out of the race with the debates, rebuilding his initial support.

The day after the TV commercials were screened in Dallas, Jordan let it be known that he wanted to quit. He felt nothing was being accomplished by the professional staff. At the time, Jordan tried to get Rollins to quit with him, but Rollins said he felt responsible for the thirty or forty professionals he had brought into the campaign. GOP National Chairman Rich Bond had warned that those who had done Republican work would get no congressional races in the fall, Rollins said. Instead of leaving, Jordan simply retreated into a shell. He mostly stayed in his office, out of the line of fire; some days he didn't even come to work. As one staffer said, he just "hung out." The big news at the Democratic National Convention on Tuesday of convention week was that Jordan was leaving the campaign. He denied the reports. According to Rollins, the reports were based on Jordan's desire to quit weeks earlier. Rollins was also assuring his friends in the media that Jordan was not leaving.

In fact, it wasn't Jordan who left, it was Rollins. On Wednesday, July 15, Luce and Meyerson went to lunch with Rollins, and he was history.

Rollins may be the best at doing what he does, according to the system as it is now defined. But who says you have to do it that way? That was Perot's point from the first, so Rollins was clearly the wrong man for the job. It was a complete mismatch. Rollins was consumed with "the game" of politics, the perceptions drawn by the media—who does the advertising, how much you spend, how long it takes to plan a traditional convention, how you treat the press, "spinning" the story your way—the kind of presidential campaigns that have become standard over the last twenty years. To him, the Republican attempts at character assassination weren't dirty tricks; they were just politics, the way the game was played. Heavy-handed, yes, but there's always an effort to "distract" your opponents, he said.

Rollins had no problem with opposition research. As he told Perot, "This is not some big CIA-type operation, it's a bunch of young researchers looking at Nexis and Lexis and finding things that have been printed." In the

Bush campaign, the "oppo unit" amounted to six paid staffers and about a dozen young volunteers, who combed old and current news stories and other public records. They were helped by a staff of twenty to forty people at the Republican National Committee, computerizing the information. The Perot campaign said it employed two researchers; there was no "oppo" unit. Perot was personally incensed by the opposition research form of campaigning. Reporters, he felt, waited for their tip of the day from the Republicans, and then called the Perot headquarters for reaction. He felt that was the way they got most of their stories. In his mind, that wasn't what a campaign ought to be about.

Perot, even though he initially agreed to the vision Rollins and Jordan had of a more "conventional" campaign, never intended a campaign like what they envisioned. He wanted a shorter campaign, one that focused on the problems of government, not the problems of politicking, one that eschewed all the trappings of today's presidential campaigns. Rollins says his only mistake was that he didn't know the candidate. The candidate's mistake was that he didn't know Rollins.

The approach of the professionals just didn't fit the "people's campaign." Gloria de la Cruz, the Hispanic coordinator on the field staff, called them the "prima donnas on the other side of the wall. They were just there, sitting in their little offices. I knew our days were numbered. The Rollins people were expending more energy running the show," she said. "The prima donnas were into role playing. There is no room in this movement for that. We the People are opposed to that. It was totally contrary to the phenomenon. I thought, 'Don't they get it?' Without us, these people have zero. Nobody needs anybody on the other side of the wall. All they're doing is having the war room meetings. They were playing battle every day; we were in the trenches. We didn't have somebody walking around with a cellular phone, somebody saying that it's okay to write a check. We were making the transformation happen strictly from within, with our own talents and abilities."

"The whole thing self-destructed," according to de la Cruz, "because of their lack of understanding of the nature of the beast. They were relying on their traditional past experience in politics, assuming that somehow this phenomenon could fit into the framework of conventional politics. It had nothing to do with convention, what we have historically experienced in this country."

Rollins tried to get Jordan, who many days earlier had expressed a desire to quit, to leave with him. Jordan, however, had been called by Perot and was asked to stay. Besides, he had just told the press the day before he wasn't quitting.

A number of the people Rollins had brought in, however, did leave with him—including Rollins's deputy Charles Leonard, advance man Joe Canzeri, media men Tony Marsh and Sal Russo, Peter Schecter from Sawyer-Miller's in Washington and adman Bob Barkin of Washington.

Shortly after the announcement that Rollins was leaving, security officials went into the offices of the departing Rollins staff members, disconnecting computers and telephones. "It was like a SWAT team descended on the office," said one Rollins aide.

It was administrator Bill Frost's responsibility to "secure" the area. "I liked Rollins and all those people," Frost said, "but in a corporate environment, that's just what you do." You protect your files, your sensitive material, your "inventory."

Maybe so, but it nonetheless confirmed the ruthless, paranoid tycoon image that was part of Perot's unmaking. Nothing was going right.

Leonard went to see Luce after Rollins returned from lunch with the news that he was out of there. Luce apologized to Leonard, and Leonard remembers Luce saying: "Nobody knew how Ross was going to react to a lot of things. I know it's been a frustrating experience, and you've worked very hard, but it's not going to work. It's going to be a different kind of campaign; we're going to go back to the old petition movement." Luce asked Leonard if he would be willing to come back to Dallas occasionally and act as an adviser, and told him the campaign would honor its commitment to pay him through November. "The next thing I know the goon squad is coming around turning off computers and telephones," Leonard said.

Later that afternoon, he was handed a typed confidentiality agreement to sign by Clay Mulford, if he wanted his salary to be continued through November 30, 1992. According to the agreement, Leonard had to refrain from making any disparaging remarks or negative comments about Perot or the campaign. He also had to agree not to reveal any information about strategy, tactics, budgets, issues, the vice-presidential selection, or any conversations with other top campaign officials or campaign anecdotes. Others on the Rollins team were also asked to sign the agreement.

Leonard was insulted by the separation agreement and said so to Tom Luce, who said he would work it out with Perot. Forty-eight hours later, Luce called Leonard at his hotel, put him on speaker phone with Meyerson and Mulford and told him that Perot was not going to pay him beyond that day. Perot believed that Leonard had been party to the leaks to the media, which Leonard vehemently denied. Leonard was "angry and disappointed" on a professional level, but he was also furious at Luce, who he felt failed to uphold their handshake deal.

It had been apparent to the staff for several days that all was not well. For the last week to ten days of the campaign, those on the professional side, even those at a lesser level, were not feeling good about the campaign. Kristen Silverberg graduated from Harvard on June 3, and started working for Luce in the campaign on June 8. She recalled that "When I got down there it had been steadily building, the excitement was growing. The polls were reflecting that we could actually win it. It was just a really exciting, hopeful time. But for the last week-and-a-half, we had had the NAACP speech. We didn't have an announcement yet, the staff was impatient about that, and we had not had a vice-presidential candidate announced. And there were other internal discussions. People were showing up (to work) and very few of them were female, and very few of them were black. There were three blacks on staff. Sharon Holman was the only woman in a high level position until Liz Maas arrived." (Liz Maas came to Dallas to work with the press operation, her three-year-old daughter and nanny in tow; she had been in town a week before the bottom dropped out of the campaign.)

"When they announced that Rollins was leaving, people thought maybe this would take care of the problems. But it was a frustrating feeling," she said. "I was very sad to see these people leaving, but on the other hand, I knew something had to be done." She said she fretted over who would be left to be in charge of the various aspects of the campaign. How were all the campaign functions going to be carried out? Perot apparently didn't want them carried out.

Things were building to a critical mass. Perot didn't want any part of what his campaign had become; it was everything he said was wrong with politics—handlers, imagery, manipulation, focusing on personal aspects of the candidate instead of what's wrong with government. He was mad about the airport press conference in Michigan, mad about how he was being treated by the press in general, mad about stories on the advertising brouhaha. He had been humiliated by the NAACP speech. His image, which had been carefully nurtured for over two decades, was going down the tubes. And there were rumors that more bad stories were forthcoming.

One was that his daughter Carolyn, who was to be married in August, was going to be splashed across the front of a tabloid, her face on another person's body, in some kind of lesbian situation. "It's crazy, but it's going to show up somewhere, even if it's not true—and it's not true," Squires said. As bizarre as it might seem, he said, it was not beyond the realm of possibility that two daughters would be smeared. Perot had told close associates that two well-known Republicans had informed him of the rumors about his daughter's wedding being disrupted. The other story was one that ABC was prepared to air on Thursday night, July 16. The report would say that an EDS employee had been fired in 1986 from the Bethesda office after he had told his supervisor that he had been hospitalized with an H.I.V.-related pneumonia.

The day that Rollins was released, Perot met with his policy staff to firm up some final positions in the economic plan. Perot wanted to make a major speech on television, outlining the economic plan and then, at the end of the speech, announce that a book detailing the plan could be purchased at bookstores throughout the country. Work on the speech and on the book had been going on simultaneously.

The positions he decided to take were tough positions, some requiring sacrifice. Some were not likely to sit well with the American people. His advisers told him there would be consequences; he would lose some support. But he either took the tough position and told the truth about the bitter medicine required, or he could gloss over it and become just like the politicians he had scorned. Social security, second mortgages—these were some of the sacred cows that had to be hit. There would probably need to be an energy tax. When all was said and done, his advisers figured he could count on keeping 20 to 25 percent of the vote.

When the issues meeting broke up about 2:00 p.m., Squires left to plug the final decisions into the economic speech. Wick Allison, who has a publishing company in New York and was once a Dallas magazine publisher, was writing the issues book. Perot called Allison at the hotel where he was working and asked him if he had everything he needed and if he was prepared to deliver the book draft. Perot gave no sign that he had any intention of doing anything but going ahead with it.

Late in the afternoon, Perot went home, where it is believed he tuned in to the Democratic National Convention. Some time between 5:00 and 9:00 p.m. he decided to withdraw. He had never officially declared his candidacy. Perot felt besieged from the inside and the outside. The media were assaulting him; the Republicans were assaulting him. He couldn't support what his own campaign had become. He saw his reputation being damaged, the reputation he had spent a lifetime developing. He saw himself as a great humanitarian being painted as a racist. Squires speculated that Perot asked why subject himself to all of that when he wasn't going to win anyway? The best he could do was throw the election into the House, where he would stand no chance of being elected.

But some close to the campaign had other ideas. When Rollins was fired, Perot was actually leading in twenty-two states with 307 electoral votes. He still had enough electoral votes to be elected. One staffer reasoned: "The man did not want to become president of the United States. He wanted to shake things up and get rid of Bush."

Another regarded it as a purely personal decision. Perot finally came face to face with what his life would be like and what his family's life would be like if he actually became president. It was not a pretty sight. His business interests would be sacrificed. Ross, Jr., would be hampered in trying to carry on the family businesses. His children would continue to be in the limelight. The worst of it was this threat that his daughter's August wedding might be disrupted.

In the end, he weighed in on the personal side, the family side. No matter that he was letting down hundreds of thousands, maybe millions, of people. As one staff member said: "He says he's a simple man, and it's true. He's into deal-making, public good and his family. This thing had gotten way out of hand; he was surf boarding on a tidal wave."

The only way to regain control of his life was to shut the campaign down.

To Squires, it all went back to the basic fabric of the man and his beliefs about presidential campaigning: "Will you sacrifice your family's reputation, will you concoct a false image, will you defend yourself against attacks no matter how farfetched, will you try to manipulate the press?" The answer to all those questions was "No."

Another one of the pros thought Perot looked at it more practically. "He believed he was going to lose. It was disrupting his family. It wasn't fun anymore. It was cruel; it was grueling. If he wasn't going to win, why go through with this?"

Luce and Meyerson were summoned to the Perot home on Strait Lane that evening. Perot informed them he was dropping out; he didn't ask for their advice. He later informed the original Team of Six who had been directing the volunteer efforts from the beginning. At 7:00 a.m. the next day, they were to put out the word to all of the field reps. The field reps were to tell their state coordinators that Perot would have a press conference that morning, and "be sure to watch."

The next morning, Perot walked into the campaign press room at 6606 LBJ Freeway and read this statement:

"Several million volunteers in all fifty states have done a brilliant job in re-establishing a government that comes from the people. Both political parties are now squarely focused on the issues that concern the American people. Being associated with the volunteers is one of the greatest experiences of my life.

"Throughout this effort, we have said that we do not want our efforts to disrupt the political process. In order to succeed, we must win a majority of electoral votes in November. If we cannot win in November, the election will be decided in the House of Representatives. Since the House of Representatives is made up of Democrats and Republicans, our group would be unlikely to win.

"Now that the Democratic Party has revitalized itself, I have concluded that we cannot win in November, and that the election will be decided in the House of Representatives. Since the House of Representatives does not pick the president until January, the new president is unable to use the months of November and December to assemble his team and prepare to govern.

"I have decided not to become a candidate because I do not believe it serves the country's best interest.

"In the states where petitions have not yet been turned in, I urge the volunteers to turn them in so that both parties know exactly who the people are who are concerned about our country's future. If the petitions are turned in, both parties will give a great deal of attention to the concerns of the volunteers. This is good for the country.

"I would like to thank the members of the press who have been assigned to this effort.

"Again, to the volunteers and dedicated teams across the country who have worked so valiantly on this effort, I compliment you on your patriotism, your idealism, your creativity and your ingenuity. The people who founded our country would be very proud of you."

Perot was unprepared for the pandemonium that would be precipitated by that announcement. His supporters were totally unequipped to handle the suddenness and apparent finality of the collapse of a campaign they felt, only days before, was marching to certain victory.

PART II
UNCONVENTIONAL
CAMPAIGN

HEARTBREAK:
THE PEOPLE REACT

VOLUNTEERS ARRIVED AT THE DALLAS PHONE BANK ON THE morning of July 16 not knowing what was in store. According to phone bank director Rose Roberts-Cannaday, people were on a high, and the phones were backed up in queues.

On the staff side, however, the atmosphere that morning was tense. When issues director John P. White walked into offices at 7:30 a.m., he found a "lot of buzzing and running around." He talked to Squires and to a couple of others who said they believed Perot was going to quit that day. Then he talked directly to Luce. Luce confirmed it.

The day before, Perot had called in Hamilton Jordan and told him he was going to get rid of Rollins. At least two weeks earlier, Jordan had told Perot he wanted to leave. "I was not making a contribution. I was not sure why we had been brought there, we weren't having any impact." Jordan said. Meyerson and Luce were in the office when Perot said he would like Jordan to "stay on and manage this thing." But if he was going to leave, to go ahead and leave with Rollins. According to Jordan, Perot went on to say, "Let me tell you, there's a chance I may pull the plug on this thing." Jordan said Perot talked about his family and the loss of his privacy. He had asked Jordan several times about the impact of the presidency on Jimmy Carter's children. Jordan always told him, "It's going to get worse, Ross, the scrutiny is going to be worse rather than better." Jordan said, "He was concerned about that. He was genuinely worried about the impact on his family." Earlier in the spring, Perot had said in interviews he didn't want his family involved in the campaign. "I don't want my family to be brutalized," he said, adding that his family was not relevant to the process of selecting a good president.

So Jordan was totally prepared for anything when he went to work the morning of July 16, including the probability that Perot would "pull the plug on this thing."

The senior staff went into a meeting about 8:00 a.m. Other staffers were advised there would be a press conference at 10:00 a.m.; they were advised to watch in the big break room. Darcy Anderson began making phone calls to state coordinators telling them to find a television and watch CNN at 10:00 a.m. Many of them were in for a rude awakening—they thought he was going to declare his candidacy.

The atmosphere at the headquarters had become one of foreboding and apprehension. Some of the volunteers sensed the gloom; they feared what was going to happen but could not bring themselves to believe it. At 9:50 a.m., Rose Cannaday was called aside and told Perot was going to withdraw. As she walked down the center aisle of the phone bank, tears streaming and hands shaking, Wes Whitlock, the in-house volunteer computer guru, knew immediately what was about to take place.

In the crowded break room, volunteers were joined by Tom Luce, Mort Meyerson, Clay Mulford and Jim

Squires. That was a giveaway; the top staffers had TVs in their offices. "He's going to back out," said Brett Basnett, looking sick. The room was filled with worried-looking volunteers.

Perot's announcement that he would not be a candidate was greeted by stunned, grim faces, and almost virtual silence. There was bedlam as soon as he finished. Volunteers clustered around Mort Meyerson, demanding an explanation. Basnett fled the room; his name tag was later found ground into the floor by his heel. Jim Serur said, "I can't believe it."

After Perot made his announcement, he walked out, got in his car and left.

The volunteers were ushered into the phone bank. Perot's photographer was allowed in, but no press. Security guarded the door to the hall leading to the phone bank. Volunteer Howard Mann was there as usual with his video camera. He had been documenting the volunteer effort all along. Everyone had become accustomed to seeing Mann with his video camera; it was like an extension of his arm. Mann had made the sign on the wall that said, "The Revolution Started With Us."

Tom Luce appeared at the front of the room, with Muffie McCoole and Bill Frost standing behind him. Luce said he wished he could think of something funny to say but "I can't really think of anything very funny right now. I wanted to come in and personally thank each and every one of you. What you have done since February 21 is extraordinary. The amount of dedication, selfless dedication you have put into this effort is really an extraordinary reflection on this country. I wish that we could have finished the mission." Luce urged the volunteers not to give up. "Keep your faith in yourself and in your country." Then he choked up.

One volunteer shouted "We hear you." Another said, "He doesn't know how much we love him," adding that if she could get near him (Perot), she would let him know. Luce, urging the volunteers to "hang in there," choked up again. He hugged phone bank director Rose Roberts-Cannaday, patted a few people on the shoulder and left.

Cannaday said, "We worked our hearts out. What makes it so hard is that everything was looking so good." She was crying, but she continued to spur on the troops. "He may have pulled out, but we still can put him on the ballot in all fifty states." Ed Campbell was in tears as well. "We have made a difference. We can continue to make a difference. Do not give up. We cannot give up. This is for our children," he said.

In shock, the volunteers did the only thing they knew to do. They started answering the phones.

Howard Mann's video tape showed one woman on the phone talking about "all this work down the drain, we're all just sick about it," and a man advising a caller to call back later. "Maybe we'll know more later," he said. Different ones on the phones could be heard telling callers "He needs to know we love him; we need him. Write him. We're keeping on going. We're not going to let him resign."

There was a United States map on the phone bank wall with pins stuck in the states where Perot was qualified to be on the ballot. The sign that day read: "Now on the ballot in twenty-four states."

That afternoon, supporters from across the state began gathering on the lawn outside the 6606 LBJ Freeway office building in Dallas. They came from Houston, Austin, San Antonio, carrying signs that said: "Ross You Can't Quit" and "Keep Your Promise" and "We Don't

Run From a Fight." Also camped out on the lawn were reporters conducting interviews and vendors hawking T-shirts, buttons and caps. The scene was a virtual kaleidoscope of angry and determined volunteers, the media and vendors selling souvenirs.

Robert Weisman was angry. He told video producer Jo Streit: "I've been here 145 days; at this time I don't feel very good." Wearing, ironically, one of the T-shirts that said, "Perot 92—The Party's Over," Weisman complained that Perot had "promised if he were elected we'd all have a take in this government. He also said if we put him on all fifty ballots he would serve as our servant. He said he didn't want anybody leaving and going home. Now he's left and gone home. I'm pretty sad and pretty mad." Weisman, who said he was trying to form a Force Perot to Run Committee, drove off in a car piled with boxes of Perot paraphernalia he was selling.

In an effort to lift spirits, some of the volunteers from the phone bank decided to have a rally that afternoon on the lawn beside the headquarters building. Brett Basnett, wearing an "I Love the Perot Girls" T-shirt, set up a sound system, and sang his song, "Don't Tread on Me, I'm American." A number of the volunteers made short, but eloquent speeches. Karoline Wilson was the mistress of the ceremonies. The sun was beaming down on the hot, hot July day as the volunteers pumped each other up and urged one another to stay involved and to keep working to change government.

Some of the volunteers coming out of the phone bank believed Perot would re-emerge once he was placed on all fifty state ballots. Raymond Lavado, a recent college graduate from Miami, Florida, had been in Dallas as a volunteer for three weeks. He felt Perot's announcement was a "calculated move" and that "Perot knew what he was doing."

"I believe the campaign was starting to fall apart on a professional level. This campaign is about volunteers and a grass roots effort. That was not the way it was being run by the professionals," Lavado said. He believed that the week after September 25, when Arizona became the last state to put Perot's name on the ballot, Perot would get back in the race.

After viewing the press conference in Dallas, Miller Hicks went back to Austin where he was a regional coordinator. Workers were still sweeping out the debris in New York's Madison Square Garden from the just-ended Democratic National Convention when he called together his volunteers. "Of all sad words of tongue or pen," he recited, "the saddest of these are 'it might have been.'"

As the Democratic convention was ending on what its leaders felt was a new high, a wave of sadness and anger was sweeping the local cells of the Perotistas—those people who had stalled their lives to back Ross Perot in an effort to promote change in the political process.

Bill Clinton was calling for a "New Covenant," and Ross Perot was breaking his—leaving a big hurt out in the land and the unanswered question of whether the new non-partisans would stay involved or retreat behind an even thicker wall of cynicism.

July 16—the day Perot got out—was the legal starting day for petitions to be signed in New York. The New York volunteers, who had been organizing for months, kicked off the drive right after midnight July 15 at a big party in their Lexington Avenue headquarters. The press had been invited and the two hundred or so volunteers were encouraged to speak out about how they were going to get Ross Perot on the ballot in New

York in what they knew would be a tough task. A cousin of the plain-speaking former President Harry Truman was there to witness the first signer, an eighteen-year-old first voter. After daybreak, they would fan out to collect signatures.

New York organizer Kurt Koenig went to his petition post that morning at the City University Graduate Center. Curtis Sliwa, founder of the Guardian Angels, was coming by with his bodyguards to sign, and a local TV crew would be there. Shortly before noon, Eastern time, a CNN crew ran up with a camera, asking: "What's your response, now that he's withdrawn?" Koenig was dumbfounded. People walking by were ridiculing him as he was being interviewed. One said: "What are you doing there, you jerk? He quit!"

In Boston, the volunteer organization was moving into newly leased offices, and technicians were putting in a cable connection. Field reps from Dallas were in town, and rep Brokaw Price had gotten a phone call about the press conference. Boston co-chairman Dick Norman went to Price's room and watched. "One of the workmen had snaked about two-thirds of the cable through the ceiling," Norman said, "when we came back and said, 'Stop.'"

Bill Anderson, the other Boston co-chairman, was in the new office space with other volunteers. It was attached to a hotel, so they ordered in beer and soft drinks, and determined to "have a good old Irish wake. We decided, let's have a party; what else could we do?" One woman was carried out on a stretcher, another volunteer went out in handcuffs. Suffice to say that, in their disappointment, the Boston volunteers exhibited the full gamut of emotions.

In Denver, Rosemarie Sax, an interior designer for

thirty years and a longtime Republican who had been involved in the petition drive since April, was the only one in the petition campaign offices when she got word from the media. Her reaction was disbelief. "The best way to explain it was like when my husband died suddenly of a heart attack. I just couldn't believe it."

Noell Custer of Denver, a fifty-three-year-old professional watercolorist and volunteer, watched the announcement on cable at home and immediately called Sax at headquarters. "Are you all right?" she asked. Sax answered: "I have three TV cameras pointed at me and two more coming in the door." Custer said, "I'm on my way." She worked at headquarters all day, and when she got home that night, there were eight messages on her recorder. "I did fine until the last one. It was from my thirty-two-year-old son, Kevin, who said, 'Mom, I just called to tell you how sorry I am. I know how much he meant to you.' I was okay until then; then I broke into tears."

All over the country, the reactions were the same—shock, fury, grief, and, for some, a refusal to accept Perot's decision. The *Political Hotline* reviewed newspapers from around the country the morning after Perot got out; all were doing Perot reaction stories. Here's a sampling of what the Hotline passed on to its subscribers:

CALIFORNIA: From the *Los Angeles Times*: "Just as survivors of an earthquake or a riot find their ways to hospitals or rescue centers, Perot volunteers found their way to local storefront campaign operations, searching for comfort, hugs and perhaps a sign that the campaign would go on.

FLORIDA: From the *Orlando Sentinel*: Supporter Miriam Lancaster: "I was on my way to a funeral, but this is the real funeral." Volunteer Shawn O'Donnell: "It's sad; this wasn't a political thing—it was an American dream." Seminole County coordinator Melissa Reed: "I wouldn't have dropped my life if I thought he would not go the course."

IOWA: From the *Des Moines Register*: Supporters reacted to his sudden withdrawal as if "they had just heard that Santa Claus was quitting the toy business."

LOUISIANA: From the *New Orleans Times Picayune*: Tulane University student Frank Wharton: "I feel like I've wasted my time." Retiree Angela Strahan: "I feel betrayed. We believed that he would fight the fight—give us a chance to see this whole thing through. I never believed he was a quitter."

MISSOURI: From the *St. Louis Post-Dispatch*: Missouri Perot chief Sandy McClure said she'll "fight to put (Perot) on the ballot—whether or not he wants to be there. We're going to draft him. We have something to say and something to accomplish."

NEW JERSEY: From *The Record*: Supporter Betsie Zak: "We're furious. We've been duped." Volunteer Ron Pondiscio: "We've become politically homeless....We've been betrayed. We've still got to pay the bills for all this stuff (buttons and bumper stickers)." Volunteer organizer Shelia Sachs: "I'm disappointed not only in the fact that he dropped out, but also because I'm not sure he stands for what I thought he did."

NEW YORK: The *New York Post* cover: "What a wimp." Albany coordinator Don Neddo: "He's going down in history as the biggest con artist in the world." New York People for Perot chairman Matthew Lifflander: "He's broken the hearts of millions." Petition volunteer Frances Lynn: "We won't stop. We're going to stay with it....Hopefully, he'll change his mind."

OREGON: From the *Eugene Register Guard*: Local Perot backers "expressed shock, hurt, anger and disbelief" at Perot's announcement. Lane County Perot campaign chair Jim Hale: "You can't be a servant of the people if you're not willing to serve."

PENNSYLVANIA: The *Philadelphia Daily News* ran a photo of Perot backers hanging a giant blindfolded Perot head in effigy, with a sign around its neck: "You left us hanging." The Perotistas "already embittered by politics...feel a strong sense of betrayal."

WASHINGTON: From the *Seattle Post-Intelligencer*: Perot director Russ Stromberg: "We got in the ring. We're going to stay in the ring....What do we know for sure? We know we're not dropping out." Supporter Adrian Van Holts: "I am disgusted in him. I have contempt in my heart for the man....He owes us all an apology, not just a thank-you." Supporter Don Gilberton: "I'm devastated. He was our only hope for the country."

The next morning a new attitude was developing in the Dallas phone bank. The attitude that prevailed was: "We're going to hold this thing together somehow. It isn't going to end. It isn't the man; it's an idea. It's us."

Mick Ulakovic, an airline pilot who lives in a Dallas suburb, stated it eloquently: "Ross made an agreement with us, back when we started this program. He said if we put him on the ballot in all fifty states, he would run. We're halfway through that process, going full steam. Yesterday, I felt very much abandoned; today I don't feel the battle is over yet. It's mid-July, the election is not until November 3. We could change his mind as easily as he decided to make his statement yesterday....It's not just his decision anymore. He made a contract with the volunteers in this room, with millions of people around the country, with fifty state organizations that have invested millions of man hours and labor to make him the next president."

"He can make a statement like yesterday and you can see the ramifications—thousands of phone calls today, fax machine going wild, people angry, people upset, people calling in and saying we're going to vote for him anyway. He can do what he wants to do, but the fact is he cannot bail out of this program without the consent of the people who brought him here. It's not his movement. It's our movement. It's a contract that at this point in time he appears to have breached. I for one am very much motivated to hold him to his word.

"I don't know what I expected coming here to the volunteer headquarters the day after the announcement; possibly people sitting back with their feet propped up, crying, moving things out of offices. I'm not seeing that. I'm seeing people who are not willing to give up hope, people who have invested not only their time, they've invested their emotions. He just can't bail out. He can't desert us."

Another volunteer wanted to know what would happen to the data base, the millions of names and addresses and phone numbers that were being collected. "I think we should stay together as a coalition to make change. Exactly how, I don't know. Hopefully, we'll find a way," she said.

The phones were going wild, again. Phone bank director Rose Roberts-Cannaday said the calls were coming in at a rate of one thousand an hour, from all over the country, and that 10 percent were being lost. "People just refuse to give up," she said. "The answer he gave them is not acceptable."

California coordinator Bob Hayden called Darcy Anderson to report that an emergency steering committee meeting had been held in California, and supporters wanted to keep moving forward. He wanted to come to Dallas to convince Perot to get back in or to somehow try to keep the movement alive. Pat Muth called from Florida, requesting a meeting with Perot. She was told she wasn't the only one. She made arrangements to fly into Dallas.

On Friday, thirty-seven state representatives were on their way to Dallas to try to convince Perot not to drop out. A block of rooms had been reserved at a nearby Sheraton hotel. "They'll all be in by tomorrow," Cannaday said. "The shock is over, the tears are over. People are more determined today than they were yesterday. They're going to conference at the Sheraton. All I know is these people are on their way to Dallas."

It was four o'clock on the morning of July 16 when Orson Swindle got an unexpected wakeup call from a field representative from Dallas who was in Honolulu. Swindle, an acquaintance of Perot since his release as a POW, had quit his job running an association of preschools two weeks before to become state coordinator and campaign manager in Hawaii, one of the states which had been having organizational problems. The field rep, a young lawyer from Dallas, said: "Orson, I've got some bad news for you. Perot's going to be on TV in thirty minutes, and he's pulling out." Swindle called Dallas and was told that many of the state coordinators were flying in to decide what to do. He got on a plane.

On Friday night, one day after leaving the race, Perot appeared on "Larry King Live"—where his candidacy had been launched five months earlier. He urged supporters to maintain a "united front" and become a power broker in the presidential and congressional elections. "Let's organize—we can provide the swing vote to who gets to be the next president of the United States," he said.

About fifty volunteers from Dallas and several other states watched the King show at the Sheraton Park Central and roared with approval when he said he would back the effort he was proposing.

But his own role as a potential candidate remained unclear.

King: You can't stop someone from voting for you.

Perot: That's right.

King: In a sense, you're still sort of hanging that leaf out.

Perot: That's the magic, Larry.

King: We've got an alternative.

Perot: We have a protest vote and that could take one of the two of you (Clinton or Bush) through the tank.

King: If (Bush or Clinton) don't satisfy your people, your people should protest vote for you?

Perot: They have the option.

Earlier in the day he taped an interview with Barbara Walters for ABC's "20/20" in which he said he would listen to his supporters' views on whether he should leave his name on the ballots. "They put my name on. It's not appropriate for me unilaterally to take my name off."

Barbara Walters asked him: "Is there any possibility that you would change your mind and reenter?" Perot replied: "I don't see a possibility unless I thought it was good for the country." She then presented a scenario in which Bill Clinton was discredited and something happens with Bush, and asked, "you might then come into the race again?"

"Well, this is all up to the volunteers," he responded. But he went on to say that he believed when the volunteers thought it through they also would be convinced that it would be disruptive. However, he did urge the volunteers to stay together as a unit "because there they have a voice." And he added that he would "provide them with any kind of help and leadership they want me to. Now they have an interesting piece of leverage....They will have both candidates giving them their full attention."

Suffice to say that Perot was sending conflicting signals to his volunteers, but they were just happy that he wasn't retreating unequivocally. It was enough to remind folks of the old Southern saying, "Every shut eye ain't sleepin', and every goodbye don't mean he's gone."

One reason for the conflicting signals was that the Barbara Walters interview was taped in the morning, and the Larry King interview was Friday night. In between, Perot had been presented with the idea of trying to affect congressional races. One of the state coordinators had gone on CNN earlier in the day, saying the Perot supporters ought to stick together and work to have an impact on congressional races.

As Perot was preparing to fly to the Larry King interview, aides were telling him about the idea. He had said nothing about refocusing the volunteer effort on congressional races when he talked to Barbara Walters. By the time Perot appeared on "Larry King," however, affecting the congressional races was one of the reasons for his getting out of the presidential campaign. Looking back on that weekend, one of the state coordinators surmised that he was just making it up as he went along.

On Saturday morning, July 18, the forty or so state leaders arrived at the Dallas headquarters by bus. They filed into the headquarters building between a row of cameras and were greeted at the door by Sharon

Holman. Perot met with them for more than two hours. The state leaders talked about moving forward with an organization, and Perot told them he would help finance their continued campaign to reform American government. The volunteers considered names for their movement, but downplayed the idea of a third party. Later, Conrad Bookout of North Carolina described Perot as being "between a rock and a hard place," when he got out of the race. "He had this grass roots movement that had a lot of passion and energy. Then he brought in these professional people who took the edge off the passion and energy. He just said this thing wasn't working, let's go back to the people. Now it's back up to the people. The ball's back in our court."

Upstairs, the phone bank was humming. It was full of volunteers and the phone lines were busy. A chalkboard at the front noted that Perot's appearance on "Larry King Live" would be rebroadcast on Sunday. Another signboard listed the options for the "Party's Name." Among those listed were American, Eagle, Patriots, America PAC, Independent, The People Lobby, Volunteer, Voice of the People, You People Party, We the People and Unity Party.

While the state representatives were meeting downstairs, some of the Dallas volunteers were in a giddy, say-it-isn't-so frame of mind. They wanted to cheer up the place. The Perot Girls had on their denim skirts, red T-shirts and Perot earrings, and were recreating their "Something's Gotta Give" chorus line. "fight, fight, fight, we're fighting with all of our might. Our man Ross is neither a left nor a right," they sang.

After the state reps boarded their bus and left for the hotel, Perot went into the phone bank to meet his Dallas volunteers face-to-face for the first time since he backed out. Perot stood on a chair and addressed them:

"Our mission is simple. We need to continue to expand our organization," he said, "to influence candidates for Congress and Senate." Then he made a telling statement. "If neither presidential candidate is found satisfactory," he said, "in the event this goes to the House of Representatives, they (members of Congress) will vote the will of their districts. You follow me?"

There's no way the election could go to the House of Representatives unless it's a three-way race. Perot was already thinking of a way to force members of Congress to vote as their districts voted, in case he got back in the race. Then, it wouldn't be a fool's mission—at least he'd have a chance, if it went to the House.

He also told the volunteers, "One of the reasons we've gone through what we've gone through here is to get rid of all of the political professionals. We're now back to the people with real innovative ideas. We've gone back to your strength. It's been a very productive day. We will put together a group of state coordinators and carefully go through all the things we think should be fixed. We will continue in all fifty states; if we're not on the ballot we have no leverage."

Perot went on to say, "One of the things we're going to do is we're going to give this thing a name." He jokingly suggested the People's Interest Group which, abbreviated, is PIG. Or, he said, maybe it will be called the the PACK, an acronym for People's Political Action Committee. "We'll do whatever we have to do in every state so that the ticking bomb is sitting in the corner. On this plan," he added, "I'm going to stick with Admiral Stockdale."

There was no press in the room that day. They had been barred, and were holding vigil outside. But Howard

Mann, with his trusty video cam, was filming away. Jo Streit, a friend of the Young Turks, was filming for her documentary. Perot even talked about going to the debates.

"We've cleaned out the pros and gone back to basics. I fired those suckers," he said. "Ham Jordan has been a loyal, good man. Some of these other guys have their own agenda; they'll self-destruct on their own."

Perot had unquestionably given some thought as to what might happen next, if the fifty-state petition drive were carried to completion. And it was very clear to some of the volunteers that his intention was to reenter the race later. Among those who thought it clear that Perot would eventually reenter the race were volunteers Karoline Wilson and Wes Whitlock, along with Tommy Attaway who had only recently joined the staff as assistant director of the phone bank. Attaway, a young army officer whose military career was cut short by downsizing, was working for the Tandy Corporation when he began volunteering, but quit his job to work full-time in the Perot effort. His reading on Perot's reentry: "You just had to look through the glass." Karoline Wilson said, "Reading between the lines was so easy." Yet, "what was clear to a few of us was not to many others. It was amazing." Those who took Perot at face value when he said he wouldn't be a candidate quickly dropped out of sight, and a few dissidents tried to reorganize the Dallas volunteers, to no avail.

When Perot finished speaking, the volunteers applauded him and clamored to shake his hand. Robert Weisman, who had been so critical two days earlier, shouted: "Let's go back to work. We've got over one thousand phone calls." Weisman said the volunteers "deserved that. The revolution started with us; it's going to continue with us. What he did today was a very necessary thing for all our emotions. We're all energized."

During the time that Perot was talking, 1,059 calls came into the phone bank. There was more phone traffic than the volunteers could handle, and working the phones was cathartic. "We could talk to others over the country, help them, help ourselves, and heal," one volunteer said. Another called the hard-core supporters who accepted the events as they had happened and remained to work, the "strap-hangers." There were plenty of them—standing in wait for someone to give up their phone spot and hanging by their straps to see what would happen next.

When Orson Swindle came to Dallas that weekend, it was the first time he had seen Ross Perot in years. They had become acquainted in 1973 after Swindle returned home from being a prisoner of war in Southeast Asia. Swindle, a Marine fighter pilot shot down over Vietnam on his last combat mission, spent six years and four months as a prisoner. Swindle had been in captivity at Son Tay, a camp that was the target of a rescue raid, and Perot hosted a party at a San Francisco hotel for those POWs to meet the Son Tay raiders. The morning after the party, Swindle happened to stroll into the dining room as Perot and his wife were having breakfast and was invited to join them. It was the beginning of a long-term relationship.

Over the years, Swindle had been drawn into politics by his outrage over former President Jimmy Carter's declaration of amnesty for Vietnam draft dodgers. He ran Ronald Reagan's 1980 campaign against Carter in the Southwest Georgia congressional district where he then lived. As a result, he was appointed to be the Georgia director of the Farmers Home Administration, the lending arm of the Department of Agriculture. He later became Assistant Secretary of Commerce in charge of the Economic Development Agency. When George Bush became president, Swindle was out of Washington; he had supported Jack Kemp for vice president at the 1980 GOP convention, when Bush became Reagan's running mate.

Swindle, having relocated to Hawaii, had written Perot a letter in March regarding his petition drive and was contacted by Darcy Anderson. Later on, with all sorts of power struggles going on in the Hawaii organization, Swindle agreed to take the leadership position there. He had just gone on the paid staff when Perot backed out.

When he got to Dallas, Swindle found Perot "obviously extremely stressed." On Saturday, the state leaders had discussed moving forward with an organization. But on Sunday, the agenda topic was how to draft Perot back into the race. Alaska coordinator Donna Gilbert was at the forefront of the effort. At one point, Nancy Bush of California wrapped her arms around Perot's ankles, begging him to stay in the race. Perot was disturbed by the level of the emotion. Swindle said, "I couldn't believe it. I'd never met any of these people. I finally got up and said, 'Folks, you're not going to impress the Ross Perot I know with all this emotion.' They were ranting and raving. It was incredible; it was uncredible. They were all signing their names to this draft statement to force him to run. He was stressed about this thing." According to Gilbert, Perot asked for twenty-four hours to think it over, then for a few hours to consult his family. But ten minutes later, the answer was no.

One of the staff members sitting in on those meetings was Russ Monroe, Perot's tax man who had worked with the field organization. Monroe was devastated when Perot dropped out, and was obviously pessimistic and depressed during the meetings with the state leaders. "I had put a lot of heart and soul into this thing," Monroe said. "There was no way he would ever rejoin the race in my opinion. It was difficult for me to understand their conviction in wanting to hang together. Emotionally, I was drained. I thought everyone else would be...They were begging and pleading with him to stay in the race. He was going through a tough time and I thought, hey, leave the guy alone."

Perot told the state leaders he thought they were too emotionally charged, to go home, let things cool down and take the pulse of their states. They would get back together in a week or so.

Swindle walked out with him. "He gave me his home phone number and said, 'I want you to call, and let's talk about this.' He allowed as how if people felt this strongly, we'll talk it over and decide what to do with the organization," Swindle said.

Darcy Anderson, who was in charge of one region of the field organization, admitted he had mixed emotions when Perot backed out. He was disappointed because "I knew we could win. When I traveled, I stopped wearing a lapel pin or button because I couldn't get any work done on the airplane. I would end up emptying my supply of buttons. Everywhere I went, it was that way; all of us were experiencing that." But he admitted to an element of relief because, "We were just working so hard."

Clay Mulford said later that his father-in-law was very surprised by the reaction to his July 16 announcement. The state leaders felt that without a charismatic leader, it would be difficult to keep the movement alive, and they were very saddened that the movement might die. Perot, he said, didn't realize that he was the personification of the movement and that they were relying on him to keep it alive.

On June 20, a Perot volunteer in Florida filed a class-action lawsuit against Perot for breaking his promise to run for office. The suit was dropped after Perot called the volunteer.

There were others, outside the Perot organization, who felt strongly about keeping a movement alive—with or without Ross Perot. The Coalition to End the Permanent Congress was meeting that weekend in Dallas, offering assistance to congressional challengers—independents, Democrats and Republicans—who wanted to open up the system and obtain real campaign reform. Perot had been scheduled to be the featured speaker at a Saturday night dinner, but obviously was a no-show. There was a good deal of hand wringing and teeth gnashing at the dinner over Perot's withdrawal, because they believed he was going to inspire a whole new independent movement in the country.

Cecil Heftel, a former congressman from Hawaii, was angry. Heftel had quit Congress after ten years in 1987, in frustration over money's domination of the political system. "Ross Perot set back the movement for a third party and independent candidates for one hundred years," he complained.

But Jack Gargen, Perot's old admirer from T.H.R.O. (Throw the Hypocritical Rascals Out) in Florida, told the group: "This is bigger than Ross Perot. This is a movement we can't let die. We've got to encourage states to put him on the ballot...Republicans and Democrats say 'Come on back.' Are you kidding? These are the guys who got us in this incredible mess....We have got to regroup this thing."

Lionel Kunst, co-chairman of the Coalition to End the Permanent Congress, suggested there might be another independent leader on the horizon. John Anderson had been such a candidate in 1980, he said, but people weren't angry enough in 1980 to elect him.

Anderson, now a college professor in Florida, thought the country was on the brink of a second revolution—a revolution that would not be coming from either of the existing parties. "Great tremors are occurring in the country today," he said. "We've been brought together," he told the group, "not to weep, not to mourn, not to grieve, but to make up our minds we are going to continue what we've begun. There is a need for a strong new independent political force in this country."

Except for his own faithful, Perot was the object of derision across the country. He took it on the chin—and in the shins—from the editorialists and columnists around the country. And for good reason. He had encouraged millions of people to get in the ring with him, and they did. But then he took a lay-down. He forfeited before the bout ever really began—but not until after millions had invested their time, energies and emotions in him and in the fight. He had energized the presidential campaign; he had brought excitement to it. And then he had snuffed out the flame almost as quickly as he had ignited it.

The New York Times editorial in its Sunday edition, July 19, offered this definition: "per-ot (puh-ro) v. 1. to give up, especially when faced with opposition, after rousing millions to a popular cause. ANT. see PERSIST." *U.S. News's* David Gergen wrote, "As much as Perot energized our politics by the way he started, he diminished it—and himself—by the way he quit."

The most hurtful to the super-competitive Perot, who prides himself on being a fighter, had to be the *Newsweek* cover story headlined: "The Quitter: Why Perot Bowed Out." Ed Rollins—who Perot always said didn't know him and had rarely met with him—conjectured later that the day Perot read that *Newsweek* cover, "He would have done anything to get back in the race. He would have paid anything to get his reputation back."

But the people he had inspired were hurting, too. They fired off hundreds of negative faxes to the Dallas headquarters. "The fax machine blew up on us," said one staffer. "These were grown people feeling enormous pain." Many of the faxes were copies of the *Newsweek* "Quitter" cover.

State leaders reconvened July 29-31 in Dallas to try to determine how they could stay together and become a national force. All the states except Rhode Island and Delaware were represented. Perot financed the conference at an Embassy Suites Hotel in Dallas. Darcy Anderson said, "They had gone home and come back a different group, more rational. They came back thinking about a movement, not a candidate."

Most of the people attending the Dallas reorganizational meetings were obsessed with the idea that the press might hear their discussions. They stood in front of the cracks in the doors to the hotel meeting rooms, because reporters were hanging around outside. The scene had a smell of paranoia to Orson Swindle. He told the others: "This is politics; we have to talk to the press. Somebody's got to go out and talk to them." Swindle started talking to the press, explaining what was going on behind the closed doors. He believes it brought some credibility to the effort.

After an hour-long meeting with Perot on July 29, Swindle emerged to say that Perot had encouraged them to put his name on all of the state ballots but reaffirmed his decision not to campaign for the presidency. Swindle said the group was evolving "into realizing that the phenomenon is not Ross Perot, the phenomenon is that critical issues facing this country need to be addressed by the major presidential candidates, and the congressional candidates."

Swindle said he saw no evidence that Perot's strategy was to "get out of the line of fire" and then re-emerge as a candidate in the fall. "He was very stressed about this dirty tricks thing. He gave me the names of the two people in the Republican Party who gave him the information about the picture of his daughter. I told him, 'If you're not prepared to give the names, don't go (public) with it.' He was sincerely disturbed, in my opinion, and made a decision I can't fault him for."

On July 30, the state leaders met and adopted a name and a mission statement. They called their organization United We Stand. The name was the same one Perot had given an organization he formed in 1969, which was a grass roots effort focused on freeing the POWs in Southeast Asia. That organization functioned through the early 1970s. A trademark search was conducted, and a gay and lesbian group in California was found to have the name United We Stand, so the new Perot group became United We Stand America.

The group decided to try to put Perot's name on the ballot in all fifty states and to urge people to vote for him if the other candidates failed to measure up. Perot agreed to fund them at $7,500 per month per state. The concept was that Perot would be leveraged against the two major-party candidates. "That was the focus of United We Stand America, that was our hammer," Darcy Anderson said. "They could say to Bush and Clinton, 'If you don't get serious, we could pull out the hammer.' Deep down inside, Ross hoped it wouldn't happen."

The founding members of United We Stand America, representing all states except Delaware, Rhode Island and Virginia, signed a mission statement that said:

> We the People...
>
> ...recognizing that our republic was founded as a government of the people, by the people and for the people, unite to restore the integrity of our economic and political systems.
>
> We commit ourselves to organize, to educate, to participate in the political process, and to hold our public servants accountable.
>
> We shall rebuild our country, renew its economic, moral and social strength, and return the sovereignty of America to her people.

Along with Ross Perot, Jim Stockdale and Sybil Stockdale, the statement was signed by the following people, representing their states.

Alabama	Mac Phillipi
Alaska	John Townsend
Arizona	Walt Peters
Arkansas	Greg Owens
California	Robert Hayden
Colorado	Lillian Bickel
Connecticut	Dennis Shay
Florida	Stu Phillips

Georgia	Ken Kendricks
Hawaii	Orson Swindle
Idaho	Shirley Hamm
Illinois	Tom Wing
Indiana	Wally Howard
Iowa	Rick Ross
Kansas	Orville Sweet
Kentucky	Gary Klier
Louisiana	Betty Moore
Maine	Steve Bost
Maryland	Joan Vinson
Massachusetts	Richard Andrews
Michigan	Susan Esser
Minnesota	Bob Laguban
Mississippi	James Smith
Missouri	Sandy McClure
Montana	Hays Kirby
Nebraska	Matt Wickless
Nevada	Jan Hunt
New Hampshire	Herb Clark
New Jersey	C.J. Barthelenghi
New Mexico	John Bishop
New York	Bill Tschudy
North Carolina	Jackie Foltz
North Dakota	Jim Kisse
Ohio	Nancy Kavanagh
Oklahoma	Jamie Hurst
Oregon	Bill Maher
Pennsylvania	David Kirby
South Carolina	Betty Montgomery
South Dakota	Dennis Olson
Texas	Jim Serur
Tennessee	Steve Fridrich
Utah	Marie George

Vermont	Wolfe Schmokel
Washington	Ed Doyne
West Virginia	David Dingees
Wisconsin	Cindy Schultz
Wyoming	Linda Stoval
District of Columbia	Gloria Borland

Orson Swindle had been the group's spokesman to the press and, as a result, was invited on "Nightline." He got rave reviews from the other state leaders, watching at the hotel. When it came time to elect a chairman, since he was doing a good job as spokesman and since he knew Perot personally, the group agreed that he should be their leader.

Swindle told the group that UWSA couldn't separate itself from Perot until after the election, and if they were successful in getting Perot on the ballot in all fifty states, maybe he would reconsider and run. After that, he said, the organization ought to have a life of its own.

Communications Director Jim Squires, asked later why Perot (instead of getting out of the race) didn't just fire the professionals and get the campaign back to the grass roots, to what it was, responded: "That's exactly what he did."

13

THE SECOND WAVE—
ISSUES BOOK AND FIFTY
STATE BALLOTS

THE IMMEDIATE INSTRUCTIONS PEROT GAVE THE STAFF WERE TO shut down the operation, to assess the financial obligations in every state and to wind it down. When he backed out, he was funding an office in every state, and campaign chairmen were in the process of being hired in every state. The paradoxical part was that the Dallas campaign apparatus was in a shutdown mode, even as the new organization, United We Stand America, was being formed. One of the commitments Perot made to the state leaders was that he would allocate $7,500 a month to the start-up of the state UWSA organizations. He would, over the next few weeks, spend much more than that to complete the ballot process in the few remaining states.

The Dallas phone bank went from seventy-two phones to forty-eight very quickly. Bill Frost, the administrator brought in by Mort Meyerson in late June, began laying people off. On the day Perot backed out, there were 178 people on the payroll. As Frost said, "It was a locomotive that had to stop." The first person he fired was his daughter, Karen Frost, who worked in the press operation. Frost was responsible for all the inventory—computers, cellular phones and the data base. He had been hired to watch over Perot's money, and none of the equipment nor the data base or files would be walking out of there if Frost could help it. In an even more assertive exercise of what happened when the Rollins people left, Frost moved aggressively to shut down the computers and phones, to seize the equipment and protect the data base. Among other equipment, more than one hundred cellular phones had to be accounted for. Within two-and-a-half weeks, he had the staff down to thirty-eight people. The joke among the paid staffers was, who would get "Frosted" that day.

Some of the field staff was being retained, however, because of the decision to continue trying to get Perot on the ballot in fifty states. And, even as they were gearing down, the diehards didn't feel their mission was over.

During the first week after Perot got out, Gloria de la Cruz, the Hispanic outreach person on staff, dealt with the "feeling of utter defeat." During the second week she said, "it was very clear to me that Perot was about to give us another mission." The focus was going from Phase I to Phase II.

In the vast phone bank room, a new sign had been hung that said: "The Second Wave Has Begun."

Meanwhile, the principal focus of John P. White, the former Kodak executive and issues guru, was to convince Perot to release the economic plan that he had been working on for two-and-a-half months.

His reaction to Perot's withdrawal was "anger and disappointment." When he heard the reasons, he said, "It was like, 'C'mon.'" Perot's main, publicly stated reasons were that the Democratic Party had revitalized itself and his candidacy would throw the election into the House, disrupting the process. "I don't think he lied.

I think it was true; it was just not very important in terms of why he did it," White said. White believed Perot quit because he was "just so upset about the press, particularly the press around his children, and he had a campaign that wasn't going well. It was going very badly from the point of view of the inability to put together a real campaign that somehow integrated this enormous grass roots groundswell with any sort of a professionally managed campaign."

White saw an inability to reconcile the volunteer effort with the professional campaign. Most of the volunteers had turned in their petitions, and there was nothing for them to do, and that became a problem. "You have the enthusiasm but you also have the uncontrollable nature of volunteers. Then you have all this positioning in volunteer organizations by people who see it as an opportunity to be somebody important."

White—who had been a top official in the Carter Administration—had joined Perot because he believed Perot was in the race for the right reasons. He was concerned about raising the level of the debate—"not that he didn't have a big ego, you could tell that by talking to him, and you knew that by his history." White's Democratic friends had cautioned him against getting involved. "People would say to me, 'He's in some ways a little strange.' I would say, 'Have you ever met Jimmy Carter?' People who run for president tend to be a little strange."

When Perot retreated, White admitted, "I was angry. But it seemed to me the important thing from my point of view was that I wanted the economic plan out. I thought it was important, and if anything was going to be salvaged from this campaign, we ought to do the economic plan, and we ought to do the book as well."

The economic plan had been finalized the day before Perot stepped down. White had met all morning on July 15 in his conference room with Luce, Meyerson, Squires, Jordan and Bob Peck. Peck was a young Rhodes Scholar member of the staff at the Perot Group who had some experience working on Capitol Hill and who had been drafted by Perot to work on the issues team. The team had all the details of the economic plan, plus charts, ready for Perot's approval. When Perot came in, White went through the actual tables of the deficit reduction with him, and Perot did some modifying and fine-tuning.

The method for getting the plan out was to be a thirty-minute television address by Perot, delivered between the Democratic and Republican National Conventions. Perot would buy the TV time. The staff had been preparing the speech by video-taping it, with John White playing the role of Perot. At the end of the speech, Perot was to say, "I understand all this is complicated, but you can read about it in my book which will be on the newsstands tomorrow."

Even though the plan was virtually finished, there had been considerable turmoil because of Rollins's exit with all of his people. White met around 7:00 p.m. the evening of the Rollins departure with Jordan, Squires, Luce and Meyerson. They talked about what the campaign was going to be like with Rollins and camp gone, and how they could get over the immediate trauma. "It was all very positive. In fact, there was some desire to have Ross postpone some appearance he was going to make that weekend. Given where we were, we thought we'd better get our act together." Meyerson called Perot from the war room, and when he hung up, said, "That's funny, he agreed right away. He just said, 'Okay.'"

Over the last two-week period, there had been clear agreement on the part of Perot and the senior staff people—White, Jordan, Luce, Meyerson, Squires and Rollins—"that we were going to go for it, that we were going to give this very deep deficit reduction plan that would be the centerpiece of the issues in the campaign," White said. The first time Jordan saw the speech and realized how deeply it did go and the sacrifices required, he turned to White and said, "My God, White, where are we all going to work?"

The economic plan was the main body of work emanating from the efforts of White and his issues staff over the ten-week period. White had packed up and moved to Dallas, into a furnished apartment, in early May. Although he had been deputy director of the Office of Management and Budget, and a former assistant secretary of defense in the Carter Administration, the enormous size of the task only hit him when he arrived in Dallas. "Here you were plugging in a computer, and you think, Oh my God, not only don't I have any help, not only am I six to nine months behind, but I can't even go to the usual sources." Being neither fish nor fowl at the time—neither Democrat nor Republican—he would have no entrée to Capitol Hill. White devised a two-pronged approach. First he would quickly hire a dozen new graduates from the best graduate schools in public policy, recommended by their advisers. Second, he would appeal to experts around the country for their advice. The staff was in place in two weeks. The recent graduates came to Dallas and were housed by Perot, two to an apartment. Finally, White said, the determination was made that the issues to be dealt with would be limited. Perot's priorities were economic issues, mainly the deficit and job creation.

White called more than one hundred policy experts at universities, public policy institutes and "think tanks," and received only one refusal to his plea for assistance. He went to people who were concerned about policy; they didn't have to support Ross Perot. He assured them their names would be kept private and told them, "I just want to know what's the best stuff on the deficit, what's the best stuff on job creation, what we should be talking about. That turned out to be marvelously successful," White said. Information also was just coming in "over the transom." People were calling, sending in material and dropping in, asking to present data on specific issues.

As a result of the research White and his staff were doing, Perot would repeatedly say that he didn't have to reinvent the wheel, that there were "plenty of good plans" available—all of which White was assembling.

In addition to budget issues, however, analysts were assigned to work on such issues as political reform, governmental reorganization, investment, education reform, inner cities, crime and drugs, health care reform, abortion, race, trade and foreign trade. Richard Fisher, a Dallas investments banker who had worked in the Carter administration and who was active in the international community, stepped in as the foreign policy adviser.

The position papers being developed by the policy staff were given to Wick Allison, who was hired to draft the issues book on a quick, three-week turnaround. A process that White thought worked beautifully was viewed by Allison with some disdain, however. The recent graduates ranged from conservative Republican in philosophy to what Allison called "leftists," so there was a considerable amount of wrangling when these young policy analysts were thrown together. "They all had the opportunity to edit each other, so they were crossing out each other's paragraphs," Allison said.

Allison said the meetings he observed were baffling. The senior staff was preparing for a speech. The "students" were preparing position papers. "The only thing Perot contributed," he said, was to ask "where are the charts and graphs?" Allison took the position papers and Perot's speeches back to his hotel room, cut and pasted according to subject matter and, he said, "proceeded to make it up." But he proceeded to make up a little too much. Squires and others thought Allison tried to put his own imprint on the plan, to inject his own ideology, which they thought was more conservative in some instances than Perot's. They edited the book. According to White and Fisher, the gist of the book came from the position papers developed by the issues staff, with Fisher contributing the last chapter, the foreign policy chapter.

The penultimate draft of the book was reviewed very carefully by Perot, to put it in his own voice. He made changes and additions, and personally wrote the foreword and titled the book, *United We Stand: How We Can Take Back Our Country*. Perot went through it "line by line, making copious comments," Fisher said.

White met with Perot in two or three very long sessions, principally on the issues of budget and economics. "We didn't get a lot of his time, so we did a lot of this on the fly," he said. In the early going, Perot was still enjoying the campaign mode, caught up in the media appearances. If there were frustrations for the policy staff, it was that there wasn't much guidance from Perot. "I think the hardest part was probably trying to get it right with very little guidance—what really he wanted and what he was going to be comfortable with. There were a lot of areas where he never did really want to get specific." One such area, for example, was gun control. As White put it, "He's against people shooting people, but tell me more. The answer is, you don't really get any more." On abortion, for example, Perot's original comments had to do with every life being precious and "We're not rabbits. People shouldn't be getting high, getting it on and having babies for which they refused to accept responsibility." However, he was pinned down on the abortion issue by Barbara Walters, saying a woman has the right to make the decision about her body, which followed in large measure his wife's strong belief in planned parenthood. That was one of the issues Allison tried to balance with his own philosophy.

The good part, however, was that there were no constraints on White. "There weren't any constituencies that had to be protected. That was very, very helpful."

A couple of weeks before he withdrew, Perot met with White, Peck and Luce, and was presented with five or six notebooks on different issues. White intended to "work through these issues" with Perot and obtain his guidance. Perot didn't want to do it that way. He felt there wasn't enough time. He wanted to focus on the economy and jobs. "Let's get that one right," Perot told White. So they proceeded, laser-beam-like, on the economic plan.

White, the former Kodak executive, was more than reluctant to see all that work go down the drain after Perot stepped aside. He believed the economic plan could provide a real contribution to the political dialogue, and wanted Perot to go ahead and release it, even though he was no longer a candidate. He talked with the other senior staff members and "lobbied to make that happen."

Likewise, there was interest among the volunteers in the issues. On the day after Perot stepped down, a phone bank volunteer was adamant in demanding that the issues book be produced. "This morning I woke up and I said to myself, 'Well, I don't think he is going to come back.' But what about the issues? They had a bunch of hotshot guys in the back there studying the issues. They were about to publish the issues book. I want to know what they found out, what about the issues? We have a right to know what they found out," she said.

On the Saturday morning after his Thursday morning withdrawal statement, Perot called White at his apartment and said he wanted to release the plan. Several news outlets had expressed interest in getting the details of the plan. White and Squires negotiated with *U.S. News* for the exclusive release. Why *U.S. News*? They wanted it to appear in a weekly instead of daily because they felt the writers and editors would have greater understanding of the issues, and the plan would get a better presentation. The *U.S. News*'s David Gergen was one of those who expressed interest; Perot liked him, and he was respected by the other professionals. Finally, it's a magazine that likes "numbers" issues. "It just seemed like a comfortable match," White said. Perot granted the news magazine a two-hour interview on the plan.

U.S. News headlined its story in the August 3, 1992 issue: "Ross Perot's bitter tonic—An exclusive look at the economic plan that could shape the debate." The story said:

> "The timing may be anticlimactic, but the contents aren't: In an act of utter fiscal daring, Perot's plan...would transform this year's estimated $340 billion budget gap into an $8 billion surplus by

1998. Over five years, it would raise more than $300 billion in new taxes on everything from cigarettes to health insurance. It would also slay a thundering herd of political sacred cows—hiking taxes on Social Security benefits, slashing Medicare, curbing deductions on pricey home mortgages and generally offending everyone from the low-income elderly to the prosperous upper middle class. In short, it's just the sort of plan no candidate has ever come close to proposing, for fear that voters would automatically say no."

U.S. News noted that Perot's package represented a blunter, more realistic approach to reducing the deficit, while Bush and Clinton were clinging to variations of the theme that the budget deficit would shrink gradually as the economy grew. Bush would grow the economy by enacting a passel of tax breaks and controls on entitlement spending, while Clinton would stimulate economic growth by spending far more federal dollars on educating people and rebuilding infrastructure.

According to *U.S. News*, Perot's "biggest contribution may be his frank admission that the budget problem can't possibly be solved without braking the growth of so-called mandatory programs like Social Security, Medicare and Medicaid, which now account for about half of all federal spending." His plan called for taxing 85 percent of Social Security benefits, instead of 50 percent, for all individual recipients with incomes of over $25,000 a year or $32,000 for couples, and for lifting the cap on Medicare taxes paid by Americans with incomes over $130,000 a year.

Perot also proposed increasing the highest income tax bracket from 31 percent to 33 percent (affecting individuals who make over $55,500 a year and joint filers who make over $89,250); taxing a portion of health insurance benefits given by employers to their workers; doubling the federal cigarette tax; and reducing the deductibility of business entertainment expenses from 80 percent to 50 percent. As first proposed by Paul Tsongas, Perot called for increasing the gasoline tax by ten cents a year for five years, to conserve energy and reduce pollution as well as raise revenue.

On the spending side, Perot proposed cutting defense an additional $40 billion over Bush's 1993 budget request; cutting 10 percent in all other federal discretionary programs; cutting the space station and weapons systems such as the Seawolf submarine; eliminating programs such as the Rural Electrification Agency, which had outlived its usefulness; reducing subsidies to large corporate farmers; and drastically cutting the White House and executive branch staffs. One target for executive-slashing would be the Department of Agriculture, which had grown from sixty-seven thousand employees when farms employed 20 percent of the population to 188,000 employees with farms employing 2 percent of the population.

The Perot plan proposed to save $52.8 billion in Medicare and Medicaid spending in the fiscal year 1998 through cost containment, but failed to explain how those costs would be reined in.

Once the plan was released, everyone's attention turned to getting the book published. After Perot withdrew, Wick Allison wrote what he called a "long, unconvincing introduction" on why Perot dropped out of the race. It was cut. The introduction made no mention of the aborted presidential race. As soon as he got back the edited version, Allison said, "I knew he was going to get back in the race."

White didn't see it that way. He knew that it was "clearly a possibility, but I didn't assume the decision had been made." He believed that "once he had quit, he had quit." And White was aware of all the work left undone, the issues left unresolved, the incompleteness of the platform. "I knew that everything else was unfinished, we boxed it all up," White said, referring to the research into the other policy areas. "We didn't have health. We didn't have education, and even in campaign finance reform, we didn't have details of how it would all work. We didn't have governmental reform that we had been working on. We were working on stuff on inner cities and crime; we didn't have that done."

The book emphasized the economic plan—specifics for deficit reduction and jobs creation. It also included some governmental reform, and a short chapter on race and abortion. To White, it was all incomplete, except for the economic plan. The foreign policy chapter was based on the concept that a strong foreign policy depended on economic strength at home. It called for replacement of doctrines of the 1940s, burden sharing by allies who still enjoy protection at U.S. expense, and consistent policies toward rogue governments.

In June, Perot had been given a two-hour foreign policy briefing by former President Nixon, but many of the foreign policy ideas were contributed by Richard Fisher.

Among the political and governmental reforms proposed in the book were restricting campaign contributions to $1,000, curbing political action committees, altering the structure of the Federal Election Commission and eliminating the electoral college. Perot wanted to cut out the perks from both the executive and legislative branches and pass tougher ethics laws.

The publisher, Hyperion, whose enthusiasm waned once Perot dropped out of the race, agreed to print two hundred thousand copies if Perot would buy one hundred thousand for distribution himself. Perot went on television during the Republican National Convention to explain the plan and announce the release of his book. Republicans and reporters alike speculated that Perot wanted to intrude on their convention in Houston just as he had on the Democrats in New York. That wasn't the case, White said. "We just wanted to get it out as fast as we could." And Perot had originally promised that he would have his "platform" out when the others did. And the others would put theirs out at their conventions.

The book took off like a rocket. The publisher was into extra printings before the week was out, and was asking Perot to promote the book. Perot said, "Why should I do that—you can't buy it." Stores across the country were sold out.

It took White three weeks to complete his work in Dallas, and then he returned to Rochester. But because of interest in the plan, he remained on Perot's payroll and spent basically full-time the next month doing talk shows, being interviewed by the media, sending people the plan and answering questions about it.

The speculation was that the plan never would have seen the light of day if Perot had not withdrawn. Analysts were calling it the program of a man who's not running. White saw no evidence, however, that Perot got out of the race because he couldn't stand the heat that the plan would have generated had he still been a candidate. "He was told by Hamilton and others that when you put this plan out, you're going to go down in the numbers. But because it is credible, because it's consistent with what you've been saying, and because it's more specific than anybody else's, you will gain a lot of credibility and come back in the polls."

Except for the TV address touting his book, Perot kept a low profile during most of August. By then, the support staff was down to a skeleton crew. The "Pentagon" had been thoroughly dismantled. Ham Jordan, Tom Luce, Jim Squires and Bill Frost were gone. Mort Meyerson was working full-time as chief executive officer of Perot Systems.

By the second week in August, the phone bank had moved downstairs into what had been the media room, which had been designed to be a central part of the campaign. The floor was wired for satellite relay. The phone bank operated with sixteen phones. The Dallas volunteer center continued to operate under the guidance of Charlene McClary, Kay Bickham and Jean Ann Reed. And the beat went on. The new United We Stand America folks were forming their organizations and efforts to finish up the petition process went right ahead.

When Perot withdrew, however, all hell began to break loose in many of the states. One of them was New York, the state that was scheduled to begin its petition drive the day Perot backed out. Right after the announcement, the headquarters in New York City was a mess, according to Manhattan organizer Kurt Koenig. The man who was running the petition drive was "tearing down posters and kicking things." An aide to Governor Bill Clinton called to ask if Clinton could come over from the Democratic Convention and express his sympathy. Matthew Lifflander, chairman of the executive committee, appeared on a platform with Clinton before the nominee left the city, giving him the backing of New York's People for Perot. Koenig was miffed because he knew that Lifflander could "only give himself over."

"The only thing that held it together," Koenig said, "was the petition drive."

Some thirty diehard New York supporters decided to go ahead with the petition drive; a meeting was called and about two hundred faithful showed up, from upstate and downstate New York. "People were fighting and screaming," Koenig said. Forty thousand New Yorkers were expected to carry petitions the first day. After Perot got out, perhaps as many as two thousand volunteers remained. To complicate matters, some of the defectors were listed on the petitions as electors. So the original petitions had to be junked. New electors had to be found, and Perot had to be convinced to pay the $30,000 cost to print new petitions. By the time they were printed, it was four weeks from deadline. While the law required twenty thousand valid signatures, Koenig said five times that amount would be needed to insure against those that might be thrown out.

New York was the toughest state in the country in which to gain ballot access. The law requires that one hundred signatures come from at least half of the congressional districts in the state. "That sounds fairly simple," said Koenig. But the technical requirements enable any political group to keep someone off the ballot, he said. No independent had ever qualified for the New York ballot; John Anderson ran as a party in 1980. "If they want to keep you out, they can keep you out. No one can satisfy all the requirements," Koenig said. "New York election law is still very undemocratic."

The first week of the drive, Koenig stood in Grand

Central Station, where he said he was "figuratively spit on" by more people than signed. "They were laughing, ridiculing me. It was humiliating. I thought, I can't last much longer." Koenig sent a fax to Dallas asking for help. Perot agreed to fund an advertising campaign. When it started having an impact, Koenig said, "we were down to two weeks to go and we had only fifteen thousand to sixteen thousand signatures."

The organization was in chaos. People were writing and calling Dallas and complaining; different ones were vying to be in control. "When I saw what was going on in our state, I knew it wasn't Dallas kicking people out, it was other volunteers kicking people out. A dozen people in the state tried to take control over the organization."

Orson Swindle likewise said he couldn't believe the turmoil that existed in almost every state organization when he stepped into a leadership role in United We Stand America. "In Florida, Oregon, Ohio, North Carolina, and California, two or three groups were at the point of killing each other. Factions were trying to gain power. I said, 'Folks, I don't know what you think power is, but this ain't power.' They were cutting each other's throats for no good reason."

In Florida, Pat Muth returned from the meetings in Dallas which followed the July 16 announcement and had to close 138 local offices. She kept working out of her home. And while new people were trying to volunteer "even as we were closing the doors," the original followers were launching splinter groups.

"Part of those who fell off went on to create other kinds of groups, many at the local level. Some lasted through the summer, some didn't," she said. "Some are still operating."

Volunteers in states across the country were demanding that Perot pay their phone bills and reimburse them for the cost of campaign souvenirs and paraphernalia. Shutting down wasn't easy.

After July 16 in New York, Koenig said, "What was left was a bunch of little splinter groups. Everyone was dancing to their own drummer."

Dallas sent about half of its remaining field staff, which was then about fifteen, to New York, along with some volunteers, to help. Temporary workers were hired from local employment agencies, and the volunteers and staff members began working as supervisors over the temps. In the final two weeks, Mike Poss from Perot's staff was overseeing the New York petition drive.

One of the staffers sent up from Dallas was Gloria de la Cruz. "I've never done anything in my life as hard as that was," she said. Every morning, the "supervisors" had to be up by 4:30 or 5:00 a.m. to get the petitions boxed up, the volunteers trained and out to their positions, carrying all their gear, including their Perot signs, on the subway. Then they had to convince people to sign the petitions. A lot of the temps quit, and the supervisors had to check on them every hour, to make sure they were still at their locations. When people were asked to sign a petition, a typical response was: "What for, man? He's out." At night, the petitions had to be checked and materials prepared for the next morning.

de la Cruz worked several days in the financial district and recalled a typical conversation on the street. "All of these Wall Street guys in their Gucci shoes and Brooks Brothers and Italian suits—obviously very successful people of great dignity—would stop and say:

'How can you do this?'

'Do what, sir?'

'How can you be for this man?'
'But sir, we believe in this man's message.'
'But look at what he did to you.'
'Yes, sir, but the message is still the same. Why are we doing this for him? We have high hopes if we honor our end of the bargain, he might honor his. We don't want to lose that opportunity.'"

"I was fascinated by that," she said. "It happened so many times."

One morning, after positioning her teams of temps, de la Cruz stopped to get a cup of coffee. A woman walked into the coffee shop, saying, "Can you believe this? All these Perot ding-a-longs are back out on the street. These ding-a-longs are everywhere."

The ding-a-longs got Perot on the ballot in New York. On August 28, the boxes of petitions were bused to Albany, where they were accepted.

Why was Perot let on, given New York's ability to deny access to anyone the political establishment desired? Insiders say that gaining ballot access depends in large measure on the governor's position, and Governor Mario Cuomo was never anti-Perot. There was speculation that Cuomo was a vice-presidential possibility on a Perot ticket, although he denied it. Democratic leaders in the state capital also believed that Perot would take away from George Bush and the Republican ticket, so it was to their advantage to have him on the ballot. Contrary to widespread press reports, Koenig said he saw no evidence that there was ever an elaborate Republican plan to keep Perot off the ballot.

The question anyone might ask was why would Kurt Koenig, a well-educated (Berkeley graduate), thirty-five-year-old financial officer for a New York advertising agency, remain steadfast and continue the effort even after Perot dropped the ball? "It was never about him in the first place," he said. "It was about the voters taking the country back. We still needed to take our country back, and we needed to have his name on the ballot to do that."

Koenig first began paying attention to Ross Perot in 1986, when General Motors bought him out. At the time, he was working on Wall Street as a broker. GM had just laid off fifty thousand employees and yet had paid Perot $750 million to get him off the board. Perot had said GM was paying him three times the value of his stock "because they're tired of listening to me. That's what's wrong with America." Koenig said, "He won my heart, right then and there."

Koenig and his partner at the ad agency, Charles Donnelly, decided to try to get in touch with Perot in early 1992 after seeing him on TV to see if he would be interested in sponsoring an ad program designed to acquaint people with issues leading to the '92 election. Perot returned the call, and Koenig discussed the ad campaign they proposed to run in the print media. Perot told Koenig he thought the print media were history. He was insistent that the only way to reach the American people was through television, particularly through an avenue by which they could respond—talk shows and the electronic town hall.

In March 1992 Perot was in New Jersey to appear on a call-in show with a studio audience at WOR, the Universal Station. Koenig and Tom O'Neill, an organizer from New Jersey, rode together to the airport in Perot's car. Koenig asked Perot about his concept of the electronic town hall and whether Perot believed Congress was still needed if there is the capability of going directly to the people for decisions on policy. "Of course, we need Congress," Perot said. "The people just need to have their voice in the process, too."

"That is when it occurred to me that the Perot phenomenon was a political revolution. He was trying to add the fifth branch. We have the legislative, executive, judicial, and the press—whether it's in the constitution or not. He wants to create the Fifth Estate. He wants to put voters into day-to-day decision making in government," Koenig said. "Did he realize it was a political revolution? Maybe not. We weren't going to hang anybody. I think he got duped into thinking he could win, he could succeed in being president. One thing we all learned is that revolutions don't come from the inside; you have to continue to fight from the outside."

From New York, some of the field staff flew to Hawaii to work in the petition drive there. Gloria de la Cruz went to Austin, Texas, where the Perot petition effort began, for a rally on her way to help with the petition drive in Arizona, where it would end. She told supporters there, "We're not just witnessing history, we're making history. The fruits of our labor will be culminated in Arizona."

Meanwhile, many of Perot's prior supporters were bouncing around, trying to determine which candidate to support in the fall. According to a story in the *Dallas Morning News*, "Nearly two months after Mr. Perot pulled the plug on his independent presidential bid, interviews showed that his supporters have not enthusiastically embraced either remaining candidate. But they remain strikingly dedicated to transforming American politics."

Quoted in the story was former Perot supporter Bob McCarthy of Denver. "If the car is out of control and you're in a neighborhood that doesn't have any cliffs, you can sit back and sort of hide. But if you're going off a cliff, you've got to do something...You can't sit in the back seat anymore."

The question was, how much longer Perot would sit in the back seat? Appearing on ABC's "Good Morning America" on August 25 to promote the issues book, Perot was asked about returning to the race. "I think it's very remote, not even worth talking about," he said. "The thing that is worth talking about is how you get the system to work."

In early September, however, Sharon Holman was telling press inquiries that "to be sure, the door is still open."

Others were making the same interpretation. Mark Petracca, associate professor of political science at the University of California at Irvine, said Perot "clearly left the door open" to coming back in. In Irvine, which earlier had been a hotbed of Perotism, he said volunteers were "acting as if Perot is still very much a part of the race."

Sharon Holman said Perot's decision would depend on whether the two candidates proposed realistic ways to deal with the deficit. But it was apparent that the nominees were not concentrating on the issues that concerned him, namely the deficit. The Republicans had staged a convention which focused on family values. Much more attention was paid at the GOP convention to Congress-bashing, media-bashing and Hillary-bashing than to economic issues. In his acceptance speech, George Bush presented only one new economic proposal—an optional income tax return checkoff for funds to be dedicated to the deficit—a move the cynics immediately labeled as a gimmick. Bill Clinton and his running mate, Al Gore, meantime, had participated in some enormously successful bus tours of the country, where they were succeeding in getting in touch with the people. But heading into the fall campaign, Clinton was campaigning cautiously, trying to sit on his lead—he was ahead by eleven to twelve points in the polls when the Republican convention ended—and avoiding any risk-taking that would include talking about economic sacrifice.

Perot was beginning to reemerge. On September 10, he toured areas of Florida recently damaged by Hurricane Andrew and the next day appeared on C-Span. Petitions had been submitted in forty-nine states. He was waiting to hear if they had been accepted in New York and Hawaii, and Arizona petitioning was underway. At that time, Perot was maintaining sixty-four field offices at a cost of $48,000 a month, in addition to the Dallas headquarters. And speculation had begun about an "October surprise." He was asked about it by C-Span's Brian Lamb.

"That is certainly not our objective," he said. "There is no chance that I would do it unilaterally. ...(But) if after we do everything we can to get the parties to face the issues—and if they won't—if the volunteers said, 'It's a dirty job, you've got to do it,' I will belong to them."

Ex-campaign manager Ed Rollins told *The New York Times*, "The only way he saves his reputation is to jump in again, and there's nobody left in Dallas to tell him not to do it." To the contrary, he was getting the opposite advice.

Orson Swindle went from Hawaii to Arizona to meet with volunteers and consummate the end of the petition drive, as Arizona became the fiftieth state to submit petitions on September 18. Arizona volunteers had collected seventy-seven thousand signatures in nine days. With the end of the drive in Arizona, more than five million voters had signed petitions in the fifty states to get Perot on the ballot. From Arizona, Swindle returned to Dallas, where he talked to Perot.

Swindle told Perot, "I can explain away what you did in July. But, Ross, we just got you on the ballot in the fifty states. You said you would run; I don't know how to explain that away. Your personal reputation is at stake. Hundreds of thousands of people busted their butts for you. They deserve for you to go out and run. And, frankly, these two turkeys nominated are not talking about the issues." He recalls Perot saying, "Let's think about it."

At that time, according to an NBC-*Wall Street Journal* poll, Perot was viewed negatively by 43 percent of the people and positively by only 24 percent. In a three-way race, Perot garnered only 18 percent support, down from 33 percent in the same poll in July. Still, however, two-thirds of those polled said the country was on the "wrong track," and 40 percent said they were worse off than they had been four years before. Clearly, the dissatisfaction was still there, but Perot had a lot of repair work to do to be a viable candidate, if he got back in the race.

Speculation was that Perot's strategy was simply to get out of the line of fire, to elude the media scrutiny for the rest of the summer, and then to run in the fall. Swindle remained unconvinced. "He is a cunning, intelligent man with great intuition. But I honestly saw no evidence that was a plan of his...As we approached October, I'm watching him, and I'm not convinced he wants to do this thing."

It was clear, however, that Perot had been thinking about it and, in some ways, was even getting ready for it. His old friend, Murphy Martin, who was working on television advertising when Hal Riney left the campaign, continued throughout the summer. He had been filming and interviewing people whose lives had been touched by Perot—unknown stories about people he had helped, including some POWs and their families. Murphy also did a number of interviews with Perot, on his life and on business, and with family members.

Martin's days with Perot went back to 1969 when, as an anchorman for the local ABC affiliate, WFAA-TV, he accompanied Perot to Hanoi on his first POW mission. In January 1970, Martin resigned his news job to become president of the original United We Stand, the corporation Perot had created in 1969. That United We Stand was formed to promote a grass roots movement to pressure the North Vietnamese to free the POWs. It existed until sometime in 1973. Perot was interested then in the concept of the electronic town hall, and Martin put together one TV program with astronaut Frank Borman and some of the POW wives. Under the aegis of United We Stand, the POW wives went to dozens of cities, stimulating a mail campaign, and made two trips to Europe. Martin later opened a small media consulting business and continued over the years to do work intermittently for Perot, including putting together an audio library of interviews with POWs, family members and government officials for Perot's personal records.

During the summer of '92, while Perot was out of the presidential race, Martin put together a number of commercials "in case he needed them, in case he decided to get back in the race. We had fifteen or twenty spots ready so he would not be caught short." They ranged from two minutes to five minutes to a half hour. Martin worked steadily throughout August, while Perot was out of the race.

But there was a parallel effort going on at the same time to see if Perot could get on TV with issue-oriented advertising, without getting back in the race. According to Clay Mulford, the attorney and Perot's son-in-law, the idea was that Perot would buy the time to offer prominent individuals an opportunity to speak from various viewpoints on five or six major national issues. Overtures were made to Senator Warren Rudman and former Senator Paul Tsongas to appear. "We would sponsor the programs. We assembled lists of people to be heard on jobs, health care and other issues," Mulford said. Perot, he said, "did not anticipate reentering the race." Inquiries were made to the broadcast networks and, after some legal wrangling back and forth, they found it wasn't workable. They were not inclined to sell Perot time because he was not a candidate.

Jim Squires, who was still on Perot's payroll doing some consulting and some media work from his horse farm in Kentucky, was convinced that Perot's major objective was to get his message on TV in October. Squires had met with Perot the day after he got out of the race on July 16, and they had talked about whether to stay on the ballot and finish the process in fifty states. "If he stayed on the ballot, he could run his ads in the fall and give people who felt strongly about it somebody to vote for. He could finish the economic plan and the book. At least he would be following through on his commitment," Squires said. "He wanted to spend his money and get on TV in October. But they wouldn't let him buy ads because he wasn't a candidate. About that time, he got on all the ballots."

On September 18, the day he wrapped up ballot access in fifty states with Arizona, Perot appeared on the "Today" show, where he said: "If the television networks will sell me time, I'm going to be talking about this economy big time....Interestingly enough, I'm trapped, they won't sell it to me unless I declare as a candidate. So I may be the first guy in history that had to declare as a candidate so he could buy TV time....So I may declare so I can buy time, the lawyer's working on it now. It's a funny world out there that you're forced to become a candidate to explain to the American people what these problems are."

14

MOUNTAIN TO MOHAMMED— BACK IN THE RACE

ON SEPTEMBER 15, 1992, the *Wall Street Journal* published a front-page article headlined, "The Fiscal Proposals of Bush and Clinton Both Flunk Arithmetic." Alan Murray began his story this way: "Is it too much to expect presidential candidates to be able to add?" The story essentially said that the economic plans put forward by George Bush and Bill Clinton failed to add up.

"Even if generous allowances are made for election-year hyperbole and estimating differences, both programs are promising hundreds of billions of dollars more in tax cuts, spending increases and deficit reduction than their specific proposals will pay for," the *Journal* said. Neither candidate, according to the story, "is giving voters—or the financial markets—grounds to expect real progress in shrinking the nation's $300 billion-plus annual budget deficit, which both agree is hobbling the country's long-term growth prospects."

Republican Senator Warren Rudman of New Hampshire was quoted as saying, "There's no question that the issue not being discussed in real detail in this campaign is A, the size of the deficit, and B, what is it doing to the economy."

The *Journal* took President Bush to task for saying he would balance the budget without raising any taxes, while proposing a variety of new spending programs and tax cuts. His spending cuts amounted to only $130 billion, compared to the $570 billion the *Wall Street Journal* said would be needed to balance his budget. Shortfall: $440 billion.

As for Governor Clinton, it said he was willing to consider tax increases and deeper defense cuts, but the money saved on defense would go for new investment in education and infrastructure. Clinton proposed only $142 billion in deficit reduction over current projected levels, and his proposal for health care reform was projected to leave a "jumbo-size" hole in his economic plan. Shortfall: $359 billion.

The *Journal* concluded that "only one presidential candidate this year has come close to proposing an economic plan that adds up, and that's Texas billionaire Ross Perot. His proposal was an eclectic blend of tax boosts and spending cuts, including a fifty-cent-a-gallon rise in the gas tax and a steep rise in the premiums paid for Medicare benefits." And that plan came after he got out of the race.

It was just the ammunition Perot had been looking for, to try to hold the party nominees' feet to the fire one final time, or to justify his own return to the race.

In an appearance on CBS's "This Morning" on September 22, he set the stage for his reentry. He said quitting the race had been a mistake because the other candidates really had not addressed the issues. That same day, Perot met separately with White House Chief of Staff James Baker (the former secretary of state brought in to shore up the White House staff for the campaign) and Democratic National Chairman Ron Brown. NBC's

Bob Sirkin reported that Perot was putting the president's chief campaign strategist on notice that he was coming back to deal with issues such as the deficit that Bush was ignoring. The meeting with Brown was designed to send the same signal to Clinton.

Perot's Dallas staff had asked United We Stand leaders to poll volunteers in their states to find out if they wanted Perot to become a candidate. The next step would be to bring the fifty state chairmen together in Dallas over the weekend to give Perot their formal blessing for him to reenter the race. Never mind that Perot failed to consult with them before he exited the race in July.

A Federal Election Commission report issued that day showed that Perot had spent $17.6 million on his campaign up to that point in 1992, and that $4 million had been spent in August, his most expensive month.

The admission that he had made a mistake and the other activity set off a frenzy among supporters and the media that Perot was indeed on his way back in. John Jay Hooker, Perot's old supporter from Tennessee, told the *Detroit News*, he "never had any doubt" Perot would reenter the race. "In all probability, he's going to dramatically change the country...He's going to create a third party in America."

Republican analyst Kevin Phillips assessed the reasons Perot might get in on National Public Radio's "Morning Edition." "One of them is the negative publicity. I think he wants to recover his pride and his macho...to lay out his views on the economy and force the other two to try to move more in his direction....He carries a few chips on his shoulder as far as the way the White House (the Republicans) and Bush went after him in June, and I think he means to repay that."

As Perot was getting pressured to reenter the race, Squires thought that a better alternative would be to get one of the nominees, namely Clinton, to adopt his positions. Clinton aide James Carville had called Squires after Perot dropped out and asked what Clinton could do to get the support of Perot and his people. Squires told him to take Perot's positions. "No," Carville came back, "what kind of a job does he want in the Clinton administration?" Squires told him Perot didn't want a job. "To get United We Stand," Squires said, "you have to be candid about the deficit."

Perot decided to give the nominees one last chance to "beg" him off. If their own economic plans didn't add up, as the *Wall Street Journal* had said, then he would provide them with the details of a plan that did add up. He offered to send John P. White to discuss with them the details of his own economic plan. The Republicans never responded. The Clinton people, however, were interested. So John White went to Little Rock and went through the material with them. Essentially, he told them: One, tell the truth about the deficit. Two, acknowledge the need for new revenues; the budget can't be balanced simply with cost cutting. Three, take back previous claims that only people with incomes of $200,000 or more would be hit with tax increases.

Clinton bought about 85 percent of the Perot plan but, according to Squires, "the 15 percent he wouldn't take were the tough steps." So Perot decided to put on a big show to put pressure on Clinton to take the tough steps. He invited both parties to send envoys to Dallas to discuss deficit reduction with his state leaders and make whatever pitch they wanted to try to win over his supporters before they voted on whether he should return to the race.

Such an action was unprecedented. Both campaigns accepted Perot's invitation to send high-level emissaries to Dallas, hats in hand, to appear before Perot's ragtag army, outlining their candidates' economic views. The *Political Hotline* headlined its advance coverage of the meeting, "Come into My Parlor, Said the Spider to the Flies."

The Clinton delegation included campaign chairman Mickey Kantor, Senator Lloyd Bentsen of Texas, Senator David Boren of Oklahoma, former chairman of the Joint Chiefs of Staff William J. Crowe, financier Felix Rohatyn, Representative Nancy Pelosi of California and civil rights leader Vernon Jordan. The Bush team included campaign manager Robert Teeter, Senator Phil Gramm of Texas, Senator Pete Domenici of New Mexico, National Security Adviser Brent Scowcroft, Housing Secretary Jack Kemp, and campaign aide Mary Matalin.

It was a remarkable day, a testament to the political power of Perot and his people. That party leaders representing both national tickets would first consent to come to Dallas, and secondly, spend considerable time talking about economic policy with leaders of the independent movement was extraordinary.

Each delegation was given two hours to defend its candidate and economic platform, followed by a press conference by both teams. The press was excluded from the actual meetings, conducted at the Doubletree Hotel in North Dallas. Perot called the meetings "further confirmation of the validity of the town hall concept," and "democracy at its finest." He said the meetings were "just bright, intelligent people talking about the future of this country." Democrats, such as Senator Bentsen, played up the similarity of Clinton and Perot proposals. Felix Rohatyn noted that Clinton had a serious deficit reduction plan, only it was for 50 percent over four years while Perot would get the deficit down to zero. The difference in their approaches, he said, was "how hard you want to step on the brakes and how much growth you want to create." He noted the risk of "stepping on the brake too quickly and too hard...It's a very delicate exercise, how to step on the gas at the same time you step on the brake."

The Perot people emerging from the meetings said they thought the Democrats came better prepared and were taking the meeting more seriously than the Republicans. They said Perot and the Democrats appeared closer than Perot and the Republicans. According to Perot's New Mexico chief Jim Bishop, however, Jack Kemp became "so worked up" at one point that he urged, "Run, Ross, Run. Let the chips fall where they may."

Various press reports called the summit meeting a "spectacle unmatched in modern political history" and a "remarkable political pageant." CBS's Scott Pelley reported that "Perot played power broker in an unprecedented meeting....It was an audition in Perot's own smoke-filled room."

After the meeting, state coordinators would fan out across the country to engage in what the *Dallas Morning News*'s David Jackson called a "predictable political exercise: asking Ross Perot supporters whether Ross Perot should run for president." Bob Hayden of California said he believed Perot to be "totally committed to running, if the volunteers want him to." And that, for all the talk of polling the volunteers, appeared to be a foregone conclusion. The "polling" was little more than a formality.

Milling around in the hotel corridors, the state leaders said they wanted to report back to the volunteers in their states before taking a final survey on whether Perot should run. "As Ross says, we're going to measure twice, cut once," said Pat Muth of Florida. Texas chairman Jim Serur pointed out that whether Perot became an active candidate or not, he nonetheless would be on the ballot across the country. And the state leaders appeared unpersuaded that they should support either the Democrat or the Republican candidate. New Mexico Perot coordinator John Bishop said, "The question is: Who would make the best leader? I feel Ross Perot is the best leader and it would be good for the country to have an independent president."

William Schneider, a scholar at the American Enterprise Institute in Washington and a political analyst for CNN, said, "I think they'll do what the hell he wants. It all depends on signals from him. I mean, the whole thing is a charade." Schneider also accused Perot of "playing sort of the ayatollah" with everyone coming to seek his blessing.

The day was a fifteen-hour media marathon for Perot, which began with an interview on NBC's "Today" show, spanned four nationally televised press conferences and ended with an appearance on CNN's "Larry King Live," broadcast live from Dallas. "We've come to the mountain," King said of the show's visit to Dallas. CNN followed Perot's every move, providing live coverage of Perot's four news conferences, including the two conducted with the high-level Republicans and Democrats.

NBC political reporter Lisa Myers, reporting on "Today," told viewers that Monday's session largely constituted "political theater. As in all Perot productions, Ross Perot is producer, director and star. And at this point, only he knows how this melodrama will end."

The *Political Hotline*, however, suggested that "heads he runs and tails he runs." By late in the day on September 29, according to Perot and his staff, Perot's 800 number had received 1.5 million calls urging him to run. "No" votes were not recorded by the 800 number.

On October 1, Perot ended the melodrama, reviving his bid for the presidency in a Dallas press conference by apologizing for his July withdrawal and saying that the volunteers in all fifty states "have asked me to run as a candidate for president of the United States. Jim Stockdale, our vice-presidential candidate, and I are honored to accept their request."

Perot appeared with members of his family and Admiral Stockdale, the fellow Naval Academy graduate and celebrated POW who had been the senior Naval officer during his years of confinement at the Hanoi Hilton. Perot called Stockdale a "hero's hero" and a "man of steel." Stockdale's only previous involvement in presidential politics was running Ronald Reagan's California campaign in 1980, which merited him the honorary post overseeing White House fellowships during the Reagan Administration.

In his statement, Perot said: "I know I hurt many of the volunteers who worked so hard through the spring and summer when I stepped aside in July. I thought it was the right thing to do. I thought that both political parties would address the problems that face the nation. We gave them a chance. They didn't do it.

"My decision in July hurt you. I apologize....I made a mistake. I take full responsibility for it. Looking back won't solve any of our problems. Looking forward, working together, we can fix anything....The American people are good. But they have a government that is a mess."

Perot went on to say that the American people were concerned about a government they pay for that doesn't produce results, about a government where people go to Washington to cash in and not to serve. "They want the government changed so that people go as servants of the people back home and do not use government service as a stepping-stone to financial success."

"The people know that it is wrong to spend our children's money...We know that we cannot constantly pass on a $4 trillion debt to our children.

"The people are concerned that our goverment is still organized to fight the Cold War. They want it reorganized to rebuild America as the highest priority. In order to do that, the highest priority of all is to rebuild the job base and the industrial base. We must make the words 'Made in the U.S.A.' once again the world's standard for excellence."

Perot said that not only is government a mess, politics is a mess and the way political campaigns are run is a mess. "The people want a new political climate where the system does not attract ego-driven, power-hungry people."

Perot said, "These are the issues we'll talk about in the coming weeks. I will not spend one minute answering questions that are not directly relevant to the issues that concern the American people."

Perot left the lecturn after his statement, but returned ten minutes later after demands from the press that he answer some questions. The news conference was termed "raucous" by the *Dallas Morning News*'s David Jackson, featuring "frequent jousts" with reporters. There were loud snickers during Perot's announcement statement when he called for a system that does not attract "ego-driven" people. Perot showed that his contempt for the media had not dissipated during his political sabbatical. "Just have fun, get raises and bonuses, play gotcha. I don't care," he snapped at reporters. Perot gave no details on budgets or travel plans. "We're not going to lay out our strategy for you," he said. "It will be unconventional, I'll tell you that." Staff members, however, said the campaign would be largely conducted on television.

Indeed, the Perot campaign moved swiftly to buy half-hour blocks of network television time. His first purchase was made within ninety minutes of his reentry into the race. Perot paid $380,000 for the half-hour spot, according to a CBS spokeswoman. Perot also bought a half-hour on ABC at a cost described as "upwards of $500,000" on a time slot leading into the news magazine program "20/20."

Perot representatives contacted CBS, ABC and NBC earlier in the week about possible ad buys and were told Perot could not buy commercial time until he became an announced candidate. The networks do not allow private citizens, corporations or interest groups to air advocacy ads of a political nature. At that time, Murphy Martin said he had thirty-five to fifty TV spots ready to go, ranging from thirty seconds to thirty minutes on subjects ranging from the deficit to jobs, health care, gridlock in Washington and on Perot himself.

A *Wall Street Journal* editorial of October 2 addressed the heads of the three networks: "Gentlemen: If your policies on political (ads) weren't so restrictive, we all might have been spared the Ross Perot spectacle."

When Perot reemerged as a candidate, polls indicated he had only 7 percent support. A CNN-*USA Today* poll showed Clinton with 52 percent to Bush's 35 percent— a seventeen-point lead. Clinton's aides claimed not to be worried, but they were far less eager to see Perot enter the race than were Bush strategists. He was too much of a wild card, too much of a loose cannon, his impact too unpredictable. Clinton pollster Stan Greenberg, however, predicted that Perot's reentry would be "anticlimactic."

The Bush campaign almost welcomed his reemergence. Bush needed something to shake up the race, and Perot had the ability to do that. Republicans feared the election was getting dangerously close to the notion of inevitability—the inevitability that Bush could not win. Bush needed a jolt, whatever the source. One Bush campaign official said, "The race wasn't going anywhere for us. Now we have a window of opportunity to change their minds. It is not a guarantee, but it is at least an opening for us."

The most realistic assessment, however, was that Perot would draw attention away from President Bush at the very time he needed it most, and that he would create new geographic complications for the president's reelection efforts. Perot obviously would confound matters in two states viewed as the anchor to a Republican victory—Texas, with its thirty-two electoral votes, and Florida, with twenty-five electoral votes. With a big Perot vote in Texas, Bush conceivably could lose his home state. And Florida, where Jeb Bush was managing his father's campaign, was only leaning toward the Republican. Other states where Perot might impact the election included New Jersey, where Perot put Bush back in competition in a big suburban struggle; Michigan, where the bigger the Perot vote, the less certain the Clinton victory; and Pennsylvania, where Clinton would have to struggle to hold on to Reagan Democrats he had lured back to the party.

While some Republicans thought Perot's late candidacy provided their campaign a last-ditch opportunity to scramble the race, enabling Bush to somehow regain lost ground, others viewed him as simply a nuisance. Former Education Secretary William Bennett called him an "egotistical pest."

Others in the political and media mainstream believed Perot cared not a whit what his impact on the race was—that he simply wanted to get rid of the tag, "The Yellow Ross of Texas," repair his injured reputation and perhaps regain his own self-esteem. After he had abruptly quit the race in July, Perot received hundreds of little mirrors in the mail from angry supporters who demanded that he "look himself in the mirror."

The print media and the political pundits were not kind to Perot on his reentry. Michael Kramer writing in *Time* magazine called him a "paranoid hoist by his own self-regard." The *New York Daily News* subhead was "Ego Man fails reality check." *Boston Globe* columnist Ellen Goodman wrote that the billionaire Texan fancied himself a "thinking man's Rambo" who was on a "national rescue mission."

Goodman wrote: "From the beginning, Perot has talked about being captive by the two parties. On Thursday, he declared that 'the issues' were still languishing, gagged and bound in some hidden cell. With his bells and whistles, his talk shows and 800 numbers, his volunteers and dollars, his straight talk and his ideas, he wants to single-handedly free democracy from the parties' old grasp. All we have to do is tie a yellow ribbon round the old Perot tree. Again."

To be sure, the issues were still languishing. President Bush had made only one major economic address since the Republican convention—a September 10 speech to the Economic Club of Detroit in which he detailed a thirteen-point agenda to cut taxes and spending and restore the nation's economic vitality. In that speech, Bush drew the most complete picture of his own economic principles and what he wanted the economy to look like in the future. His *Agenda for American Renewal* was published for distribution, but Bush failed to make it a prominent part of his campaign speeches. It received scant attention as the political dialogue went on.

By getting back in the race, at least Perot could refocus the debate on the issues that mattered to him and should have mattered to everyone else. After all, none of the other issues would count in a country that lost its economic underpinnings. As he and his supporters had been saying since the onset of the Perot phenomenon, it matters not how you divide up the pie when there is no pie left to divide.

Goodman correctly saw, however, that Perot was reentering the race with a big wart on his nose—his abrupt July exit. "Across the country," she wrote, "people had left their jobs, upended their lives, to work for Perot. They had put Perot first. Unfortunately, so had Perot. In a critical decision, he behaved like the most ruthless businessman who closes the factory, abruptly, when the bottom line starts to fall. Workers be damned. If he treated his own people that way, with such personal disregard, how would he treat the country?"

Perot's reappearance obviously would be met with considerable skepticism. However, by getting out, he had managed to divert the press from continuing to riddle the legends of his life; he had gotten rid of the political professionals he abhorred; he had tamed an unwieldy network of volunteers, including purging the charlatans who were trying to either make money or gain power from his candidacy; and he had returned to a political time frame that was manageable. It would be a sprint to the finish, the kind of race he liked. In that sprint, he had the opportunity to repair his damaged image and to reinvigorate a new political movement that could impact the system beyond the November 3 election. There was no way that Perot would reenter the race as the powerful third force he was when he got out. But there were other compelling reasons—besides winning—for him to return.

And the question yet remained: Did Perot actually want to *be* president? John P. White believed not, and said so in a speech at American University the day Perot reentered the contest. Perot, he said, "doesn't want to be president of the United States," and never did. He said Perot simply wanted to bring his economic issues— including a plan to cut the U.S. budget deficit—into the debate.

When Perot got back into the race, it was with a new cast of characters. Longtime aides Tom Luce and Mort Meyerson had ended their active involvement in Perot's political career. Meyerson—who many said was the only person who could disagree with Perot and get away with it—had become chairman and chief executive officer of Perot Systems; Luce had returned to his law firm. Relations between Luce and Perot had become strained when, after Perot withdrew, Luce had accepted an invitation to the White House. Luce, a lifelong Republican, never shared Perot's animosity toward Bush and considered endorsing the President, but never did. One staff member explained that Perot "has a way of exhausting personal relationships." They had been emotionally spent by the first campaign.

Republican consultant Ed Rollins, of course, was out. He became a harsh critic, on television and in interviews with the print media, saying Perot didn't deserve a second chance. Rollins wrote a scathing indictment of Perot for the *The New York Times* op-ed page on the eve of Perot's reentry, in which he recalled that in his first meeting with Perot, he had written two words on a blackboard: "hope" and "kook." "I told him that for him to win, he would have to cast himself as the agent of hope. I also told him that every day, the Republicans and Democrats would attempt to cast him as a kook. Little did I know no one could make him look more kooky than he has himself." Rollins told anyone who would listen that Perot had offered him a half-million dollars to keep his mouth shut when he left the Perot I campaign and that he believed Perot was temperamentally unsuited to be president.

Democratic consultant Hamilton Jordan had returned to Whittle Communications in Knoxville, Tennessee, and was maintaining silence regarding the first campaign. He was still considered a friend by Perot, although he was uninvolved in the fall campaign, and had no further contact with Perot after leaving Dallas.

John White supported Perot through the day of the summit, when the emissaries from both parties came to Dallas. He was available in Dallas to answer questions from volunteers about positions taken by the Democrat and Republican leaders. The next morning he informed Perot that he couldn't remain on the team, and explained why. White said he had made a personal decision not to support Perot if he got back in the race. "It seemed to be wrong to be out for what was two-and-a-half months, and basically not to have any platform other than the economic plan," White said. "This was a man who had been standing around making quotes like, 'Don't quit' and 'Never give up.' I couldn't support him, knowing what he had done."

White said Perot was very gracious during a forty-five-minute conversation. "He said, 'All of us have to do what we have to do, and you've been very helpful to me. You've done good work, and I appreciate it.'" Perot was less gracious, however, when White, who went back to work for Eastman Kodak, openly endorsed Bill Clinton.

Jim Squires, the former communications director, remained on the Perot payroll and handled media inquiries from his Kentucky horse farm. He stayed in touch by phone, did some consulting for Perot, and wrote some advertising copy.

The new guard consisted of Clay Mulford, who would become the campaign manager; Sharon Holman, the press secretary; Orson Swindle, the head of United We Stand America; adman Murphy Martin and the Dallas advertising agency of Timerlin-McClain, which was headed by Perot's longtime friend, Lanier Timerlin.

Some of the original Young Turks from Perot businesses were still on board—including Mark Blahnik and Darcy Anderson. "It was humorous," Anderson said. Perot had sent his announcement statement around to a handful of staff members—Mulford, Swindle, Sharon Holman, Blahnik, Anderson and the other regional coordinators. "We had no advance preparation. Here it was October 1, and we had thirty days to run a campaign. I looked around the room and said, 'What do we do now?'"

Orson Swindle said he never intended to stay in Dallas during the fall, but "things just started spinning. I was just pushed out the door to talk to the media. Nobody was comfortable talking to the media." Once he returned to Dallas after Arizona became the fiftieth state to put Perot on the ballot, he never returned to Hawaii until after the election.

When Perot got back into the race, Swindle said Perot "obviously was going to do it by TV, but he wasn't sharing anything with us." Sharon Holman asked Swindle to talk to the reporters who were hanging around the headquarters.

"I told them, 'I'm an amateur. I would appreciate your suggestions. Do you want a press conference every day?' They said, 'Yes.' I said, 'Okay, 10:00 a.m.' I told them two things: 'I will listen to you, and I will be polite.' I expect you not to be rude to me. If you do the same, I will be accessible." Swindle thus became the defacto press spokesman for the Perot campaign from October 1 through November 3. He became the most visible spokesperson for the campaign on all the national news and political programs. He had the advantage of having almost daily access to Perot, but that doesn't mean he knew everything that was going on.

"Nobody knew what was going on," he said. "I'm not sure I ever did know totally what was going on. That's the way Ross operates; he does a lot of it on his own."

FIVE WEEKS TO FINISH— INFOMERCIALS AND DEBATES

WHEN ROSS PEROT DECLARED HIS PRESIDENTIAL CANDIDACY, there were only thirty-three days until the November 3 election—not quite five weeks. His preoccupation was with accomplishing two feats: getting his advertising on television (and producing more advertising), and gaining access to the nationally televised debates. That would be his fall campaign: TV ads and debates. He would hardly be seen in the flesh.

Traditional candidates kick off their campaigns by hitting the hustings. In the three days after the GOP National Convention in August, President Bush made campaign stops in seven cities in six states. Bill Clinton and Al Gore embarked on a bus tour of eight states on the heels of the Democratic convention. Not Ross Perot. After a flurry of media activity leading up to his announcement, he virtually dropped out of sight while he worked on his advertising. Clay Mulford took charge of negotiations to get him on the debates.

MADE-FOR-TV CAMPAIGN—THE INFOMERCIAL
All told, Perot would produce eleven thirty-minute commercials, fifteen sixty-second commercials and five thirty-second commercials, and air most of them in a

whirlwind of advertising. Perot persuaded the Timerlin-McClain advertising agency, Texas's largest, to handle the advertising campaign. Lanier Timerlin was Perot's longtime friend, and Perot had asked the agency to work on Perot I, but the agency normally didn't do political work because it took too much time away from the normal client base. Timerlin and Dennis McClain, the agency's president, reconsidered for Perot II. "We figured we could do anything for five weeks," McClain said. He put together a group of less than a dozen people, who would work nonstop for the duration of the campaign. "It was like taking a five-week sabbatical, but it was doable," he said. In the first two or three days after McClain became involved, he and Perot brainstormed sixteen different programs. The first four spots were done in two days.

While Perot was portrayed in the print media as the "stealth candidate" for receding from public view, he was hard at work on the television ads. He announced on Thursday, October 1, and over the weekend he was meeting with his advertising team and filming his first thirty-minute program, titled "The Problems—Plain Talk about Jobs, Debt and the Washington Mess," which would run on Tuesday night, October 6, less than one week after he entered the race. It was filmed in a Dallas studio, with Perot sitting at a desk in front of a bookcase, and produced by the 270 Group, set up by Timerlin-McClain and named for the number of electoral votes needed to win the election.

On his first thirty-minute program, Perot walked the American public through the causes of the country's economic problems, armed with two dozen charts and a metal pointer. He blamed the Reagan and Bush administrations for an economy that he said was in "deep voodoo." One chart showed that for every year of the Bush presidency, the nation lost more jobs than it did the year before, a figure that peaked with the loss of seven hundred thousand jobs in 1992—"when the Republicans said things were getting better." Perot spent most of the time talking about the deficit, the recession, GNP growth, lobbying by government officials and government expenditures. He presented no solutions, saying they would come in a later program.

The first thirty-minute program cost Perot $380,000, and attracted a higher rating than most regularly scheduled entertainment shows on all three networks. It even beat the National League playoff game, which followed the airing of his "infomercial" on CBS, as well as two shows on NBC and one on ABC. The A.C. Nielsen company listed the total number of households watching at 11.4 million and estimated 16.5 million people had watched the program. *The New York Times* commented that Perot's first thirty-minute program "had all the vitality of a low-budget corporate training film. But it made curiously compelling viewing nevertheless." Perot bought another thirty-minute block of time on ABC on Friday night, October 9, at a cost of $620,000 for his second presentation.

When McClain got involved, polls were showing Perot had the support of 7 percent of American voters, at the most. McClain met with Perot to sell him on the idea of doing something other than just Ross Perot appearing in front of the camera. "Clinton was running positive commercials about himself, which nobody believed. Bush was running positive commericals, which nobody believed. Soon, they would start running negative commercials about each other," McClain said. He told Perot, "There is an opportunity for somebody to come in who can be believed. It won't be you; you dropped out." The point was that it shouldn't just be Perot on camera; his issues should be on camera.

The concept would be brief issue-oriented ads, each with a simple visual. One ad showed a fluttering piece of red fabric to illustrate a new war against red tape and red ink that would replace the Cold War. The point was: "The great fear today is not the red flag of Communism but the red tape of government bureaucracy." Another message, illustrated by water droplets, was that trickle-down economics didn't trickle. The finish line: "It's time for a candidate who will get down to business. It's time for Ross Perot." One ad showed a huge storm cloud rolling across the screen. Against a backdrop of jagged lightning bolt and thunderclaps, a narrator spoke of the national debt as "a massive storm that is clouding America's future, an ill wind that is destroying jobs."

The sound of a beating heart with a visual of an electrocardiogram were used for the health care message. Against a backdrop of falling dollars and a drumroll, the wasteful spending of government programs was discussed. Again, "It's time for a candidate who will get down to business. It's time for Ross Perot." Another ad, discussing the problems of the inner cities, pictured graffitti on a wall. "The writing is on the wall. This is no time to waste our vote on politics as usual. It's time for a candidate who will get down to business. It's time for Ross Perot." Another favorite closing line was to specify the issue, such as "The issue is leadership. The candidate is Ross Perot. The choice is yours." Or, "The candidate is Ross Perot. The issue is the national debt. The choice is yours."

One of the sixty-second ads featured a close-up of a Purple Heart medal sent to Perot as a good luck charm during the campaign by Dennis Skirvin, a Vietnam veteran from Wilmington, Delaware. A narrator read excerpts from a letter from Skirvin to Perot, as the words scrolled across the screen. "Dear Ross, I was awarded this Purple Heart for wounds received during a Vietnam ambush. Over the years its value to me has grown significantly. And, like my family, it is priceless. I would be honored if you would accept the loan of my Purple Heart to keep with you throughout the campaign. I believe that it can serve as a compelling reminder that the hard battle ahead can, and must, be won. Let it also remind you of the army of ordinary citizens that has mustered to your call and looks to you to stop the hemorrhaging of the American spirit, and to restore honesty, integrity and responsibility to our government."

The concept for this series of short ads was to just scroll the copy up and off the screen. It was simple and direct. No fancy video tricks, no location shooting. They didn't require a lot of production work or editing. Because the format was simple, the ads could be churned out more quickly. The thirty-second and sixty-second ads began running one week after Perot entered the race. "The simple scrolls, for example," Murphy Martin said, "all we had to have was the right background and music. What's more simple than holding flip charts at a desk and turning them down and talking about them?" In addition to getting the ads on air quickly, the concepts fit Perot's personality and his idea of how the advertising campaign should be conducted.

McClain also said that one aim was to present Perot not as a product—which was standard for political advertising—but as a service. For years, political candidates have been marketed as products, focusing on selling that product on Election Day. The difference in marketing, McClain explained, is to create a relationship, not promote a single transaction that would take place on Election Day.

Perot's thirty-minute programs were somewhat interrupted by the nine days—October 11-19—in which three presidential debates were crammed. The night after the second debate, however, Perot unveiled his economic plan on NBC in a thirty-minute infomercial. Utilizing his cherished charts, Perot explained the plan that was detailed in his issues book, *United We Stand: How We Can Take Back Our Country.* The next night, Perot bought sixty minutes on ABC at a cost of $540,000—the first half hour was used for biographical material; the second half hour was a repeat of the economic plan.

Perot used the "Solutions" infomercial to outline $754 billion in tax hikes and budget cuts that would balance the budget over six years. To answer critics, Perot said the program could be phased in so as not to add to the woes of the sluggish economy. Detailed in the same program was his plan for political reform, including reduced staffs and perks for the White House and Congress and lobbying restrictions.

In the program, Perot called for higher income tax rates on the top 4 percent of the population, increased tax bills for some Social Security and Medicare recipients, a fifty-cent gas tax increase over five years, and higher tobacco taxes. Perot also proposed spending cuts in discretionary programs that included "science grants, farm supports, government operations, etc., etc." He pledged to eliminate $22 billion in "business subsidies," and said he was confident his administration could reduce federal health care costs by $141 billion through elimination of inefficiencies. While most of the increased revenue would go toward decreasing the deficit, Perot also proposed spending $46 billion on research and development, $40 billion on infrastructure, $12 billion on education and $11 billion on aid to cities.

The New York Times editorialized that Perot (whom it previously had criticized for being "all hat and no cattle") presented "some beef." *The Times* said that Perot is "much more credible" than Bush, who wouldn't raise taxes at all, and Clinton, whose spending and revenue projections are "wildly optimistic."

The Times also said Perot's weekend advertising blitz was "cause for admiration, regret and frustration. Admiration because he gave viewers a high-minded seminar on America's fiscal problems—and because he offered a serious and mostly honest program to address those problems. Regret because Mr. Perot's ideas would surely have challenged his opponents and elevated the tone of the campaign—if only he had presented them earlier and not cravenly quit the race in July when his candidacy had credibility. Frustration because Mr. Perot insists even now on presenting his detailed remedies in hermetically sealed TV studios, avoiding cross-examination."

Perot had yet to make a public appearance in the fall campaign, but he was nonetheless having an impact on the political discourse.

Of the economic plan, Rich Thomas wrote in *Newsweek*: "The Perot plan is under attack from both ends of the political spectrum. Some liberal economists think it will hurt the U.S. economy by cutting federal spending too quickly, while conservatives say it will hurt the economy by raising taxes too much. Both criticisms are arguably off the mark. At $3 trillion and growing, the federal debt is already smothering economic growth by keeping long-term interest rates high—and left unattended, the deficit could eventually trigger a national financial crisis. That means the next president will have to confront the deficit sooner or later—and when he does, he will owe a political debt to Ross Perot. It's just that simple."

Time magazine said the Perot plan could be a landmark in American politics. It quoted Rudolph Penner, a former Congressional Budget Office director, saying: "This is the most detailed austerity program ever put in front of people...It is distinguished mainly by its honesty."

Even as he touted his economic plan, Perot went into the fall campaign woefully short of positions on other issues, with only vague stances on education, cities and crime. Nonetheless, it was clear that Perot was gaining attention for the issues that concerned him. But was he being taken seriously as a presidential candidate? Probably not. He was viewed rather as a sort of sidebar to the "real" presidential race, between Bush and Clinton. Some speculated that as Clinton became more and more a cinch to win, the more voters were willing to cast a "protest vote" for Perot. It's not apparent that Perot regarded himself that way. The closer it got to the election, the more he concentrated on convincing voters they would not be throwing their vote away if they voted for him.

With two weeks left in the campaign, he was flooding the market with fifteen-second and sixty-second ads, in addition to his thirty-minute time segments. Those buys, many of them in major sports time slots, included $3.2 million for time on ABC and at least $2.6 million on CBS to air nineteen commercials. His NBC thirty-minute purchase, with fifteen one-minute time slots in prime time, and eight fifteen-second spots during the Tonight show, cost between $2.1 and $2.6 million. When Perot reappeared after the debates with his commercial programs, it was image makeover time. He was literally buying all the good thirty-minute time blocks he could get. There was the Perot biography, a conversation conducted by Murphy Martin. There was "The Best of Ross Perot by his Family," which included testimonials by the Perot offspring and Perot talking about his family. Ross, Jr., called his father "my hero" and daughter Suzanne talked about his "warm, soft, sweet, caring side." One of the stories was about Suzanne's Christmas wish in 1976—twenty new horses for the New York City police department for their mounted force. Perot complied with her wish. Suzanne named the horses, calling one "Ross."

The third installment of that series was "The Ross Perot Nobody Knows," which was hosted by Perot's secretary, Sally Bell. "The Ross Perot Nobody Knows" ran on CBS before the World Series, and featured previously anonymous acts of charity by Perot for various people—soldiers in the Persian Gulf, Dallas police officers, neighbors and employees.

"People had a vision of Ross Perot which had no depth. We were trying to give depth to who he was," said McClain. People also were trying to portray him as a "nut case," he said. Perot's family, which had not been visible during the petition drive, was an obvious asset. "Can a guy who people are saying is crazy raise a family like this? These are people with core values."

The "Ross Perot Nobody Knows" showed a man of great compassion who has performed extraordinary individual acts of charity for people. Todd Reed, a disabled Persian Gulf veteran, was one example. Perot had paid for a high-tech prosthesis for Reed, who lost his leg below the knee after stepping on a land mine in the Persian Gulf. Perot also came to the rescue of a police officer hurt in a skiing accident and a neighboring youth who was involved in an auto accident. On the day he spoke to a petition rally in Arkansas, Perot had rushed back to Dallas to attend the young man's wedding.

The half-hour program in which Perot introduced his family attracted 10.5 million viewers, according to Neilsen Media Research.

Perot paid more than $1 million to broadcast four half-hour programs about himself over an eight-day period. Most of it was information that the mainstream media, which he so despised, would never have brought out. The image Perot had of himself and the image of him that had been portrayed by the media throughout the campaign were obviously two different breeds of cat. He wanted his version to be seen.

The New York Times media critic Walter Goodman had this to say: "The latest Perot performances are plainly meant to soften the impact of his first two commercials, which were all stark graphs and gloomy statistics....(But) instead of staying with the problems and developing approaches to them, the campaigner has turned to selling his image. That progression or descent from tough talk to soft soap is a bow to the conventions of both television and politics. It is not enough that the candidate be respected, even admired for daring to call for a tax on gasoline; he also has to be a warm human being."

Up to the last week of the campaign, Perot spent $19.8 million on network commercials, the most of the three candidates. Before Perot was through, Murphy Martin estimated he had spent $30 to $35 million buying commercial time. In the last week, he blanketed the airwaves, including one of the most popular thirty-minute shows, "Deep Voodoo, Chicken Feathers and the American

Dream," which aired the Sunday night before the election. In one of the thirty-minute programs, Perot talked about "how to build a business."

On most of the "infomercials," Perot spoke extemporaneously for about forty-five minutes and the tape was edited to thirty minutes by the advertising team. Using simple infomercials was Perot's idea. His notion all along was to have Ross Perot get in front of the American people with flip charts and give them the unvarnished facts. "He absolutely wanted to do that. He was convinced it was something the American people were hungry for," McClain said. McClain didn't know the thirty-minute infomercial was going to be "a real powerful tool" until he saw the first thirty minutes edited.

Perot wanted to use a lot of thirty-minute commercials, which had not been popular tools for advertising in presidential campaigns for some three decades. Adlai Stevenson used them in the 1952 campaign. Political candidates used them sparingly in the 1960s, before television time became outrageously high. They were used, for example, in U.S. Senate races in the 1960s. Former U.S. Senator Ralph Yarborough of Texas used thirty-minute time blocks in his 1964 election—just Yarborough speaking in front of a camera. But it was widely believed at the time that the greatest impact of such advertising was to "fire up" supporters to go out and work the grass roots. It was questioned whether thirty minutes of a candidate talking would hold the attention of a nonsupporter.

Perot, however, was not just preaching to the choir; he was trying to convert the nonbelievers. McClain theorized that people would be channel-flipping or tune in to watch for two or three minutes and end up watching the entire thirty-minute program. "We decided to run them until we lost our audience. And we never did," he said.

The infomercials were filmed at a Dallas commercial studio, using a set that Texas Instruments was using for a training film. The set was called a cross between a "Ward Cleaver study and the Oval Office" in the press. Actually, said McClain, it was just a set that existed. The charts were created by Mike Poss, the Perot Group financial officer who became a jack-of-all-trades during the petition drive and campaign.

Perot was involved in the advertising on a day-to-day basis. "He was always accessible, always involved, always in the decision-making process," McClain said. "He is a hands-on guy. He totally erases every layer. I couldn't imagine I was going to pick up the phone and call the guy and he was going to discuss what we were doing. That's exactly what happened. Even if he was on his plane going to a rally. He doesn't have to prepare for things; Ross is prepared. He doesn't have to spend his time getting focused; he is focused."

Most of the ideas either originated with Perot or were finalized by him. In some cases, the advertising team took the issues book, *United We Stand*, and came up with ideas to present. Perot was in his element. He was utilizing his own creativity with people he trusted. He still felt the unpleasantness of the advertising brouhaha with Ed Rollins and Hal Riney earlier in the summer.

"He was stung by the so-called outsiders," Murphy Martin said. "There was such a relief to be able to accomplish what he had in mind and do it with people at the local level he had a comfort level with; it kind of reinvigorated his thinking," Martin said, recalling Perot's comment: "After we got rid of the Pentagon, we were able to accomplish some things."

McClain predicts lasting impacts from Perot's television campaign, including less slick political ads. "I don't think there's any question we'll see an explosion of infomercials," he said. "Once you see it in the advertising business and it works, you see it again." But he added, "I can't wait until other candidates try to hold people's attention for thirty minutes." Perot had a charismatic ability to hold people's attention. "It is an extraordinary talent," McClain said, "and very, very few people have it."

During the fall campaign, Perot was intent on getting his message out, unfiltered by journalists, and without any distracting "noise" from media appearances that would "step on" his message. He declined to appear on even the morning chat shows that he had previously enjoyed. Thus, the only opportunity voters had to satisfy their curiosity about him was to watch his thirty-minute commercial shows. Also, he was working night and day to put them together, even during the debate period. He had little time for other media appearances, given the intensity of the advertising campaign and his own personal involvement in it.

THE TRILATERAL DEBATES

The other major element of the fall campaign for Perot was the debates. Perot wanted his ads on TV as soon as possible after getting back in the race so that he would "qualify" for the debates. He was then at 7 percent and going down. Clay Mulford, who was handling the debate negotiations, feared that if Perot got down to 3 or 4 percent, it would be difficult to distinguish him from other alternative candidates, and that would make it more difficult to get him on the debates. "Without a more activist campaign, the question was whether we would meet the qualifications of the Commission on Presidential Debates," Mulford said.

As it turned out, it wasn't up to the commission but to the major party candidates, who had negotiated their own agreement. Mulford extracted from the counsel to the Clinton campaign the draft agreement between the candidates, which specified that Perot would be invited. The Bush people, he said, wanted Perot in the debates to try to split the "change" vote between Clinton and Perot. When Mulford saw the draft agreement on October 4, he immediately wrote a letter to Bush campaign manager Robert Teeter and to Mickey Kantor for the Clinton campaign saying that Perot "accepted." A press release was then issued saying Perot would be participating in the debates, to put pressure on the commission and the candidates not to alter the agreement. The commission initially said he could be included in the first debate, after which his popular support would be assessed to determine whether he could appear in debates two and three. Over the next couple of days, the commission met and decided to sponsor the debates, with the inclusion of Perot. The deal was set; he would be on all three debates.

The final agreement was a thirty-six-page document which detailed who got which dressing room, the height of the podium, the location of the TV camera and other particulars, much of which seemed to be foolish minutae to the Perot camp.

Before the debates began, Perot was viewed fairly negatively. A *Newsweek* poll indicated 60 percent of voters were influenced by his decision to pull out in July. Sixty-one percent questioned whether he had the temperament to be president, and 63 percent thought he was manipulating his volunteers instead of following them.

The first debate was set for Sunday, October 11, at Washington University in St. Louis. The Perot camp sent three people to handle the advance work. When they arrived in St. Louis, they found that all the hotel rooms had been blocked up; the Bush campaign had 350 people there and the Clinton campaign had 250. "The argument stretched over eighteen hours over such things as who got which bathroom," Mulford said. Representatives of the major-party candidates were dividing up the waiting rooms and other areas, and what was left over was going to Perot. He would be put in the basement. "It was irksome to the people who were there negotiating for us. We would remind them that this is all nonsense. These are things that don't matter," Mulford said.

The first debate was a ninety-minute event featuring questions from three reporters. Jim Lehrer, of PBS's "MacNeil/Lehrer NewsHour," was the moderator. Panelists were Ann Compton of ABC, John Mashek of the *Boston Globe*, and Sander Vanocur, a freelance journalist whose debate credentials went back to the Kennedy-Nixon debates.

Perot was his usual plain-talking self, exhibiting occasional displays of humor. His responses largely were the well-practiced remarks he had made repeatedly in speeches, and during numerous talk show and TV interviews. Still, he seemed as much at ease as did the traditional party candidates who have been through the same process many times.

He was the king of the soundbite, when he commented he was "all ears." Mashek had asked Perot, "As part of your plan to reduce the ballooning federal deficit, you've suggested that we raise gasoline taxes fifty cents a gallon over five years. Why punish the middle-class consumer to such a degree?" Perot responded: "Why do we have to do it? Because we have so mismanaged our country over the years, and it is now time to pay the fiddler. And if we don't we will be spending our children's money. We have spent $4 trillion worth...We've got to clean this mess up, leave this country in good shape, and pass on the American dream to them. We've got to collect the taxes to do it. If there's a fairer way, I'm all ears."

His second sound bite concerned his experience in government. Perot said, "I don't have any experience in running up a four-trillion-dollar debt."

Perot also registered with viewers when he responded to a question about "Why should American taxpayers be taxed to support armies in Europe when the Europeans have plenty of money to do it for themselves?"

Perot replied: "If I'm poor and you're rich, and I can get you to defend me, that's good. But when the tables get turned, I ought to do my share. Right now we spend about $300 billion a year on defense; the Japanese spend around $30 billion in Asia; the Germans spend around $30 billion in Europe. For example, Germany will spend a trillion dollars building infrastructure over the next ten years. It's kind of easy to do if you only have to pick up a $30 billion tab to defend your country. The European Community is in a position to pay a lot more than they have in the past. I agree with the president: When they couldn't, we should have; now that they can, they should."

Perot skewered Bush and helped Clinton on at least one answer. On the question of Clinton's draft and antiwar record versus Bush's presidential performance, Perot said: "When you're a senior official in the federal government spending billions of dollars of taxpayers' money and you're a mature individual and you make a mistake, that's on our ticket. If you make (a mistake) as a young man, time passes."

Perot got good marks after the debate, which was viewed by an estimated forty-seven million households. ABC analyst Cokie Roberts said, "Let's call a spade a spade here. Ross Perot won this debate." An overnight poll of debate viewers by CBS showed 33 percent of those surveyed thought Perot had won, while 30 percent thought Clinton won and only 16 percent thought Bush had won. So much for Bush's strategy to get Perot to shake things up.

The *Dallas Morning News's* media critic Ed Bark wrote that "Perot stood out in a three-man crowd... Unquestionably, his stature as a candidate grew considerably...Perot showed he shouldn't be undersold." CBS's Scott Pelley said: "Many voters had been willing to write off the Perot candidacy, but now they're beginning to remember why they liked him in the first place." And ABC's Jeff Greenfield said: "If Ross Perot had stayed in this race...we would be looking at a very different campaign."

In three post-debate polls—CBS, CNN and *Newsweek*—registered voters picked Perot as the winner over Clinton and Bush. But only 12 to 14 percent said they would vote for him. However, 70 percent told Newsweek they would take Perot more seriously as a presidential candidate, and 64 percent said they would watch the remaining debates.

Perot was loose about the whole thing. He visited with his family in his basement waiting room and had a handful of people milling around the media area after the event—including Orson Swindle, Clay Mulford, Sharon Holman and Ross Perot, Jr.,—as hordes of Bush and Clinton surrogates put the campaign spin on their candidate's performance. Swindle deplored the whole idea of "spin alley," where the spinmeisters gather at the end of the debate to comment to the press on their candidate's performance, but said the Perot team had to participate. "It's ludicrous, the most absurd thing I ever saw in my life, but you're put in a position you have to do it....If you aren't there defending yourself, you're going to be adversely affected. So we're talking against all these high-powered people"—senators and cabinet members and White House aides, party leaders and movie stars.

The Perot defenders were like water pistols against heavy artillery. They had even enticed Mort Meyerson to come back for the debates. The *Washington Post* wrote: "All the strangeness of the evening was apparent on Mort Meyerson's face as he wandered, aimless and skittish, through the media center in the nervous hours before the debate and the frantic moments afterward. He looked a little bemused, a little confused and a little amused. A stalwart of the Perot business empire, Meyerson is no pro when it comes to politics."

What was apparent is that the debates are no longer simply debates, designed to put one candidate up against another in front of the camera and therefore the American people. They are giant, professionally-organized circuses, media events, second only to the national conventions in the elaborate staging and attempts at media manipulation by the "spin doctors." Perot would later ridicule the debate-making process, saying that Bush and Clinton insisted on forty-eight-car motorcades while he "rented one car from Avis."

Two nights after the first presidential debate, the vice-presidential candidates debated at Georgia Tech University in Atlanta. Retired Admiral Jim Stockdale, Perot's running mate, was clearly out of his element. Stockdale made a promising start, stressing his nonpolitical background by asking "Who am I? Why am I here? Don't expect me to use the language of the Washington insider." As Democrat Al Gore and Republican Dan Quayle swapped charges, Stockdale drew an appreciative laugh from the audience when he said, "I think America is seeing right now the reason that this nation is in gridlock."

At one point, watching Gore and Quayle slug it out, Stockdale said he felt like an "observer in a Ping-Pong game." Otherwise, however, it was downhill for Stockdale. A philosopher and a thinker (he had recently been writing a book on a Greek philosopher), Stockdale was neither glib like the two practiced politicians, nor was he as well grounded on the questions of public policy. On two occasions, he had to admit he had nothing further to say. At one point, he had to admit to having his hearing aid turned down.

To his credit, Stockdale displayed courage in getting on the stage with the two professional politicians, since he didn't even have a practiced stump speech. He simply had not done that kind of campaigning. Perot had virtually been a one-man band. Appearing on the morning talk shows the next day he said, "I enjoyed the challenge." But he admitted, "I was just kind of out of it, because I don't have a speech I give when somebody pushes the abortion button or economy button, and thoughtful is my line. It's not just a barrage of facts." Stockdale stressed the fact that he had been "a leader in the most extreme circumstances you can imagine."

Clay Mulford later explained away Stockdale's performance by saying that Stockdale was up against two people who were propelled into politics at a young age, classic twentieth century political people, who had a lot of experience in TV campaigning. "Admiral Stockdale is a man of profound intellectual accomplishment, but he does not have that background."

Mulford said the "comical stories" on debate planning continued with the vice-presidential debate. Vice President Quayle's representatives refused to let Admiral Stockdale use a room that was available in the debate hall because he would have to use the same staircase used by Quayle and his staff. The debate staff was going to put Admiral Stockdale in a separate building and have him walk to the debate room, but were told Stockdale's war injuries precluded him from walking that far. The first offer was to provide him with a golf cart. Later, the decision was made to put a trailer in the back of the building so he would have a bathroom.

Orson Swindle pointed to Stockdale as another indication that Perot didn't plan to run all along, that Perot was really running by the seat of his pants. "Our lack of organizational structure was reflected most profoundly and most tragically with Jim Stockdale. It was like night on a carrier deck, pitch black and raining. We were not prepared for that phase."

Stockdale, Swindle reminded, "was merely placed in there to meet technical requirements. When Perot pulled out, it eliminated the possibility of getting anybody else to run with him. So here we go roaring into a presidential campaign with a guy who has no interest, wasn't intending to be the vice-presidental candidate and wasn't suited to that environment. Jim Stockdale was put in a situation that caused him embarrassment; that disappointed me. He's probably smarter than anybody we've had in the White House in my lifetime. He's a brilliant man, a brilliant leader. Those other two guys don't even belong on the same continent with him, but their forte is showmanship. They've been debating all their lives. He looked like he wasn't even there. One thing that was a negative for Perot was picking Jim Stockdale, as he appeared to be on that debate, because perception becomes reality."

The *Washington Post's* E.J. Dionne called it a "painfully uncomfortable performance." Some analysts speculated it might reverse Perot's mini-surge from the debate two nights before. But the second debate in the nine-day marathon was coming up, another opportunity for Perot to shine. And pollsters for the *Wall Street Journal* predicted that a strong performance on Debate No. 2 from Perot, who was then running between 12 and 15 percent, "could push him up to 20 percent, despite the disappointing performance" by Admiral Stockdale in the vice-presidential debate.

The second presidential debate drew the highest viewership of the 1992 debate series. CBS researchers estimated that with other networks factored in, the debate was seen by more than 90 million people. Nielsen estimated the debate attracted 43.1 million households or 69.9 million households. (Nielsen numbers do not include C-Span or PBS audiences). It was the largest audience for any presidential debate, with the exception of the Ronald Reagan-Jimmy Carter debate on October 28, 1980.

A different format was used for the second debate which was staged at the University of Richmond in Richmond, Virginia. The candidates were perched on stools as moderator Carole Simpson directed questions from an audience of 209 uncommitted voters in an unprecedented town hall-type format. That ordinary people were selected to ask the questions was an obvious concession to the newfound power of the people in this election.

Those in the audience clearly set a different tone, scolding the candidates for personal attacks and asking strictly issue-oriented questions. In a question that virtually sealed George Bush's fate, one woman wanted to know how the massive national debt had affected the lives of the three candidates. President Bush didn't get it. At first he started talking about interest rates, and then asked her for help with the question. Finally, he talked about mail to the White House from people in distress. Perot said, "It caused me to disrupt my private life and my business to get involved in this activity. That's how much I care about it."

The second moment in the debate came when a citizen spectator, prompted by Simpson to deplore negative campaign attacks, asked the candidates to talk about "our needs instead of yours,"—i.e., the needs of the people, not the needs of the politicians. In an instant, this voter stripped away the trivia, the pregame hype, the post-game show, the emphasis on tactics and strategy, the character assassination, the obsession of the insiders with polls and the "sport" of the campaign, to get to what the crux of the campaign should be about. The needs of the people.

In coverage of the second debate, the *Washington Post* wrote that the voters gathered to ask the questions were the "clearest victors in tonight's debate. As has happened all year, they proved themselves at least as good—and often better—than the professional question-askers at pushing the campaign toward the realities of crime, economic sluggishness, expensive or nonexistent health insurance, faltering schools and deteriorating race relations."

The final debate of the nine-day marathon—regarded as President Bush's last major chance before a national audience to light a fire under his lagging campaign—was October 19 at Michigan State University in East Lansing, Michigan. It featured forty-five minutes with PBS's Jim Lehrer as the lone moderator and forty-five minutes with a panel of journalists—Gene Gibbons of Reuters, Helen Thomas of United Press International, and Susan Rook of CNN. President Bush turned in his strongest showing of the three debates, but Perot had his moments, as well. Perot had to defend his honor at several points, arguing against the premise of questions that suggested he had a pattern of walking away from difficult business and political challenges or ordering investigations of his critics.

On the question of his penchant for investigations, Perot said, "If you look at my life, until I got involved in this effort, I was one person. And then after the Republican dirty tricks group got through with me, I'm another person...They investigated every single one of my children. They investigated my wife...They went to extraordinary sick lengths, and I just found it amusing that they would take two or three cases where I was involved in lawsuits and would engage an investigator. The lawyers would engage an investigator, which is common...So that's just another one of those little fruitloopy things they make up to try to—instead of facing issues—to try to redefine a person that's running against them....I will do everything I can, if I get up there, to make dirty tricks a thing of the past."

Perot disputed having a pattern of quitting. In the case of General Motors, he said he did everything he could to get General Motors to face its problems in the mid-1980s when it was still financially strong. They wouldn't do it, he said, and they paid a terrible price. They asked to buy his remaining shares and he sold, "because it was obvious we had a complete disagreement about what should be done with the company." Perot said the GM experience was relevant because "our government is at that point now. The thing that I am in this race for is to tap the American people on the shoulder and to say to every single one of you, fix it while we're still relatively strong."

As for what happened in July when he withdrew, he said: "In terms of the American people's concern about my commitment, I'm here tonight, folks; I never quit supporting you as you put me on the ballot in the other twenty-six states; and when you asked me to come back in, I came back in. And talk about not quitting: I'm spending my money on this campaign....I put my wallet on the table for you and your children. Over $60 million at least will go into this campaign."

Perot attacked Bush's handling of U.S. relations with Iraq, and also pricked Clinton. Experience running a small state such as Arkansas is "irrelevant," Perot said, comparing it to the owner of a corner store boasting that he could run Wal-Mart.

Also, in the final debate, Perot presaged later criticism of the North American Free Trade Agreement, with the comment: "You're going to hear a giant sucking sound of jobs being pulled out of this country, right at a time when we need the tax base to pay the debt and pay down the interest on the debt and get our house back in order."

Perot used his closing statement in the last debate to tout his thirty-minute commercials that would be on all three networks on Thursday, Friday and Saturday of that week. He urged people to "stop letting these folks in the press tell you you're throwing your vote away. You got to start using your own head."

He then asked: "Who's the best-qualified person up here on the stage to create jobs?...I suggest you might consider somebody who's created jobs. Who's the best person to manage money? I suggest you pick a person who's successfully managed money. Finally, who would you give your pension fund and your savings account to to manage? And, last one, who would you ask to be the trustee of your estate and take care of your children if something happened to you? Finally, to you students up there, God bless you, I'm doing this for you: I want you to have the American dream. To the American people, I'm doing this because I love you."

Did Ross Perot really want to be president? Probably not. But at this point, he wanted to win this election. He looked at the other two men who had been on the debate stage with him three times and he was absolutely convinced he was the best of the lot.

A FATAL MISTAKE AND A FEW FALL RALLIES

Perot was coming up in the polls. There were reports that the race was tightening, that Perot's support was surging, and that he was altering the shape of the campaign. Such a story appeared in the *Wall Street Journal* on Monday, October 26. "The dynamic of the last several days is basically clear: Mr. Perot is the only candidate who is showing any growth in support...a Perot victory, totally unimaginable before last week, can no longer be summarily dismissed. Democratic polltaker Peter Hart said it wasn't clear whether the Perot phenomenon was a "fever or a virus. If it's a fever, it will hit its peak and come down. If it's a virus, we don't know where it will spread."

Whichever it was, the Perot phenomenon suffered a shot of the wrong medicine. Perot was at 21 percent, aiming at 25 percent—the threshold his supporters thought necessary to begin attracting voters who thought he couldn't win—when he made a fatal mistake. He agreed to appear on CBS's "60 Minutes" on Sunday, October 25. (The *Wall Street Journal* story was written before the fatal appearance, although published the next morning.) Perot was told that "60 Minutes" was going to air the story about the potential disruption of his daughter's wedding in August, and he wanted to tell his side of it. Orson Swindle called it "Black Sunday." "We were on an upswing. Clinton was coming down, we were picking up a point or two a day. Bush was holding steady; his hard core was around 37 percent," Swindle said. Then Perot appeared on "60 Minutes."

Without offering any proof, Perot said a smear campaign aimed at embarrassing his daughter forced him to abandon his campaign in July. Perot said several Republicans on separate occasions warned him about a plan to disrupt his daughter's wedding by showing up at the church with a doctored photo of the daughter that placed her head on another body. Perot said the photos were "destined for use in supermarket tabloids." Perot said he had not gone public with the story in July because he wanted to protect his daughter's privacy and because it would have distracted from his message.

Once again, Perot became that paranoid and bizarre person who had sabotaged his own campaign in July. And now he was sabotaging Perot II. White House spokesman Marlin Fitzwater reemerged, calling Perot a "paranoid person" and denouncing "this crazy man's theories."

"It was like a big rock dropped on my head," said

Kurt Koenig, who was still leading the fight for Perot in New York. Koenig had been passing out leaflets in Westchester County, where "people were coming up to me in droves saying they wished they could believe Perot could win. It was exciting to all of us out there. We actually thought we had a chance." A state poll in New York was showing 25 percent support for Perot. "If people actually believed he could win, we thought he would really take off."

"Why did he allow them to do this to him?" asked Koenig. "Why did he allow himself to be dragged down? They made him look like some kind of paranoid. Either he was tricked, and he's too smart for that, or it's his way of finally derailing this campaign, of saying 'I don't want to be president.' Because there's no way he's going to win after this. The next day, I'm out there with my leaflets, and our 25 percent has plummeted. There was no momentum after that."

Perot also alleged on "60 Minutes" and in an exclusive interview with the *Boston Herald* that, after he left the race, the Bush campaign hired ex-CIA contract employee Scott Barnes "to tap into his computerized stock trading program, hoping to prevent (him) from bankrolling a revival candidacy." The *Boston Herald* reported that "The FBI in Dallas is investigating that report, according to Perot, who said he has given investigators a twenty-minute videotape of a meeting in downtown Dallas between (Barnes) and a senior member of the Bush campaign."

While the Bush-Quayle campaign denied all aspects of the charges, Perot said that after he told authorities what he knew about the wiretap scheme, they asked him to make a tape recording of his own voice as bait for a trap. As part of the sting, an undercover FBI opera-

tive went to see Bush-Quayle Texas chairman Jim
Oberwetter and offered him the tape. Oberwetter's re-
sponse was "Haven't you ever heard of Watergate?"
He kicked the man out of his office and called the Dallas
Police Department.

The morning after the episode on "60 Minutes,"
Orson Swindle, Sharon Holman and Ross, Jr., were conducting the morning news briefing, trying to deflect
questions about the "60 Minutes" report, when Perot
walked in and compounded the damage. Perot had been
watching on CNN down the street in his Merit Drive
office. A volunteer saw him pull up in front of the headquarters to a screeching halt in his green, bulletproof
vehicle, which he had been persuaded by security-conscious aides to drive. He was livid. He chastised reporters who pressed him to substantiate the charges, saying,
"I am sick and tired of you-all questioning my integrity
without a basis for it." He was frustrated and confrontational, and the briefing was being broadcast live on
CNN. As Swindle said, "When the sharks are in a frenzy,
you don't just get in there with them." The story would
remain active all week.

The whole episode derailed whatever momentum the
Perot campaign had going into the final week. Ironically, Perot believed that he had to make the story about
his daughter public because he thought it was the only
thing in the way of his actually winning the race. One
associate called it the "biggest issue standing between
him and the presidency." People wondered why he
dropped out; this was the reason, and he wanted to say
so. The result, however, was just the opposite. His support began to drop in the polls and he never recovered.

According to a *Newsweek* survey, Perot's support
dropped from 22 percent to 14 percent between October

23 and October 28, a devastating loss so close to Election Day. More than half of *Newsweek*'s sample disbelieved a Republican plot to smear his daughter and 48 percent said they thought Perot "relies too much on stories that are not backed up by hard evidence."

During the fall campaign, Ross Perot brought new meaning to the phrase made-for-television—as it applies to presidential politics. Up to the last week before the election, his only public appearances had been in conjunction with the debates—rallies for supporters in the debate cities and news conferences after the debates. He finally agreed, however, to do a series of public rallies in the waning days of the campaign. Altogether, he would have only eight such public rallies during his five-week period of active candidacy.

Once having returned to the race, Perot paid almost no attention to the people who got him on the ballot. Even Orson Swindle, the executive director of United We Stand America, spent all of his time on television, and very little working with the troops. Swindle had nobody working for him. What contact there was with state leaders was by the field reps who remained on Perot's payroll. "We needed a single organizational entity, but that gap was never bridged," Swindle said. Essentially, there was no campaign in the states other than whatever people could put together themselves at the local level.

In many locations, while supporters conducted voter registration and get-out-the-vote campaigns, there were no brochures, no phone banks, no lists of registered voters—none of the usual tools of a traditional campaign.

The determination had been made to launch an air war rather than a ground war. Alex Rodriguez, the Manhattan coordinator, complained that New York City was only budgeted $1,850 a month for the fall campaign. "There was no money for the ground troops at all," he said. Rodriguez threatened to close the New York office if it didn't get some materials. "We had been promised supplies were coming for three weeks," he said. "When they got here, it was like three hundred buttons. Everybody emptied their pockets to keep this place going."

Volunteers, however, were improvising. They copied newspaper articles to hand out. There were speaker's bureaus to send surrogates out to speak in Perot's behalf. Dallas volunteers organized "Team Perot," a group of volunteers to fulfill requests for programs on Perot. One appearance by Team Perot representatives was to an elementary school in a high crime area of Dallas, where a mock election was staged. Two second grade couples dressed up as the Perots and the Stockdales. The children couldn't vote, which makes one wonder if the Perot campaign wasn't involved as much in a national civics lesson as an election.

Members of Team Perot bought matching outfits, so they would present a unified appearance. It was all volunteer-driven, because there was no one in a real position of authority in Dallas to authorize what the volunteers were doing. If nobody said, "No," they just did it.

People were clamoring for yard signs. Nancy Mulford, Perot's daughter and the wife of Clay Mulford, bought some signs and brought them to the Dallas headquarters. Dressed in jeans, she—with the help of other volunteers—stapled the signs to stakes for distribution to people that were coming in asking for yard signs.

"Ross's Rangers" was another group organized to register voters and get out the vote. Two Dallas volunteers, Jeffrey King and Tom Hall, manned a booth at D/ FW Airport twelve hours a day, seven days a week for three weeks in October. They handed out thousands of the September 15 *Wall Street Journal* article that said neither Clinton's nor Bush's economic plan added up. The Dallas phone bank returned to its big room and went back up to seventy-two incoming lines. In the last week of the campaign, it was taking ten thousand to fifteen thousand calls a day.

Swindle became, essentially, a super public relations man, making media appearances and holding the daily news briefing in Dallas. He was on "Nightline" three or four times, "Larry King" three times, all the morning shows, the Sunday morning news shows—"I lost track," he said. And for the duration, he was winging it. He admitted to not knowing what Perot was planning or thinking. Every day, the press was asking "when is he going to hit the road?" Swindle kept saying, "he's going to be out there." He said, "I was doing a tap dance." Most of Perot's "young lieutenants," he said, feared for Perot's safety and didn't want him out in crowds that could get out of hand. And they're the ones he talked to. Swindle told Perot, "You've got to go out." But he believes it was Perot's wife, Margot, who finally talked him into hitting the road.

The first two rallies were in Flemington, New Jersey, and Pittsburgh on Sunday, October 25. In New Jersey, volunteers were planning a rally for thousands with three days' notice.

Jeff Zucker, one of the field reps, called Joe Canzeri, a Washington events specialist who had worked on the campaign during the days of the "Pentagon" but who had gotten along well with the local Perot loyalists. Canzeri got the call after midnight on Friday and was at the Flemington fairgrounds by 7:30 the next morning, where he worked around the clock helping to stage the Sunday afternoon event. He figured the event would draw fifteen hundred to eighteen hundred. Twenty thousand showed up at the Flemington racetrack, starting at 7:00 a.m. Police projected another ten thousand were backed up in traffic when Perot appeared. "It was the damndest thing I've ever seen," Canzeri said. "I've seen big crowds in the last two to three days of a campaign, but nothing put together that fast with so little work."

Canzeri said he left as soon as Perot arrived and was driving down the road where traffic was bumper-to-bumper for twelve miles with people trying to get to the event. "It was extraordinary, truly the silent majority," Canzeri said. "I thought, These people are still out there and are still looking for somebody to represent them."

At both the Flemington and Pittsburgh rallies, Perot repeated the stories about the threatened disruption of the wedding as the reason why he believed he had to step aside. He refused to take questions about the allegations, saying he mentioned them only because of "60 Minutes."

Perot's top campaign officials, meanwhile, struggled to squelch the controversy over Perot's allegations, insisting that Perot would be sticking to the issues for the rest of the campaign. But the crossfire between Perot and Bush over the alleged political skullduggery undoubtedly stalled the surge precipitated by Perot's performance on the debates and his millions of dollars of advertising.

In Denver on Wednesday, October 28, Perot gave a rousing speech to five thousand supporters; again, he maintained "my integrity was never questioned until the Repubican dirty tricks guys started after me." The

Denver crowd gave Perot a two-minute ovation when he stepped to the podium. He proceeded to belittle Clinton without mentioning him by name, calling him the "candidate from a rural state whose principal industry is raising chickens." Much of the new material Perot used in his rallies came from material in his TV ads.

Over the last weekend of the campaign, Perot did a cross-country blitz with rallies Saturday in Tampa and Kansas City; two on Sunday in California; wrapping up his campaign with an election eve rally in Dallas.

In Kansas City, Martin Gross, author of *The Government Racket: Washington Waste from A to Z,* spoke before Perot. Gross detailed how things have gone awry in the bureaucracy, using anecdotal stories from his book. The audience was enthralled throughout his forty-five-minute speech. Jeff Zucker, the aide who said he signed on with Perot as much for the message as the messenger, was thrilled to see the audience reaction to Gross as well as to Perot, because it meant the message was getting across—regardless of who the messenger was.

A cheering crowd of more than ten thousand greeted him in Long Beach, California, where—to claim the polls and the media were wrong—he held up a copy of the *Chicago Daily Tribune* that erroneously proclaimed a Thomas Dewey victory over Harry Truman in 1948. He also continued his attack against Clinton. Echoing the words from a TV ad, he said, "If you look at every single factor in his twelve years in Arkansas, you'll realize that when you're at the bottom of everything, there's no place to go but up." In Santa Clara, California, Perot said Clinton's response to all problems was "we fixed that in Arkansas." "I studied Arkansas," he said. "That's where the chicken feathers come from. I don't have to tell you in Silicon Valley where the high-wage jobs come from. But it's not from raising chickens." Perot said that compared to companies on the Fortune 500 list, Arkansas "ranks below Toys 'R Us and Chiquita Bananas."

As Perot was wrapping up his campaign with the rallies, he was also filling the airwaves with his half-hour television shows over the final weekend. He continued his attacks on Clinton's Arkansas record in "Chicken Feathers, Deep Voodoo and the American Dream" on both NBC and ABC on Sunday night, November 1. On the eve of the election, he spent $2.9 million for network air time, including one-hour slots on NBC on November 1 and November 2. *The New York Times* reported that his total expenditures during the five-week campaign for television time was $34.8 million.

Kevin Nealon humorously summed up the campaign on NBC's "Saturday Night Live" on October 24: "Daylight savings time ends tonight. Normally Americans would set their clocks back and get an extra hour of sleep. Unfortunately this year, that hour has been purchased by Ross Perot."

16

CRAZY—PEROT AND PEOPLE POWER

ACCORDING TO AN OLD TEXAS FOLK TALE, after Huey Long was assassinated, the people of Louisiana elected as governor his crazier brother, Earl, who eventually was sent over to Texas to a mental hospital. As the story is recounted by political humorists, Earl Long was kept in the Texas hospital for only about six weeks and then turned loose. He looked like a perfectly normal governor to people in Texas.

Call them crazy or call them eccentric, but politicians who seem a bit peculiar have long been part of the colorful tradition of Texas politics. Ross Perot, to a lot of Texans, looked like a perfectly normal president. Others found him and his fanatical band of supporters somewhere between weird and loony. The Perot people heard it so often, they began referring to themselves as the "crazies."

In Flemington, New Jersey, on October 25, at Perot's first public rally after his reentry, he said: "They say I'm crazy and everyone who supports me is crazy. You're driving them all crazy down there in Washington."

On the stage at the final Perot rally, at noon in Dallas on election eve, Bob Hoyt, a Phase II Perot supporter who became a regional coordinator in Abilene, sauntered to the microphone and introduced himself to the crowd. "Hi. My name's Bob, and I'm crazy," he said.

When Perot took his turn at the mike, he picked up the theme. "You are crazy," he said, "crazy about this country." And he joked: "We've got buses outside to take you back to the insane asylum." He talked about the "crazy" public opinion polls and about the next day being a "crazy day" at the polls.

He asked the band to play his new theme song, the old Willie Nelson tune popularized by the late country singer, Patsy Cline, called "Crazy." Apparently having the time of his life, a grinning Perot grabbed his youngest daughter, Katherine, a college student, and danced around the stage.

Some teenage girls in school uniforms waved a sign that said "Save Us Daddy Warbucks." Another said: "No Foreign lobbyists. No PACs. Just red-blooded Americans." Still another: "Vote for Perot and Make the Press Eat Crow." And "Four trillion reasons to vote for Ross Perot."

While Bush and Clinton were conducting their last-day frantic fly-around of the country, Perot was cavorting with a hometown crowd, his sole appearance for the day. The rally would be replayed that night during an hour of commercial time on NBC. Perot had paid $2.9 million for two hours of election-eve television—thirty-minute blocks on ABC and CBS, and an hour on NBC. One of the programs would be a repeat of "Chicken Feathers, Deep Voodoo and the American Dream," already seen by thirty-two million people, and another was titled, "Ross, You Bet Your Hat He Can Win."

The traditional candidates were doing the traditional thing—a fly-around designed to generate high turnout for their candidacies. Clinton was winging around the country in thirty hours of ceaseless campaigning, hitting nine states in a 4,106-mile trip from the East Coast to western Texas. Bush spent his last day blitz hitting six states whose electoral votes were crucial. Perot was dancing.

At the end of his speech, he seemed reluctant to leave the stage, calling on the band to play song after song— "Crazy," "America the Beautiful," "Way Down Yonder in New Orleans," and "When the Saints Go Marching In." He danced with Margot, and with all of his daughters.

It was the kind of unconventional, in-your-face strategy that was Perot-ic: "We'll landslide this thing, if people vote their conscience." In other words, we'll show you how crazy we are on Election Day.

The whole Perot phenomenon played to the traditional Texas political mythology. The state's larger-than-life politicians have long been known for having a strong sense of self, saying what they think and, yes, having a few idiosyncrasies.

Among the big Democrats were Lyndon B. Johnson, the majority leader cum president, whose complex persona has provided the impetus for lifetimes of research by political historians, and powerful U.S. House Speakers Jim Wright and "Mr. Sam" Rayburn. Among the outspoken Texas politicians was Republican governor Bill Clements, who trained as a young man for Texas politics as a youthful oil field roughneck. More recently, there was Clayton Williams, a cattleman and unsuccessful GOP gubernatorial nominee against Democrat Ann Richards in 1990. Williams once stormed the Texas state house on horseback. His campfire joke during a cattle roundup that bad weather was like rape ("you might as well lay back and enjoy it") began the downfall of his candidacy. And Ann Richards could easily go from governor to stand-up comedienne. Before becoming a national political figure, she entertained wearing a pig's nose and impersonating a male chauvinist pig.

In earlier days, Ma Ferguson succeeded her husband Jim Ferguson as governor in 1924 after his impeachment, using the slogan: "Two governors for the price of one." Ma had the title, Pa made the decisions. W. Lee (Pappy) O'Daniel, a flour company sales manager, stumped the state with a hillbilly band and spouted Scriptures to be elected governor in 1938. From the unlikely President George Bush to presidential wannabe John Connally, Texas has been both blessed and cursed by its own paradoxical brand of politicians.

Russell Baker wrote about the mystique of Texas politicians in a *New York Times* column—how there has hardly been a time since World War II that Texans were not sitting tall in the Washington saddle. "Isn't it strange for a presidential campaign to be so dominated by Texas? Not at all," Baker wrote. "It just shows once again how determined Texas is to save the United States from itself."

"The Shakespearean tragedy that was Lyndon Johnson was about a Texan who believed he could single-handedly, with Texas strength and Texas compassion and Texas largeness of vision, make life better for millions...could make a whole country sit tall in the saddle.

"Are we talking about a touch of madness? Or just a presumption so breathtaking that if it weren't so funny it would seem like childish arrogance? The Perot candidacy raises these questions about Texas once again," Baker wrote.

Perot was never a politician in the truest sense. But he fits the tradition of Texas political characters who are colorful, outspoken, ambitious, risk seeking and idio-syncratic. He reflects the larger-than-life mythology that is the fabric of Texas political history. He's strong-willed, a super patriot with a militaristic bent, a populist, a billionaire man of the people who embodies a conservative philosophy with a fierce independent streak. His meritocratic instincts have sometimes outweighed his populist impulses; his outspokenness has never been contained by fear of ruffled feathers. During his work on education reform in Texas, when parents worried that creating special classes for the brightest kids smacked of elitism, he said sarcastically. "Fine. Let's put all the fat girls on the drill team. Let's let everyone play quarterback."

Perot appreciates the impetuous, the creative and the humorous. He's not afraid to try something different. Politics need not be conventional or boring. As he suggested to his followers on the election-eve rally: "Turn on the headlights, honk the horn, raise a little hell on the way home."

But he also appeared at times to be acting out the myths he created for himself—the rawhide Texarkanan who broke and traded horses as a boy, grew up in a traditionally strong family unit, became a straight-laced Naval officer, grew impatient with IBM and launched a company that would be worth $4.4 billion when he left it, a super salesman who never gave up the traits of an eagle scout. As if he knew he would have a place in history, Perot has enshrined what he believed to be the important aspects of his life. He bought and maintained the home he grew up in. If the only way to erase the mistake somebody made by painting his old Texarkana homestead white was to turn the bricks inside-out, by God, he would have it done. For Perot, everything had to be "world-class"—from the rescue mission of his Electronic Data Systems employees in Iran, to the doctors he would provide for a Desert Storm victim or a Vietnam veteran or a critically ill volunteer. Margot was super-wife and super-mom, and his five children were "world-class"—"five precious gems."

Russell Baker wrote that Perot was hard to decipher from the TV imagery. "Sometimes he seems fired with the true believer's zeal, convinced the nation is headed for doom unless it lets him save it. Other times he looks like a man squandering millions for the pure boyish fun of making a little mischief. Then we see the egocentric Perot, the master salesman showing off his skill with a sample case. Then there are moments when something disturbing flickers in his eyes and the mouth sets in a suddenly angry expression, and you wonder: Is he maybe just a little too Texas for comfort?"

Like Lyndon Johnson before him, Perot manifests a complex personality. Despite his personal fortune, he liked to eat in the company cafeteria or at Dickey's, his favorite barbecue place. His personal warmth to his volunteers turned to ice when confronted by a swarm of press. But when he met with a reporter one-on-one, he was often effusive, chatting on for one or two hours in some interviews. There's no question, however, that he was thin-skinned, accusatorial, conniving and willing to bend the truth about even the smallest things (such as saying he voted absentee so as not to be followed to his polling place by reporters on Election Day.) NBC's Tom Brokaw said he combined a Texas "country boy charm with the impatience of a CEO billionaire." And so he did. Like LBJ, he had to be in control, in charge of every situation. And, also like LBJ, he drew his sustenance from the people. But Johnson believed strongly in the power of government—that government ought to do things for people—while Perot believed that government ought to get out of the way and let people do what they are capable of.

Perot appeared truly a man with a split personality. He wanted to change the system; he wanted to be the man who changed the system. He wanted to win the election, but he really didn't want to serve as president. ABC's Jeff Greenfield said on "Nightline" just prior to the election, "It is possible to see in this remarkable Perot campaign a series of contradictory impressions. A candidate whose instinct and actions sometimes are at war with each other...There was this year, this time...a move that would have made a third party, or independent candidate, properly financed, a really credible alternative. And, in my view, Perot could have won." Ted Koppel, host of "Nightline," agreed that some of the things Perot had done and said were "a little weird. That's also part of his charm, his attraction," Koppel said. "If he had acted more predictably we might have become bored with the Perot phenomenon long ago."

In some ways, Ross Perot was almost a caricature of himself. His colorful, folksy and blunt comments provided plenty of fodder for cartoonists and comedians, including Dana Carvey of "Saturday Night Live," who Perot concluded was "more like me than I am."

If John Anderson was the Doonesbury candidate, Perot was the candidate of "Saturday Night Live" and "Washingtoon," a political cartoon that appears in the *Washington Post*. Washingtoon's creator Wayne Stamaty calls Perot "H. Raw Pile'O-Dough." This is Pile'O Dough on Bush and modern campaign tactics: "You won't catch me doing any negative campaigning against this here fool!...I drink coffee with ordinary folks every morning!

I don't need a focus group to tell me about 'em, ' cause I'm just so ordinary myself." In another panel, "Washingtoon" shows Perot giving double-talk answers to a voter's questions about congressional gridlock and his electronic town hall. "H. Raw Pile'O-Dough" says, "I've got all the Congress we need right up here in my head, and there won't be any gridlock. I pledge allegiance to the flag of the United States of my mind..."

Jonathan Alter wrote in *Newsweek* that Perot's "Chihuahua persona is so original that he's ridiculously easy to parody."

But no one was ridiculing him on Election Day, when he captured 19 percent of the vote, a higher share of the popular vote than any third-party candidate in eighty years. He scored a more impressive showing than any third-party candidate since Theodore Roosevelt captured 27 percent on the Bull Moose ticket in 1912. The 19.7 million Americans who voted for Ross Perot, in raw numbers, was nearly twice the total cast for any previous third-party candidate. Even after he pulled the plug on his supporters on July 16, nearly one in five voters cast ballots for Perot. Both parties knew when the election results were tallied that the Perot vote—crazy Texan or not—was a force to contend with in the future.

Although Perot personally campaigned in only sixteen states, he received more than 20 percent of the vote in thirty-one states. He outscored what all the polls were saying would be his maximum vote—14 or 15 percent. His support cut a wide swath through the Reagan coalition that had dominated the last three elections. It was absolutely grounded in the small towns and suburbs that have come to be known as middle America.

Bill Clinton, running as a "new Democrat" on a message of "change," won the election with 43 percent of the popular vote, carrying thirty-two states. His election was heralded as a new beginning for the Democratic Party, perhaps erroneously so. To suggest that Bill Clinton magically reconstituted the Democratic Party is to ignore reality. Clinton's 43-percent share was the fourth-lowest for anyone elected president. (Only John Quincy Adams in 1824, Abraham Lincoln in 1860 and Woodrow Wilson in 1912 won with lower percentages.) Clinton won a smaller percentage of the vote than Michael Dukakis did in 1988, but captured the White House because Ross Perot took huge chunks out of the Republican coalition—in essence, forming a new party of "independents." On Election Day, Perot voters said they thought of themselves this way: 43 percent as independents, 31 percent as Republicans and 25 percent as Democrats.

Some analysts suggested that there would have been no difference in the election had Perot not been on the ballot—that a two-way race would not have turned out much differently. Had Perot not been on the ballot, his voters would have split about equally between the two other candidates. According to the Gallup Poll, 43 percent of Perot voters said they would have backed Clinton and 41 percent would have picked Bush. "Perot did not cost Bush the election. Bush cost Bush the election," said William Schneider of the American Enterprise Institute, who analyzed election results for CNN.

But Perot had done his damage to Bush long before Election Day. By focusing the race on the problems in the economy, the deficit and wasteful government spending, Perot took away Bush's argument that things weren't as bad as they seemed. Voters wanted to know what Bush was going to do at home, and that stemmed in part from Perot's ceaseless snapping at the president's heels. Bush was done in because he had gotten too far away from the people—just as the political power of the people was being re-energized—and he was never able to offer a compelling picture of what he would do to make things better for Americans in the future. After weeks of Ross Perot blanketing the airwaves and talking about the economy, the deficit and jobs, the Republican Convention—with its emphasis on family values, it's mean-spiritedness and lack of attention to an economic agenda—seemed silly, divisive and counter-productive.

Perot also changed the dynamics of the race, getting out on the eve of Bill Clinton's acceptance address, thereby focusing attention on the Democrats, and getting back in just before the debates. He set the tone for political rhetoric. As a businessman, he was able to make the economy a more credible issue than Bill Clinton could have done alone, as a politician. He awoke the American populace to Washington's overwhelming absorption with power, perks and influence-peddlers. He was the national civics teacher.

While the Republicans were happy to see Perot get in the race in the fall in hopes of shaking it up, the Democrats had been just as happy to have him around in the spring and early summer. Perot provided a resting place for voters who were unhappy with the Republican incumbent but who were not yet ready to move over to the Democrat. The late Democratic strategist Paul Tully said that during the spring and early summer, Perot "de-partisanized the critique of George Bush," forcing down his job rating and creating an opening that the then unpopular Bill Clinton was able later to take advantage of. When Perot got out, declaring the Democratic Party revitalized just as Clinton and Gore appeared to be running as mainstream, middle Americans, many of those voters took the other half-step and moved into the Democrats' column. Throughout the rest of the summer and well into September, Clinton held a huge lead over the incumbent president. Perot essentially dislodged the GOP in many of its bastions after having kept the president off balance through much of the year.

Moreover, he convinced millions of disenchanted voters to return to the ballot box. Invigorated by the contest, Americans registered to vote in record numbers. The Perot campaign brought millions out to vote who had not participated in presidential elections in years. Turnout was 55.24 percent of the nation's estimated voting-age population of nearly 190 million, the highest turnout rate for any national election since 1968. A total of 104.4 million voters cast ballots in the 1992 presidential election, easily eclipsing the 92.7 million of 1984. Curtis Gans, director of the nonpartisan Committee for the Study of the American Electorate, attributes the twelve-million-plus increase to Perot. "In what was clearly a repudiation of the two major political parties, the entire increase in participation can be traced to Perot's candidacy," Gans said.

Perot's impact cannot be taken lightly. It bodes ill for both parties, but particularly for the Republican Party. Frank Luntz, research director for the Perot Petition Committee, said two-thirds of the Perot vote came from the forty-four-and-under voters. Republicans have won a majority of the forty-four-and-under voters in every election since 1972, and their attraction to Perot spells serious trouble for the GOP unless it can win these voters back. This is particularly true in the Plains and Rocky Mountain states and in California, regions of enormous Perot strength that Republicans used to take for granted, he said.

House Republican Leader Bob Michel of Illinois warned a Republican breakfast group at the height of Perot I of the dilemma presented the GOP by "Perot-stroika." Michel said, "All I see when I turn on the TV to watch Perot volunteers is suburbanites and older Americans and younger folks and farmers—exactly the people we thought were in our Republican camp."

Exit polls showed Perot won support from a diverse group—Westerners, union households, first-time voters, eighteen-to-twenty-nine-year-olds, parents with children under eighteen, suburbanites and Reagan Democrats. Overall, he was strongest in fiercely independent New England and in the frontier states of the West. His highest percentage, 30 percent, was in Maine—where President Bush has a vacation home.

In nine states, he received more than 25 percent. If there was a common thread in those states—Alaska, Idaho, Maine, Montana, Nevada, Oregon, Utah, Kansas and Wyoming—it is a history of intensely independent, often adversarial politics. Kansas boasted one of Perot's strongest state organizations and pioneered what came to be known as the "wave campaign." Perot supporters lined highways to shake banners and wave placards at passing motorists.

Bush managed to carry his home state of Texas with 40 percent, while Perot drew 22 percent. But some two dozen Texas counties, mostly in the environs of Dallas, gave Perot over 30 percent of the vote. He carried four Texas counties, including Grayson County, where he maintains a vacation home on Lake Texoma.

Perot also was strong in the high-tech and industrial areas from Route 128 around Boston to Florida's Cape Kennedy, Dallas's Silicon Prairie and California's Silicon Valley,

But the key factor was that Perot's strength was in the socioeconomic middle—in the ordinary suburbs, the moderately prosperous rural areas and in the anonymous small towns and small cities. Like the Teddy Roosevelt voters of 1912, Perot voters are widely distributed rather than concentrated in one or two regions, making it more difficult for either party to preempt them.

Frank Luntz says the element of greatest concern to the parties should be that Perot captured more than a quarter of the under-thirty male vote and 22 percent of all first-time voters, while he convinced disgruntled voters to return to the ballot box.

"This newly expanded electorate holds the key to America's political future," Luntz wrote in *Policy Review*. "Whichever party wins the lion's share of the Perot vote will be guaranteed a governing majority for the next decade, if not the next generation."

But there's no guarantee that either party will be able to co-opt the Perot voters. In fact, voter identification with the traditional parties has been declining in recent years, for reasons that have become well-known—gridlock, Washington's failure to respond to the real-life problems of people, the arrogance of power and the party hierarchy's preoccupation with power for power's sake. Another reason, however, is that the parties don't need to rely on volunteers as they once did. Campaigns are run by professionals, who hire other professionals to carry out the work that used to be done entirely by volunteers. The people, more and more, feel cut out of the process.

Finally, the parties have increasingly failed to provide a solid foundation of beliefs which inspire strong allegiance from voters as they once did. Rather, they have come to exist primarily to provide the framework for nominating candidates and to offer access to fundraising.

The proliferation of the primaries and the decline of the caucus or convention system of selecting candidates has added to the decline of the parties. The nominees are no longer selected by party notables and workers but by expensive campaigns, taken directly to the people, and sorted out by the media. University of Texas political scientist James Fishkin believes party loyalty is at an extraordinary low level for both parties and that the country may be seeing an historical realignment of parties. "We've created an environment of self-selected candidates for the party nomination. Now we have a candidate who has selected his own party as well, created his own party," he said, of Perot's party of independents.

The problem faced by the Democrats with their newly elected president and their control of both houses of Congress is that they no longer have any excuses. They can't blame divided government or partisan gridlock for inaction on such problems as the deficit, health care, job creation and economic competitiveness. If Clinton can't govern and mold a majority coalition, the Democrats will be in serious trouble in 1996.

George Christian, former press secretary to President Lyndon Johnson, said, "I think the two political parties are in trouble and I don't think this election is going to change that. Democrats did a lot of shaping up during this campaign. Republicans really have some work cut out for them. They're fractured. They're beginning to act like Democrats more and more—too much infighting, jealousies, bitterness. They're going to have to regroup as a White House party. People may wind up continuously frustrated. It's hard to believe that Clinton

is going to be able to make any magical difference overnight. There's going to be a lot of impatience; he's got a
lot to do to get this country squared away. Clinton may
be forced to move before he's ready to, and there's still
going to be a lot of angry folks out there. Who knows?
Perot may stick around, and he may try again."

The truth is that Perot wasn't crazy, at all, and neither were his supporters. He intuitively recognized the
dissatisfaction that was just beneath the surface and
brought it out into the open. He energized and empowered people as they haven't been in decades. The interest was also seen in the debates, which exceeded the
ratings of the debates four years prior.

Many feel Perot's greatest contribution in 1992 was
to refocus the election-year debate. With his paperback
best seller and his unremitting media appearances, Perot
almost single-handedly forced the issue of the deficit
and the country's economic backsliding onto the national playing field. There was little or no indication
that Clinton or Bush would have picked these as the top
priority issues, had it not been for Perot. These issues
were not even part of the discussion before Perot.

One fact is certain: His candidacy could not have
happened without the force of his personality, his unbelievable wealth and the vacuum on issues from the
other candidates. Perot could not have achieved what
he did without his own tens of millions. Final Federal
Elections Commission reports showed at year's end that
Perot '92 had spent $69.6 million, with the Perot Peti-
tion Committee spending $18.5 million of that. But nei-
ther could it have happened without the "crazies"—the
people who put him on the ballot and the millions who
voted for him on Election Day.

As The New York Times put it, for all his money spent,

"The public was under no obligation to respond to his appeal, and it does appear that Mr. Perot may have mobilized a brand new army." That army was described as being primarily under forty-five, overwhelmingly white, and one that considers itself neither Republican nor Democrat, but independent. It was further described as a corps of voters highly distrustful of politicians, who by and large felt the country was "on the wrong track."

Newsweek wrote that the demographic data suggest that Perot scored best with independents with incomes of more than $50,000 a year and with voters in their thirties and forties—the upper-middle segment of white-collar, suburban America, and people in their most productive years. "This is hardly a profile of true believing zanies—and these are not people who, as some have suggested, can rightly be seen as proto-fascists yearning for a dictator."

Bill Clinton surely saw some sanity in what Perot was doing and saying. If imitation is the sincerest form of flattery, Perot should have felt complimented; Clinton and the Democrats repeatedly borrowed from the Perot playbook. Campaigning in Michigan in the final days of the campaign, Clinton said: "I am nothing more than a temporary tenant and your chief hired hand. And if it hadn't been for you I would not be here."

On "Good Morning America" during the last week of the election, Clinton was listing deficit reduction as his number-two priority after job creation. Even in the summer, the Perot vocabulary had become the vocabulary of the campaign. The Democratic platform talked about the government treating Americans as the customers and bosses they are. The Democratic platform appropriated one of Perot's favorite terms, "world-class." The whole message of the Democratic platform, in fact, was to make government work for the people. Even Clinton's phrase, "the people's mandate," seemed to be whisked from Perot's vocabulary. Clinton also utilized the town hall meeting concept and the half-hour infomercial among tactics that were identified with Perot.

Clinton recognized the importance of the Perot phenomenon; he moved both during and after the campaign to address the concerns of "the people" and to provide for greater involvement by average people in his campaign and administration. An example was the Economic Summit, which brought 329 business and labor leaders and economists together for two days in Little Rock a month before Clinton's inauguration. "This is all a part of the kind of effort that we have to continue to reconnect the American people to their government," he said.

Unquestionably, Perot's ability to refocus the debate was important for 1992 and for the future. But Perot's most singular accomplishment was to empower the American people, to restore their appetite for democracy and the perception that each individual can make a difference.

And the devotion of his supporters—his volunteers— was incredible. Grady Hendricks, who introduced Perot at that election eve rally at Reunion Arena in Dallas, was an eighty-two-year-old retired paper salesman who began volunteering at the Dallas phone bank in March. He became seriously ill and was hospitalized, but obtained a two-week pass to return to the phone bank during the campaign. Hendricks said that working in the phone bank and introducing Perot at the rally made 1992 the greatest year of his life.

Few of these people were profiled in news reports, although there was considerable coverage given to those who left the ship. Certainly, he lost some of the people along the way. Among them were volunteers and state leaders who claimed their credit records had been checked, those who claimed they had been pushed aside by operatives from Dallas, those burned by Perot's withdrawal, and those who merely decided that the skipper and his crew were a little too strange to stay the course.

Columbia University's Alan Brinkley found in Perot an unlikely populist because "real wisdom, he seems to believe, lies not in the people but in himself." Yet Brinkley found an important populist element to the Perot campaign nevertheless. "It is the passion that millions of voters seem to have found in becoming part of a popular movement. Unlike the major party candidates, whose media-driven campaigns leave almost no room for citizen involvement, Perot has actually given his followers something to do." They had to collect signatures, organize committees, figure out new ways to promote a new candidate with limited direction and limited local funds, without relying on party machinery and party money. It was old-fashioned grass roots politics with a new sense of urgency. It was intoxicating. One after another, the Perotistas called their involvement the most rewarding work of a lifetime.

"Perot's campaign has shown, if nothing else, that despite decades of declining voter turnout, yearning for political empowerment is still strong. For many, Perot's position on issues (or his unwillingness to take positions on them) is beside the point. He has given them something they consider more important: a chance to feel democracy at work," Brinkley wrote in the *New Republic.*

And they did it well. Not only did they engineer Perot's petition campaigns in almost all of the states, they also planned and executed the rallies. Joe Canzeri, a long-time special-events man who worked for Republicans before getting involved in the Perot effort, said he was "astounded" at how well the volunteers staged their events with little professional assistance, and how smoothly the Perot events went without the usual "advance teams" utilized by the parties.

Supporter Jan Garb said at Perot's election-eve rally, "People from all walks of life can think for themselves. We don't need to be managed. We need the freedom to think for ourselves. We will no longer sit still for government that has an apparent condescension for the average working American."

Susan Esser, Michigan chairperson and a volunteer going back to the original "Larry King Show," said on Election Day: "I never met a higher caliber of people in my life. Now I know exactly what they mean by 'family of man.' It's been one of the most incredible experiences of my life."

Rosemarie Sax of Denver found a unity among the people who volunteered in the Perot effort she had never experienced before. While the people were much more disparate than those she previously worked with in the Republican Party, she said, "I had never encountered this immediate bonding of people."

Perot had frequently said he once wanted to be a beautiful pearl. "But I looked in the mirror and decided that wasn't in the cards," he said. Then he hoped to be the oyster that made the beautiful pearl. That didn't work either. Finally, he had come to realize that his lot in life was to be the grain of sand that irritates the oyster. On election night, speaking to a hotel ballroom full of supporters in Dallas, Perot praised the millions who came together to take back their country. "You have done an incredible job of getting this country turned back around. It's been an honor to be your grain of sand."

Then he quickly added, "Let's forget the election; it's behind us. The hard work is in front of us." He admonished his supporters, "Don't lose your enthusiasm. Don't lose your idealism. Don't lose your love of this country. Don't feel, Gee, I'm powerless again. We will stay together and we will be a force for good for our country."

Perot knew he held the hammer. Displaying a bumper sticker someone passed up to the lectern that said "Perot '96," Perot said on election night he would remain a "safety valve." If the Clinton administration doesn't perform to satisfaction, if the parties don't reform to meet the needs of the people, Perot said: "You can bring that old stray dog out from the dog pound again."

Crazy? Yes, as was often said about Perot, like a fox.

PART III
THE NEW AMERICAN POLITICS

17

COMMUNICATIONS REVOLUTION: NEW MEDIA VS. OLD MEDIA

Ross Perot ushered in a new era of American politics in 1992—one based on the empowerment of people and the communications revolution. He opened a passageway for a more participatory electorate grounded in the "new media" of television talk shows and other direct forms of communication. For better or worse, Perot recognized that television and other new technologies could augment, if not replace, the old technologies of the parties. Talk shows, 800 numbers and facsimile machines became the new media of influence during the '92 campaign. It was "Speak Up, America," time. People wanted to be heard, to be part of the process, and they could do that with the "new media" in which they asked the questions in forums without the traditional journalistic filters. One indication of the vox populi was that ordinary voters, not reporters, asked questions of the presidential candidates in the Richmond debate.

But the greatest manifestation of Speak-Up America could be found in the TV talk shows, such as "Larry King Live," where Perot had unceremoniously announced his own candidacy. "This is a year in which people want to be heard," said Ann Lewis, a Democratic political consultant. She told *The New York Times*,

"They have sent a very clear message: 'We want a candidate who hears what we have to say.' With a call-in show, millions of voters can watch you listen and respond courteously to people just like them."

These kinds of shows tapped into the voters' sense of alienation. "Talk radio and talk television are a phenomenal thing that's happened to the disenfranchised in this country," said Michael K. Deaver, a former aide to President Ronald Reagan. Deaver told *The Times*, "The other channels have been closed off to them. It's like a flow of water that gets dammed up and finds another way to go."

That this happened in 1992 should have come as no big surprise, given the political climate and the fact that dramatic changes, spurred by the communications revolution, were occurring around the world. As Americans were seeing other countries become more democratic, they sensed their own stake in democracy was floundering.

In the face of global change, it was preposterous that American politics not change—that this nation's party structure, election mechanisms and political traditions are somehow sacrosanct. The walls of communism collapsed in part because people were able to gain direct access to information through an open communications network.

Despite the complacency of the two major political parties, the American political system is neither immune from revolution, at most, nor evolution, at the least.

On three occasions over the last one hundred years, technology and politics have intersected with such force that the political landscape was unalterably changed. The first was when William Jennings Bryan used the railroads to take his presidential campaign directly to the people at the end of the last century. The second was when Franklin D. Roosevelt reached into living rooms throughout the country with his radio "fireside chats." The third such change occurred with the televised Kennedy-Nixon debates in 1960.

The sea change of 1992 was the emergence of "electronic campaigning" largely exploited by Ross Perot— talk shows, cable TV, electronic town halls, infomercials, campaign videos, satellite television, faxed information, computer bulletin boards—all aimed at a more participatory democracy.

In 1982, John Naisbitt predicted in his groundbreaking book, *Megatrends*, that America would move away from representative democracy toward a more participatory democracy. The guiding principle of this participatory democracy, he said, is that people must be part of the process of arriving at decisions that affect their lives. It was a theory that would be validated by the Perot phenomenon.

Recognizing the unprecedented growth in the use of referenda and initiatives in the 1970s, Naisbitt noted that "participatory democracy is revolutionizing local politics in America and is bubbling upward to change the course of national government as well." He forecast further that the end of representative democracy would sound the death knell for the two-party system.

In a representative democracy, people do not vote on issues directly but elect someone to do the voting for them. "We created a representative system two hundred years ago when it was the practical way to organize a democracy," Naisbitt wrote. "Direct citizen participation was simply not feasible, so we elected people to go off to the state capitals, represent us, vote and then come back and tell us what happened. The representative who did a good job was reelected. The one who did not was turned out. For two hundred years, it worked quite well," he said.

"Then along came the communication revolution and with it an extremely well-educated electorate. Today, with instantaneously shared information, we know as much about what's going on as our representatives, and we know it just as quickly.

"The fact is we have outlived the historical usefulness of representative democracy, and we all sense intuitively that it is obsolete. Furthermore, we have grown more confident of our own ability to make decisions about how institutions, including government and corporations, should operate," he wrote.

Naisbitt concluded that we continue to elect representatives because this is the way we've always done it, and because it is politically expedient. We don't really want to vote on every issue, he said, only the ones that we feel make a difference in our lives.

Perot recognized the power inherent in participatory democracy and in the communications revolution that had been manifest on a global scale.

Alvin Toffler, author of *Future Shock* and *Powershift*, told the *Los Angeles Times* that, "Representative democracy is increasingly giving way to direct democracy, a trend facilitated in no small part by a communications revolution that provides global information directly to electorates in a way intelligence channels once informed leaders."

"The growing complexity and speed (of change) make it difficult to govern in the old way," Toffler said. "It's like a computer blowing fuses. Our existing political decision-making structures are now recognized to be obsolete."

Ken Auletta, a journalist and author, said the effort of people to interact directly in the process will be a permanent part of American presidential campaigns. He is quoted in a special election report of the Freedom Forum Media Studies Center at Columbia University as saying, "That's what happened, in fact, in Eastern Europe when they overthrew the middleman, the socialist government; it's what we see happening with home banking, home computers and the mail-order catalog business; what we see in TV clickers that gives us the choice of what we want to watch and when we want to watch it. Throughout our society, we are seeing a move to get rid of the middleman. That's what happened this year in politics."

So significant was Perot's contribution to a direct electronic democracy that the University of Miami (Florida) School of Communication conducted as "Electronic Democracy" seminar in early 1993, during which Ed Pfister, dean of the school, talked about a "new page" being turned in the American democratic process. One of the speakers at the seminar was Larry Grossman, former president of NBC News and of the Public Broadcasting Service (PBS).

Grossman said he believed Ross Perot was "on to something, and indeed, his ideas of direct electronic democracy may well end up being his most enduring, and certainly his most interesting, contribution to American politics...It used to be that you had to wait until you could have an election day and get your views expressed in the voting booth. Today it can be done instantaneously, and with the rise of telecomputers, people will be punching buttons at home letting congressmen and congresswomen in Washington know exactly how they feel at the instant on any particular issue."

Grossman attributed the rise of electronic democracy not just to technology, but also to the sense of alienation, frustration and anger that the American people have with their government. He quoted a Louis Harris poll taken just before the November election that found that 72 percent of the electorate felt their leaders were out of touch with the voters, 66 percent felt powerless with regard to their government, and 61 percent felt political leaders did not care about their fate or their lives. That hostility, he said, gave rise to "this powerful new movement of direct democracy."

Grossman pointed to the dangers as well as the advantages of direct democracy, asking the question of whether elected officials should be following public opinion or leading public opinion. "How do we have strong, enduring, intelligent leadership if the leaders are simply testing the wind and doing exactly what the public wants at any particular moment?" he asked.

Grossman concluded, "It is very clear that if the public is, as I believe it is, inevitably going to be more of a participant, a new fourth branch of government alongside the executive, the judiciary and the legislative, then our information systems have got to be enhanced enormously." He cited the need, for example, for the public to be given the opportunity to wrestle with issues, one at a time, in between election campaigns. He called for the political parties to organize the debate, one issue at a time, to make sure that the American people are well informed enough to be full-time players in the process.

"Unless we pay attention to that," he said, "we are going to be in very deep trouble in terms of the future of our democratic system. And in order to make sure that politics continues to work...we are going to have to take account of the new, the rise of direct democracy, which is now replacing what has been a two-hundred-year-old tradition of a representative republic."

Perot indicated early in his petition drive that his intent was to rely on the "new media." Perot was uninterested in the "political press," the political reporters, both print and broadcast, who have had a lot to do with setting the political agenda in recent presidential campaigns.

His communications director Jim Squires said in May 1992, that Perot "does not like to talk to people the way the political process talks to people." His inclination was to largely ignore the national press and rely on live television talk shows, some of which would be paid for and hosted by himself. Squires said Perot wanted to "pay for the studio, cameras and satellite time for numerous talk shows on cable outlets and network affiliates across the country." The shows would have a live audience, perhaps with studio audiences in other cities watching via satellite. Anyone in any of the audiences would be able to ask him a question. During the petition drive, he never fully developed this concept, and the compressed nature of the fall campaign did not allow him the time to carry out his idea. But during the spring and early summer, Perot did rely almost entirely on TV talk shows and appearances on morning news shows, where his message was not squeezed into a normal news broadcast or relinquished to a sound bite of 9.8 seconds—the average in the 1988 election.

Because of the Perot candidacy, the media became divided into "old news" and "new news," with the old being the print media—both newspapers and news magazines—and the regular broadcast news, and the "new media" being the Larry Kings and Phil Donahues. The five most common talk show venues for the presidential candidates were the three morning network shows—CBS's "This Morning," ABC's "Good Morning America," and NBC's "Today"—along with "Larry King Live" and "Donahue." The three candidates appeared a total of ninety-six times on these five shows from January 1 through Election Day, according to the Freedom Forum Media Studies Center at Columbia University. Waking up to one of the presidential candidates became de rigeur. Clinton actually appeared even more often than Perot; he made forty-seven such appearances to Perot's thirty-three. Bush, making only sixteen appearances, arrived late to the "new media" phenomenon; he thought it undignified for the president to appear on such shows as "Arsenio Hall" and MTV (Music Television). Clinton appeared sixteen times on "Good Morning America," while Perot appeared fifteen times on the "Today" show. And Larry King conducted thirteen interviews with the three major presidential candidates.

Even the late-night comedians such as Jay Leno of "The Tonight Show" and Dana Carvey of "Saturday Night Live" were purveyors of information in the '92 election campaign. A poll by CBS News found that 30 percent of the eighteen-to-twenty-nine age group and 18 percent of all respondents said they heard some presidential campaign news for the first time from late-night comedians.

In its report, *The Homestretch: New Politics. New Media. New Voters?*, Columbia University's Freedom Forum Media Studies Center concluded that the different media reached a different audience, especially the young, which probably contributed to the largest turnout in recent history.

To illustrate what a difference four years can make, Phil Donahue tried and failed to get Michael Dukakis on his television show. And, in 1988, television news was covering photo opportunities such as flag factories, George Bush in Boston Harbor and before Veterans of Foreign Wars, and Dukakis in a tank. In 1992, the contrived photo-ops all but disappeared.

The salutary effect of talk show politics was that the average American citizen had far greater access to the candidates and what they were saying. "Let's face it," said National Public Radio's political editor Ken Rudin, "the public is not sitting home watching 'Meet the Press.' It's watching 'Arsenio Hall' and 'Donahue,' and people are talking about the candidates because they have far better access to them than they ever had before."

Contrary to critics' predictions that the talk show phase of the campaign would end after the national conventions, talk show appearances by the candidates rose to a fever pitch during the final months of the campaign. All of a sudden, it seemed, the once-alienated American people were enamored of presidential politics. In the aftermath, Ross Perot was given much of the credit for the revived interest in the presidential election. But that credit was slow in coming. Susan Page, White House correspondent for *Newsday*, said in the Columbia report that one of the greatest shortcomings of news coverage of the election year "was our failure to understand and take seriously enough the candidacy of Ross Perot and what it signaled about the electorate."

One of the developments of the '92 campaign season was that the modern information age began catching up with today's politics and with the traditional news media. The public need not rely on only a handful of major news outlets for campaign information. "They can click on their computers, link up to scores of information services and locate whatever data they want," wrote Carl Sessions Stepp, a journalism professor and senior editor of the *Washington Journalism Review*. Perot reminded people of this during the final debate when, in talking about President Bush's relations with Saddam Hussein, he said, "Go through Nexis and Lexis, pull all the old news articles" and see for yourselves the contradictions in administration statements about Iraq.

That the "new media" had bumped the evening news on campaign coverage was apparent when ABC's Peter Jennings opened an hour-long ABC News documentary about Perot with pictures of Perot on the "Phil Donahue Show."

To be sure, the political reporters and the Sam Donaldsons and Dan Rathers who were being bypassed by the talk shows weren't happy about the development. The "newsies" complained about the Politainment Era. Bill Clinton playing the saxophone on "Arsenio Hall" was criticized as infotainment—although Clinton engaged in prolonged conversation with Hall about the Los Angeles riots and reconnecting inner-city kids with society. Candidates, the hard-core journalists said, needed to be subjected to the harder questions posed by journalists. In fact, a review of the hundreds of questions posed to the presidential candidates showed a striking difference between those that came from ordinary citizens and reporters. A story in *The New York Times* noted that "reporters dwell on the process, asking about polls, tactical strategy and, of course, the story of the day. Questions from the public are far less confrontational, and an overwhelming number of people ask candidates how they would solve problems that affect the questioner." In most cases, it was to the candidate's advantage to bypass the Washington-based elite corps of reporters who concentrated more on process and character. But the striking factor was that the public thought it also was to their advantage for the candidates to leap-frog the traditional media.

Media critic Jon Katz, who coined the phrase "new news" and "old news" in relation to this campaign, delivered one of the most on-target documentaries of the campaign on National Public Radio when he talked about the trend toward getting journalists out of the way so the candidates could talk directly to the voters. "Everyone but reporters seem to like it. Using 800 telephone numbers, talk shows and cable broadcasts, they (the candidates) found new ways to get through to one another that energized presidential politics. Never was it clearer that journalism and the electorate have radically different agendas. Reporters, determined to function as a sort of campaign FBI, were obsessed to the end with sex, lies and transcripts, scrambling to catch candidates with their memos and their pants down—alleged mistresses, Iran-Contra, decades-old draft letters. It was the public—not the media—that pressed concerns about the economy, women's issues, health care, race and poverty."

The *Washington Post*'s ombudsman Richard Harwood suggested in an op-ed piece on "The Growing Irrelevance of Journalists" that the new immediacy of the television camera was reducing the need for a "surrogate witness," i.e., the journalist. He cited the live coverage of the Gulf War, the military briefings on the war and the talk show candidacies of the presidential candidates. Dan Rather took exception to that, responding that reporters ask sharper questions with follow-ups. The public, however, said loudly in 1992 that it didn't care much for the sharp questions with follow-ups that the journalists asked.

Harwood further quoted a Twentieth Century Fund study of the network news coverage during the early months of the 1992 primary campaign which found that 72 percent of the air time was monopolized by a handful of reporters and commentators. Only 13 percent of the time went to candidates actually speaking on camera, and only 15 percent to voters, experts and other sources. "What these numbers mean is that journalists—not the politicians and not the people—dominate the conversations of democracy in the United States."

Phil Donahue defended talk-show politics because it's "closer to the street" and it's free. "They're free, at a time when we're all horrified at the amount of money we're spending during campaigns," Donahue said, on "Good Morning America." For years, public advocates have been trying to open up the airwaves to candidates and campaigning. Public financing is regarded as laudatory by some because it enables challengers to compete with incumbents in financing media campaigns. But with adequate free air time, who needs taxpayer-funded campaigns? Also, Donahue pointed out, "The serious shows...are the same shows that missed Iranscam, missed the S&L crises, missed BCCI, missed the HUD scandal and missed a lot of other stories. So when these serious journalists uncover those stories, then they can preach to us and tell us we're not serious."

As a result of the "new media," campaigns should be conducted and covered differently in the future. Perot demonstrated that there's no need for a candidate to frantically fly around the country making photogenic media appearances, largely to get snippets shown on network news. Nor is there need for the press planes and the press buses to haul all the reporters around. "It's silly business, getting on and off airplanes, dragging huge numbers of press behind you," says Squires. "It does not make for good political dialogue." Perot's idea was to stage relatively few events and give reporters who wanted to cover them the opportunity to get there on their own. With so much happening on television interviews and talk shows, the "Boys on the Bus"—the reporters on the road—with Bush and Clinton were missing much of the action because they were away from a TV. By spending all of their time in the campaign's cocoon, they were also missing the real story of the year—what was going on in the hearts and minds of the American people.

But the lack of press charters and statements and press conferences left the traditional journalists scrambling for ways to cover the Perot campaign. As a result, they turned to dissecting Perot's business dealings and his private life—which was cataclysmic for him.

"I will have to have privacy. I will not live my life, you know, 100 percent exposed," Perot told *Time* magazine, in a May question-and-answer interview. "This business of the press following the President if he goes out to have dinner with a friend at night—I'm going to work that out with the press."

The fact is that Perot never worked anything out with the press. As his popularity grew and the press scrutiny intensified, his appetite for the contest dissipated and his hatred for the media mob escalated. As Hamilton Jordan said, "He'd had this kind of business-hero press worship. He just wasn't prepared for what happened to him. No one is. Clinton wasn't either. All you can tell people is that it is rough in the big leagues. I found him both a master at manipulating this business-press image and naive as to how the political press treated him."

As the campaign progressed, the mutual hostility

between Perot and the "old media" grew. Perot repeatedly accused the press of practicing "gotcha" journalism and of being conduits for negative stories supplied by Republicans and other members of the political establishment. His names for reporters included "teenage boy" and "jerk." He began the "Blame the Media" assault picked up by Republicans at their national convention, which Bush carried over in the fall campaign—holding up his favorite bumper sticker: "Annoy the Media—Re-Elect Bush."

It was good political strategy because the public distrusted the traditional media as much as it distrusted the entrenched politicians. *Newsweek*'s Jonathan Alter reflected that "There's almost two rebellions at once going on. There's a rebellion against politics as usual and a rebellion against media as usual."

David Awbrey, editorial page editor of the Wichita (Kansas) *Eagle-Beacon*, in a column explaining why he was rejecting Washington-based pundits on his op-ed page, wrote that many Americans feel instinctively that "presidents may come and go but the Washington journalistic, governmental and influence-peddling establishment is eternal. They are a self-perpetuating elite, more concerned to promote their personal goals than the national purpose, more motivated by career status than the national interest. As the 1992 election showed—from the Ross Perot phenomenon to the turnover in Congress—it is a group out of touch with America and trapped in old mindsets."

Perot cast the media as part of the political establishment, which he was fighting. And, in fact, there is something to be said about "media incumbency." The elite, Washington-based political press corps operated according to the delusion that they were as important to the process as were the candidates. It was a rude awakening, in 1992, when they discovered that at least one candidate could do without them.

Appearing on ABC's "20/20" news program in early October, Perot said, "Anybody who's not trying to be politically correct would make it clear that journalism needs to clean up its act. They've got their agendas; they've got their candidates," he said.

William Greider wrote in *Who Will Tell the People* that as upwardly mobile people have taken over our newsrooms, they have "gravitated toward elite interests and converged with those powerful few who already dominate politics." In this new journalism the lives and concerns of ordinary people count for less than connections with the powerful. The people's uprising in 1992 was as much about media-as-usual as it was politics-as-usual.

Even Ellen Goodman, the *Boston Globe* columnist, who annihilated Perot in her column when he reentered the race after dropping out, admitted that she had been uneasy earlier in the campaign "when my media mates came down on Perot with such a heavy hand. I think it showed how conservative we have become as professionals—too much a part of the system, too comfortable with the old names on our Rolodexes. For all our overt passion for news, new-ness, change, some of us were hostile to the notion that a Ross Perot might really throw the whole process up for grabs. Reporters who had trudged through months of primaries, commentators who had nurtured all the right (and left) contacts in Washington, were not friendly to the new outsider, the nobody."

Squires, the former editor of the *Chicago Tribune*, wrote in *Nieman Reports*, after Perot got out of the race: "Of all the good reasons why Ross Perot quit running for president, only one is personally embarrassing. For me, not him. After nearly thirty years as a reporter and editor, going to work for a presidential candidate gave me the extraordinary opportunity to see what I had been doing all my life—from the other side. It was not a pretty sight.

"For one hundred days, I truthfully answered thousands of questions from dozens of reporters on subjects on which I had firsthand knowledge and then watched them played back on front pages and television screens. Watching the press cover the Perot campaign underscored my growing conviction, shared by many veteran journalists, that the traditional institutions of the press of which I was so proud is no more; and that the news media that have replaced it are so rife with careerism and incompetence and so driven by marketing compulsions that they have ceased to be a positive force in the democracy."

His was a damning indictment of the press's role in the presidential campaign.

Tom Luce, who headed Perot I, was also critical of the press. He believes one of the great mistakes the media have made in the last twenty years has been in assigning reporters to be "political reporters." He cited as one example a story on employment discrimination lawsuits filed against EDS while Perot was head of the company. It was probably the smallest number a company that size had, he said, but the political reporters didn't understand the context of those lawsuits. There was nothing inaccurate about the story, but a business writer instead of a political reporter would have had a better frame of reference for writing the story. Luce believed the problem with the Perot campaign was that political reporters were dealing with a different breed of candidate, outside of their frame of reference. They couldn't go back to his political record, to previous campaign speeches or voting records. "Perot was outside the mold," Luce said, "and it was hard for the press to adjust."

Perot, however, can't blame the media for his own quirkiness—the split personality that he exhibited to the press and to the public unfiltered by the press. In the final days before he quit the campaign in July and in the five-week fall campaign, Perot appeared agitated and accusatory in his dealings with the press—a contradictory personality to the folksy and issues-oriented persona he portrayed on his infomercials. After one debate, he attacked what he called a "hostile media," saying reporters "have less respect in this country than Congress." That wasn't an original thought; it was expressed repeatedly at the Republican National Convention in August in Houston.

However, Perot fostered the "paranoid" image that he developed with the press. In some cases, he treated the press as badly as it treated him. At a California appearance the last weekend of the campaign, Perot actually worked the crowd into a frenzy against the press. After the speech, people in the audience began rocking a satellite truck outside the event, and members of the media were actually fearful they would be hurt.

"It was the last trip of the campaign," said *USA Today*'s Debbie Howlett. "It was also the first one where the campaign made any provisions for the press at all. There was a charter plane and buses to take us to the venue." The press paid for their transportation, but the charters enabled the reporters to get to the events on time. During the speech, Perot had railed against the media. When it was over, a confrontation developed outside the arena between people attending the event and a woman broadcast journalist who was doing a "stand-up" report. "People were really upset because they didn't think we were giving Perot a fair shake; they thought we were biased," Debbie Howlett said. One of Perot's staff people, April Cotton, finally went in and faced down the crowd.

Another reporter complained that Perot refused to conduct press conferences in a civilized manner, on the rare occasions that he had them. Rather than acknowledge a questioner, he would let the reporters shout out questions and then he would pick the one he wanted to answer.

But Perot's major shortcoming in dealing with the press was that he simply failed to share any information. He was a closed book. Even the people who were reportedly speaking for him, such as Orson Swindle during the fall campaign, had no idea what he was doing. Karen Frost, a former ABC producer who managed the media room at the Dallas headquarters during the fall campaign, said she believed the press did the best job they could with what they had to work with. "Mr. Perot was just not sharing any information. That's just the way he is. The press worked openly and fairly, and they did get frustrated," she said. She could only count three press conferences conducted by Perot during the campaign, including a spontaneous appearance at Swindle's daily briefing after the infamous "60 Minutes" "conspiracy" appearance. It was unfortunate, she said, that Perot regarded the press as the "enemy" because an open and honest relationship with the press would have benefited his candidacy.

Newsweek reported in its November 9, 1992 issue that Perot "could not stand the press corps' skepticism, its relentless search for critics from his business years and, most of all, its interest in his family. He probably never understood that reporters were paid to ask impertinent questions and that somewhere in the hazing process a truer portrait of the candidate would emerge. The newsies, on the other hand, were mostly uninterested in the issues Perot was trying to promote and almost obsessive in their conviction that a major character flaw was lurking somewhere in his past. What they found, for the most part, was a culture clash—the conflict between Perot's straitlaced, military style and their own irreverent disregard for Norman Rockwell pieties."

The question remains as to whether it is the role of the press to "haze" someone who is running for the highest office in the land, or to act as a sort of character police. Most agree, however, that it is a legitimate role of the press to put forward the issues that should be on the public agenda. Many issues, such as those pertaining to the economy and budget, including the deficit, are not popular issues with reporters and their editors; they're regarded as complex and dry. It's much easier to get one's teeth into a good scandal—such as the check-kiting scandal—than it is to wrap one's arms around public policy issues like the deficit, even though the deficit has far more impact on John Q. Public than does a congressman's hot checks.

Whether the press treated Perot badly or Perot treated the press badly, the fact remains that the public regards the press as biased, non-objective and a deterrent to the democratic process. When ABC's "Prime Time Live" asked for examples of press bias for a report aired on March 11, 1993, it received eight thousand individual responses. The citizen complainants mentioned photo selection, headlines, interpretation and commentary in their examples of bias.

Thomas Oliphant wrote in the *Boston Globe* in June 1992, about the time that the "new news" programs were threatening conventional journalism that "at half-time of the quadrennial national ordeal, it ought to be clear that, along with the Republican and Democratic parties, the other institution in deep doo-doo is journalism."

Looking back on the mass of material written and broadcast since the beginning of the 1992 primary campaign, Oliphant said, "one inescapable conclusion emerges, based solely upon the press coverage." That conclusion was that "none of these people deserves to be president because they all are fools, liars, cheats, crooks and failures. The truth, of course, is that all of them are human beings, with defects and strengths, good ideas and bad ones, accomplishments and flops; but in the distorting, supermagnification of modern media, the defects, bad ideas and flops are the news. Worse, the dominance of 'gotcha' stories, scandal and rumor mongering is so great that perspective (once the signal contribution of good journalism) has been lost."

Oliphant lamented the fact that the coverage has "lost the distinctions between personal and public character, and between insider speculation and old-fashioned reporting." For the moment, he said, the antidote may be direct access events like "Arsenio Hall." "For the future, it would be better if the press itself responded by getting out of the people's way more and letting the candidates speak. We have gotten too big for our britches, and our kind of pride usually precedes a serious fall."

It took a Ross Perot candidacy, with his emphasis on participatory democracy and utilization of the myriad tools of the communications revolution—his own novel brand of telepopulism—to bring forth such introspection from some members of the media. It will, however, take much more to force a course correction.

18

LESSONS FOR THE FUTURE AND THIRD-PARTY POLITICS

W HEN THE DUST SETTLED ON E LECTION '92, the people's revolt had left its imprint. American voters had elected 110 new House members, and fourteen states voted in favor of term limitations of officeholders. Voters very deliberately cast their votes to redirect a government that had become too arrogant and too self-indulgent to listen and respond to the needs of its average citizens. The people hoped to change both the executive and legislative branches. And Perot's army had grown large enough to do real damage to either political party—or both—in the future.

The Democrats were reasserting their power in Washington, celebrating their return to the White House for only the second time in six elections. But even as Democratic leaders rejoiced at the inauguration of Bill Clinton, they were warned against taking too much for granted. President Clinton's pollster Stan Greenburg told the Democratic National Committee: "We need to understand that the Republican coalition collapsed in 1992, but we have not yet formed a new Democratic majority," he said. "We need to take those Perot voters seriously. I view that as our primary task if we are going to turn this election from a Republican collapse to a genuine Democratic victory."

Clinton's advisers were saying the only way to convince skeptical Perot supporters that things were really changing in Washington was to move forward on both deficit reduction and political reform.

Elaine Kamarck and Bill Galston wrote in the Democratic Leadership Council's publication, *The New Democrat*, in January 1993: "The lasting contribution of the Perot voters to the political system may turn out to be that for the first time in a long time the balance of power does not reside in the hands of those who would wage a fruitless cultural war. The construction of a durable Democratic presidential majority may well hinge on an effective appeal to independent voters demanding progress on two fronts (political reform and deficit reduction) that have long been anathema to political incumbents of all persuasions."

Analysts from both political parties agreed that the Perot vote was a powerful new force, and Perot himself continued to present a dilemma to both parties. John Sears, who served as Ronald Reagan's campaign chairman in 1976 and 1980, wrote in a December 1992 op-ed piece in *Newsday*: "Even though Perot carried no states, has no backers in Congress and holds no office, the 19 percent of the vote that Perot received rendered Bill Clinton a minority president and deprived the Republicans of total claim to the role of the loyal opposition."

"Instead of having a mandate," Sears said, "Clinton is a dog on a short leash, and the Republicans, if they can't unite, face a possible challenge to their status as a major party. While Clinton and Bush were busy trying to get elected, Perot ran off with the power."

Indeed, if the Democrats are unable to build that governing coalition, and if the Republicans prove not up to

the task of refashioning their party around new defining principles and a moderate, mainstream core, the
future still holds the promise of an eventual new party
emerging, or the takeover of one of the existing parties
by the Perot faction.

But the prevailing question after the '92 election was:
What would Ross Perot do with his power? What would
Ross do next? He had energized people, and he had
brought new modes of communication into the political
process. There was no way the communications revolution would be turned back. With the expansion of cable,
even more channels of communication will be open
before 1996. *Advertising Age*, the newspaper of the advertising industry, named Perot "Adman of the Year"
because of his innovative use of political advertising—
which suggests that his advertising approach also is here
to stay. In its February 1993 issue, *Advertising Age* called
Perot "a winner after all" for altering the face of political marketing.

But what would happen to Perot's followers? Would
they stay together to fashion a new political force? A
new political party? Columbia University's Alan
Brinkley wrote in the midst of the 1992 campaign that
Perot's strength was "a reflection of changes in our politics much larger than anything he himself has created
or can hope to control. America in the 1990s appears to
be in the midst of a major political realignment." Writing in the *New Republic*, Brinkley said, "A realignment
occurs when the two-party system is no longer able to
contain the demands and grievances of the electorate,
when old allegiances snap and new ones are formed."

"Perot's movement is likely to produce its most enduring legacy not through its own political successes
but through the way it facilitates the passage to a new

political order...Perot is not just a product of a moment of rage. He is part of a process by which the major parties and even the institutions of government may finally be forced to confront their growing irrelevance to the concerns of many, if not most, American voters," Brinkley said.

To be sure, the climate was ripe in 1992 for the development of a third political party. If Perot had been a long-distance runner, staying in the race all the way without interruption—certainly if he had won the election instead of serving as a vehicle for protest—that third party likely would have emerged.

The sentiment for a new reform party was substantiated by a survey conducted in May 1992 by Dr. Gordon S. Black, chairman of the Gordon S. Black Corporation, a Rochester, New York, research firm. Black's survey, sponsored by Paychex, indicated that political discontent in the United States had reached levels unprecedented in modern times—the greatest dissatisfaction since the beginning of polling in the 1930s. "Not even in the Depression were we this mad," he said.

Not since the founding of the Republican Party in 1854 had there been so much potential to create a full-scale national political party, according to Black. Moreover, he predicted that the new political party would emerge as a "centrist" or "moderate" party, directed primarily at the reform of American political and electoral institutions and long-standing national problems.

Pollster Frank Luntz agreed with Black's assessment of Perot supporters as moderates or centrists. Luntz called them "Radical Centrists"—middle-class moderates who once made up much of Richard Nixon's Silent Majority, but decided in 1992 to remain silent no longer. While Perot never acknowledged that he had a pollster,

Luntz was authorized by others in the Perot I campaign to conduct some focus group sessions—which he did during the third and fourth weeks of June 1992 in Philadelphia, Memphis, Detroit, Los Angeles, Denver and Tampa. One of his most interesting findings was that not once did a Perot supporter identify himself as liberal or conservative. "This suggests that ideology is irrelevant to Perovians," Luntz wrote in a spring 1993 *Policy Review* article entitled "Perovian Civilization." "The term conservative, so useful in the 1960s through the 1980s, has only limited appeal to the Perot constituency," he wrote.

Black determined in May 1992 that the public's agenda was political and institutional reform, and 57 percent wanted to see a national political party created to run candidates for office at every level of government. The "consistent partisans" for a new party, based on answers to several questions, amounted to 30 percent of the American electorate. Black's study also found a wide range of support for overhauling long-standing public policies, including the welfare system, defense spending, and trade policies with Japan. Supporters of a new reform party, however, would want it to stay away from the abortion issue.

Black's study also reinforced a conclusion that became more apparent as the 1992 campaign progressed, that the American public was as angry at the national news media as with the institutions of government and politics. In Black's study, 89 percent agreed that newspapers would rather "take cheap shots at the personal lives of candidates than help voters understand the issues," and 73 percent agreed that the national networks "have gotten way out of touch with what most Americans really think."

Black wrote: "The cozy, symbiotic relationship between the national media and the national party leadership may be appropriate for understanding what is happening inside of Congress, the White House, and the national party organizations, but it has been a disaster for understanding what is happening across the breadth of the United States. As a result, the national media have misunderstood the mood of the electorate, underestimated the strength of Ross Perot, and still do not understand the size and scope of the political upheaval that is in progress. Nearly all of the so-called 'experts' that are put on national television are pulled from the existing parties, or from organizations inside the 'beltway,' and they are 'insiders' who largely represent the political interests they have served in the past. They operate within the existing political paradigm...As a result, they both misrepresent what is happening and misunderstand the mood of the country."

In June 1993, one year after his landmark poll establishing the level of voter dissatisfaction in the country, Black said he had continued to poll the topic and found that the discontent levels on all key indicators "are back up and are as high as they were in May 1992. That says there's a market if you can organize. If you can find leaders, you've got followers. What's ironic is that there is no dearth of followers, there are not enough leaders; of all the people of wealth and stature in the United States, only Ross Perot is doing what he's doing."

Another who put stock in the validity of a third-party movement was Theodore J. Lowi, the John L. Senior professor of American Institutions at Cornell University. Lowi wrote in *The New York Times Magazine* on August 23, 1992, that "whatever the outcome of this year's presidential race, historians will undoubtedly focus on 1992 as the beginning of the end of America's two-party system. The extraordinary rise of Ross Perot and the remarkable outburst of enthusiasm for his ill-defined alternative to the established parties removed all doubt about the viability of a broad-based third party."

Lowi contended that the parties have atrophied because they have been in power too long, and the monumental growth of the federal government's role has overwhelmed them.

He wrote: "Back when the federal government was smaller and less important, the two parties could be umbrella parties—organizing campaigns, running elections and getting the vote out—without much regard to ideology or policy. But with the New Deal and the rise of the welfare state, the federal government became increasingly vulnerable to ideological battles over policy. None of this was particularly noticeable while the government and the economy were expanding, but in the early 1970s, class and ideological conflicts began to emerge more starkly."

Thus were born the familiar "wedge" issues, he said, issues such as crime, welfare, prayer, economic regulation, social regulations that drove a "wedge" between people. (Republicans were particularly successful in 1988 with gun control, prayer in schools, flag flying and revolving door criminal sentences.) "No matter what position party leaders took on such issues, they were bound to alienate a substantial segment of their constituency," Lowi said. "While the Democrats were the first to feel the cut of wedge issues—particularly concerning race—Republicans are now having their own agonies over abortion, foreign policy and budget deficits. Wedge issues immobilize party leadership, and once parties are immobilized the government is itself immobilized."

Lowi made the case, even before the November election, that "One of the best-kept secrets in American politics is that the two-party system has long been brain dead—kept alive by support systems like state electoral laws that protect the established parties from rivals and by federal subsidies and so-called campaign reform. The two-party system would collapse in an instant if the tubes were pulled and the IV's were cut."

Perot tried to jerk some of the tubes during the '92 election. But loosening the hold of the two parties over the political system is a monumental undertaking that will not be accomplished without a great deal more exertion and stamina.

The fact that Perot's supporters were able to get him on all fifty ballots is, in itself, a sign of the declining importance of parties. It is now easier for third-party candidates to qualify for the ballot. That diminishes the need for presidential hopefuls to fight through the primaries to gain party nomination, which usually means running for president for two full years.

Ballot access activists such as Richard Winger continue to work for uniform laws of ballot access. One bill introduced in Congress in the spring of 1993 was that no third party or independent candidates for federal office could be required to submit petition signatures amounting to more than one-half of one percent of the votes cast in that district in the last election. Introduced three times before, the bill had never gotten a hearing. Moves were also afoot in at least fifteen states to reduce the cumbersome restrictions on ballot access. "Perot showed that a lot of people sometimes want to vote for somebody other than the Democrat or Republican," Winger said.

Perot also proved that a candidate can be successful

without all the accouterments now associated with presidential campaigns. He has pointed a new way, if only the parties would follow it. Special events coordinator Joe Canzeri was astounded at how well the less-is-more method of campaigning worked for Perot—staging fewer public events, having the volunteers arrange them, and not having huge staffs of people working on them.

"I was used to staying up all night, talking to local officials and a bunch of advance people—who's meeting us at the airport, where are the planes going to land, who are the county chairmen and elected officials who will be there," he said. Perot didn't have the traditional staff at the locations working on the events. "The volunteers did all the work. I would go in and make sure the press platforms were firm and the cameras weren't pointed into the sun and that the backdrop was attractive. But we didn't travel with a cadre of speech writers and these kinds of things," Canzeri said, adding that he was impressed by the way it worked.

"What happens on other campaigns is that you have a huge staff, and that huge staff creates more staff. So you have a lot of strap hangers wanting to travel, wanting to go on the trip. Consequently, you have to have bigger everything, bigger motorcades, bigger airplanes, staff offices to handle the press," he said. If press planes follow the candidate, he said, "you have to have filing phones at the airport, with a lot of crew standing around when you arrive" to accommodate the press. "With the new cellular phones, you don't need this kind of stuff anymore," he said.

It is possible to have a couple of public events in one day, in the same geographic area, and allow the press to travel to the venue on their own, as Perot did. And with greater utilization of the diversity of communication, numerous events crammed into one day and designed to get coverage in different local media markets are unnecessary. Satellite hookups with local news media can perform the same function. Satellite hookups, call-in TV and the electronic town hall can provide the public access to the candidate.

"I think Perot was on to something," Canzeri said, "that will absolutely impact the campaign in 1996." Yet, while the traditional campaign operations will no doubt follow the leader on media utilization, the Democrats and Republicans likely will resist shaving their staff operations. Because such a cottage industry has been built up around campaigns, candidates will be under enormous pressure to continue to have the huge staff operations and continue to employ numerous "consultants." What's happened in presidential campaigns is similar to what's happened in government. "What we've done," Canzeri said, "is just continue to expand and expand, and never cut back."

Much of that expansion has been in political consultancy. The consultancy explosion has changed the role citizens play in political campaigning and has resulted in consultants controlling the direction of campaigns even more than the candidates. It was this phenomenon that Perot rebelled against when he "fired those suckers" who were brought in to give him professional support. Mark Petracca, associate professor of political science at the University of California in Irvine, has written that "the penetration of political consultants into every level of American politics displaces political amateurs from the political system." And consultants emphasize those aspects of a campaign which are least conducive to participatory politics. Not only have consultants contributed to the rapidly rising costs of political campaigns, they have also brought about a shift in expenditures by candidates from grass roots activities to the high-tech and more expensive strategies of permanent campaigning. Petracca conducted a study which determined that consultants do not generally provide such services as precinct walking, phone banking or turnout efforts. Rather, they specialize in direct mail, fundraising, advertising, issue analysis, and survey research.

Tom Luce said at the University of Miami seminar on "Electronic Democracy" that he believes that consultant-driven politics attempts to keep the people out. He cited California in the Perot petition drive as an illustration of what the people can do, without consultants or staff direction. "The volunteers that wanted to put Perot on the ballot in California self selected their own leadership, opened twenty statewide offices, had forty-six thousand volunteers going door to door, and collected 1.5 million signatures in six weeks," he said, all before he had even met the California state chairman.

"In two Pacific Northwest states," he added, "more than 50 percent of the registered voters signed petitions. That is the mood of the population in terms of their attitudes about wanting to be involved. I think the consultant-driven world in which politics has lived for the last ten years doesn't want people involved, doesn't believe they are interested in issues and that's just not correct."

Before there will be any changes in the role performed by consultants in political campaigns, the public has to recognize how great that role is. Perot did his part to put the power of consultancy on the big screen..

Another election reform brought to the forefront by the Perot candidacy is the outmoded throwback to horse-

and-buggy days—the electoral college. Perot's candidacy, and the potential of deciding the election in the House of Representatives, caused voters and political theorists alike to reexamine the need for the continuation of the electoral college. The question was repeatedly raised: Why not just have a direct popular vote for president? One possibility would be to abolish the "winner-take-all" system in favor of apportioning electoral votes by congressional district. That way, if a candidate led in some congressional districts, he or she would get the electoral votes of that district. Another option is to provide for a mechanical conversion of the popular vote into electoral votes, thus eliminating the need to have actual electors who are not bound to vote for the candidate who won their state.

Perot personally called for elimination of the electoral college, which some editorialists have labeled an obsolete impediment to the expression of the democratic will. Arkansas Senator David Pryor introduced a constitutional amendment providing for popular election of the president and vice-president. The House approved such a proposal in 1969, but the Senate squashed it. Pryor has said he feared a "constitutional crisis" in which a discredited Congress would be seen as usurping the voters' will in a three-way race by denying the seating of the voters' choice. They have that opportunity if there is no electoral college majority in a three-way race. That happened after the 1824 election, when the House chose John Quincy Adams over Andrew Jackson in a four-way contest. And, as recently as 1968, when George Wallace ran as an independent, the country had a close call. Had Wallace won about sixty thousand more votes in three states, neither Richard Nixon nor Hubert Humphrey would have won an electoral majority.

The intent of the Founding Fathers in setting up the system was the essence of the federal system—the American idea of a union of states. As a practical matter, the electoral system has had the effect of supporting the two-party system and thwarting the rise of splinter parties. Continued reliance on the electoral college, in an age of instant communication and the concept of one man-one vote, is viewed by many as totally out of step. Editorialists have said (and rightly so) that to guarantee that the choice of the people is not denied the presidency, the House of Representatives should move to abolish the electoral college and abdicate its own undemocratic role in the presidential selection.

The influence of money in elections also continues to be a problem. Perot said repeatedly he was buying this election for the people because they couldn't afford it. However, the ability of a billionaire to stake his own presidential campaign raises serious questions: For example, if someone is precluded from spending millions on someone else's campaign for the presidency, why is he allowed to spend that amount on his own campaign? Millionaire candidates have begun to emerge at the state and local level, as well. Los Angeles elected millionaire attorney-businessman Richard Riordan as mayor in June 1993 after he spent $6 million of his own money on the campaign. Given the lock the two major parties have on politics, however, about the only way an independent or third-party candidate can get noticed is to spend vast sums of his own money.

Tom Luce doesn't believe a candidate has to have a billion dollars to run. He contends that, in today's world, anybody who can capture the imagination of the public via direct-access television can potentially run for president. Luce suggested that such figures as CNN president Ted Turner or entertainer Bill Cosby, for examples, could conceivably run for president, because they have the ability to get on the talk-show circuit. The information age, he contends, has opened up new avenues for entrance into politics.

Speaking at the Miami University conference, Luce said: "Bill Cosby could get on the "Larry King" show. Bill Cosby could speak to national issues. And I would submit to you, the American people will decide whether or not they want Bill Cosby to be president, and *The New York Times* won't decide that, the Republican Party won't decide that, and the Democratic Party won't determine that...It says where we are today is we have an enormous potential for good or an enormous potential for wreaking havoc when it comes to the information age."

In the case of a billionaire businessman such as Perot, however, most journalists would agree that Perot could not have gotten the attention of the media nor of the public had he not had the ability to fund his own campaign—Tom Luce's opinion notwithstanding.

Lawrence Barrett, who covers politics for *Time* magazine, has argued that Perot's performance in the '92 election proves the need for a twenty-seventh amendment to the Constitution—the "Perot Amendment." The Supreme Court's ruling in Valso vs. Buckley equated spending one's own money on a campaign with protected free speech. A so-called "Perot Amendment" would authorize Congress to exclude spending in campaigns for national office from that protection.

Fundamental reforms in campaign financing were high on President Clinton's priority list when he assumed office. Included in the congressional dialogue were limits on campaign expenditures, expansion of public financing to congressional candidates, and limits on the use of "soft money"—unregulated money raised outside federal rules, ostensibly to be spent on party activities.

In 1992, Bush and Clinton both received $55 million in public funds after their nomination. The Democratic Party raised an additional $71 million in soft money, while the Republican Party raised $62.4 million. So, the Democrats actually spent $126 million on the presidential election, and the Republicans spent $117.6 million. Perot spent $69.6 million, according to Federal Elections Commission reports, which included $63 million of his own, in contributions or loans.

Soft money came into being after Jimmy Carter and Gerald Ford spent the bulk of their publicly funded war chests on media advertising in 1976, the first election after the Watergate-inspired campaign finance reforms. There was precious little money left for the traditional grass roots activity which included political paraphernalia and volunteer-driven get-out-the-vote efforts. In 1979, Congress acted to restore grass roots activity by allowing national parties wide leeway in spending for voter registration and get-out-the-vote drives, and to buy unlimited materials for volunteer activities. Soon, millions of unreported, unregulated dollars were flowing to the parties—ostensibly for "grass roots" campaigns, but used for a wide variety of activities supporting the presidential tickets. Fifty percent of the "soft funds" in 1992 were donations larger than $20,000—including hundreds of thousands of dollars from single large conglomerate corporations. The "fat cat" contributions led to cries for reform, once again.

Ironically, very little of Perot's money went for grass roots campaigning. He spent $18.5 million on the petition drive. In the fall campaign, having opted to conduct an "air war" instead of a "ground war," precious little money went for grass roots activity.

After the election, some state leaders theorized that one reason Perot "stepped back" on July 16 was that he was getting ready to drop a bundle on field operations. Three days before he got out, he had authorized a field operations budget that was going to cost about $50 million. This was money he couldn't control. Plus, he was convinced that he would get a higher return on his money, in votes cast, by spending it on TV. The field offices operated on a shoestring—in many cases out of the pockets of the volunteers. That reality would cause him grief later, as disgruntled volunteers began demanding reimbursement for their expenses.

According to Professor Lowi, a multiparty system would not immediately wipe out capital-intensive mass politics, but it would eliminate many of the pressures and incentives that produce its extremes, because of the tendency of third parties to rely on labor-intensive politics. "Third parties simply do not have access to the kind of financing that capital-intensive politics requires. But more than that, there is an enthusiasm about an emerging party that inspires people to come out from their private lives and to convert their civic activity to political activity."

Lowi suggested that a third party could play the role of honest broker and policy manager because it would hold a balance of power in many important and divisive interests. But to be effective, it had to be built from the bottom up. Such a party, in his opinion, needed to nominate and campaign for its own candidates at all levels, and not simply run somebody for president. And it must attract regular Democrats and Republicans by nominating some of them to run as candidates with the third-party nomination as well as that of their own party.

But the United We Stand America that began emerging in the spring of 1993 didn't appear to fit that description at all. Perot, in fact, didn't see it as a third party; he saw it as a "watchdog" organization.

Certainly, the sentiment remained, both for a potential third party and for Perot to stay involved after the election. Some people questioned who designated Ross Perot the official watchdog of the new Clinton administration. The answer was simple: almost twenty million voters did. And many of them remained vocal about it.

Letters from readers to the *Dallas Morning News* included one from Paul Coughlin of Dallas nominating Perot as director of a new "People's Lobby" in Washington to continue the job he had started. Another, R. M. Anglin of Richardson, Texas, wrote about the "nineteen million voters out here (who) are not very happy with either political party."

"We would like to see more fiscal responsibility. We'd like to see Congress be more responsive to the desires of our people. Polls show that most of us favor such things as 1) term limitations for members of Congress, 2) shorter political campaigns, 3) less money spent on political campaigns, 4) elimination of political action committees, 5) less influence by lobbyists and 6) a balanced budget amendment. How many of these would pass a vote by Congress? Zero!

"Maybe there will be another presidential candidate in 1996. Maybe Mr. Perot will run again. Maybe by then there will be a viable third political party. And, hopefully by then, the surviving members of Congress will be more to our liking," the reader wrote.

A letter to *People* magazine from Candice Kern of

Corsicana, Texas, put it even more bluntly. She was replying to the Clinton insider who said that in the new administration, George Stephanopoulos "would be the ass to kiss" in Washington. "That kind of brownnosing game-playing that goes on in Washington is exactly why Clinton did not get my vote and Ross Perot did," she wrote. "The politicians just don't get it. You work for us, we pay your salary—start kissing our butts."

Perot, indisputably, had amassed a tremendous amount of political capital. It was a unique franchise, but how he would utilize that franchise was uncertain. Would it simply serve as a backdrop for his rhetorical watchdoggery? Would it become a permanent outside political force, impacting future elections? Or would it provide a new core of support for one of the existing parties? That was the big uncertainty halfway into 1993.

19

UNITED WE STAND AMERICA

FOR MANY PEOPLE, THE PEROT CAMPAIGN NEVER ENDED. At least, they never wanted it to end. In the two months following the election, United We Stand America activists across the country recognized the power of their force and were trying to "stay together" to continue exercising it. They were calling Dallas wanting to know, "What are we going to do now?" In January 1993, Perot told them. United We Stand America would solicit members at $15 a membership and would become a nonpartisan, not-for-profit citizens' action group. Its national spokesman would be Ross Perot.

As Perot envisioned it, UWSA would be organized in every congressional district to put pressure on lawmakers for governmental and political reform and debt reduction. He envisioned a people's agenda that would be developed during electronic town hall meetings which he would conduct. Candidates committed to UWSA priorities would be identified, and members of Congress would be held accountable by the large block of voters amassed through the membership drive. As Perot said, "It gives the little guy a voice by putting him together with other little guys."

In the first twenty-four hours, Perot asserted that four

hundred thousand people had signed up. But after claiming a membership of over one million Americans, Perot and his UWSA spokespersons refused to release any other numbers, even to the membership. Perot said in June the number of members would be announced when all states were organized. "It will all be done by the end of the year," he said.

The membership money that came in was being banked until UWSA was organized at the local and state levels; Perot continued to finance the organizational setup and the membership drive. "I want to be in a position to send everybody their money back if we don't reach critical mass, or if we decide there's no reason to be doing this," Perot said, in the early stages of the organization.

In the reconstituted United We Stand America, most of the small national staff had been staff members in the Perot campaign and/or came from Perot businesses. The names were familiar. Darcy Anderson was executive director. The board members were Perot, his attorney son-in-law Clay Mulford and accountant Mike Poss. A handful of field reps—a few of the Young Turks—were carryovers from Perot I (before the campaign pull-out) and II (the 1992 fall campaign).

The initial instructions to state leaders and workers was to get more members, while the national headquarters in Dallas set about hiring executive directors in each state. The idea was that once the executive directors were in place, then the states could organize themselves and elect their own leaders.

"When you're trying to reorganize people in every city and town in the United States, it's a huge undertaking. You have to give them time," Perot said. But he added that "By 1994, we will have an organization that can be a swing vote in every congressional district in the country. Our objective is so simple—to reconnect Congress with the people, not the lobbyists and special interests. Congress must be sensitive to the will of the people."

While that goal was not in question, some supporters wanted to do more. They wanted to get involved in local and area elections, supporting and endorsing candidates, lobbying at all levels of government—in essence, moving forward, exercising influence, flexing muscle. Perot wanted to build membership. So, local members were distributing membership applications, as Perot embarked on a nationwide tour, speaking at membership rallies.

His first appearance at a public event after the November 3 election was in early February, shortly after Clinton's inauguration. Perot went first to Maine, the state that gave him the highest percentage of the vote—30.4 percent, the same percentage given its occasional resident, George Bush. Perot's message had broad appeal in Maine, a state which had experienced gridlock in state government and a loss of industry. Maine was still at the far end of economic recovery when Perot showed up, decrying the $25 million cost of the Clinton inauguration. "They in Washington just don't get it," he said. "You and I get it. I don't understand a $25 million inauguration at a time when people are hurting."

Perot was not the first independent to captivate people in Maine. In the 1970s, Maine voters elected independent Jim Longley as governor. "Despite warnings by the two parties that an independent could not work with a Democratic House and a Republican Senate, he (Longley) was able to do that," said Steve Bost, state UWSA director in Orono, Maine.

When Perot arrived in Bangor on February 6, 1993, Maine was experiencing one of its worst cold snaps of the season; it was thirty-seven degrees below zero. Despite the weather, people drove four to six hours from the Canadian border to the University of Maine site for one of the three Perot appearances. With their families, they stood outside with their thermoses and bags of doughnuts waiting for the doors to open for the 1:00 p.m. event.

After the second appearance, at the high school in the coastal fishing community of Rockland, Steve Bost followed Perot to the airport in a staff car. He remembers the most haunting vignette—a family standing on their front lawn, bathed in the light of a full moon, waving an American flag as Perot went by. "It was about the most moving experience I can recall," Bost said.

Seventy-five hundred Maine residents saw Perot during his appearances there, and he would continue to find large and enthusiastic audiences at his UWSA rallies, including large numbers of young people who showed up at rallies on college campuses. He appeared to be on a mission to visit every state in the union.

In Colorado in early March, the scene was similar. In Fort Collins, Perot not only packed the main auditorium but also two smaller auditoriums where his speech was broadcast over television monitors. People who could not get into either auditorium waited patiently in the chilly Rocky Mountain night. In Grand Junction, fifteen hundred heard him speak in the high school auditorium; another five hundred were in the cafeteria, listening to the piped-in address.

All of the post-campaign rallies were similar. They were held indoors, in ordinary places such as high school auditoriums and Holiday Inns—places where common people felt comfortable and would come in their every-day clothes. There was no big head table, no dignitaries, just the volunteers, the curious and Ross Perot talking. A small but lively band always played the theme song, "Crazy." Supporters wore Perot T-shirts and buttons and held up homemade signs. Local USWA workers gave out membership applications.

In Denver on March 6, John Mara, a retired fireman and author of a senior citizens' column for the *Pueblo Ledger*, walked around wearing a sandwich board that said, "UWSA Says Cut Spending First." The message to President Clinton and the Congress was to cut spending before passing massive new tax increases. One woman held up a sign that said, "Let's put Congress on a low-fat diet." That day in Denver, where five thousand people gathered, Perot's speech was interrupted no fewer than fifty times by applause. The kind of crowds he was drawing are often seen during the height of a presidential campaign. But this was four months after the election. The scope of Perot's appeal was rare, if not unprecedented.

A typical rally would begin with the reading of UWSA's mission statement "We the people of United We Stand America, recognizing that our republic was founded as a government of the people, by the people and for the people, unite to restore the integrity of our economic and political systems. We commit ourselves to organize, to educate, to participate in the political process, and to hold our public servants accountable. We shall rebuild our country, renew its economic, moral and social strength, and return the sovereignty of America to her people."

While the Denver UWSA leaders recognized that their strength was in numbers, they also recognized the importance of Perot's continuing in his role as national spokesman. "Because of his position, he can get into the media. I couldn't do that; they wouldn't pay attention to me," said Rosemarie Sax, Denver UWSA office manager. But, she added, the more members UWSA gains, the louder the voice. She said that every time either President Clinton or Ross Perot appeared on television, people called wanting to join. Sax, an interior designer, was doing a lot of her professional work at night to accommodate her UWSA work. "I wouldn't be working so hard," she said, if she thought UWSA was just a "flash in the pan."

Gaynor Miller, a sixty-one-year-old small-business man and former Vail real estate developer, who served as state co-administrator during the presidential campaign, agreed there was a need for a Perot. "People in Washington, D.C., are not going to call a Ron Ellsworth (Colorado state chairman, a former pro football player now in the cattle business) or a Gaynor Miller. We need somebody in the limelight; we need all the exposure he can give us," Miller said. It's necessary to balance the prevailing views of the media, he said.

Noell Custer, a Denver native and professional artist, believes the influence of UWSA will continue even if Perot's visibility diminishes. "I think he has raised public awareness to a new dimension, and it cuts across party lines. He has told people, if you don't like what they're doing (in Washington), tell them, pick up the phone. I think that's why they're having such an outpouring in Washington, reacting to President Clinton's budget plan and to Zoe Baird (Clinton's first choice for attorney general who was forced to withdraw). He told the country, 'Hey, you don't have to put up with this and not say anything.'"

But even as Perot was drawing record crowds in his personal appearances, reports were emerging of trouble in "Perotdise." The organizational pains in United We Stand America were acute.

Orson Swindle, the original spokesman for UWSA, bailed out early, because he had a different concept for the organization. Swindle thought it needed more "intellectual capacity," rather than Perot as its sole idea man. "The guy is brilliant. His intuition is staggering. I admire him greatly, but he's just one person," Swindle said. Swindle also thought it should be a Washington-based organization, set up to lobby Congress. When it became clear Perot was going to build the organization from Dallas and that Ross would be boss, Swindle bowed out— no doubt fortuitously, avoiding a clash of two hearty egos. Swindle said, "I'm a big supporter of his, but there was no way it was going to work. My strong feeling of what we had to do was just too different from his."

Swindle became an associate director with Empower America, a group intent on rebuilding the Republican Party. It included former Secretary of Housing and Urban Development Jack Kemp, former United Nations Ambassador Jeanne Kirkpatrick, former Education Secretary and drug czar William Bennett and former congressman Vin Weber. A Republican since he left the military, Swindle decided to work to redefine the Republican Party, rebuild the Reagan coalition and change the makeup of Congress in 1994—all within the context of the two-party system. In fact, he made the suggestion to Perot several times during the presidential campaign that if he wanted to be president, he ought to try to take over the party that lost the election.

Swindle also feared that UWSA wasn't being set up to have a real capacity to listen to the grass roots. "From the Perot (campaign) experience, I can tell you that the one thing you must do is create a mechanism by which people can talk to you. I think Ross still has a problem with this. They don't have the staff to assimilate all that's coming in," Swindle said.

Swindle left on good terms with Perot, though, and maintained that Perot's effect on politics had been positive. "I don't think politics will ever be the same. The country ought to feel darned good about Ross Perot's involvement in politics," he said.

Others who had been involved in the 1992 campaign did not leave on good terms. And some did not feel nearly so good about their year's involvement with Perot-politics.

As UWSA reorganized, some of the most loyal volunteers from the 1992 campaign were getting off the bandwagon. Only about half of the UWSA founders remained as state directors as of June 1993, although UWSA executive director Darcy Anderson said that of the first twenty-nine state directors hired, all but three had been state coordinators or in a senior leadership role in their states during the fall campaign.

Some of the dissidents had a different idea of how the organization should be structured and run. And they complained that the state leaders were never brought together to determine the format for the newly constituted UWSA. Others felt the folks in Dallas wanted a different kind of state leader in the "new" UWSA, one that would be more acquiescent to Perot's plan of attack. Orville Sweet, an original Perot leader in Kansas, felt "they just want to delete us."

In February 1993, there was an uprising of state leaders who had remained involved after the election. They were fed up with the direction they were getting from

Dallas, and talked about it on a twenty-two-person conference call. They were unable to get membership lists, the number of members in their states or the names of current state leaders. They were precluded from getting involved in local races, from endorsing candidates, and from meeting as a group to influence the organizational process. After the conference call, according to one state director, "Dallas went ballistic." Shortly thereafter, several of the old state directors either dropped out or were pushed out.

Cindy Schultz, state director in Wisconsin, was one. She was concerned about the lack of direction of the organization and upset with the way some of the state leaders were being treated. She wanted to get involved in the open race for the congressional seat of Les Aspin, who had joined the Clinton administration as Secretary of Defense. She had been told Dallas would charter the state organizations when Dallas was ready. "We didn't know where we were going or how we were going to get there," she complained.

On March 5, 1993, after investing more than a year in the Perot movement and being one of the original July 30, 1992 incorporators of UWSA, she quit. She told her Dallas contacts: "You people really don't know what the hell you're doing and you're never going to know, and I'm out of here."

Later, she said, "They don't want people who know what they're doing. They just want robots. That was my frustration."

A new term was coined that would be heard over and over from a growing group of dissenters—former state leaders and volunteers who left the organization. "Perotbots," they said, were those who stayed aboard and simply did as they were told, continuing blind allegiance to their political guru.

Perot and his senior advisers for UWSA—executive director Darcy Anderson and counsel Clay Mulford—attributed the dissension in the ranks to the normal growing problems of building a permanent, long-standing national organization. Building the foundation included hiring a full-time director in every state. Then the organization would build from the ground up, beginning with the election of leaders in each congressional district, who would elect their own state leaders—operating under the paid staff director. Perot and his spokesmen initially said only about a half-dozen malcontents were involved, and they were people who were upset because they didn't get the paid jobs.

Cindy Schultz said she had plenty of work as a political consultant (she worked in nonpartisan and Republican races before getting involved with Perot) and she wasn't concerned about getting a paid position. But she was bothered that other state chairmen who had "paid their dues" during the campaign were being "jerked around."

A common complaint was that leaders who quit got stuck with the last month's expenses—or worse. They said they were promised reimbursement for expenses. According to Clay Mulford, after the fall campaign, volunteers came out of the woodwork demanding that all sorts of bills be paid, including their personal phone bills and campaign materials they had contracted to buy and sell on their own.

Sharon Holman said every legitimate expense was paid, but some expenses had not been authorized. "Some people just went out and spent large sums of money and wanted Mr. Perot to pay," she said, adding that reimbursements were not denied because people quit, but because "they incurred expenses that we had not authorized or had no knowledge of."

Ken Kendricks of Georgia was another one of the initial signers of the UWSA charter, which was established on July 30, 1992, who dropped out. Kendricks had been head of the committee that drafted the original UWSA preamble. He came up with the idea to put it on a big parchment and have all the state leaders sign at that meeting two weeks after Perot had dropped out of the presidential race.

Kendricks, a lawyer with an Atlanta firm, wasn't looking for a job, either. He was disappointed that the organization was not going to be able to use its political muscle, that it was going to be simply a membership organization. He had tasted success, and knew what the group was capable of doing—if turned loose to do it.

In the fall of 1992, the Georgia UWSA had laid down the prototype for how UWSA could be an effective political force—providing the margin of difference in the U.S. Senate race between Democrat Wyche Fowler and Republican Paul Coverdell. Those who had worked to get Perot on the ballot in Georgia turned their efforts and their funds during the general election campaign to trying to impact the Senate race, creating a data base of Perot petition signers. That data base was promised to any candidate who took the Lead or Leave tax reduction pledge. Coverdell took the pledge; Fowler, the incumbent, didn't. UWSA sent a newsletter to five thousand people who had circulated petitions and also produced a postcard which Coverdell mailed to a hundred thousand names taken from the data base, emphasizing his tax reduction stance. Coverdell won by fifteen thousand votes, and the Georgia UWSA declared victory.

"We had managed to pull off a strategy we had put in place with no help from Dallas," Kendricks said.

In January, when the directive came down from Dallas that UWSA chapters weren't to get involved in endorsing candidates, Kendricks quit. At the time, he said, the Georgia UWSA was already organized at the congressional district level. "It just evaporated," he said. "We needed infrastructure support, an office, a newsletter, feedback—but after November, that didn't exist."

What made the Perot movement a powerful force in the spring and summer of '92, he said, was the quality of the people. "They were not flakes. They were professional people, community leaders, who put their lives on hold to come save their country." The one motivating factor he heard over all others as to why people got involved in the Perot petition drive and his presidential campaign was: "The country is at risk; it's not going to last forever on automatic pilot."

Kendricks wasn't mad that he wasn't going to be involved anymore, but he was disappointed over what he believed was a "tremendous missed opportunity to capitalize on an organization that existed, as of early July last year, as of the day of the election." He believes the opportunity to seize the moment was lost—that UWSA could have become a centrist third party dedicated to supporting candidates who cared only about fixing government and then going back home. But, he said, that would have required Perot to step aside as the centerpiece.

That's not to say that the UWSA Perot was building in the spring of 1993 won't eventually get to the same place. But it will be more difficult to create it without the energy of presidential politics, and having lost much of the initial momentum and many of the initial leaders. "It's the opportunity that was there versus trying to pull off what they're doing now. A lot of people never understood how large the ground swell really was," he said.

Kendricks acknowledged, however, that some of the people were getting re-involved after the new UWSA had been in operation for several months.

Over the long term, Kendricks believes that the frustrations that caused people to come together so quickly and to organize so well behind Ross Perot suggest that something else will happen. Someone else may come forward. "Hopefully, it won't be a demagogue. For a lot of people, unfortunately, that's what Ross Perot has become. I'm not sure he ever asked for that, so I don't think it's something to blame him for. But I'm disappointed that the opportunity to capitalize on what was in place has been lost."

By May, press pellets were being fired at Perot's balloon. "Fissures" in the organization were being cited— disputes within local chapters. Several state leaders appeared in television interviews claiming the new organization was dictatorial and secretive and that they had been thrown out. They criticized Perot for being more interested in making ego-gratifying speeches and television appearances and signing up new members than in lobbying legislatures and supporting like-minded candidates. Some claimed he had inflated the membership numbers, or that the numbers weren't being revealed because they were disappointing.

Splinter groups and off-shoots of UWSA were showing up, such as United We Stand Idaho and, in Arizona, United We Stand Everywhere. Several dissidents spoke on NBC's "Dateline" and on ABC's "Nightline" in late May 1993. Some of the rebels told *Time* magazine that there could be as many as one hundred small splinter groups. Clay Mulford confirmed that groups were adopting different names in order to take more activist roles that they couldn't take in the name of Perot or UWSA. But some of the dissidents were clearly angry over the turn taken by UWSA.

Former Indiana UWSA coordinator Wally Howard was among those on the May 27, 1993 "Nightline" broadcast, "Ross Perot: The Man, the Message, the Movement." Howard called the new UWSA movement a "dictatorship" because "There's nothing flowing from the bottom up to reflect the concerns of people. State coordinators have never been asked, in concert, a thing about what they think ought to be done."

Tom Wing, former Illinois coordinator, said, "I believe them to want puppets. I believe them to want people who are malleable, who will do as they're told, who will go along with the program from Dallas and not put up an argument."

Wing told *Dallas Morning News* reporter David Jackson that Dallas officials told him he was in line to be named state director, but they kept delaying the appointment. They finally told him he wouldn't be getting the job. "It seemed to me they wanted to milk every ounce of volunteerism out of us before we were replaced."

Another disgruntled former worker complained of the Perot "management style," which was reflected in the national staff of UWSA. "Perot's management style is to create a golden apple—which you never quite get—to string you along. He gets people to do remarkable things."

Dee Zuber of Dublin, Ohio, a fifty-one-year-old mother of two and wife of a corporate executive, identified with the dissenters who were on TV. She was still trying to recover, both financially and emotionally, from the drain of the campaign. Zuber and a fellow supporter had each invested $5,000 to launch a magazine, America Speaks, which sold upscale Perot collectibles for the movement. But Zuber was called a "profiteer." She also was told she was being investigated by Dallas, and was ostracized when she tried to work on the fall campaign. She begged for vindication from Dallas, without response, even as she continued to work for Perot's election behind the scenes. Sharon Holman said Dallas never promised any support for her magazine.

Zuber disputed claims by Perot and his senior advisers that there were only a half-dozen disgruntled former supporters. "There are thousands of us," Zuber said, "not six. The six that were on 'Dateline,' four were his state leaders during the campaign." Zuber said she couldn't believe Perot "didn't reach out to the six people on 'Dateline,' who were some of the finest people who worked for him." Instead, they were castigated in comments from Perot and UWSA officials. "He's treating us Americans who would have walked through fire for him very shabbily." she said. "I feel I have been very used and very abused. I believe in the message fully, but I'm frightened of the messenger, of his organization. He must clean up his own barn, to ever get my vote for anything again."

Joyce Shepard, a Long Island clinical social worker, accused Perot of becoming the proprietor of the "biggest little whorehouse in Texas—called United We Stand America. All we heard was 'Get memberships, get memberships.' It was like a pyramid scheme." Shepard, who at one time was the campaign coordinator in Queens, was organizing a dissident network she called DUPED,

for Disenchanted United People for Equality and Democracy. Shepard claimed her network included dissident leaders in forty-seven states. "We're hearing from
people all over the country who were used and thrown
away like dirty dish rags," she said. The objective of the
dissident network, according to Shepard, was to "start
the phones ringing in Dallas" and make Perot listen to
the complaints, and to let people know that Perot was
all talk and no action.

"We need a United We Stand," she said. "He has
attracted the politically homeless, the apathetic, but the
reality of United We Stand and his reality are two different things. In essence, his ego won't let anybody—
volunteers, Rollins, Swindle, anybody—advise him."

Shepard was one of the people who went on "Dateline." She said she felt like she had "remarried an abusive husband," because she had quit the campaign once
and then later returned to work as a volunteer in UWSA.
"When we were on 'Dateline,' he said we were into criminal activities and we were publicity seekers. He attacked
us instead of meeting with us," she said.

Alex Rodriguez, who had been elected Manhattan
coordinator, said he was "canceled out by the state coordinator," but continued operating under United We
Stand America New York.

Rodriguez said, "When we were really hot, we were
doing incredible things, with no money from Dallas.
All of it came from the creativity of the volunteers. All
of that stopped; they killed it with the screws and the
tight controls. You get rid of the craziness, but you also
stifle the creativity. They're spending all their energy
on control. There's no way in '94 they are going to be
able to run congressional campaigns because there's
nobody they trust."

Rodriguez said, "We were promised a grass roots organization with people participating. That's not what we have. I want a democratic organization. No matter what, this country is a democracy and we operate within the context that a democracy works. If there is no democracy, it's not going to work."

Many of the complaints went back to the campaign. Walt Peters, another UWSA founder, said he was relieved as state coordinator in Arizona in October and made the victim of a "brutal smear campaign" for reasons he never figured out. He described "secret meetings" conducted by staff from Dallas, the changing of the locks on the office and dumping of the leadership team only a month before the election.

Even before the election, at least eight former Perot volunteers from several states claimed the campaign had investigated them and gained access to their credit histories without permission. In June 1993, however, the FBI ended its investigation into allegations that Perot campaign workers had stolen security codes and broken into computer systems of companies that issue credit reports. The investigation was dropped after the U.S. attorney's office in Dallas declined to prosecute the case.

Among the UWSA dissidents, the grievances went from one person who felt she had spent a "wasted year" to another who called her involvement in the Perot movement "the worst experience" of her life. Many told stories of the "crisp white shirts" coming in, wearing their "Arnold power suits," creating havoc with the operation and then whipping out their pocket phones and retreating to a corner to talk to Dallas.

The unkindest cut of all came from a state leader who had worked for the Perot candidacy from February to

November of 1992 and who had become convinced that it would be a "disaster" for Perot to be president.

Perot's response to all the discord was: "I deeply regret any single individual out there who's unhappy." But he added that the disgruntled people who were not reelected to leadership positions or who stole money from the organization are "ones and twos," while there are millions of others "who are out there building the organization. There's no interest in them." And, indeed, for every one who quit, there were another one hundred waiting to sign up or write letters to the national office in Dallas.

"Part of organizing from the bottom up is you will have disputes. You will have turf battles. People will be displaced. It's just people being people," Perot said. "It takes a while to get organized. You can't rationally select your state volunteer leaders until you have your local leaders in place." Eventually, he said, the members would approve their budgets and determine how the money would be spent. Part of it would be spent at the local level, part of it on TV and part on national staff, he said. "We'll have all of this done by the end of the year."

On the two-part program produced by "Nightline" on May 27 and May 28, 1993, featuring the disgruntled former supporters, Koppel claimed erroneously that Perot had been planning this organization, United We Stand, for nearly twenty-five years. Koppel produced some twenty-three-year-old film, in which he had interviewed Perot about a grassroots organization called United We Stand. Only Koppel never made it clear that the original United We Stand was set up to try to gain the release of POWs in Southeast Asia—and had nothing to do with the current organization, presidential politics or congressional races.

But Koppel was right when he said Perot's idea of the electronic town hall meeting was at least that old. Perot said he got the idea when he was working on the POW project in 1969 and 1970 and that Frank Borman, the ex-astronaut, was going to run the electronic town hall, but the networks weren't interested. (Borman said in 1992 he was no longer in favor of the concept because issues are too complex and the forum had "enormous potential for manipulating the emotions of people.")

The Dallas headquarters was peppered with phone calls from grass roots workers who were upset with the "Dateline" and "Nightline" shows. Some wrote to the networks. James Boutelle, interim state chairman in Connecticut, wrote Ted Koppel with the objection that "Nightline" researchers only sought out former state leaders with negative opinions of the organization. "I'm sure plenty of state leaders would have been willing to appear on the record to present a balanced view of how we in the field view 'Dallas,'" he said. Boutelle also said that he had been provided with a list of members, and that he and others in Connecticut had taken part in the formulation of policy through conference calls and separate conversations with national staff members in Dallas.

"Further," he wrote, "we are free, for the most part, to focus on issues at the state level. Thanks in part to the efforts of many United We Stand Volunteers, the Connecticut State Legislature passed a revolving door bill, prohibiting state legislators from becoming lobbyists immediately after leaving office. This is only one of many pieces of reform legislation we have pursued in Connecticut. We did not have to seek the permission of Dallas to do this."

Boutelle said Tom Wing had expressed concerns to him and he had urged him to be patient. "Unfortunately," Boutelle said, "he was not. Those of us who got into this movement to turn this country around realize that this will be a long and difficult process. The only way to do this is to educate our members on the key issues and then urge them to get involved. We are doing this at the grass roots level."

Some of the dissenters were critical of the bylaws, because they fostered control from Dallas, and of the original three-man board of directors. Clay Mulford, one of the three board members, explained, however, that "We have to be off within a year, and we will be. It's a mere technicality, to form the corporation. Elections will be held to fill the board seats." A board with fifty members would be unworkable, he said, so the eventual board will probably be twelve to fifteen members. However, all fifty elected state chairpersons were to function as a national advisory board.

Mulford acknowledged that there had been some dissension in the ranks because some people who worked in the presidential campaign wanted to form a political organization that would be fielding and endorsing candidates. Mulford believes UWSA will "endorse" candidates in 1994—but that is different from "running" candidates. The candidates, instead, would endorse the UWSA platform, and UWSA members would get behind whichever candidate is most receptive to UWSA goals. "We don't need to put money in paper bags; we don't have to field candidates," Mulford said. "We're trying to assemble the largest organized block of voters, so that we offer votes to people, so they will seek the support of this block."

And that's exactly what was done in the special U.S. Senate election in Texas—even though Perot's former foreign policy adviser Richard Fisher of Dallas was running, and running on a Perot-style platform. Perot passed up the opportunity to support Fisher, who styled himself as a "Perot Democrat"—emphasizing reform issues. Fisher had some of Perot's key Texas people working for him, including former Texas state coordinator Jim Serur and former director of the national phone bank, Rose Roberts-Cannaday. But without Perot's endorsement or formal backing from the Texas UWSA, Fisher was unable to attract more than 8 percent of the vote; he finished fifth in a twenty-four-person field.

UWSA's role in that special election campaign was to stage forums to present the candidates to voters, including one forum for all twenty-four Senate candidates and another limited to the top six contenders. After the field was pared to two, UWSA sponsored a one-on-one debate between the appointed incumbent, Democrat Bob Krueger, and Republican Kay Bailey Hutchison, moderated by Sander Vanocur. Local chapters of UWSA also held separate forums, many of which were attended only by surrogates and the lesser-known candidates. Yet, the candidates openly touted their UWSA membership during the race, and four of the top five finishers were UWSA members, including both of the runoff candidates.

In the final weeks of the Texas Senate election campaign, UWSA mailed out postcards asking its Texas members whether they wanted to support one of the two runoff candidates and, if so, which one. Hutchison won the postcard poll. Two days before the runoff election, Texas UWSA Director Bill Walker, with Perot looking on, announced at a news conference that one-third of the Texas members responded to the postcard survey and 84 percent of those who responded favored Kay Bailey Hutchison. By that time, the die was cast in the

Texas Senate race. That same day, a poll was released showing Hutchison had a seventeen-point lead over Krueger. Hutchison was an overwhelming winner in the runoff election. Walker refused to say how many postcards were returned or what the size of the Texas membership was at that time.

Hutchison was going to win the election, with or without the UWSA-announced support because of dissatisfaction with the Clinton administration and because Texans weren't enamored of Bob Krueger. Nonetheless, there was some UWSA impact on the election simply from the fact that the candidates were campaigning on many of the UWSA issues. Hutchison, who had fervently courted UWSA members, reiterated her support for the group's goals when the UWSA support was announced.

Perot explained the concept. "We're not trying to tell our members how to vote. We're saying our people have been active in debates, they've listened to the debates and here's where they come out. We'll probably have a better way to do that in 1994. Each state will do it their own way."

Other meet-the-candidates nights were sponsored in New Jersey, California and Wisconsin—some with live television or radio coverage.

UWSA was forging ahead—but it was a different kind of operation than the 1992 presidential campaign had been. Many of the campaign volunteers had gone back to their lives and UWSA was seeing a lot of new people, according to staffer Jeff Zucker. Zucker pointed out that in several elections around the country it was becoming apparent that UWSA didn't need to endorse candidates. "They're embracing us," he said.

Tommy Attaway, director of the UWSA phone bank in Dallas, observed a difference in attitude. "The people in the campaign were more emotional. The volunteers now are much more deliberate in their approach. They realize it's going to be long-term." Nor were the volunteers devoting the kind of energy and time they did in the campaign. That kind of slavish devotion is impossible to maintain. Volunteering for UWSA was becoming "a more regular part of their lives rather than an overwhelming passion," Attaway said.

Additionally, more of the work with UWSA revolves around the mail, rather than the phones. Cases of mail arrive daily to the mail center, where it is sorted and prepared for response by a staff-volunteer team. The heaviest day brought in sixty-five thousand pieces of mail to the Dallas headquarters.

Attaway said in late May 1993, he believed the organization was at or near the point at which it could stay alive with or without Ross Perot,

The dissenters begged to differ. Cindy Schultz predicted UWSA would self-destruct just as Perot did during the campaign. "I don't think it's going to have any effect on any elections, unless he cleans house down there and gets some people in with political smarts and people smarts." In a year's time, she predicted, "it's going to be a big nothing."

They believed Perot was looking for a different kind of person to head up the new UWSA—people he could control. Directors who were hired could also be fired. It's much harder to "fire" volunteers. They talked of storm-trooper, strong-arm tactics to get the right people in and the wrong people out. They claimed the "Perotbots" who stayed on board were not strong people, not independent thinkers.

But that wasn't the total truth, either. There were plenty of strong, smart, impressive people still on board with UWSA. Take Carolyn (C. J.) Barthelenghi, for example. C. J. Barthelenghi was state chairman in New Jersey, having replaced Tom O'Neil, a Lawrenceville, New Jersey, businessman who claimed he was moved aside. (O'Neil had told *The New York Times* in September that there were no "volunteers" in New Jersey, only "Perot's people.") Barthelenghi's husband, George, had worked on Perot's campaign for class president at Annapolis. They had helped get Perot on the ballot, and she became one of the founders of United We Stand America on July 30. Barthelenghi was a former corporate executive for Scott Paper Company, in charge of strategic planning and organizational development in Europe.

Barthelenghi questioned whether the term "grass roots organization" wasn't an oxymoron. "Grass roots" she said, implies "we can do whatever we want," while "organization" suggests a "top-down" approach. "We are trying to employ the best of both, so that within boundaries, people will be free to play the game however we can." The guidelines, she said, include a consistency of mission and some principles—including the fact that "we're not going to play politics as usual while pursuing our mission."

She suggested that some of the dissidents "got in for the wrong reasons" or "felt jilted at the altar." And she disputed charges that Perot was propelled simply by ego. "You'd have to be crazy to do this for your ego. Look at the grief he's taken. He has a healthy ego; it doesn't require the care and feeding from a lot of people."

But it's difficult even for her to forecast how the new "Perotdigm" will evolve. "It's a new form of political force, unlike any other. It offers the opportunity to counter balance the special interests that the parties and officeholders have to cave in to." While she doesn't see it becoming a party "like the others," she believes millions of people have been attracted to the movement.

Steve Bost of Maine was another. Bost served ten years in the Maine legislature, retiring in early 1992 after he became disaffected with the gridlock in Augusta. He had planned to take a break from politics before Perot appeared on the scene. Bost volunteered and ended up running Perot's presidential campaign in Maine and became a UWSA paid staff member. Like Barthelenghi, he also predicted the organization will have staying power. "We have not yet reached our stride. It will develop and mature as an organization, and I think over time have both credibility and influence, certainly in the halls of Congress and with the American people as well—particularly if they view it as a catalyst for meaningful change."

In California, the state director was a longtime associate of Perot from IBM days, James Campbell. Campbell had been the president and/or chief executive officer of such companies as Greyhound Computer Corporation, Xerox Computer Services, the Shurgart Corporation (Manufacturers of floppy disks) and Fortune Systems Corporation.

Among '92 state coordinators remaining on board as paid state directors in 1993 were Joan Vinson in Maryland, Susan Esser in Michigan, Betty Montgomery in South Carolina, Pat Muth in Florida, and Sandy McClure in Missouri.

Darcy Anderson, UWSA executive director, disputed claims that state leaders were not involved in the planning process and that UWSA is a top-down organization. The first meeting of state leaders, he said, was conducted about two weeks after the election. A representative group of fifteen state leaders was brought to Dallas; others were polled by telephone. The basic concepts of the organization were developed, he said, including the nonprofit (rather than political organization) approach, the $15 memberships and the focus on elected leadership at the state and congressional district levels.

"Some may have had their feelings hurt because they were not asked to come in for that meeting," Anderson said. "

Afterwards, organizational guidelines were drafted and, during January and February of 1993, those guidelines were circulated and refinements were sought from state leaders. A workshop for state directors was conducted in April and another planned after more state directors were hired.

The decision was made to hire state directors to serve as a stabilizing force for the organization, because elected leadership is expected to turn over every year, Anderson said. The role of the state director, as he described it, will be to help the state organize, administer elections of leaders at the regional and congressional district level, and to provide continuity and stability over the long term.

As for the dissenters, he said, "In the big scheme of things, it's still a very, very small number...We would have been very naive to think that we, as an organization, wouldn't go through some growing pains—as large as we are." And, he added, "It's the nature of the people. They're very passionate about solving the problems the country faces. They're independent by nature; they're critical by nature. They're in this because they're frustrated about where the country is headed, and they're impatient.

Part of the frustration has been with the lengthy startup period and with the deliberation with which

UWSA is being organized for the long term. "People would have loved to have seen us get organized quicker. It certainly could have moved faster if we wanted it to be a top-down dictatorial organization. We spent a good three months getting input and moving forward in a very sensitive yet deliberative way," Anderson said. Rather than being headed for destruction, he sees the organization building momentum with every passing week.

Jeff Zucker, who is editor of the UWSA newsletter, which was published in the summer of 1993 as a twenty-page tabloid newspaper, feels as a result of working in the national office in Dallas that "there's a depth to this movement that goes beyond the Perot groupie. A twenty-nine-year-old political science graduate with an MBA in international finance, he joined the Perot movement in 1992.

The publication of the full-blown newsletter was a concession made to improve communications, according to one of the resigned state leaders. Perot, he said, "saw everybody going out the door," so he consented to make some changes. But that leader is skeptical that Perot will ever be able to loosen his own grip on the organization enough to let nature take its course.

However, even Dee Zuber, the Ohio dissident, admitted that "Perot did one very good service; he got people off their couch potatoes. I was one, as a college grad in economics. I'll never return to the former status." And, she said, "I have many fine friends who still love him with all their heart."

Syndicated columnist Jack Germond observed during a trip to Texas in June 1993 that the political future of Ross Perot and the movement he represented depended in large part on "how aberrationally he behaves." But he conceded that a love affair still exists between Perot and many Americans. Germond, who writes a column for Prodigy in addition to his syndicated column, said, "If I write a column critical of Perot, I get inundated with responses. There are two sacred cows," he said, "Ross Perot and Rush Limbaugh," the conservative talk show host.

By June, speculation was that UWSA had more than two million members. In a *Time*/CNN poll in mid-May, 12 percent of those polled said they would consider joining UWSA, and one percent volunteered that they were already members. That would more or less square with reports of a two million membership at that time. Obviously, Perot wanted to get closer to the nineteen million figure that represented his 1992 vote before he announced the membership number. And he wanted the group to be completely organized in every state first.

When asked in June, five months after the membership drive began on January 11, 1993, when he might know if the money would be sent back, he replied: "We're past that point now."

Without ever forming a third party, Perot had created a third political force that had the potential of overwhelming the other two. "This thing is working so well," he said, "it scares me."

Still, if UWSA is going to be successful over the long term, several refinements need to be embodied in the organization. One includes abandoning the secrecy and closed-door policies with the press that were so much a part of the Perot campaign. If normal modes of communication are ignored, the organization will continue to be stung by one-sided press reports. Credibility will require periodic reports on the number of members and the activities of the state chapters. The organization will not be taken seriously in the future if candidates are supported based on member surveys which fail to reveal how many members participated in that particular poll, as in Texas's special U.S. Senate election of 1993. Percentages are meaningless without total numbers reflected. Nor will it be taken seriously unless it begins to demonstrate accomplishments in the political arena—to collect some scalps for the UWSA belt, as was done in Georgia, or influence legislation, as was done in Connecticut.

THE SHADOW PRESIDENCY

BY JUNE 6, 1993, Perot had appeared at more rallies in 1993 than he did during his presidential campaign—fifty rallies in twenty states: Maine, Florida, Texas, New Mexico, Colorado, South Carolina, North Carolina, Virginia, Utah, Montana, Washington, Oregon, Louisiana, Minnesota, Kansas, Missouri, Kentucky, West Virginia, New Jersey and Michigan.

And his television talk show tour was just as heavy. Perot was all over the airwaves, on all the network morning shows, and others ranging from "Joan Rivers," to "Donahue," "Tonight" with Jay Leno, "Regis and Kathy Lee," "MacNeil/Lehrer," "Maury Povich," "Larry King Live," the "David Frost Show," C-Span, and NBC "Nightly News."

He appeared before a Joint Congressional Committee on Governmental Reform, testified on the North American Free Trade Agreement before a House Committee and the Senate Banking Committee. And he had bought thirty-minute segments on NBC for infomercials.

That Congress was awed by the potential power of Perot was evident when he appeared before the Joint Committee on Governmental Reform. Senator William Cohen, a Maine Republican, told Perot at the hearing: "I walked in here from a meeting with the President, and there were as many people waiting to get in to see you as there had been waiting to see him. And I said, 'Who won the election?' You have a tremendous amount of support out there." Democratic Senator Harry M. Reid of Nevada was the only member of the joint House-Senate reform panel who put Perot through rigorous questioning. After challenging Perot on his facts and accusing him of playing to the applause, Reid returned to his office to find a number of negative phone calls. He told the *Washington Post* he later got some positive calls, as well as plaudits from some fellow members of Congress for standing up to Perot.

Senator David L. Boren, Democrat of Oklahoma and co-chairman of the panel, said he too got calls from constituents, but virtually all were praising Perot's testimony. He told the *Washington Post*, "We sit there and the average insider says, 'What technical suggestions did he have? What did he add?' But the folks back home say, 'That was the best thing...that I ever saw.' We forget the general citizenry doesn't talk our language, but they talk his."

On the Sunday morning after Perot's appearance, Cokie Roberts of ABC News said that members of Congress were "scared to death" of Perot. "I think there is true fear of Ross Perot in the halls of Congress...people bowed and kowtowed to him for the most part. The fact that he got 19 percent of the vote—nineteen million voters—everybody's worried sick about who those voters are and whether they're going to be with the Democrats or the Republicans."

Fellow commentator Sam Donaldson weighed in on the situation saying, "Well, Ross Perot is a force, no doubt, but so is a hurricane which knocks down all the houses."

And George Will, in his own haughty assessment, allowed as how he couldn't understand Perot's hold on people. "I listen to the sentences. There's a subject, an object, a predicate, but I don't get it. I just don't understand the hold he has on people, and hence, I don't understand the fear he instills." It was another reminder of the need for the inside-the-beltway commentators, such as Will and Donaldson, to get out of their insulated bubbles and talk to some real people.

Perot became such an effective watchdog over the first few months of the Clinton administration that the *U.S. News*'s David Gergen (who later accepted the job of special counselor in the Clinton White House) said on "Nightline" on May 27, 1993, "There's no question who won the first one hundred days, the first 150 days. It's been Ross Perot."

Perot was in a unique position. He could concentrate on the problems, without being held accountable for the solutions. It was the best of all possible worlds. He was the country's most powerful political gadfly, the "shadow" president. He had a position of influence with no strings attached. All he had to do was say what was wrong.

Perot was also continuing to try to air more infomercials. Only NBC was willing to sell him time, opening up the network airwaves to the long-format "advocacy ads." Former NBC correspondent Marvin Kalb, director of the Joan Shorenstein Barone Center on the Press, Politics and Public Policy at Harvard University, noted the significance. He called it "another large step in the direction of the electronic democracy that Ross Perot alerted us to last year. We're moving into uncharted terrain where technology and economics are going to determine the political landscape. And we must all be alert to the implications. If you sell that time to Ross Perot, then why not sell it to Lyndon LaRouche or the National Rifle Association?" he asked. Indeed, why not? With hundreds of channels to choose from, none has a captive audience anymore. In fact, advocacy groups already are running infomercials on cable TV.

NBC's acquiescence to Perot's demands allowed him to begin conducting his great experiment with the electronic town hall. On Sunday, March 21, 1993, NBC aired "Ross Perot Presents: The First National Referendum—Government Reform." Perot purchased the network time for $400,000 on behalf of UWSA, and viewers were asked to vote by ballot on seventeen questions ranging from debt reduction to eliminating the electoral college. The ballot appeared in *TV Guide*, and copies were sent to ten thousand newspapers, asking that it be reprinted as a public service. It also was made available to electronic bulletin boards. Perot said the responses would provide a "quick, crude...dipstick check of public reaction."

The questions were widely criticized for being "loaded" so as to achieve a desired response. Professional pollsters suggested the survey would reflect the views of Perot partisans rather than those of the public at large. As a result, Perot engaged pollster Gordon Black to follow up with a statistically sound poll on Perot-driven issues.

Perot promoted the referendum as a voice for the people during a speech to the National Press Club. "We're going to give them a bullhorn and everybody in Congress a Miracle Ear to make sure they can hear the people," he said.

In California, he urged drivers to turn on their car lights on the day after his TV show if they favored government reform. "We'll ask stations to play the old gospel hymn, 'I See the Light.' I hope Washington will see the light....This is going to create a number-ten migraine headache inside the Beltway," Perot said, adding that officeholders would be saying, "Oh my God, all those crazy people are out there again."

UWSA spokeswoman Sharon Holman said more than 1.3 million people sent in ballots following the March 21 program. Not surprisingly, the balloting reflected overwhelming support for the Perot issue positions. Each of the seventeen questions resulted in a "yes" response rate of between 93 and 99 percent. The ballots were tabulated according to congressional districts and states, and delivered to each member of Congress and each senator by UWSA members.

Gordon Black said his poll (of 1,733 adult respondents) produced the following findings on his issue questions: 92 percent favored a proposal for a quarterly audited financial report so they could know whether deficit reduction was being achieved; 71 percent favored a balanced budget amendment; 61 percent favored the line-item veto; 78 percent favored automatic term limits if Congress fails to meet a publicly accepted deficit reduction timetable; 78 percent favored reducing the role of domestic lobbyists and 67 percent favored the elimination of foreign lobbyists; 69 percent favored the elimination of political action committees; 90 percent favored reducing the president's and Congress's salaries, and their respective retirement plans, to bring them in line with American workers.

Black also found public support for the elimination of the electoral college, replacing it with a direct, popular election of the president by a margin of 73 percent to 21 percent.

But the most extraordinary figures produced by Black

indicated that UWSA could become the largest political movement in the history of the nation, with up to 40 million adult members. Twenty percent of the Black poll respondents said they would join the grass roots group. "What does 20 percent mean?" Dr. Black asked at a news conference. "Obviously, if everybody who said they would, joined, the sheer size would be staggering—it would be forty million adults. If even half the people were planning on joining, you're talking about twenty million Americans and a political movement larger than has ever been seen in this country before." An organization of twenty million would be larger than the entire labor movement in the United States.

Viewership of Perot's thirty-minute "First National Referendum" was slightly less than he drew during the campaign, although Black estimated that more than twenty million adults heard or watched Perot's broadcast. Other polls were beginning to show that Perot was gaining popularity. An NBC poll in early March 1993, showed Perot's favorable ratings had risen from 35 percent to 47 percent since December, and his negatives had dropped from 33 percent to 24 percent. *USA Today* reported after the referendum broadcast that Perot's favorable rating was up from 44 percent to 66 percent. And Perot's former research director, Frank Luntz, found that 38 percent of voters were more favorably disposed toward Perot than they were on Election Day, and 25 percent said they would vote for Perot for president. The range of the numbers in the polls indicated the mercurial nature of Perot's popularity. Even so, anybody in Washington who wasn't taking Perot seriously needed a math lesson.

As analyst Kevin Phillips said on National Public Radio the morning after the referendum broadcast, Perot represented "a threat to anybody who's trying to tell the American people that Washington is working again, because Ross Perot's underlying premise is, 'It ain't working. These guys don't know how to get under the hood, and you can't trust them when they're under there.' So, at this point, he's a threat to the Democrats as much as the Republicans."

Perot's electronic town halls served to stimulate an American populace that had become more vocal with the 1992 election. The *Washington Post* reported that in the first eight days of the 1993 legislative session, the Capitol switchboard logged 1.6 million calls, compared to seven hundred thousand for the same time period in the 1992 session. Thousands more calls and fax transmissions were placed directly to senatorial and congressional offices.

The stampede included public response to two emotional issues: 1) the nomination of Zoe Baird, the $500,000-a-year corporate lawyer who delayed paying taxes for illegal immigrants hired for child care, and 2) Clinton's proposal to repeal the ban on homosexuals in the military. "I've been jokingly saying those folks out there are really taking this democracy thing seriously," Democratic Senator John I. Lieberman of Connecticut, told *The Post*.

In the Dallas phone bank for UWSA, where volunteers continued to man a dozen to eighteen phones daily, numbers are listed on a message board for both the White House and for Capitol Hill to be passed along to callers.

As the spring of 1993 wore on, Perot continued to turn up the heat on President Clinton, assailing the President's economic package and urging television viewers to call the White House and Congress to express opposition to higher taxes unless accompanied by government reform and a solid program to pay down the debt. Perot said he felt "a great sense of responsibility" for the increase because of his campaign's emphasis on tax increases to attack the deficit. In the three days following the second thirty-minute infomercial by Perot, White House and Capitol Hill telephones were flooded with calls from people across the country expressing their opinions on the need to cut government spending before increasing taxes.

Telephone company sources told UWSA that Perot's infomercial, "The Tax Increase, Analyzing the President's Economic Plan," resulted in over one million phone-call attempts to the White House over a forty-eight-hour period. Callers to the UWSA headquarters in Dallas complained of getting a continuous busy signal or rerouting of their calls to the White House.

Perot's stepped-up attacks appeared to be a growing irritant to the President. But Paul Begala, political adviser to Clinton, urged the President to concentrate on issues that would appeal to Perot's supporters and not worry about the man himself. "What I see too much of in Washington is people who either want to suck up to Mr. Perot or strike out at Mr. Perot," Begala told *The New York Times*. "Let's eliminate the middleman and address the issues that his voters care about," he advised.

Perot also published his second book, called *Not for Sale at Any Price*, which included his economic plan, his opposition to the North American Free Trade Agreement and information on United We Stand America. It soared to number two on *The New York Times*'s paperback bestseller list in its second week in print. His first book stayed on the bestseller list for sixteen weeks.

Perot's popularity continued to climb through April.

A poll conducted jointly by Democratic pollster Celinda Lake and Republican pollster Ed Goeas found that Perot was viewed favorably by 64 percent of the electorate and unfavorably by 29 percent. Celinda Lake called Perot a "serious force in American politics" and a "threat to both parties." The survey found that Perot had eclipsed the GOP in the eyes of voters as the loyal opposition to the Democrats. And he was just getting warmed up.

Perot went on to launch a major initiative against the North American Free Trade Agreement, and to issue even more stinging personal attacks against President Clinton. His third thirty-minute electronic town hall, "Keeping Your Job in the USA," was a ringing indictment of NAFTA. His favorite line was that the agreement would create a "giant sucking sound" of jobs going from the U.S.A. to Mexico—even though American companies can move to Mexico without the agreement, if they want. Perot questioned the wisdom of creating enterprise zones in the inner cities at the same time low-wage jobs were being moved south of the border.

Asked why this had become such a huge issue for him, he replied: "If I wanted to make money, I'd keep my mouth shut and quadruple my net worth. Way back, philosophically, I was for it. I used to say, in '86 or '87, if we're going to send jobs, send them to Mexico, not to Asia." What changed his mind? "The deal. We're stuck with a bad deal," he said. "What they finally negotiated is a deal that wouldn't work. It's destructive to the country. It will really hurt our ability to strengthen our tax base. You cannot reduce the standard of living when you're $4 trillion in debt."

And his harshest attack against Clinton—issued just four months into the new administration during an interview by David Frost—was that Clinton was so poorly

prepared for the presidency that "you wouldn't consider giving him a job anywhere above middle management if he applied for a position in private industry."
He also suggested Clinton might be trying to deflect
attention from his faltering presidency by starting "a
little war" in Bosnia.

On May 17, 1993, the cover story in *U.S. News and
World Report* featured Perot and the headline, "Why is
this man smiling? Ross Perot may be the most importance force in American politics." The story included a
poll which said 45 percent would consider voting for
Perot for president—a fourteen-point increase since the
start of Clinton's term. In a hypothetical race, Perot was
running dead even with the President.

The *U.S. News* poll described Perot's supporters as a
movement of the alienated American middle—as large
as 25 percent of the electorate—who had no interest in
being siphoned off by either major party. "These people
are not in transition," said Democratic poll taker Celinda
Lake, who conducted the survey with Republican pollster Ed Goeas.

Comparing Perot to previous third-party contenders, analyst Kevin Phillips said, "It's unprecedented.
Even if Perot has peaked for now, he's achieved an unprecedented reemergence. No previous major third-
party contender has been able to play this role just six
months after being defeated...Indeed, Perot's resurgence
means he could be the first third-party candidate to in-
stitutionalize a major new political force since the 1850s."

For the moment, Perot was keeping Clinton—the 43
percent president—from building a governing majority, which Richard Nixon was able to do after winning
by the same plurality in a three-way race in 1968. But
would the force be institutionalized? Would UWSA stay

alive—with or without its charismatic leader?

"We couldn't kill it if we wanted to; it's got a life of its own," said Carolyn (C. J.) Barthelenghi, the New Jersey UWSA state chairman. "If the problems we are experiencing in government were an aberration, this might be a flash in the pan, but the problems are not transient. They're systemic. That's why we will have a life." She added that, "It's great to know we do have the best salesman in the country at the top of our organization, but millions of people are dedicated to this cause."

And there were other unanswered questions. What would be the effect of UWSA on the 1994 mid-term congressional elections? And would UWSA become the vehicle by which Ross Perot would seek the presidency again in 1996?

William Schneider, a political analyst on CNN, believes UWSA is aiming for a membership of ten million by the end of the year which will enable Perot and the organization to have real clout in the 1994 congressional elections. UWSA could then act as a powerful pressure group. If Perot announces a huge organization and then proceeds to endorse candidates, or even just announces which candidates its members "support," members of Congress would sit up and take notice. And that could have serious implications on such issues as the North American Free Trade Agreement. NAFTA could become a litmus test issue for UWSA support of congressional candidates in 1994.

Pollster Frank Luntz suggests that 1994 could be the best year for challengers in fifty years, with a large number of incumbents going down to defeat.

Doug Bailey, a former Republican consultant with Bailey, Deardorf, and the publisher of the *Political Hotline*, agrees with other analysts that UWSA's role in 1994 could be significant. UWSA could be the margin of difference in every contested congressional election by putting forward a platform which stresses deficit reduction and governmental reform and requiring allegiance to that platform for support of candidates. Anticipating that considerable sentiment will be focused on "tossing the ins out," he said, "that could be very impactful."

There's another side to the congressional coin, as well. If Perot were to be an independent presidential candidate in 1996, after backing congressional candidates in '94, he would have some leverage with Congress, some members beholden to him.

If there are wholesale changes in the Congress in '94, the new members likely will go in on reform agendas, and that will produce some change. But the ultimate fortunes of both parties depend on their presidential nominees. The Democratic Party will rise or fall on the performance of Bill Clinton. While Clinton's first few months in the White House were inauspicious, even Perot noted that he's bright and a quick learner. And he has a reputation for being the "comeback kid."

The situation for Republicans is a bit more complex, although Republicans were more than optimistic about their chances of recapturing the White House after Clinton's first few months. Many Republican leaders felt that the party seriously lost its way in the 1992 election and essentially had nothing to say. They'll be trying to change that situation before 1996. According to Doug Bailey, "there is a broad interest by the party organization to change the face the party has shown in the 1980s, to move on to a new definition of the party in 1990s. My guess is that the Republican Party will choose a new face, not a Washington face, not an eighties face—

to present the party, the Perot supporters and the people of the country with a more attractive image. And not necessarily a hard-core conservative face. My sense is that the party is ready without anger to turn the page." If that happens, then the power of the third-force candidacy would not be as great. While a "new look" nominee would be partly a result of Perot and UWSA, it would undermine Perot's strength if he were to be a candidate.

But Bailey adds that Perot would make a serious mistake to think he can be as viable in 1996 as he was in 1992. The press, he said, "will do a job on him." And, he added, Perot won't measure up to the image people have of a president."

In 1992, he said, "Clinton was elected president. Hillary was elected first lady. And Perot was elected first kibitzer." It's a role that fits him precisely. "He's earned that right," said Bailey. But he added, "It's one thing to have him as first kibitzer and another thing to have him as president. A lot of people are glad to have him out there keeping Clinton's feet to the fire, stirring the pot, but don't believe that by temperament he's qualified to be president of the United States."

Perot has been conjectured as a potential candidate in the Republican primaries in 1996. It's entirely possible that Perot with his army can flood the GOP primaries and caucuses and take the Republican nomination. Such a happening is fraught with problems for Republicans. A Perot nomination could very well split the GOP. Republican officeholders and "professional Republicans" might well become a rump group, either failing to endorse Perot or running a candidate of their own. Or it might be a rump group of establishment Republicans who would urge Perot to run in the GOP primaries.

On June 24, 1993, when he appeared in Washington to deliver 2.5 million signatures gathered by UWSA members telling Congress to "cut spending first," balance the budget and institute government reforms, Perot was joined at his news conference almost exclusively by Republican members of the House and Senate. Congressional Budget Office chief Robert Reischauer said: "As long as Ross Perot is circling like a vulture over the two existing political parties and making deficit reduction his primary focus, the parties are going to scrap and fight and show that they, too, are concerned about this problem."

While Republicans were being publicly supportive of the Perot agenda, it can be expected that, at some point, the many Republicans angling for the presidential nomination in 1996 will turn on him—in an effort to keep him out of the Republican presidential primaries.

Perot, however, told Larry King he had no intention of running in the Republican primary. "No, I don't intend—See, if I ever have to run in 1996, we have failed. We don't have four years to wait. We want the two-party system to work." But if that failure occurs, King asked, "Would you enter the Republican primaries or run independently?"

Perot: We would just probably go through the petition-signing process—never having even had a conversation about it.

King: But you wouldn't run in either party's primary?

Perot: No, I'm sure we'd just run as an independent.

Stuart Rothenberg, author of a Washington political report, says that "In a sense, the strength of a Perot party is that it's not a party, it can criticize the other guys. When you view it as a way to power, you undercut that public rationale for a Perot. ...You become part of the system, an insider, making deals and running candidates."

If history repeats itself, one of the two major parties will reach out and envelop the Perot voters by co-opting their issues. By midsummer 1993, the Republican Party had an initiative in place to do just that. Republican National Chairman Haley Barbour unveiled a plan called the National Policy Foundation by which Republicans would try to reconnect with grass roots America. The nationwide development of "policy councils" was a massive effort to try to bring Perot voters back to the GOP fold and to redefine the party's mission in the post Reagan-Bush era.

Through the National Policy Foundation, Republicans acknowledged that the answers to the problems facing the country will not be found in Washington, but will come from the "workplaces, meeting halls, local council chambers, churches and civic groups, board rooms and the living rooms of America...from the common sense of hard-working America." It sounded very Perotesque.

The NPF's one-year search for solutions would include the largest survey ever attempted—a questionnaire to six hundred thousand GOP activists—followed by regional conferences of elected officials and by two meetings to bring ordinary citizens into the process. It wasn't electronic, but it was town hall. The final product of the National Policy Foundation was scheduled to be a comprehensive report, "Listening to America: Republican Ideas that Work."

The Democrats were doing some introspection, as well. The Democratic Leadership Council (DLC) conducted a poll of twelve hundred Perot voters, to determine what President Clinton needed to do to win them over. Results of the poll, conducted by White House pollster Stan Greenberg, were announced in early July, 1993. The Democrats took solace in the poll's finding that the Perot bloc didn't appear interested in returning to the GOP. Pollster Greenberg contended that while the Perot voters have a largely Republican voting history, "they are refugees" from the GOP now and "up for grabs" if Clinton can win them over by his performance during the next three years,

But neither did Perot voters appear interested in attaching themselves to the Democrats. Unlike supporters of previous independent presidential candidates, the Perot backers were not drifting back to either the Democratic or Republican Party, but rather remained a solid, defiant voting bloc with considerable staying power. Included in the Democrat poll's conclusions were that the "Perot voters remain committed to their 1992 vote and, for the moment, want to stick with Perot in 1996—even if he were to run as a Republican."

The DLC poll suggested that Perot voters had grown increasingly skeptical about President Clinton's ability to deliver change. It concluded that to win over the Perot supporters, Clinton needs to live up to his campaign promises to provide jobs and economic growth and reform how government does business—to be a "new kind of Democrat." However, Clinton had developed a reputation during the first few months of his administration of being, instead, an old-style tax-and-spend Democrat. DLC President Al From suggested that President Clinton needed to "emphasize personal responsibility and advance a governing agenda that rewards Americans who work hard and play by the rules." Again, it sounds like Perot.

What distinguishes the Perot voters from both Clinton and Bush voters is that they are antigovernment and antiestablishment. "These attitudes are less about ideology and more about the failure of public trust that characterizes their view of almost all big institutions," according to the survey. Nonetheless, From contended that the survey results provided the benchmark for a "base-expanding strategy" for Democrats. To expand the base, he said, "the President must go hunting where the ducks are. That means targeting the nearly twenty million voters who backed Ross Perot."

Ironically, the survey offered anecdotal evidence that the Perot voters were even a little doubtful about Perot. Although they view him as being all the things Congress is not—honest, a straight shooter, someone who can get things done—they also said that his independence could produce the kind of gridlock in Washington that people are upset about. Greenberg noted that, even to his own supporters, Perot's temperament makes him unpredictable.

There still remain, among many Americans, questions about how temperamentally suited Perot is or would ever be as a president. He was probably right when he said, long ago, that he wasn't suited for it. But for the moment, "Where he is a profoundly useful influence is as a national watchdog. They (people) have a skepticism about the temperament. But it doesn't get in the way of liking the role he is playing and the desire for a new party. Up to a point his quirks make him unique and successful," analyst Stuart Rothenberg said.

Hamilton Jordan hasn't talked to Perot since July of 1992 when Perot called him to say he had done a good job on the campaign. "Which was kind of ironic. In sixty days, we'd taken him from first place to third place. But I like the man. I think he's an American hero. He's done a great thing, but the way history judges him is still to be decided, how he handles this political movement he has developed."

Jordan said, "What we'll only know four or five years from now is whether this thing so personally identified with Ross moves beyond him—whether he has a cult following of four or five million people and whether that just withers and goes away, or whether he has the discipline and ability to separate his ego from this movement. Those are questions nobody can answer today...Does it stay narrowly defined as a Ross Perot movement, or does he help it become something larger than himself? He would suggest he's already done that. I'm not sure. A lot of both the strength and weakness of what he's done is connected in the minds of the public with him personally."

Jordan, who returned to Whittle Communications in Knoxville, Tennessee, after Perot's July 16, 1992, withdrawal, disputes reports that Perot offered him a half million dollars to keep his mouth shut on the presidential campaign. Jordan said he was paid $75,000 a month for three months—even though he offered to advise Perot for free. He says today he believes Perot would find it very frustrating to be president. "You can say that about a lot of people in the private sector—not to be able to make things happen, not to have more accountability, to have all these extraneous factors that would detain you from your goals."

When Jordan first got involved in Perot's aborted presidential bid, he thought he "had a decent shot at being president." In June 1993, he said: "I don't think Ross Perot will ever be president today. I don't think he wants to be. He likes to be a gadfly. I thought he had a chance to change the course of history, and he still does. But it gets back to whether ultimately this thing is built around him and is a cult following or whether it matures into a real movement with agenda and discipline."

Jordan believes "It's not enough to be a gadfly. If you create a political force in this country, you've got some obligation to have an impact in a practical way. How will that happen? It all has to do with power, and to have power you have to take risks and whether he's going to take it from national rhetorical level to a state-by-state, congressional district level."

(Author's note: I asked Perot in June 1993, what were his hopes for United We Stand America. He responded, "Look at our mission statement, our goals. It's spelled out as clearly as we're capable of doing in that book.")

Among the goals listed in *Not for Sale at Any Price* are: To recreate a government that comes from the people—not at the people. To reform the federal government at all levels to eliminate fraud, waste and abuse. To have a government where the elected, appointed, and career officials come to serve and not to cash in. To get our economy moving and put our people back to work. To balance the budget, pay off our nation's debt, build an efficient and cost-effective health care system, get rid of foreign lobbyists and political action committees. To make our neighborhoods and streets safe from crime and violence and create the finest public schools. And, finally, to pass on the American Dream to our children, making whatever fair, shared sacrifices are necessary.

As for himself, Perot states that his intention is to "build a selfless organization for the good of the country...Every now and then someone will say, 'What's in it for me?' I say, 'Nothing, except a better country for your children.'"

Perot admits that he is a "whole lot more comfortable just working for a good cause rather than being a candidate." That, he is. His best role is being the watchdog, the gadfly, even the "shadow" president. He is doing precisely what a lot of people had in mind when they voted for him in 1992.

As he has said many times, he is the grain of sand that irritates the oyster that makes the pearl. As irritating as he may be to Bill Clinton, to the Democrats and the Republicans, and even to some ordinary citizens, Perot has reshaped American politics in the course of little more than one year. He is providing a valuable function by forcing the traditional parties to try to reconnect with average citizens and reexamine their own missions. If the parties don't respond, they very well may not have seen the last of Ross Perot—or perhaps even someone more ominous.

Looking back on 1992, I asked Perot whether he would want to do it again. " I didn't want to do it the first time," he said. I believe that. And I believe he doesn't ever really want to *be* president—to live in the White House and do what presidents have to do. For a period of time, in 1992, he got caught up in the excitement of it and, for a period, as competitive as he is, he even wanted to win. But winning and governing are two different matters. Ross Perot, Jr., now warns that his dad had better be careful or he'll get swept up in the same tidal wave for 1996.

What did Perot learn from his 1992 candidacy? "I don't spend a lot of time reflecting, I just keep going," he responded. "Looking backward does not accomplish much. I learned the obvious—there are no rules in politics."

Knowing what he knows now, would he still have done it in 1992? "I would have to," he said. "If you just go down the list and see what people are focused on now that they never talked about before. Look at Washington, see the sensitivity moving back to the people. I'm not the only guy on the road every weekend. Both parties now have $15 memberships. I would have to do it, to get the total focus on getting our financial house back in order."

What would he have done differently? "I don't spend a lot of time looking back. Obviously, I wish we hadn't gotten some of these political pros around. That was a major mistake, to put it kindly. Not Squires or Ham. But the others, who contributed nothing and created all kinds of problems. It was just a really dumb move.

"But I'm focused on what we've got to do in the future. When this thing (UWSA) gets in place, in every town and city, it will have great two-way communications. This is a major undertaking. We've got to have communication, computer networks, faxes and phones....A year from now, our network will have to be much better."

C. J. Barthelenghi, the New Jersey UWSA chairman, credits Perot with "resurrecting the real spirit and intent of democracy. It will be the spirit that revitalizes it for the twenty-first century."

For Perot, the best part of his involvement in politics over the last eighteen months has been the letters "from the heart" he gets from people—he has racks of boxes of them—and being in touch with the American people.

"The best part of it is the people," he said. "de Tocqueville's statement is still true," Perot said, referring to Alexis de Tocqueville, the French writer who conducted a nine-month journey in search of *Democracy in America* in 1831. "de Tocqueville said that America is great because it's people are good. If the people cease to be good, America will cease to be great."

"The people," Perot said, "are as good as gold."

"A lot of people are motivated by the right purposes to do a good job for the country....Ordinary people, they have control of this country if they want it."

However much the reigning political class inside-the-Beltway might have sneered at Ross Perot in the beginning, less than eighteen months after that fateful night on "Larry King Live," it was evident—to them and to all the world—that it would be a huge mistake to underestimate Perot and his people.

★ ★ ★ ★ ★ ★ ★ ★ ★ ★

APPENDIX

Official 1992 Presidential Election Results
(Based on reports from the secretaries of state for the
fifty states and the District of Columbia)

State	Bill Clinton (Democrat)		George Bush (Republican)		Ross Perot (Independent)	
	Votes	%	Votes	%	Votes	%
Alabama	690,080	40.9	804,283	47.6	183,109	10.8
Alaska	78,294	30.3	102,000	39.5	73,481	28.4
Arizona	543,050	36.5	572,086	38.5	353,741	23.8
Arkansas	505,823	53.2	337,324	35.5	99,132	10.4
California	5,121,325	46.0	3,630,575	32.0	2,296,006	20.6
Colorado	629,681	40.1	562,850	35.9	366,010	23.3
Connecticut	682,318	42.2	578,313	35.8	348,771	21.6
D.C.	192,619	84.6	20,698	9.1	9,681	4.3
Delaware	126,054	43.5	102,313	35.3	59,213	20.4
Florida	2,071,651	39.0	2,171,781	40.9	1,052,481	19.8
Georgia	1,008,966	43.5	995,252	42.9	309,657	13.3
Hawaii	179,310	48.1	136,822	36.7	53,003	14.2
Idaho	137,013	28.4	202,645	42.0	130,395	27.0
Illinois	2,453,350	48.6	1,734,096	34.3	840,515	16.6
Indiana	848,420	36.8	989,375	42.9	455,934	19.8
Iowa	586,353	43.3	504,891	37.3	253,468	18.7
Kansas	390,434	33.7	449,951	38.9	312,358	27.0

	Clinton		Bush		Perot	
Kentucky	665,104	44.6	617,178	41.3	203,944	13.7
Louisiana	815,971	45.6	733,386	41.0	211,478	11.8
Maine	263,420	38.8	206,504	30.4	206,820	30.4
Massachusetts	1,318,639	47.5	805,039	29.0	630,731	22.7
Maryland	988,571	49.8	707,094	35.6	281,414	14.2
Michigan	1,871,182	43.8	1,554,940	36.4	824,813	19.3
Minnesota	1,020,997	43.5	747,841	31.9	562,506	24.0
Mississippi	400,258	40.8	487,793	49.7	85,626	8.7
Missouri	1,053,873	44.1	811,159	33.9	518,741	21.7
Montana	154,507	37.6	144,207	35.1	107,225	26.1
Nebraska	216,864	29.4	343,678	46.6	174,104	23.6
Nevada	189,148	37.4	175,828	34.7	132,580	26.2
New Hampshire	209,040	38.9	202,484	37.6	121,337	22.6
New Jersey	1,436,206	43.0	1,356,865	40.6	521,829	15.6
New Mexico	261,617	45.9	212,824	37.3	91,895	10.1
New York	3,444,450	49.7	2,346,649	33.9	1,090,721	15.7
North Carolina	1,114,042	42.7	1,134,661	43.4	357,864	13.7
North Dakota	99,168	32.2	136,244	44.2	71,084	23.1
Ohio	1,984,919	40.2	1,894,248	38.3	1,036,403	21.0
Oklahoma	473,066	34.0	592,929	42.6	319,878	23.0
Oregon	621,314	42.5	475,757	32.5	354,091	24.2
Pennsylvania	2,239,164	45.1	1,791,841	36.1	902,667	18.2
Rhode Island	213,299	47.0	131,601	29.0	105,045	23.2
South Carolina	479,514	39.9	577,507	48.0	138,872	11.5
South Dakota	124,888	37.1	136,718	40.2	73,295	21.8
Tennessee	933,521	47.1	841,300	42.4	199,968	10.1
Texas	2,281,815	37.1	2,496,071	40.6	1,354,781	22.0
Utah	183,429	24.7	322,632	43.4	203,400	27.3
Vermont	133,592	46.1	88,122	30.4	65,991	22.8
Virginia	1,038,650	40.6	1,150,517	45.0	348,639	13.6
Washington	993,037	43.4	731,234	32.0	541,780	23.7
West Virginia	331,001	46.7	241,974	35.4	108,829	15.9
Wisconsin	1,041,114	41.1	930,855	36.8	544,479	21.5
Wyoming	68,160	34.0	79,347	39.6	51,263	25.6

Source: *Congressional Quarterly*, Jan. 23, 1993

On the Ballot in the Following States

State	Date	Signatures Needed	Total
Tennessee	March 29	275	275
Utah	April 30	300	8,000
Delaware	May 12	2,900	8,000
Maine	May 13	4,000	21,000
New Jersey	May 18	800	67,997
Wyoming	May 22	9,400	20,000
Kentucky	May 22	5,000	40,729
Texas	May 27	54,000	231,000
Florida	May 27	60,000	260,000
Idaho	May 29	4,100	34,000
Alaska	May 30	2,000	10,000
Arkansas	June 1	0	0
Kansas	June 16	5,000	50,000
New Hampshire	June 17	3,000	12,000
Massachusetts	June 19	10,000	100,000
North Carolina	June 19	65,000	185,000
Alabama	June 26	5,000	35,000
Nevada	June 26	9,362	50,000
Nebraska	June 30	2,500	18,000
California	July 2	135,000	1,400,000
Washington	July 2	200	55,000
Colorado	July 9	5,000	139,569
Montana	July 10	9,500	46,235
Oklahoma	July 13	35,000	106,000
Indiana	July 17	30,000	200,000
South Dakota	July 17	2,500	15,000
Connecticut	July 22	14,000	125,000
Ohio	July 23	10,000	15,000
Rhode Island	July 29	1,000	15,000
Minnesota	July 29	2,000	55,000
Maryland	July 31	63,186	150,000
Michigan	July 31	25,646	300,000
West Virginia	August 6	6,500	20,000

Pennsylvania	August 10	37,000	302,000
Iowa	August 11	1,000	55,000
D.C.	August 19	2,600	7,000
Louisiana	August 20	0	68,000
South Carolina	August 21	10,000	55,311
Virginia	August 24	13,900	92,000
Oregon	August 24	1,000	130,000
Missouri	August 28	21,000	125,000
Georgia	August 28	27,000	137,182
Illinois	August 28	25,000	106,000
Wisconsin	September 4	2,000	125,000
New Mexico	September 9	12,000	70,000
North Dakota	September 9	4,000	13,000
Mississippi	September 9	1,000	15,000
Vermont	September 11	1,000	7,000
Hawaii	September 15	3,606	13,000
New York	September 18	15,500	91,000
Arizona	September 18	10,600	<u>74,000</u>
			5,278,298

★ ★ ★ ★ ★ ★ ★ ★ ★ ★

BIBLIOGRAPHY

BOOKS

Barlett, Donald L., and Steele, James B. *America: What Went Wrong?* Kansas City: Andrews and McMeel, 1992.

Bennett, W. Lance. *The Governing Crisis: Media, Money and Marketing in American Elections*. New York: St. Martin's Press, 1992.

Bisnow, Mark. *Diary of a Dark Horse*. Carbondale and Edwardsville, Illinois: Southern Illinois University Press, 1983.

Black, Christine M., and Oliphant, Thomas. *All by Myself: The Unmaking of a Presidential Campaign*. Chester, Connecticut: The Globe Pequot Press, 1989.

Coyne, James K., and Fund, John H. *Cleaning House: America's Campaign for Term Limits*. Washington, D.C.: Regnery Gateway, 1992.

Cramer, Richard Ben. *What It Takes*. New York: Random House, 1992.

Dionne, E.J. Jr. *Why Americans Hate Politics*. New York: Simon and Schuster, 1991.

Ehrenhalt, Alan. *The United States of Ambition*. New York: Random House, 1991.

Fishkin, James S. *Democracy and Deliberation: New Directions for Democratic Reform*. New Haven, Connecticut: Yale University Press, 1991.

Foudy, Michael. *Reinventing America: The Common Sense Domestic Agenda for the 90s*. Scottsdale, Arizona: The Institute for American Democracy Press, 1992.

Germond, Jack W., and Witcover, Jules. *Whose Broad Stripes and Bright Stars? The Trivial Pursuit of the Presidency 1988*. New York: Warner Books, 1989.

Goldman, Peter, and Mathews, Tom, et al. *The Quest for the Presidency 1988*. New York: Simon and Schuster, 1989.

Greider, William. *Who Will Tell the People*. New York: Simon and Schuster, 1992.

Mason, Todd. *Perot, An Unauthorized Biography*. Homewood, Illinois: Dow Jones-Irwin, 1990.

Naisbitt, John. *Megatrends: Ten New Directions Transforming Our Lives*. New York: Warner Books, 1982.

Osborne, David, and Gaebler, Ted. *Reinventing Government: How the Entrepreneurial Spirit is Transforming the Public Sector*. New York: Plume, 1993.

Perot, Ross. *United We Stand: How We Can Take Back Our Country*. New York: Hyperion, 1992.

Perot, Ross. *Not for Sale at Any Price: How We Can Save America for Our Children*. New York: Hyperion, 1993.

Phillips, Kevin. *Boiling Point: Democrats, Republicans and the Decline of Middle-Class Prosperity*. New York: Random House, 1993.

Sabato, Larry J. *Feeding Frenzy: How Attack Journalism Has Transformed American Politics*. New York: The Free Press, 1991.

Squires, James D. *The Corporate Takeover of America's Newspapers*. New York: Times Books (Random House), 1993.

Taylor, Paul. *See How They Run: Electing the President in an Age of Mediaocracy*. New York: Alfred A. Knopf, 1990.

Troy, Gil. *See How They Ran: The Changing Role of the Presidential Candidate*. New York: Macmillan, 1991.

REPORTS

"An Uncertain Season, Reporting in the Postprimary Period," The Freedom Forum Media Studies Center at Columbia University, New York, September, 1992.

"The Homestretch. New Politics. New Media. New Voters?" The Freedom Forum Media Studies Center at Columbia University, New York, October, 1992.

"The Finish Line, Covering the Campaign's Final Days," The Freedom Forum Media Studies Center at Columbia University, New York, January, 1993.

"People Versus Politics: Citizens Discuss Politicians, Campaigns, and Political Reform," The Public Accountability Project, Centel Corporation and the Joyce Foundation, October, 1991.

"Our Turn: Politicians Talk About Themselves, Politics, the Public, the Press and Reform," The Public Accountability Project, Centel Corporation and the Joyce Foundation, March, 1992.

"Reflections: The Press Looks at Itself, Politicians and the Public," The Public Accountability Project, Centel Corporation and the Joyce Foundation, September, 1992.

"Citizens and Politics. A View from Main Street America." Prepared for the Kettering Foundation by The Harwood Group, Bethesda, Maryland, Summer, 1991.

INDEX

A

ABC 102, 110, 212, 213, 230, 249, 269, 305, 320, 331, 334, 336, 343, 345, 362, 364, 369, 392, 399, 403, 437
ABC News 394, 456
ABC News/*Washington Post* 214
Abilene, Texas 363
Act Up 216
Adams, John 202
Adams, John Quincy 79, 371, 418
"Adman of the Year" 409
Advertising Age 409
Agenda for American Renewal 323
Alabama 76, 84, 120, 122, 155, 281
Alaska 34, 51, 120, 281, 374
Albuquerque, New Mexico 34, 127, 129
Aliso Viejo, California 224
Allen, Fredrick 120
Alliance Airport 19, 25, 192, 212
Allison, Wick 188, 250, 290, 291, 292, 295, 296
Allred, Gloria 225
Alter, Jonathan 370, 398
Altshuler, Ruth Sharp 139, 223
Amarillo, Texas 58
America Speaks 439
America Video Productions 210
America, What Went Wrong 73, 88
American Agriculture Movement 144
American Enterprise Institute 138, 317, 371
American Newspaper Publishers

Association 102, 107
American Party 77
American Society of Newspaper Editors 102
American University 324
Amherst, Massachusetts 86
Anchorage, Alaska 29
Anderson, Bill 164, 165, 263
Anderson, Darcy 31, 32, 33, 34, 47, 48, 116, 117, 151, 258, 267, 275, 276, 279, 281, 326, 426, 432, 434, 449, 450, 451
Anderson, John 76, 85, 103, 111, 113, 115, 128, 278, 299, 369
Andrews, Richard 282
Anglin, R. M. 423
Annapolis, Maryland 131, 134, 163, 201, 203, 207, 208, 209
Anton, Alida 56
Apple 148
Apple, R.W. 153, 208
Arens, John 143, 144
Arizona 85, 111, 217, 262, 281, 304, 306, 307, 310, 327
Arkansas 55, 84, 141, 208, 281, 338, 361
Arkansas State Council of Vietnam Veterans of America 136
Arlington, Texas 51, 58, 84
Armitage, Richard 195
Armitage story 195
Arnold, Matthew 3
"Arsenio Hall" 156, 176, 392, 393, 394
Ash, Jim 50, 51
Aspin, Les 433

Associated Press   29
AT&T   186
Atlanta   32, 34, 347, 435
Atlanta Constitution   194
Attaway, Tommy   273, 446
Augusta, Georgia   449
Auletta, Ken   389
Aust, Linda   158, 159
Austin, Texas   28, 33, 34, 55, 58, 59, 95, 135, 260, 262, 304
Australia   43
Awbrey, David   398
Aynesworth, Hugh   198

B

Babbage, Bob   61
Bach, Ernie   121
Bailey, Doug   39, 65, 99, 465, 466, 467
Baird, Zoe   430, 461
Baker, Howard H. Jr.   81
Baker, James   312
Baker, John   152
Baker, Russell   366, 368
Balkin, Bob   16, 17
Ballot Access News   112
Baltimore Sun   207
Balz, Dan   154
Bankrupting of America, The   70
Barber, Dan R.   16
Barbour, Haley   469
Bark, Ed   105, 212, 345
Barkin, Bob   246
Barlett and Steele   74, 88
Barlett, Donald L.   73
Barnes, Fred   239
Barnes, Scott   355
Barr, Thomas D.   32, 112
Barr, Tom   223, 224
Barrett, Lawrence   420
Barthelenghi, Carolyn (C. J.)   282, 448, 449, 465, 475
Barthelenghi, George   448
Bartles & James   182
Barton, Joe   35
Basnett, Brett   210, 259, 261
Bastrop, Texas   49, 58
Beaumont, Texas   49
Beckel, Bob   242

Begala, Paul   462
Bell, Sally   27, 36, 125, 337
Bennett, William   322, 431
Bentsen, Lloyd   315
Berger, Marilyn   224
Berkeley University   185
Bernalillo County   127
Berwyn, Illinois   41
"Best of Ross Perot by his Family, The"   337
Bethlehem, Pennsylvania   36
Beverly Hills   148, 159
Bickel, Lillian   281
Bickham, Kay   60, 298
Bill of Rights   197
"Billionaire Boy Scout"   195
Bishop, Jim   316
Bishop, John   129, 282, 317
Black, Charles   198
Black, Dr. Gordon S.   195, 410, 411, 459, 460
Black, Merle   120
"Black Sunday"   354
Black's survey   410, 411
Blahnik, Mark   31, 32, 33, 116, 117, 179, 180, 326
Bledsoe, Bev   127
Blumenthal, Sidney   193, 194
Boerne, Texas   49, 58
Bond, Rich   204, 205, 243
Bookout, Conrad   271
Boren, David L.   315, 456
Borland, Gloria   283
Borman, Frank   308, 443
Bosnia   464
Bost, Steve   282, 427, 428, 449
Boston, Massachussetts   65, 163, 164, 166, 167, 263, 374
Boston Globe   203, 227, 322, 343, 399, 404
Boston Harbor   88, 393
Boston Herald   355
Boston Phoenix   105
Boston rally   167
Both Sides   102
"Both Sides with Jesse Jackson"   232
Boulder, Colorado   127
Boutelle, James   443
Bradford National Corporation   191
Brinkley, Alan   380, 409

Brinkley, David 102
Brodbeck, Jack 149
Broder, David 67, 146, 183
Brokaw, Tom 368
Brown, Jerry 67, 68, 93, 123, 141, 154, 155
Brown, Murphy 110
Brown, Ron 312, 313
Brown, Willie 109
Bruno, Hal 110
Bryan, William Jennings 126
Bryant, Betsy 148
Bryant, David 214
Bubba Eppes 58
Buchanan, Patrick 66, 69, 141, 154, 155, 181
Buffet, Warren 242
Bull Moose Party 77, 370
Burka, Paul 193
Bush, Barbara 47
Bush, George 21, 47, 51, 52, 55, 56, 66, 69, 78, 80, 106, 109, 115, 122, 123, 127, 128, 134, 135, 147, 150, 154, 155, 156, 159, 163, 174, 175, 183, 196, 198, 202, 203, 208, 209, 214, 230, 238, 240, 251, 269, 275, 281, 302, 311, 312, 320, 321, 322, 329, 330, 331, 336, 342, 344, 350, 364, 365, 366, 374, 377, 392, 393, 394, 397, 408, 421
Bush, Jeb 321
Bush, Nancy 275
Bush-Quayle 197
Butler, Samuel 223
Button Lady, The 84
Butts, Calvin 223, 233

C

C-Span 15, 21, 37, 102, 120, 123, 124, 126, 306, 349, 455
Caddell, Pat 12
California 45, 66, 79, 112, 128, 145, 146, 151, 152, 153, 155, 156, 162, 164, 182, 194, 218, 264, 268, 281, 300, 361, 373, 446, 449, 458
California Democrats 155
California Dolls 46, 47
California Poll 153
California primary 154, 171

California Republicans 155
Call to Arms, A 165
Calleo, David P. 70
Campaign press room 252
Campbell, Ed 34, 52, 60, 260
Campbell, James 449
Canada 43
Canzeri, Joe 182, 227, 231, 246, 359, 381, 415
Cape Cod 165, 168
Cape Kennedy 374
Capitol Hill 289, 461, 462
Capra, Frank 125
Carrick, Bill 147
Carroll, Ginny 39
Carter Administration 90, 287, 289
Carter, Jimmy 12, 173, 182, 258, 274, 287, 349, 421
Carvey, Dana 369, 392
Carville, James 314
"Cascade Curtain" 216
Castagne Communications 131
CBS 12, 102, 230, 316, 320, 331, 336, 337, 345, 349, 354, 364, 392
"CBS Morning News" 238
CBS News/*New York Times* 54
CBS Radio 103
Centel Corporation 65
Centel Public Accountability Project xxi
Central Florida Fairgrounds 119
Charlottesville, Virginia 123
Chehalis, Washington 216
Chiapparone, Paul 20
Chicago 65, 123
Chicago Mercantile Exchange 123
Chicago Tribune 88, 89, 361, 399
"Chicken Feathers, Deep Voodoo and the American Dream" 364, 362
Christian, George 376
Churchill, Winston 163
CIA 197
Citizens and Politics: A View from Main Street America 64
Citizens Party 104
City University Graduate Center 263
Clark, Herb 282
Clark, Tony 155
Clay, Henry 79
Clements, Bill 86, 365

Clift, Eleanor 190
Cline, Patsy 364
Clinton Administration 382, 423, 433
Clinton, Bill 13, 17, 55, 61, 67, 68, 76, 80, 93, 103, 110, 123, 127, 128, 141, 153, 154, 155, 156, 163, 174, 176, 183, 198, 208, 214, 221, 226, 238, 239, 243, 262, 269, 281, 298, 299, 305, 311, 312, 313, 314, 320, 321, 326, 329, 331, 336, 342, 343, 344, 352, 361, 364, 370, 372, 376, 377, 378, 379, 392, 394, 397, 407, 408, 420, 421, 430, 461, 463, 464, 466, 467, 470, 474
Clinton, Hillary 467
CNN 37, 102, 106, 120, 126, 155, 176, 177, 193, 207, 232, 258, 263, 270, 317, 345, 351, 371, 465
CNN-USA Today 320
Coalition for a Better Government 14, 159
Coalition to End the Permanent Congress 16, 114, 277, 278
"Coast to Coast" 102
Cohen, William 455
College Station, Texas 53
Collins, Jim 139
Colorado 60, 66, 70, 85, 125, 217, 228, 281, 455
Colorado House 127
Colorado Springs 96, 135
Columbia report 393
Columbia University 380, 389, 392, 409
Commission on Presidential Debates 342
Committee for the Study of the American Electorate 373
Committee to Study the American Electorate 68
Common Cause 66
Commoner, Barry 104
Compton, Ann 343
CompuServe 96
Congress 21, 22, 23, 27, 39, 63, 65, 66, 70, 71, 73, 78, 79, 121, 272, 304, 334, 370, 376, 414, 421, 427, 429, 431, 456, 458, 459, 461, 466
Connally, John 82, 366
Connecticut 68, 84, 130, 167, 281, 443, 453
Connecticut State Legislature 443
Connor, Rich 192
Conrad, Kent 70

Contel Corporation 94
Conway, Yvonne 216
Cooper, Gary 124
Cornell University 412
Corpus Christ 58
Corpus Christi 48, 58
Cosby, Bill 420
Cotton, April 402
Cotton, Shelton 233
Coughlin, Paul 423
Coverdell, Paul 435
Crabb, Norma 84
Craft, Libby 50, 62
"Crazy" 364, 429
Crenna, Richard 20
Cronkite, Walter 242
"Crossfire" 83, 242
Crowe, William J. 315
Culver, Chris 60
Cuomo, Mario 302
Custer, Noell 264, 430

D

Dallas 16, 17, 23, 26, 29, 32, 33, 35, 36, 40, 43, 48, 49, 50, 52, 54, 57, 58, 82, 83, 90, 94, 130, 138, 172, 184, 217, 218, 260, 261, 268, 275, 277, 279, 289, 297, 300, 301, 306, 307, 314, 315, 327, 374, 432, 433, 436, 439, 440, 441, 443, 446, 450
Dallas Arboretum 192
Dallas Morning News 16, 17, 26, 93, 102, 105, 109, 110, 198, 212, 304, 316, 319, 345, 423, 438
Dallas Observer, The 11
Dallas phone bank 257, 285
Dallas Public Library 26
Dallas/Fort Worth 51, 212
"Dateline" 437, 439, 443
"David Frost Show" 455
David Jay's Ice Cream shop 52
de la Cruz, Gloria 219, 234, 245, 246, 286, 301, 302, 304
de Tocqueville, Alexis 14, 475
Dean, Mort 227
Deaver, Michael K. 386
Debates 341, 342, 349

"Deep Voodoo, Chicken Feathers and the American Dream"   338
Defamation League of B'nai B'rith   215
Delaware   120, 279, 281
Deming, New Mexico   128
Democracy in America   475
Democratic Leadership Council   469
Democratic Leadership Council's publication   408
Democratic National Chairman   312
Democratic National Committee   407
Democratic National Convention   161, 214, 222, 232, 239, 243, 244, 250, 262, 288, 298
Democratic Party   80, 253, 286, 371, 372, 466
Democratic platform   378
Democrats   122, 133, 161, 165, 171, 175, 183, 233, 252, 277, 297, 315, 316, 317, 325, 371, 372, 376, 378, 407, 408, 421, 422, 456, 470, 471, 474
Denver   126, 163, 217, 263, 264, 304, 360, 381, 411, 429, 430
Denver Post   127
Department of Agriculture   275
Des Moines   105
Des Moines Register   265
Desert Storm   63, 116, 134, 135, 167, 368
Detroit   19, 227, 411
Detroit News   313
Deukmejian, George   182
Dewey, Thomas   361
"Diane Rhem Show"   102
Dickelman, Kathleen   121
Dickey, Dorothy (Dot)   45
Dingees, David   283
Dinkins, David   232
Dionne, E.J.   349
Dionne, E.J., Jr.'s, *Why Americans Hate Politics*   88
"Dirty tricks"   206, 196, 203, 205, 223, 244, 360
Disenchanted United People for Equality and Democracy   440
District of Columbia   283
DiVall, Linda   78
DLC poll   470
Dobie, Bruce   10, 11, 36
Dole, Elizabeth   241

Dominici, Pete   128, 315
Donahue, Phil   22, 23, 40, 102, 110, 193, 391, 392, 393, 394, 396, 455
Donaldson, Sam   39, 105, 394, 456, 457
Donnelly, Charles   130
"Don't Tread On Me, I'm American."   210
Doonesbury   369
Doubletree Hotel   315
Douglass, Peggy   127, 128
Downs, Hugh   108
Doyne, Ed   283
Drew, Elizabeth   193
Dublin, Ohio   438
Dukakis, Michael   166, 204, 213, 371, 392, 393
Duke University   185
DUPED   439
Dyer, James   78

E

East Coast   51
East Lansing, Michigan   351
East Texas   45, 48
Eastman Kodak   90, 326
Economic Club of Detroit   323
Economic Summit   379
EDS   19, 20, 32, 48, 57, 86, 91, 94, 108, 116, 127, 138, 181, 186, 191, 192, 215, 249, 400
Eisele, Bob   57
Eisenhower, Dwight D.   12, 127, 135, 201
El Centro   148
Election Day   370, 371, 381
Election Day in California   155
Election eve rally   379, 381
Electoral College   78, 297, 419
Electronic Data Systems   18, 368
"Electronic Democracy"   417
"Electronic Democracy" seminar   389
Electronic town hall   303, 461, 463
Elkind, Peter   11
Ellsworth, Ron   430
Embassy Suites Hotel   279
Emory, Texas   58
Emory University   120
Empower America   431
England   43
Esser, Susan   282, 381, 449

Eugene Register Guard   266
Evans and Novak   106
Evans, Rowland   213

F

Fairfield, California   148
Farmers Home Administration,   275
Fayetteville, Arkansas   136, 142
FBI   197
FEC   81
Federal Elections Commission   86, 217,
    296, 313, 377, 421
Feed the Children   142
Ferguson, Jim   366
Ferguson, Ma   366
Ferren, Don   149
Ferren, Marcy   149
Field Institute   153
Fifth Estate   304
Final Perot rally   363
First Commit the Nation   23
"First National Referendum"   460
Fisher, Richard   224, 290, 291, 296, 444,
    445
Fishkin, James   376
Fitzgerald, Ginny   218, 219
Fitzgerald, Virginia (Ginny)   185
Fitzwater, Marlin   197, 354
Flagpole Hill   54
Flemington, New Jersey   359, 363
Florida   34, 35, 45, 55, 66, 67, 84, 101, 112,
    113, 120, 121, 122, 228, 264, 268, 277,
    281, 300, 306, 317, 321, 449, 455
Florida rally   122
Flynn, Raymond   167, 242
Follett, Judy   28, 29, 31, 84
Follett, Judy and Russ   26
Follett, Ken   20
Foltz, Jackie   282
Foraker, Joy   160
Foraker, Timothy   160
Ford, Gerald   132, 421
Forgan, duPont Glore   86, 91
Fort Collins, Colorado   428
Fort Devens, Massachusetts   167
Fort Riley, Kansas   116
Fort Smith, Arkansas   137
Fort Worth   30, 33, 56, 58, 91, 137, 186

Fort Worth Star-Telegram   30, 192
Foster City, California   151
Fowler, Wyche   435
Franklin, Jay   57
Fredericksburg, Texas   58
Freedom Forum Media Studies Center
    389, 392
Fridrich and Clark Realty   36
Fridrich, Steve   36, 282
From, Al   470
Frost, Bill   186, 246, 259, 285, 298
Frost, David   104, 106, 463
Frost, Karen   285, 402
Fulani, Lenora B.   113
Future Shock   388

G

Gaebler, Ted   73
Gallup Poll   371
Galston, Bill   408
Gans, Curtis   68, 373
Garb, Jan   381
Gargan, Jack   15, 16, 17, 113, 277
Garin, Geoffrey   228
Garrett, Ruthie   50
Gayden, Bill   181
Gaylord, Bill   20
Gaynor, John   148
General Motors   19, 32, 81, 87, 91, 182,
    192, 212, 226, 303, 351
George, Marie   282
George Washington University   132
Georgia   84, 274, 282, 435, 453
Georgia Tech University   346
Gergen, David   155, 198, 203, 222, 278,
    293, 457
Germond, Jack   156, 451
Gibbons, Gene   351
Gibson, Charles   39, 99
Gilbert, Donna   275
Gilberton, Don   266
Glenwood Springs, Colorado   126
Goeas, Ed   463, 464
Goldwater, Barry   127, 129
"Good Morning America"   39, 47, 99, 102,
    238, 305, 378, 392, 396
Goodman, Ellen   322, 323, 399
Goodman, Walter   338

GOP   373
GOP convention   305
Gordon S. Black Corporation   410
Gore, Al   226, 243, 306, 329, 347, 372
Gossick, Amanda   211
Gossick, Pam   211
"Gotcha" journalism   398
Goucher College   201
Government Racket: Washington Waste from A to Z, The   361
Gramm, Phil   141, 315
Gramm-Rudman-Hollings   69
Grand Central Station   300
Grand Junction, Colorado   428
Grayson County   374
Green, Mark   33, 137
Greenberg, Ace   223
Greenberg, Stan   321, 407, 470, 471
Greenfield, Jeff   68, 345, 369
Greenwich, Connecticut   185
Greider, William   73, 74, 75, 76, 399
Greider's, *Who Will Tell The People*   88
Gross, Martin   361
Grossman, Larry   389, 390
Gulf War   27, 134, 395

H

"H. Raw Pile'O-Dough"   369, 370
Hale, Jim   266
Hall, Tom   359
Hamm, Shirley   282
Hannah, John   62
Hanoi   19, 308
Harrill, Randy   57, 58
Hart, Gary   70, 101
Hart, Peter D.   65
Hartford, Connecticut   208
Harvard University   87, 89, 140, 164, 185, 194, 248, 457
Harwood Group   64
Harwood, Richard   64, 395, 396
Hawaii   51, 85, 112, 268, 275, 282, 306
Hayden, Bob   149, 267, 281, 316
Healy, Bernadine   241
Heftel, Cecil   277
Hendricks, Grady   379
Hennessy, Patrick   8
Hepburn, Katherine   131, 224

Herndon, Virginia   19
Hicks, Henry   35
Hicks, Miller   262
Hill, Anita   65
Hines, Cragg   203
Hitler   124
Hollywood   153
Holman, Sharon   25, 31, 33, 36, 151, 248, 271, 305, 326, 345, 356, 434, 439, 459
Holmes, Lucretia   35
Holmes, Sherlock   213
Holmes, Steven A.   111
Home Shopping Network   35, 93
Homestretch: New Politics. New Media. New Voters?   392
Honolulu   268
Hooker, John Jay   10, 11,12, 16, 69, 313
Hooks, Benjamin   231, 232
Hoover Institute   114
Hope, Arkansas   142
Hotline, The   16, 17, 39
House Committee   455
House of Representatives   71, 252, 272, 418
House Republicans   179
Houston   28, 57, 59, 186
Houston Chronicle   161, 203
Howard, Wally   282, 438
Howell, Paul   136
Howlett, Debbie   401, 402
Hoyt, Bob   363
Hubbard, Ed   122
HUD scandal   396
Hughes and Luce law firm   32, 86
Hughes, David   96
Hughes, Ray   128
Humphrey, Hubert   77, 418
Hunt, Al   105
Hunt, Jan   282
Huntington Beach   159
Hurricane Andrew   306
Hurst, Jamie   282
Hussein, Saddam   21, 106, 124, 134, 394
Hutchinson, James   46
Hutchison, Kay Bailey   445, 446
Hyperion   297

I

Iacocca, Lee   241
IBM   18, 49, 148, 367, 449
Idaho   120, 282, 374
Illinois   67, 85, 217, 282, 438
Independent Broadcast Network   102
Independent Party   112
Indiana   282
Infomercial   329, 331, 339, 340, 379
"Inspector Perot"   195, 197
Iowa   85, 265, 282
Iran   368
Iran-Contra   192, 395
Iranscam   396
Iraq   106, 154
IRS   197
Irvine   149
Irvine rally   158

J

Jackson, Andrew   79, 418
Jackson, David   316, 319, 438
Jackson, Jesse   102, 144, 233, 241
Japan   227
Jarvis, Howard   153
Jennings, Peter   212, 394
"Jewish professor"   214
"Joan Rivers"   455
Joan Shorenstein Barone Center on the
     Press, Politics and Public Policy
     457
Jobs, Steven   148
Johns Hopkins University   70
Johnson, Lyndon   66, 366, 368, 376
Joint Congressional Committee on
     Governmental Reform   455
Jones, Larry   142
Jones, Ollie   122
Jordan, Hamilton   171, 173, 174, 175, 176,
     177, 178, 179, 180, 184, 187, 189, 229,
     236, 237, 239, 240, 243, 244, 245, 246,
     257, 258, 273, 288, 289, 298, 325, 397,
     471, 475
Jordan, Vernon   315
Joyce Foundation   65
Judiciary Committee   109
Jurkowitz, Mark   105

Jurow, Martin   223

K

Kalb, Marvin   457
Kamarck, Elaine   408
Kansas   85, 120, 282, 374, 455
Kansas City   16, 361
Kansas City Star   16
Kantor, Mickey   315, 342
Katz, Jon   395
Kavanagh, Nancy   282
Kearse, Amalya   241
Keating Five   66
"Keeping Your Job in the USA"   463
Kemp, Jack   173, 242, 275, 315, 316, 431
Kendricks, Ken   282, 435, 436, 437
Kennedy-Nixon debates   387
Kentucky   55, 61, 84, 89, 101, 120, 282, 309,
     455
Kern, Candice   423
Kerrey, Bob   242
Kerrville, Texas   58
Kettering Foundation   64
King, Jeffrey   359
King, Larry   3-8, 13, 26, 105, 190, 209, 269,
     270, 391, 468
King, Rodney   146
Kirby, David   282
Kirby, Hays   282
Kirkpatrick, Jeanne   241, 431
Kisse, Jim   282
Klier, Gary   282
Knoxville, Tennessee   172, 325, 472
Kodak   91, 286
Koenig, Kurt   130, 263, 298, 299, 300, 302,
     303, 304, 355
Koppel, Ted   105, 369, 442, 443
Korean War   136, 193
Kovach, Bill   194
Kraft, Tim   182
Kramer, Michael   322
Kritchfield, Phylis   148
Krueger, Bob   445, 446
Kunst, Lionel   114, 278
Kuwait   154

L

Laguban, Bob 282
Lake, Celinda 117, 463, 464
Lake Dallas 105
Lake, Darrell 31, 32, 34, 116
Lake Texoma 374
Lamb, Brian 306
Lane County 266
Lansing, Michigan 226, 227, 229, 230
Laredo, Texas 58
LaRouche, Lyndon 458
"Larry King Live" 3, 10, 13, 16, 23, 25, 26,
    27, 30, 33, 36, 37, 40, 43, 56, 87, 102,
    106, 122, 125, 128, 132, 191, 204, 205,
    209, 238, 268, 269, 271, 317, 359, 381,
    385, 392, 420, 455, 476
Las Cruces, New Mexico 34, 128
Lauder, Leonard 223
Laufer, Joanne 150
Laughlin, Kevin 218
Lavado, Raymond 261
Lawrence Welk music 107
Lawrenceville, New Jersey 448
LBJ Freeway 40
Lead or Leave 435
League of Wives of American Vietnam
    Prisoners of W 115
Lehrer, Jim 343, 351
Leno, Jay 392, 455
Leonard, Charlie 179, 180, 181, 182, 184,
    187, 246, 247, 248
Leubsdorf, Carl P. 109
Lewis, Ann 385
Lewis, Kathy 110
Lexington Avenue 262
Libertarian Party 18
Lieberman, John I. 461
Lifflander, Matthew 265, 298
Limbaugh, Rush 452
Lincoln, Abraham 371
Lion Country Center at Frasier Park in
    Irvine 157
Lion Country Park 160
Lippman, Walter 133
Little Rock, Arkansas 141, 142, 214, 314,
    379
Livingston, Texas 58
Llano, Texas 58

Long Beach, California 361
Long, Earl 363
Long, Huey 363
Long Island 439
Longley, Jim 427
Los Angeles 146, 153, 162, 175, 411
Los Angeles riots 154, 394
Los Angeles Times 13, 107, 151, 204, 217,
    264, 388
Louis Harris poll 390
Louisiana 45, 265, 282, 363, 455
Louv, Richard 96
Lowi, Theodore J. 412, 413, 414, 422
Lubbock, Texas 58
Luce Law 32
Luce, Tom 18, 32, 86, 87, 90, 100, 145, 172,
    173, 177, 178, 180, 181, 182, 185, 186,
    187, 190, 207, 213, 215, 219, 220, 221,
    222, 225, 237, 238, 239, 240, 242, 244,
    247, 248, 252, 257, 258, 259, 260, 288,
    289, 292, 298, 324, 400, 401, 417, 419
Luna County 128, 129
Luntz, Frank 181, 188, 207, 243, 373, 375,
    410, 460, 465
Lynn, Frances 265

M

Maas, Liz 248
"MacNeil/Lehrer NewsHour" 22, 155,
    189, 343, 455
Madison Square Garden 232, 262
Maguire Associates 17
Maher, Bill 282
Maine 117, 120, 167, 282, 374, 427, 449, 455
Mainferme, Monique 158
Manes, Susan 66
Manhattan 131, 357
Mann, Barbara 187
Mann, Howard 218, 259, 260, 273
Manson, Lewis 56
Mara, John 429
Marcus, Bernard 223
Marie-Walters, Hope 126
Marsh, Tony 182, 246
Martin, Murphy 20, 235, 308, 320, 326,
    333, 337, 340
Martinez, Bob 197
Maryland 123, 132, 282, 449

Mashek, John   203, 227, 343

Massachusetts   84, 164, 166, 282

Massachusetts Miracle   166

Matalin, Mary   315

Mathews, David   64

Matthew Arnold   3

"Maury Povich"   455

May Day rally   151

McCarthy, Bob   304

McCarthy, Eugene   53, 66, 113

McClain, Dennis   330, 331, 333, 334, 337,
    339, 340, 341

McClary, Charlene   60, 298

McClure, Sandy   218, 265, 282, 449

McCoole, Muffie   34, 259

MCI Communications   95

McKamy, Anne   139

McLaughlin, Ann   241

McWethy, John   212

Medicaid   191

Medicare   191

Meet John Doe   124

"Meet the Press"   233, 393

Megatrends   387

Memphis   411

Merit Drive   25, 32, 35, 41

Mexico   226

Meyer, Fred   198

Meyerson, Bernice   210

Meyerson, David   225

Meyerson, Mort   91, 92, 172, 173, 177, 178,
    180, 181, 185, 186, 187, 189, 213, 215,
    218, 220, 222, 224, 225, 231, 236, 238,
    239, 240, 244, 247, 252, 257, 258, 259,
    285, 288, 289, 298, 324, 346

MIAs   20, 131, 197

Miami, Florida   261

Miami University conference   420

Michel, Bob   197, 374

Michigan   67, 85, 226, 228, 249, 282, 321,
    378, 381, 449, 455

Michigan State University   351

Middle Tennessee State University   89

Midland, Texas   58

Miller, Don   121

Miller, Gaynor   430

Minnesota   282, 455

Mission Beach, California   152

Mississippi   282

Missouri   85, 218, 265, 282, 449, 455

Monroe, Russ   31, 32, 33, 116, 117, 219, 276

Montana   84, 155, 282, 374, 455

Montgomery, Betty   282, 449

Moore, Betty   282

Moore Motor Sales   49

Moretti, Ron   135

"Morning Edition"   313

Morton H. Meyerson Symphony   92

Mounce, Ophelia   56

Moyers, Bill   242

MTV   392

Mulford, Clay   25, 32, 86, 112, 184, 214,
    240, 247, 258, 276, 309, 326, 329, 341,
    347, 358, 426, 434, 438, 444

Mulford, Nancy   358

Murray, Alan   311

Murray, Richard   97

Mussolini   193, 198, 204

Muth, Pat   122, 123, 268, 300, 317, 449

Myers, Dee Dee   208

Myers, Lisa   189, 317

N

NAACP   230, 231, 232, 233

NAACP speech   240, 248, 249

Naisbitt, John   387

Nashville, Tennessee   8, 36, 37, 69, 230,
    231

Nashville Banner   11

Nashville Scene   10, 11

National Advisory Panel   223

National League of Families of POWs and
    MIAs in Southeast Asia   132

National Network   102

National Policy Foundation   469

National Press Club   21, 23, 37, 39, 102,
    149, 458

National Press Club speech   50

National Public Radio   313, 395, 460

National Rifle Association   458

Naval Academy   18, 152, 164

NBC   102, 189, 317, 320, 331, 334, 336, 362,
    364, 368, 389, 392, 437, 455, 457

NBC Poll   460

NBC-*Wall Street Journal* poll   307

NCR   127

Nealon, Kevin   362

Nebraska   282
Neddo, Don   265
Nelson, Jack   107
Nelson, Willie   143, 144, 223, 364
Nevada   55, 282, 374, 456
New Braunfels, Texas   58
"New Covenant"   262
New Democrat, The   408
New England   164, 166, 374
New Hampshire   66, 67, 69, 167, 282, 311
New Jersey   84, 120, 122, 130, 155, 265, 282, 321, 446, 448, 455, 475
New Jersey UWSA   465
"New media"   391, 392, 394, 396
New Mexico   34, 60, 85, 128, 155, 282, 316, 317, 455
New Orleans Times-Picayune   265
New Republic   193, 202, 380, 409
New York   84, 111, 112, 130, 131, 188, 194, 233, 262, 265, 282, 298, 299, 301, 302, 304, 355
New York City   232, 358
New York Daily News   108, 322
New York People for Perot   265
New York Post   265
New York Primary   68
New York Times Magazine, The   72, 412
New York Times, The   13, 68, 71, 91, 111, 112, 130, 139, 153, 190, 194, 208, 227, 230, 278, 306, 325, 331, 335, 338, 362, 366, 377, 385, 386, 394, 420, 448, 462
New York Times/CBS News poll   198
New Yorker, The   193
Newsday   145, 203, 393, 408
Newsweek   16, 39, 102, 182, 190, 192, 279, 335, 342, 345, 356, 370, 378, 398, 402
Nielsen, A.C.   331
Nieman Reports   399
"Nightline"   78, 105, 175, 213, 228, 283, 359, 369, 437, 438, 442, 443
"Nightly News"   455
Nitze, Paul   223
Nixon, Richard   47, 77, 296, 410, 418, 464
Nixon White House   192
Noriega, Manuel   21
Norman, Dick   164, 165, 166, 263
North American Free Trade Agreement (NAFTA)   352, 455, 462, 463, 465

North Carolina   76, 84, 111, 112, 271, 282, 300, 455
North Dakota   70, 282
North, Oliver   192
North Vietnamese   131, 308
Northern California   157, 163
Not for Sale at Any Price   462, 473
Novak, Bob   213

O

Oakes, Mary   158
Oakland Hills   146
Oberwetter, Jim   356
"October surprise"   306
O'Daniel, W. Lee (Pappy)   366
O'Donnell, Shawn   265
Office of Management and Budget   289
Ohio   84, 85, 113, 120, 155, 282, 300, 451
Okamoto, Merrick   157
Oklahoma   66, 84, 218, 282
"Old media"   398
Oliphant, Thomas   404
Olson, Dennis   282
Olympia, Washington   216
Olympian, The   216
O'Neill, Tom   303, 448
Orange County   148, 149, 157, 160, 223
Orange County Register   151
Oregon   112, 153, 216, 266, 282, 300, 374, 455
Orlando, Florida   119, 120, 121
Orlando rally   122, 141
Orlando Sentinel   89, 120, 264
Orono, Maine   427
Osborne, David   73
Osgood, Charles   103
Owens, Greg   281

P

P. J.'s Crystal Bowl   48
Page, Susan   393
Panama   21
Park Avenue   131
Parker House Hotel   167
Patriot Party   56
Paychex   410
PBS   156, 349, 389

Peck, Bob   288, 292
Pelley, Scott   316
Pelosi, Nancy   315
Penner, Rudolph   336
Pennsylvania   84, 266, 282, 321
"Pentagon"   235, 298
People Magazine   423
People Vs. Politics: Citizens Discuss
    Politicians, 65
Performing Arts Center   120
Perkins, Ralph   116, 117
Permanent Promotions   84
"Perot Amendment"   420
Perot, Bette   236
Perot, Carolyn   249
Perot Girls   271
Perot Group   19, 25, 26, 32, 116, 149, 181
Perot I   35, 190
Perot, Katherine   364
Perot, Margot   18, 25, 139, 180, 201, 223,
    241, 359, 365, 368
Perot, Nancy   214
Perot Petition Committee   33, 57, 93, 191,
    373, 377
Perot Petition News   151
Perot Phenomenon   199, 379
Perot, Ross - birthday   209
Perot, Ross Jr.   19, 25, 36, 192, 212, 235,
    251, 345, 356, 474
Perot, Suzanne   337
Perot Systems   19, 35, 92, 132, 214, 324
Perot Volunteer Appreciation Rally   157
"Perotbots"   433, 447
Persian Gulf   21, 27, 64, 337
Persian Gulf War   106
"Peter Jennings Show"   213
Peters, Walt   281, 441
Peterson, Nancy   9
Petracca, Mark   305, 416
Pfister, Ed   389
Philadelphia   411
Philadelphia Daily News   266
Philadelphia Inquirer   73
Phillipi, Mac   281
Phillips, Kevin   72, 145, 147, 313, 460, 464
Phillips, Stu   281
Phoenix   217
Phone Bank   40, 41, 267
Pincus, Ted   217

Pippin, Jerry   102
Pittsburgh   359
Plains and Rocky Mountain States   373
Plocek, Jerry   41, 42
Policy Review   375, 411
Political Hotline   99, 155, 164, 197, 205, 208,
    264, 315, 318, 465
Political Media Research   17
Pomona   158
Pondiscio, Ron   265
Poss, Mike   31, 32, 301, 340, 426
Poteet   58
POW/MIA   136, 142, 192, 196, 212
Powell, Colin   240
Powershift   388
POWs   19, 20, 46, 53, 122, 136, 161, 162,
    195, 235, 268, 280, 308, 318, 442
Preston Forest shopping center   50
Preston Royal shopping center   50
Price, Brokaw   263
"Prime Time Live"   403
Prisoner of War   114, 274
"The Problems—Plain Talk about Jobs,
    Debt and the Washington Mess"
    330
Prodigy, CompuServe   96, 148, 452
Proposition 13   147, 153
Proxmire, William   242
Pryor, David   418
Public Philosophy, The   133
Pueblo Ledger   429

Q

Quayle, Dan   110, 173, 182, 197, 347, 348
Queens   439

R

Raatz, Jim   53, 54
"Radical Centrists"   410
Rallies   216
Rally   208, 226
Rand Corporation   91
Rand University   185
Rather, Dan   394, 395
Rayburn, "Mr. Sam"   365
Reagan Coalition   176
Reagan Democrats   321

Reagan, Ronald   38, 153, 163, 173, 182,
    236, 274, 318, 330, 349, 386
Record, The   265
Reed, Jean Ann   60, 298
Reed, John Shelton   76
Reed, Melissa   265
Reed, Todd   337
Reed, Tom   167
Rees, Diane   127
"Regis and Kathy Lee"   455
Reid, Harry M.   456
Reinventing Government   73
Reischauer, Robert   468
Republican Coalition   371
Republican Congressional Committee   175
Republican National Committee   224, 245
Republican National Convention   110,
    161, 223, 288, 297, 401
Republican Party   77, 127, 203, 205, 280,
    373, 381, 410, 420, 421, 466, 469, 470
Republicans   133, 161, 165, 171, 174, 183,
    196, 209, 215, 245, 250, 252, 277, 305,
    314, 317, 325, 372, 376, 408, 422, 456,
    466, 467, 468, 474
Reunion Arena   379
Reuters   351
Reynolds, Ed   55
Rhode Island   79, 167, 279, 281
Rhodes, David   29, 33, 34, 59, 217
Richards, Ann   59, 68, 365, 366
Richardson, Charlie   52
Richmond Debate   385
Richmond, Virginia   349
Riley, Lynda   46, 47, 48, 59
Riney, Hal   182, 224, 234, 235, 236, 238,
    308, 340
Riordan, Richard   419
Roberts, Cokie   345, 456
Roberts, Jerry   146
Roberts-Cannaday, Rose   43, 140, 257, 258,
    260, 267, 268, 445
Rochester, New York   90, 297
Rockefeller, Nelson   182
Rockland, Maine   428
Roden, Dan   135
Rodriguez, Alex   357, 440
Rohatyn, Felix   315
Rollins, Ed   171, 174, 175, 176, 177, 178,
    179, 180, 181, 182, 183, 184, 185, 187,
        189, 215, 220, 222, 224, 229, 230, 235,
        236, 237, 238, 239, 241, 242, 243, 244,
        245, 246, 247, 248, 249, 251, 257, 279,
        288, 289, 306, 325, 340, 440
Rollins, Sherrie   175
Rook, Susan   351
Roosevelt, Franklin D.   92, 387
Roosevelt, Theodore   42, 77, 370
Ross, Gary   35
"Ross Perot Nobody Knows, The"   337
"Ross Perot Presents: The First National
    Referendum"   458
"Ross Perot: The Man, the Message, the
    Movement"   438
Ross, Rick   282
Ross, Steven R.   122
"Ross, You Bet Your Hat He Can Win"   364
"Ross's Rangers"   358
Rothenberg, Stuart   468, 471
Round Rock, Texas   59
Rudin, Ken   393
Rudman, Warren   69, 240, 309, 311
Russert, Tim   104, 105
Russo, Sal   182, 246

S

Sachs, Shelia   265
Sacramento   148, 157, 163
San Angelo, Texas   58
San Antonio   260
San Diego   96, 148, 149, 152, 158
San Francisco   149, 274
San Francisco Bay   151
San Francisco Chronicle   146
Santa Clara, California   361
Santa Fe, New Mexico   129
Santa Monica, California   91
Santa Ynez, California   160
"Saturday Night Live"   362, 369, 392
Sausalito, California   124
Sawyer-Miller Consulting Group   174,
    175, 179, 246
Sax, Rosemarie   263, 381, 430
Schecter, Peter   246
Schenk, John   125, 126, 217
Schmitt, Harrison   127
Schmokel, Wolfe   283
Schneider, William   138, 317, 371, 465

Schnur, Dan   146, 163
School of Communication   389
Schultz, Cindy   283, 433, 434, 447
Schwarzkopf, Norman   241
Scowcroft, Brent   315
Sears, John   408
Seattle   216
Seattle Post-Intelligencer   266
Seguin, Texas   58
Seigenthaler, John   9, 13
Senate   70, 71, 173, 272, 418
Senate Banking Committee   455
Senate Judiciary Committee   65
Senate Reform Panel   456
Serur, Jim   48, 60, 282, 317, 445
Shapiro, Walter   103
Shaw, Bernard   37
Shay, Dennis   281
Shea, Anthony   50
Shepard, Joyce   439, 440
Sheraton Park Central   269
Shields, Mark   193
Shockman, Eric   153
Siegel, Bob   185
Silicon Prairie   374
Silicon Valley   148, 374
Silverberg, Kristen   140, 185, 188, 248
Simon, Bull   20
Simpson, Carole   349
Simpson, O.J.   224
Sirkin, Bob   313
"60 Minutes"   40, 45, 102, 354, 355, 356, 360
Skidmore, Eric   52, 60
Skilman, Toni   150
Skirvin, Dennis   333
Slick Willie   67, 208
Sliwa, Curtis   263
Smith, James   282
Snavely, Bobbie   151
Socorro County   129
Soft money   421
South Carolina   84, 282, 449, 455
South Dakota   282
Southeast Asia   196, 274, 280, 442
Southern California   157
Southern Methodist University   87
Southwest Corporation   87
Speech in Tampa   18

"Spin doctors"   346
Springfield, Virginia   95
Squires, Jim   88, 91, 106, 178, 180, 196, 198, 214, 215, 220, 225, 231, 237, 238, 242, 249, 251, 257, 259, 283, 288, 289, 291, 293, 298, 309, 314, 326, 391, 475
St. Louis   343
St. Louis Post-Dispatch   154, 218, 265
Stalin, Joseph   124
Stamaty, Wayne   369
Stanford University   114, 185
State Department   109
State of the Union   124
Statehouse Convention Center   142
Stephanopoulos, George   221, 424
Stepp, Carl Sessions   394
Stewart, Martha   223
Stockdale, James   114, 229, 242, 272, 281, 318, 347, 348
Stockdale, Sybil   281
Stoval, Linda   283
Strahan, Angela   265
Streit, Jo   165, 168, 261, 273
Stromberg, Russ   266
Super Tuesday   29, 30, 68
Superconducting Super Collider   92
Supreme Court   109
Sweet, Orville   121, 282
Swindle, Orson   268, 274, 275, 276, 280, 282, 283, 300, 306, 307, 326, 348, 354, 356, 357, 359, 402, 431, 432, 440
Syracuse University   185

T

T.H.R.O. (Throw the Hypocritical Rascals Out)   14, 16, 113, 277
Taft, William Howard   77
"Talk of the Nation"   102
Talmey, Paul   127
Tampa   14, 15, 16, 65, 121, 122, 160, 361, 411
Tandy Corporation   273
Tanner, Adam   9
Tarrant County   33
"Tax Increase, Analyzing the President's Economic Plan"   462
Tay, Son   274

"Team Perot" 358
Teeter, Robert 197, 315, 342
Teflon Texan 213
Telematch 95
Temple, Arthur 223
Tennessean, The 9, 10
Tennessee 37, 84, 120, 282, 313
Texarkana 80, 101, 138, 367
Texas 36, 55, 62, 66, 79, 84, 111, 115, 120,
    196, 282, 321, 363, 374, 455
Texas Instruments 26, 340
Texas Legislature 192
Texas Monthly 193
Texas Poll 78
Texas Primary 30, 31
Texas Rally 55
Texas Rangers 51
Texas Secretary of State John Hannah 55
Texas Senate Election 445
Texas UWSA 445
Texas UWSA Director 445
Texas's special U.S. Senate election 453
"The Tonight Show" 392
"This Morning" 312, 392
"This Week with David Brinkley" 39
Thomas, Clarence 65, 109
Thomas, Helen 351
Thomas, Rich 335
Thompson, John 136, 142
Thompson, Kathryn 223
Threlkeld, Tom Steinert 93
Thurmon, Strom 76, 77
Time Magazine 102, 103, 104, 230, 322,
    336, 397, 420, 437
Time/CNN poll 452
Timerlin, Lanier 215, 326, 330
Timerlin-McClain 326, 330
Times Mirror survey 54
Tisch, Andrew 223
"Today" 37, 102, 130, 156, 204, 209, 233,
    238, 310, 317, 392
Toffler, Alvin 388
"Tom Snyder Show" 102
"Tonight" 336, 455
Town Hall 213, 379
Townsend, John 281
Tracy, Spencer 124, 125
Truman, Harry 77, 135, 263, 361
Tschudy, Bill 282

Tsongas, Paul 67, 68, 69, 123, 164, 165,
    166, 240, 309
Tucson 217
Tully, Paul 372
Turks 218, 219
TV Guide 458
Twentieth Century Fund study 396
"20/20" 20, 25, 102, 107, 269, 399
270 Group 330
Tyler, Texas 45, 46, 47, 48
Tyler State Park 45
Tyson Foods 141

U

U.S. Naval Academy 134, 201
U.S. News and World Report 155, 156, 198,
    203, 278, 293, 294, 457, 464
U.S. News poll 464
U.S. Senate election in Texas 444
Ueberroth, Peter 241
Ulakovic, Mick 266
United Press International 351
United We Stand America 280, 285, 300,
    308, 326, 340, 357, 423, 425, 426, 431,
    432, 433, 435, 436, 438, 440, 441, 442,
    444-449, 451, 452, 458, 459, 462, 464-
    466, 468, 473, 475
United We Stand America New York 440
United We Stand Everywhere 437
United We Stand Idaho 437
United We Stand: How We Can Take Back
    Our Country 291, 334
University of California at Irvine 305
University of California at Irvine Medical
    Center 161
University of California in Irvine 416
University of Houston 97
University of Maine 428
University of Miami 389
University of Miami seminar 417
University of North Texas 116
University of Pennsylvania's Wharton
    Graduate School 150
University of Richmond 349
University of Southern California 153
University of Texas 91, 376
University of Virginia 86
USA Today 108, 136, 401, 460

USA Today-CNN   163
Utah   120, 282, 374, 455
UWSA phone bank   446, 461

V

Valso vs. Buckley   420
Van Holts, Adrian   266
Vanderbilt University   37, 214
Vanocur, Sander   343, 445
Ventura, California   149
Vermont   283
Veterans of Foreign Wars   393
Vetter, Nina   45, 46, 56
Vietnam   19, 21, 114, 131, 143, 161, 197,
    274, 368
Vietnam Veterans Memorial   136
Vietnam Veterans Shelter   167
Vietnam War   143
Vigil, Dr. Steve   129
Vinson, Joan   131, 132, 133, 134, 202, 282,
    449
Virginia   218, 281, 455
Visalia, California   148
Vokey, Roy   27, 136
Vokey, Virginia   27, 84
Von Drehle, David   209

W

Waco, Texas   58
Wal-Mart   141, 352
Waldman, Gene   153
Walker, Bill   445, 446
Wall Street   131
Wall Street Journal 13, 178, 205, 236, 239,
    311, 312, 314, 349, 353, 354, 359
Wall Street Journal-NBC News poll   104,
    138
Wallace, George   53, 76, 113, 418
Wallace, Henry   77, 113
Waller, Calvin A. H.   135
Walter, Tom   181
Walters, Barbara   20, 25, 102, 107, 108, 109,
    214, 225, 269, 270, 292
Walton, Sam   142
Wang   166
Warfield, Paul   223

Washington   25, 51, 63, 75, 85, 115, 138,
    153, 184, 266, 275, 283, 320, 455
Washington D.C.   101, 134, 136
Washington, Jack Anderson   102
Washington Journalism Review   394
Washington Post   67, 103, 154, 174, 183, 195,
    196, 202, 203, 205, 207, 209, 220, 346,
    349, 369, 395, 456, 461
Washington Times   198
Washington University   343
"Washingtoon"   369, 370
Watergate   194
Wattleton, Faye   241
Wayne, Len   47, 160
Wayne, Len and Janet   160
WBAP radio   30
"We Own This Country" speech to the
    National Press   37
Weber, Vin   431
Weicker, Lowell   241
Weisman, Robert   261, 273
Welfare Billionaire   191
West Coast   51
West Texas   58
West Virginia   112, 283, 455
Westchester County   355
Western New Mexico University   59
Wetsel, Allison   210
WFAA-TV   308
Wharton, Frank   265
Wharton University   185
"Wheel of Fortune"   105
White House   22, 121, 153, 173, 203, 313,
    334, 348, 350, 461, 462
White, John P.   90, 91, 154, 173, 185, 224,
    257, 286, 287, 289, 291, 292, 293, 296,
    297, 314, 324, 325
White, Mark   87
White Shirts   219
White, Vanna   105
Whitlock, Wes   258, 273
Whittle Communications   172, 325, 472
Who Will Tell The People   73, 74, 399
Wichita   121
Wichita (Kansas) Eagle-Beacon   398
Wichita Falls   58
Wickless, Matt   282
Wilder, Doug   17, 241
Will, George   457

Williams, Clayton   58, 68, 365
Williams, Hank   143
Williams, Larry   165, 168
Willow Run   226
Wilmington, Delaware   333
Wilson, Karoline   41, 49, 163, 210, 261, 273
Wilson, Pete   146
Wilson, Woodrow   77, 371
Wing, Tom   282, 438, 443
Winger, Richard   18, 112, 414
Wirth, Tim   70
Wisconsin   85, 283, 433, 446
Witcover, Jules   156
Wizard of Oz   204
WLAC radio   8
Woodward, Bob   195
WOR   303
Wright Asphalt Products   50
Wright, Jim   365
Wyoming   120, 283, 374

Y

Yarborough, Ralph   339
"Yellow Ross of Texas, The "   322
"You people"   233
Young Turks   117, 186, 217, 273, 326, 426
"Your people"   231, 232

Z

Zak, Betsie   265
Zeldin, Rae   159, 160
Zuber, Dee   438, 439, 451
Zucker, Jeff   359, 361, 446, 451